W0091139

(Un)Familiar Femininities

(Un)Familiar Femininities

Studies in Contemporary Lesbian
South Asian Texts

ANEETA RAJENDRAN

OXFORD
UNIVERSITY PRESS

OXFORD
UNIVERSITY PRESS

Oxford University Press is a department of the University of Oxford.
It furthers the University's objective of excellence in research, scholarship,
and education by publishing worldwide. Oxford is a registered trademark of
Oxford University Press in the UK and in certain other countries

Published in India by
Oxford University Press
YMCA Library Building, 1 Jai Singh Road, New Delhi 110 001, India

© Oxford University Press 2015

The moral rights of the author have been asserted

First Edition published in 2015

All rights reserved. No part of this publication may be reproduced, stored in
a retrieval system, or transmitted, in any form or by any means, without the
prior permission in writing of Oxford University Press, or as expressly permitted
by law, by licence, or under terms agreed with the appropriate reprographics
rights organization. Enquiries concerning reproduction outside the scope of the
above should be sent to the Rights Department, Oxford University Press, at the
address above

You must not circulate this work in any other form
and you must impose this same condition on any acquirer

ISBN-13: 978-0-19-945491-4
ISBN-10: 0-19-945491-4

Typeset in Adobe Garamond Pro 11/13
by The Graphics Solution, New Delhi 110 092
Printed in India by Rakmo Press, New Delhi 110 020

For all my families

Contents

Acknowledgements

This book has been a test of many things: rectitude, endurance, patience, and above all, of self-belief. If I have managed to emerge from the lion's den, it is because of the many humane creatures who stood by and waited to take care of me at every step of the way. Colleagues from different universities and continents have contributed in its creation. I would like to express deep gratitude to Professor Makarand Paranjape, my doctoral supervisor, for his patient guidance and unstinting encouragement over the course of this project. I would also like to express my very great appreciation for the generous mentorship, support, constructive criticism, and personal warmth that Professor J. Devika, Professor Jens Rydstrom, and Professor Surinder S. Jodhka have extended to me. To all colleagues, including administrative staff, at the Centre for English Studies, Jawaharlal Nehru University, New Delhi, where I did my doctoral work, and at the Centre of Gender Studies, Lund University, where I spent time as an Erasmus Mundus postdoctoral scholar, my sincerest thanks for the kind, enriching atmosphere you have all helped create and sustain. Both places will always be special in my heart for having helped shape not only this book, but also my confidence in being able to participate in the process of knowledge creation. So many friendships have been formed here too, to which I owe so much. I must also thank my editors at Oxford University Press for having gently but ably kept things on schedule.

Closer home, the *homo sapiens* members of my families have again created space for me to be able to think, read, and write, often at great expense to themselves: I do not know at all how I can ever begin to thank any of them. The other members of the family, Pinchu, Tau, and now Kali, have been very enthusiastic academic assistants: without them, the work may have finished in half the time, but would not have been half as rich nor half as joyous, for their canine selves have helped me understand how othering might feel far better than any amount of book-study would have.

I also wish to acknowledge and thank the publishers who brought out the earlier versions of some of the chapters in this book. Chapter 2 draws upon 'Lesbians in the House: Female Queerness in Bend It Like Beckham (Gurinder Chadha, 2002) and Chutney Popcorn (Nisha Ganatra, 1999)', which appeared in the 'queer cinemas' special issue of *New Cinemas: Journal of Contemporary Cinema* (2012, 10[2–3]: 145). The concluding chapter is based on 'Popular Forms, Altering Normativities: Queer Buddies in Contemporary Mainstream Hindi Cinema', in V. Kishore, A. Sarwal, and P. Patra, eds. 2014. *Bollywood and Its Other(s): Towards New Configurations*. London: Palgrave Macmillan.

An Introduction

Subsequent History

In one of the stories in Suniti Namjoshi's *St Suniti and the Dragon*, a woman befriends a wolf:

> And so the two friends walked away and when at the third village they were rudely greeted by sticks and stones, because it was claimed, their reputation had preceded them, they were not greatly surprised, but just walked on until, at last, they entered *a realm that is not as yet familiar to us*. (Namjoshi 1998: 87, emphasis added)

Namjoshi's story 'Subsequent History' carries the tale forward from 'Wolf,' where 'once a young woman … made friends with a wolf' (Namjoshi 1998: 85). Initially, all the men are full of admiration, because they think the woman has tamed the wolf. Rubbish, the narrator tells us, 'there had never been any question of taming' (Namjoshi 1998: 85), but simply that woman and wolf got on together, and 'frequently went for walks together'. Soon, the men, seeing both creatures retain their earlier shapes and propensities, spread a rumour. They set up a wolf-hunting expedition, where the wolf is to be captured with the woman serving as bait. The woman tries to get out of it, but they truss her up as bait anyway and begin the hunt; but woman and wolf somehow manage to disappear, and the men, elders now after what appears an infinite period of waiting, 'put up a sign on the edge of their town in large red letters warning the unwary that there were wolves about' (Namjoshi 1998: 85). 'Subsequent History' tells us that the woman and wolf have wandered around looking for a new home. Where they are not greeted literally by sticks and stones, a metaphor for heteronormativity, the woman is frequently told to get married; or tranquilisers to capture the wolf are forced upon them as 'options'. Finally, they leave the realm of the realistic convention, disappearing from both the story and the book into 'a realm that is not as yet familiar to us' (Namjoshi 1998: 87).

The title of this book, *(Un)Familiar Femininities*, is inspired by Namjoshi's story which tells us not only how lesbianism is perceived (the 'wolf') but also how lesbian women continue to exist in the everyday world around us, albeit wandering through one or other kind of homophobic realm, and also how new spaces/histories are created by continuing to resist heteronormativity ('just walked on until'). Namjoshi's post-modernist fabular spaces do not identify 'a woman', 'a wolf', 'men' and 'villagers', and instead they locate the woman who argues with normative femininity—heterosexual femininity that privileges reproductive temporality including motherhood in the service of the nation—as an Everywoman, locate homophobias as everyday as homosexuality; promising at the same time that there will be a 'subsequent history' after oppression based on one's sexuality is endured. This 'woman' who argues with normative femininity is our '(un)familiar' of the title of this book; this book traces histories, representations, legacies of femininities that are at odds with, that queer 'heteronormativity'. Namjoshi's articulation of the vulnerability of the 'wolf' as an animal amongst the alien culture of 'homo sapiens' is a fantastically pertinent trope for how sexual othering comes to be vilified as the non-human other to the universally human heterosexual. Terry Castle, in her magisterial anthology, *The Literature of Lesbianism* (2003), shows that one of the first, almost primordial responses to the idea of the lesbian when first encountered is that of its 'monsterisation', pervaded by a feeling of bewilderment or astonishment. The life narratives of Indian women from various locations and temporalities suggests that at least as far as welding a space in India is concerned, monsterization is hitherto the routine response on the part of much of civil society, a fact very much visible when one considers certain inconsistences in the Indian public discourse on sexuality. This aspect of the word 'familiar' as monster, discussed in greater detail later, connects 'woman' with the human other, 'wolf'— the lesbian woman, the other, to heterosexuality, becomes as much of a monster as her companion wolf. While the 'wolf' of Namjoshi's story might look like the more likely 'lesbian' by virtue of immediate vilification—monsterization literally s/he attracts, the 'woman' does as much as to challenge reproductive temporalities and heteronormative expectations as the word 'wolf' does to dislocate our compulsory anthropomorphisms. Woman and wolf together, taking long walks, talking to one another, upset reproductive temporality. That is—the expectation that individual temporalities are organized to service heteronormative requirements—and immediately attract censure much as particular kinds of same-sex female couples might. Their otherness from everyone else's organization of their own socialities becomes rather immediately dangerous, but they are able to walk to another realm of freedom or safety of which this story is a 'subsequent history' also, suggesting that the act of writing, the rendering of lives in narrative, representations of (un)familiarity exist in the quotidian world both as trope and as literal presence.

The (un)familiarity of the subject matter at hand requires me to elucidate, problematize, and, often provisionalize, a number of key words in my title, whose meanings are often transparent. So as not to risk complete unintelligibility, let me define 'lesbian' now. *Webster's Ninth* defines lesbian as a woman 'characterised by a tendency to direct sexual desire toward another of the same sex', while the *Encarta* calls a lesbian 'a woman who is sexually attracted to other women', while lesbianism is 'sexual attraction and sexual relations between women'. But what does this mean? What does it mean to be 'sexually attracted to another woman', or to 'direct sexual desire' towards another of the same sex? Would a woman have to sleep with, make love to, have sex with another woman in order to qualify as a lesbian? Is lesbian then as lesbian does? But if that is the case, then what about women who have erotic fantasies about other women but have never acted on them? What exactly qualifies as 'sexual attraction'? What about women who have lived with other women all their lives, and have certainly had sexual relations with them, but who all the same refuse the label 'lesbian'? What about all the women who did not even know there was a word for them because they always assumed that to be lesbian is to be something other than a lover? Or for, our purpose, would a woman qualify as a 'lesbian' writer if she wrote another woman a romantic poem, or a piece of erotic literature? But then, what about the non-erotic or non-romantic output of the 'confirmed' lesbian writer? Would it be unworthy of study by definition? What about the men who write about lesbianism? Would their literature then of necessity be disqualified?[1] This is not a problem with just the term 'lesbian' in particular; it is notoriously difficult to define what 'homosexuality' is for that matter. As David Halperin asks,

> Does the 'pederast,' the classical Greek adult, married male who periodically enjoys penetrating a male adolescent share the *same sexuality* with the 'berdache,' the Native American Indian male adult who from childhood has taken on many aspects of a woman and is regularly penetrated by the adult male to whom he has been married in a public and socially sanctioned ceremony? Does the latter share the same sexuality as the New Guinea tribesman and warrior who from the ages of eight to fifteen has been orally inseminated on a daily basis by older youths and who, after years of orally inseminating his juniors, will be married to an adult woman and have children of his own? Does any of these three persons share the *same sexuality* with the modern homosexual? (Halperin 1989: 46)

For the purposes of this research, we shall use Bina Fernandez's and Gomathy's definition of the term lesbian to include 'women who are in or desire to be in, emotional and/or sexually intimate relationships with other women. This definition therefore does not exclude women who are bisexual or women who do not use the word 'lesbian' to describe themselves' (Fernandez *et al*, 2003: 6). This definition offers a very broad range of possibilities as to the erotic/genital desires and intentions of individual subjects, and also allows us to go beyond the homo/hetero binarization of lesbians as other to heterosexual women.

This book, then, looks at lesbianism not exclusively as lived experience, but as Terry Castle suggests, as '*locus communis*, as site of collective imaginative inquiry, as topic of cultural conversation,' and 'its role as rhetorical and cultural topos' (Castle 2003: 6). It examines the creation of the 'idea' of the lesbian as she appears in the texts that I have chosen. Tagging this idea of lesbian, as it were, with a radio-isotope I attempt to follow its trail inside and out of other bodies of discourse that have been produced in the space of India's recent past. The endeavour, then, is to study how lesbianism has been seen, spoken about and written in contemporary South Asian narrative spaces of literature and cinema both. At the outset, I must state that this project is underwritten by the assumption that the study of love between women is a topic of 'serious and abiding human significance—bound up in as yet unfathomed ways with our deepest beliefs about nature and culture, sexuality and desire, femininity and masculinity, women and men,' as Castle puts it (Castle 2003: 1). It is a study of 'lesbian' texts, but not necessarily by 'lesbians' (self-proclaimed or suspected or otherwise), authored by women of Indian origin, at first or second remove sometimes. By way of a small, but growing and rather interesting corpus of literature written by women of Indian-origin on the subject of desire for other women, I study the re-worlding of the world, snatching often out of unimaginable pain a small space for subjectivities that do not fit within heterosexuality.

The 'lesbian writers' approach, focussing on the output of 'confirmed' lesbian writers, does indeed have many strong points in its favour; there is no denying the filiational or community-building power of such works, identified by the sexuality of their authors. The works of Suniti Namjoshi, one could argue, are particularly open to such an inspection, as are the works of Monique Wittig (1992), or Jeannette Winterson (1991), or Clarice Lispector (2012), or earlier still, Radclyffe Hall (1982/1928), and so on. All of them have acknowledged their lesbianism, militant or otherwise, with open literary and other avowals, which have made it possible for later writers and readers to know unequivocally that their personal lives are testaments to the possibilities open to the lesbian in real life. The 'lesbian writers' approach while it is indeed a useful one in affirming identity and in creating a community of beloved writers, foremothers and other such useful points of reference for potential lesbian/lesbian-friendly readers and writers, and indeed, for the public in general, is, especially in the Indian context, an approach that is pulled up by frustrating biographical ambiguities, especially those necessary in a public culture where sexual disclosure must at best be partial, an approach that has by and large guided the Indian English literature publicity machine. Other inconsistencies in the larger public discourse also necessitate that one need not put all one's eggs into the identify-the-lesbians basket: male homosexual writers have always had more press and better press too, than female homosexual writers, as the instances of Vikram Seth and Raj Rao vis-à-vis Suniti Namjoshi show. While viewers see *Fire* as a 'Lesbian' film, Deepa Mehta insistently repeated that neither the film nor she was lesbian.[2] Similarly Kamala Das (1988) after the 'lesbian episodes' of *My Story* and *The Sandal Trees*, while younger writers like Abha Dawesar (*The Three of Us* (2003), *Babyji* (2005), *That Summer in Paris* (2007)) prefer to keep us guessing. The texts I study are not necessarily written by lesbians, either confirmed or suspected. While I agree entirely that the presence of 'validated' lesbian figures is very important in the forging and maintenance of viable lesbian identities, but at the same time, because the required biographical sleuthing is beyond the scope of this project, it will forgo unproductive and unsatisfying recces into the private lives of the writers chosen in favour of a 'lesbian texts' approach, which will concentrate on identifying the thematic, stylistic and other narrative descriptors of the 'lesbian text,' if there is such. I propose then, to follow the 'who wrote about lesbianism and how' approach rather than be confined by the 'who did what in bed' path.

In the Realm of the (Un)Familiar

The word '(un)familiar' in the title—with its parenthetical play— suggests both the unfamiliarity as well as the familiarity of the category of the lesbian in a literal sense. The word 'familiar,' according to the OED, pertains 'to one's family,' or 'to one's own kind,' and this meaning I shall extend to the homogeneity that the word 'homosexuality' seems to suggest. Thus, play of the word 'familiar' can suggest that lesbianism is a liking for one's own kind, for those akin to oneself (in terms of gender, biology, sex, etc.). Appending the 'un' to familiar to make the word 'unfamiliar', besides calling attention to connotations of 'familiar' that imply undue intimacy, suggests a gulf between the supposedly reassuring familiarities of heterogeneity, and by extension of certain forms of sexuality (here, the heterosexual), as opposed to the unsettling intimacies of lesbian love for one's own kind. At the same time, the parenthetical (un) suggests that the unfamiliar is already 'within' the familiar, and vice versa: interpreting this linguistic condition for my purpose, I shall take it to mean that homosexuality and heterosexuality are not in a relationship of duality or opposition, but are in a state of dialogue with one another, whether consciously or not. Thus, the (un)familiar is, to summarize, both a defamiliarization of the normal/normative, as also a comment on the unfamiliar propensities of what appears familiar. Further, the parenthesis in my use suggests that homosexuality and heterosexuality function within a 'spectrum' rather than within a polarized dichotomy. This is particularly important, because as we shall see, many of the texts that I deal with do not feature 'exclusively' lesbian subjects, but subjects which are imbricated in a variety of other sexual and affectional economies. Examining the construction of lesbian subjectivities in contemporary Indian and diasporic texts, studying these representations vis-à-vis perceptions of not only a normative heterosexuality, but also of a normative homosexuality, if there is such a thing, this book theorizes spaces beyond those of identity, presence.

A 'familiar' can also mean someone whose duty it is to perform certain menial duties, and equally, can also mean a demon or evil spirit one can call up at will: thus, the word has a number of connotations that range from the comforts of the congenial, the suitable, and the habitual, to the disturbingly different realms of fear, secretiveness, wariness. The word 'familiar' thus can be used as a point of departure to scrutinize the various tropes that several theorists have identified in lesbian writing, such as that of metaphoric reticence, often to the point of invisibility and erasure about sexuality, desire, orientations and preferences, and to uncover their existence or otherwise, similarities and deviations, in the textual corpus I propose to examine. The 'familiar,' I would argue, asserts difference proactively—it is at the same time, so 'familiar' (connoting here the reassuringly familiar), but also so '(un)familiar' (meaning here that which is devilish or evil), that it has been erased out of being, either by making it invisible, or by channelizing such energies into heterosexual relationships, or by disguising its truth in several other ways.

The familiar is demarcated from the unfamiliar by a very fine, porous line at best. The 'transgression,' to invoke Foucault, that permits the incursion of the unfamiliar upon the familiar is often provided by the presence of the 'fantastic', the radically different, that which seems barely possible, except within the realm of the imagination, or its lesser Romantic minion, fantasy. Tzvetan Todorov's distinction between the genre of 'fantasy,' and 'the fantastic' as a mode of writing, along with Kathryn Hume's definition of the fantastic as 'any departure from consensus reality' (Hume 1984: 21) both provide useful entry points. Todorov's definition of 'the fantastic' is worth quoting in full here:

> The fantastic [is] a hesitation common to reader and character, who must decide whether or not what they perceive derives from 'reality' as it exists in the common opinion. At the story's end, the reader makes a decision even if the character does not; he opts for one solution or the other, and thereby emerges from the fantastic. If he decides that the laws of reality remain intact and permit an explanation of the phenomena described, we say that the work belongs to another genre: the uncanny. If, on the contrary, he decides that new laws of nature must be entertained to account for the phenomena, we enter the genre of the marvelous. (Todorov 1975: 41)

The space of the (un)familiar, I argue, is generated by the existence of 'the fantastic' within what are otherwise works within the realist mode. However, following Christine Brooke-Rose (1981), we shall discard Todorov's requirement of the supernatural as the agency via which the fantastic enters the text. Brooke-Rose's notion (1981) that the moment of hesitation, between the uncanny and the marvellous, is sufficient for the fantastic to produce itself is more useful for our analysis. But since most of the texts that we analyse, however, are neither post-modern in technique and ambition, nor outside the conventions of realism, the word 'fantastic' itself might be a misleading analytical category for the purpose of our study, given its critical path this far. For our purpose then, we shall incorporate the above insights on 'the fantastic' in our understanding of the '(un)familiar'. Queer desire itself, interpreted in the light of the above formulations, constitutes a moment of unresolved ambiguity wherein lies an (often) unspoken challenge to heteronormative consensus reality. The realm of the (un)familiar then, is one that exists 'within' the familiar, and one that exists momentarily—flashing up within view when certain connections are activated by incursions into the counter-realistic, or the fantastic. The term '(un)familiar' has an advantage over 'the fantastic' in that it keeps alive for the reader the co-existence of both the familiar and the un-familiar, in space and in time, with the parenthesis at the same time calling to mind the strategies that push the unfamiliar to the boundaries of the familiar where it might languish as invisible or unsought.

Desire, in requisitioning the presence of an object of desire, is, in many senses, the self's encounter with the non-self, with the unfamiliar. Todorov himself distinguishes between the 'themes of the self' and the 'themes of the other' in the realm of the fantastic, noting that desire and sexuality constitute the distinction between the two. The analytic of the (un)familiar, I hope, will keep within our cross-hairs both the annihilation of difference between the familiar and the unfamiliar when desire makes its presence felt, as well as call to mind the subversion of 'consensus reality' by desires that are either not acknowledged or are proscribed by normative standards. In keeping both the familiar and the unfamiliar within sight all the time, the '(un)familiar' helps see the constant and at the same time, the constantly evolving nature of the threat posed to the normal/abnormal binary by queer desire, which makes its entry in what are often banal familiar spaces like the home.

Sexuality, along with spirituality and insanity, figures among the themes that are constantly dealt with through counter-realistic rather than realistic genres, and even within realist genres, as Todorov notes, these are precisely the themes of the fantastic as it were. The use of the fantastic as a mode permits these 'themes of the other' to make incursions into a 'consensus reality' that actively represses or punishes them:

> The fantastic permits us to cross certain frontiers that are inaccessible so long as we have no recourse to it. Summarizing the supernatural elements, as previously enumerated, we shall see the justice of this observation. Take, for example, the 'themes of the other': incest, homosexuality, love for several persons at once, necrophilia, excessive sensuality... It is as if we were reading a list of forbidden themes, established by some censor: each of these themes has often been banned as a matter of fact, and may still be so in our own day. (Todorov 1975: 158)

The social function of the fantastic then, as Todorov envisages it, is of use to us in our study of lesbian themes in the chosen texts. As we see it, the use of the '(un)familiar' by characters and authors permits texts to venture into the proscribed with the alibi of innocence. The realm of the (un)familiar then, is a realm where new cognitions enter the mind, *re*-cognitions are possible, and new selves that may be 'impossible' within familiar territories are suddenly possible. Identity formation is a process, a continuum. Identities once formed in the (un)familiar can rupture the seamless continuity of the familiar, the normative, thus forcing these, yet again, to shape themselves anew, possibly more inclusively. The (un)familiar then, helps question hegemonic ways of being and desiring, offering a multi-layered, intersectional rubric to think of lives that stand at a tangent to heteronormativity.

One intersectional dimension that is vital to this project is that of space—the 'realm' not as yet familiar to us in Namjoshi's fable. I conceive of sexual and other identities as both made in space as well as making space. On the one hand, 'alternative' sexualities are gradually achieving a mainstream presence, and are literally moving into central academic, spatial and socio-cultural locations. Sexual identities are not performed, inhabited or produced in a vacuum, but in a surrounding context, of heterosexuality, of class, of caste, of race, of age/generation, etc. The many constituent elements of one's sexuality thus express themselves in terms of spatialization—what entities of what manner of sexuality are allowed to occupy for example the space of the marketplace, the mall, the educational institution, the home, the nation, the diaspora? The various potentialities embodied in and expressed through various spaces within public and private spheres create subjectivities. 'Space,' by and large, is treated as intrinsically empty, attaining meaning only when it is filled, when vacuum is filled by matter, as it were. This conception of space as emptiness, as void, is unhelpful as its presumption of stasis means that space is necessarily viewed as ahistorical, value-neutral, and free of, say, the contaminations of power relations.

Scholarship since the 1980s has tried to problematize this positivistic characterization of space, revealing the constructedness of space itself, even in disciplines like geography. Steering away from a passively depoliticizing space, *(Un)Familiar Femininities* views space itself as a construct, a creation of different ideologies and governed by the rules of time. After Michel de Certeau, one can perhaps define 'space,' as distinct from 'place,' as not normatively stable or empty of significance; space is 'a practised place,' that is, as a place gaining significance or meaning depending on what happens in it and who uses it (de Certeau, 1984: 117). Re-worlding the world, to use a formulation from Judith Butler (1990), has long been the political aspiration of queer studies. The question of space is all the more poignant for non-normative subjectivities, particularly feminine ones in a country where property rights for women are fictive on the ground and ill-understood even by well-educated women. Access to suitable spaces, as V. N. Deepa of Sahayatrika notes, is often the criterion that determines whether or not a lesbian existence is unliveable, even in a state like Kerala that, at least on paper, has the best social development indices for India (Deepa 2005: 187–92). Spaces, to live in, work in and to achieve dignity in are often, as we shall see below, wrought out of older, often patriarchal, heteronormative and repressive spaces. How have they been imaginatively transfigured?

While Indian feminist scholars have been attentive to the gendering of space in Indian contexts, and much important work has been done on the 'centrality of women to the formation and continuation of the domestic space' (Niranjana 2001: 108) their studies have been implicitly, exclusively heteronormative in perception and expectations of the various terrains of spatialization they have mapped out, as for example Seemanthini Niranjana's *Gender and Space* (2001). Meenakshi Thapan's *Embodiment: Essays on Gender and Identity* (1997: 3), for instance, makes available a revisionary formulation of space in noting that the 'woman's body is … central to understanding unequal gender relations', but does not concurrently theorize how the same women's bodies might also be sites where sexualization is actively played out, debated and constructed. Niranjana's work (2001), like Michel de Certeau's (1984), offers useful pointers on how a study of space as active may go beyond an oppositional binaristic formulation of space as full/empty, pure/impure, etc. Space, Niranjana notes, is gendered to produce insides and outsides, with the inside being associated with purity, sacrosanctness and auspiciousness, vis-à-vis the outside which lies beyond the threshold for attainment of these. The inside is also a space for security and inviolability, not necessarily only a space of subordination as the domestic/public sphere dichotomy would imply: this binary

treats the domestic as subordinate because the domestic by definition implies lack of participation or control on public, political and
economic matters. Inside/outside goes, in Niranjana's formulation,
beyond merely physical, immobile space—'space' is defined not by
where it is, but by the bodies that inhabit it, and what they are
permitted to do in varying contexts. But even so, the inside/outside
relational unit does use the woman's body to draw lines between
communities, for example, with the result that women are in turn
restricted with regard to certain contexts and opportunities even as
they may be empowered in others. Spaces, then, also signal what
bodies may or may not do in them. Homoerotic desire re-draws some
of these lines; making women available to one another when they
are forbidden to men of corresponding communities for instance, or
transforming notions of purity, inviolateness and chastity by revealing them to be always already under siege within the very homes
that are supposed to keep them safe. Space thus may be sexualized
differently from how it is gendered. Where Partha Chatterjee (1989)
posits a difference between inner 'private' and outer 'public' spaces
at least in the context of Indian anti-national movements and indigenous modernity, the above sequence of ideas illustrates that the
inside/outside dichotomy is not so easily evident in the question of
sexuality, where presumably 'private' and privatized behaviours not
only have public consequences, but are also shaped, disciplined and
modelled by public structures or 'networks of desire,' as Elizabeth
Grosz (1994) calls the circuits of meaning-making systems we are
all part of and within which alone our 'emotions' attain meaning.

Shilpa Phadke *et al.* (2011) in *Why Loiter?* imagine feminine occupation of public urban spaces in extraordinarily empowering ways,
though even here the overt focus is the unsexed 'female' body that is
implicitly heterosexual. Phadke's typologies for women's occupation
of street spaces is nevertheless able to normalize women in the public
sphere, theorize the role street spaces play in the construction and
enactment of notions of femininity, masculinity and gender-based
violence in ways that are useful to this project. Extending Phadke's
questions, this book asks how the non-heteronormative sexualization
of the body of the woman transforms the space of the street and thus
of society beyond the domestic sphere of the home, and in turn,
do particular kinds of spaces allow for particular expressions of (un)

familiar femininities? Chapter 1 studies the 'lesbian vernacular,' the butch female body as an 'event' in urban space, in the street, at work, in school, that impinges on the implicit compulsory heterosexuality of the public sphere. Such performances of female masculinity, transitory as they are in their interruption of the public sphere's heteronormativity, 'produce a space of public culture that powerfully critiques ... the hegemony of dominant nationalist ... formulations' (Gopinath 2005: 30), besides serving as a critique of the variously normative practises of less fleeting media—like the published texts of the film, the book, the song and so on. Such 'queer ephemera' (Munoz 1996: 433) which would otherwise be 'lost in relation to the space of heteronormativity,' help us map a number of subjectivities that would otherwise not be registered within the dominant protocols for the study of the nation or the production of subjectivities within it. Further, such moments of performance enable us to locate the nation itself, accessed through imaginations of the city, of subjecthood within larger forms of community than that of family, within transnational flows of capital—both economic and intellectual, all the more significant almost an absolute majority of the organizations in the area of sexuality activism are non-governmental and receive funding from mostly Western agencies.

Coming Out into (Un)Familiarity

Transnational political work, particularly work that has been performed by NGOs, has increasingly privileged the figure of the 'out' homosexual as the ideal, normative version of homosexuality. Two contexts in which female homosexuality is made visible, albeit only to the careful observer, are those of the scandalous twin-suicide or lesbian-suicide, where both partners have either successfully committed suicide, or were 'saved' therefrom, and that of the lesbian marriage, whose successful completion is usually prevented at the nick of time. Sometimes the two collide, as in reports on television channels of a lesbian marriage in small-town Punjab that fell apart[3] when one of the partners announced to the district magistrate that she no longer wished to live with the 'boy,' who then tried to commit suicide. The report, which ran the same footage without any contextualization, also mentioned another such marriage in the region. It also carried prominently the views of the 'girl's' side; the father of the girl said the 'boy' had dressed as a man and had lured his daughter with promises of taking her to Canada. Another typical kind of programme is the more supportive reality feature on the lived conditions that greet lesbian existence in India.[4]

Lesbianism does not have the 'talkability' that male homosexuality, with its culturally empowered location within patriarchy and male homosociality, still has in many contexts in India. As such, in a society with hardly any precedents for their behaviour, no role models to identify with or emulate, lesbian subjectivities are fashioned through considerable pain. These (un)familiars became visible only when the dizzying levels of everyday violence they have had to encounter, from being given shock therapy as a 'cure' for homosexuality, to being disinherited, abused physically and psychically, to being denied life itself, crossed a particular 'limit,' and then acquired a name and a history. A community of suffering and solidarity as much as a community of desire shapes the realm of the (un)familiar of lesbian desire. Their bodies are the sites that queer, feminist and other theories have been labouring over, their rights are the rights that jurisprudence has been steadfast in not granting, their desires are those desires that evoke a self-righteous shudder in every self-respecting heterosexual woman, and either a grin of voyeuristic pleasure or righteous disapproval in (mostly) the heterosexual person. Within this framework, the question of the coming-out story is a significant one. How is (un)familiarity to be placed in relation to the discourse of coming out?

The genre of the coming-out story is perhaps the pre-eminent one in gay, lesbian and transgendered narratives. To use a rather reductive definition, it is the tale of 'an individual's path to gay, lesbian or bisexual identity' (Saxey 2008: 1), but as Eve Kosofsky Sedgwick has shown persuasively, a necessary tool for homosexual survival, given how the lack of a 'gay' heritage or history has meant that homosexuals have 'always with difficulty and always belatedly have had to patch together from fragments a community, a useable heritage, a politics of survival or resistance' (1991: 81). In this light, the coming-out narrative may be seen as a necessary survival story of the history of non-heterosexuals in a world of 'high ambient homophobia' (Sedgwick 1991: 81). The centrality of the narrative has not gone unquestioned.

Judith Roof maps out the key plot points of the coming-out story thus:

> Each narrative features a protagonist who somehow feels that she does not fit into the role typically assigned to women in the larger heterosexual cultural story....The lesbian protagonist experiences an internalized struggle between her discomfiture with the known heterosexual part and an unknown, but intuited, correct identity. She pretends to be straight, affects an unfelt stereotypical femininity, and feigns an interest in boys. Solving the conflict between inner and outer by aligning the inner lesbian with the ultimate truth of lesbian identity finally expressed in self-affirmation and visible 'lesbian' behavior, the lesbian protagonist's assertion of lesbian difference becomes the victorious truth of lesbian identity and the end of the story. (Roof 1996: 104–05)

For one, the coming-out story is repeatedly excoriated for mimetically reproducing structures of heteronormativity within a homosexual framework. It might even be possible to argue that the coming-out story produces a narrative of 'alternormativity,' or in other words a normativization of how to be homosexual. The coming-out story is also deeply connected to visibility, with its concomitant baggage of recognition, social endorsement and/or censure. Frequently, criticism has centred on how the coming-out story celebrates the creation of stable lesbian/gay (and far more infrequently, transgendered) identities and generates such catharsis around this process of creation that other structures of oppression that persist beyond these celebrations are ignored and sometimes even valorized. The coming-out story, in this line of thinking, loses its opportunity to take on structures of hetero-dominance in its hurry to validate conservative models of self-fashioning. The coming-out story has also been criticized for its strong Western roots—the post-Stonewall era is after all the heyday of this narrative—and for thus seeking to validate Western epistemologies and models for political work unquestioningly (Gopinath 2005). Calling Audre Lorde's *Zami* (1982) a coming-out story hardly describes that text fully or well. Yet, like all coming-out stories of great value, Lorde's 'biomythography' as she calls it, is also at heart a story about understanding the relationship between one's different erotic needs. Her 'mytho-graphy' of the coming of age of a lesbian is presented in terms of her own life, a feature that many coming out narratives share. As Esther Saxey shows in *Homoplot*, the coming-out narrative is heavily invested in the truth value of the story in question, 'narratives typically express or assume autobiographical verity and claim to represent truthfully the story of a gay/lesbian hero or heroine's life' (Saxey, 2008: 35–36). A.C. Liang argues that there is 'no prototypical meaning of homosexuality,' any more than there is a 'central definition of coming out' (1997: 291), but critiques of the form have typically argued that the coming-out story is related to the individual's awakening to what appear to be 'true,' prior, unitary, stable, essentialist sexual identities. In other words, the coming-out story appears to merely provide examples for a pre-existing type. These narratives then appear to have disturbingly ahistorical implications too that needs to be carefully unravelled.

Journeys into Visibility

The coming-out story however has a vital role to play in the creation of viable non-heterosexual life-possibilities. Narrativizing (un)familiar journeys becomes thus a fraught, high-stakes project. For as long back as I myself can remember, Malayalam language newspapers carried accounts of groups of girls who had killed themselves by jumping in front of trains, into water bodies, consuming poison together and so on. The frequency of these suicide reports meant that one took them for granted, hardly ever asking why so many of them took place and equally important, why the young women in question had companions in each of these efforts. What explains this terrible phenomenon in a state that is apparently developmentally ahead of its other Indian counterparts? The famous 'Kerala model' of development has to be problematized and understood anew, as many scholars have shown, to arrive at answers. Ligy Pullappally, then a lawyer in Chicago, set out to make a direct political intervention after receiving an email about yet another 'lesbian suicide' from Kerala, Her film *Sancharam* makes a powerful case for representing lesbians and lesbianism positively. An affirmation of female–female desire that does not end in suicide was long overdue, and Pullappally's text, like Deepa Mehta's *Fire*, must be studied as a campaign document at the very least. Unlike *Fire*, *Sancharam* wishes also to make the case that lesbianism does not have to flow from heterosexual angst, disturbance, or deprivation. Pullapally's self-awareness about her location within the projects of queer studies and sexuality studies perhaps prevents her from making disingenuous defences of her film, unlike Deepa Mehta who at one point had said that *Fire* was not about lesbianism at all, and was instead about 'choices.' Where *Fire* intervened to 'invent' lesbians in India, Pullappally sought to show that 'lesbians' do and did exist in India anyway, actively placing her act of making *Sancharam* in Malayalam rather than in English within the framework of queer political work. This is an important gesture, as the space devoted to feminine development and growth is near zero in terms of screen time allocation, as the hero's development gets the bulk of onscreen time; in fact, the heroine's growth might be placed exclusively in terms of getting her to compliantly accept a subordinate place within a heteropatriarchally defined Malayali modernity. The diegetic placing of Malayali heroines is always within a frame that marks desire as heterosexual; heroines are also constantly being shaped for a heterosexual future existence. Female subjectivity that is not exclusively defined by male requirements is an unfamiliar type in Malayalam cinema; *Sancharam*'s representation of a female homosociality that also has within it an active sexual component is almost unthinkable, explosive even.

Sancharam (2005) tells the story of two girls whose lives are disrupted in their final year of school by their desire for one another. Kiran and Delilah are neighbours in a small Kerala village; schoolmates who do everything together; they end up falling in love. Their intimacy is discovered by a teacher and a fellow-student; the latter tells on them while the former communicates the template of impending social disapproval in her reaction to what she has discovered. Once their families come to know about their love, efforts to separate Kiran and Delilah are put in motion, prime amongst which is the quick arrangement of Delilah's marriage to Sebastian, a doctor who is shortly to settle in the USA. Delilah's marriage to such a man will of course put her physically out of Kiran's reach; Kiran's despair pushes her to think of suicide. The film begins with her standing on the brink of a waterfall, poised to jump, even as Delilah's wedding is underway in the village church. Delilah has what seems to be a nervous breakdown just before she is supposed to say 'I do,' and the energies of her dithering communicate ethereally to Kiran, who finally decides not to jump, but to go on with what at least for the present is an attenuated life. *Sancharam's* representation of its protagonists' relatively cloistered home-lives frees the screen of the hypermasculinity it is constantly in danger of descending into. In a major symbolic departure in terms of cinematic history, *Sancharam* places love between the women at the centre of the story, not as one of two equal or unequal subplots, a move that makes evident its politics—that of claiming an autonomy for female homosexual subjectivity that is not dependent on male–female erotic structures.

While *Sancharam* locates love between women within the familiar realm of the home, it in unable to make this space itself (un)familiar because of its unreflecting invocation of various stereotypes, such as the wandering soothsayer—female here—to contest the claim that lesbianism is neither 'traditional' nor 'Indian'. The soothsayer's likening of Kiran's and Delilah's love to that of the ideal deified couple of Shiva and Parvati is an effort to say traditional epistemologies have means of cognizing non-normative loves; yet, ultimately, the model is the normative heterosexual couple of Shiva and Parvati. While this heterosexualization of lesbian romance can be seen to be expressive of the lack of a heritage that gay and lesbian people feel, the film maker's own historical location gives her access to ground-breaking pioneering scholarship on histories of non-normative sexuality in Indic contexts, such as Ruth Vanita's and Salim Kidwai's anthology *Same Sex Love in India: Readings from Literature and History* (2000) or Ashwini Sukhthankar's *Facing the Mirror* (1999), an anthology of lesbianism as lived experience for Indians today. Scholarship of this kind has been invested in rigourous historical materialist analysis of how modern heteronormativities have come to be created and maintained. *Sancharam's* political project of representation then does try to depoliticize its own creation of the figure of the 'Indian lesbian'. Again, the soothsayer herself represents the immobile Malayali nation, beyond modernity, in a timeless neverland where Kiran's homosexuality is the first, the unique expression of difference. The force of consensus reality is that proscribes (un)familiar desire in a 'land steeped in tradition' is also represented as so exceedingly powerful as to evict the desiring woman from her home. In other words, (un)familiar desire itself is, in a sense, presented as 'unusual' even as the film tries to show that unusual does not mean abnormal. All the same, casting homosexual love as a clearly labelled 'difference' separate from the meanings and intentions of the society it develops within, *Sancharam* is in a sense a step backwards from *Fire* where the intensely gender-segregated homosociality of the joint family is itself seen as a point of origin for (un)familiar desires. As depicted in *Fire*, the space of the home, of the family, of the nation are all, as we shall see below, always already marked by this desire: there were no pure spaces to begin with, and (un)familiar love can be present anywhere.

At the same time, *Sancharam*'s choice of adolescent protagonists permits us to dwell on etiologies of the lesbian, of the (un)familiar. The underwriting assumption of the coming-out narrative is that there is a core lesbian identity that will come out. In placing the growth of their love in the home space and following it from childhood to late adolescence, Pullapally reinforces lesbian love as identity, as elemental to the self, as constitutive, and places lesbian experience amongst one's most primary experiences through a number of episodes and stories that resonate with a number of foundational lesbian 'moments' in mainstream Western lesbian texts. *Sancharam* acknowledges the very porous borders that keep female homosociality and female homosexual desire apart. Where the same-sex spaces of the women's hostel or educational institution are also important, it is often possible to isolate these as finite experiences separate from what is to come after. Lesbian desire can often be cleanly relegated to spaces that one outgrows; by extension, leaving these spaces behind also means leaving the desire behind. Yet, at the same time, in presenting this very lesbian love as something that disrupts 'a land steeped in tradition,' *Sancharam* has the effect of cleanly separating lesbian love from the familiar spaces wherein it first erupts, a removal that is problematic in its surrender of the home as a possible space for (un)familiar love. Further, the girls' love for one another is uncluttered by any other encumbrance: no other attachments to spouses/children, etc, which in some ways renders the exile of the lesbian subject unproblematically cathartic and freeing.

Next, the picturesque local traditions and spaces through which local contexts are invoked for the viewer also encode privileges connected to caste rather than only suggesting traditional female homosociality, though these can be indeed spaces for the latter. The traditional *thiruvathirakkali* dance, the *sarpa-kaavu* or serpent grove, and the *kulippura* or bathing pond, to name but a few are spaces that are by and large gender-segregated. The bathing pond where the two girls consummate their love is a space that is also at the same time an instance of a space that is grounded in caste-arrangements but presented in a decontextualized way within the plot. Such a private bathing enclosure, contrary to what outsiders might believe, is not available to all Malayalis. Instead, it forms one of those special enclosures of the *tharawad* or upper-caste ancestral house that in contemporary Kerala is more of an exception for use as an everyday bathing enclosure rather than the norm. The film though is set somewhere in the post-globalization phase, as one frame each of a film magazine and a scene in the street with telephone booths indicate. In the last two decades at least, the use of such a location for one's daily bath is an unlikely fact; its presence in one's life's pattern suggests the continuance of older feudal property arrangements that benefitted the uppermost castes in particular. The film locates Kiran in one such feudal, ancestrally matrilineal household; however, matrilocal residence does not guarantee an emancipatory approach to desire. Contrary to lay perceptions on the subject, matrilineal arrangements such as the ones the Nairs followed were not necessarily empowering to women either as propertied or as sexual subjects. Effective control of the homestead and its properties usually lay in the hands of the *karanavar*, one's mother's brother. While the Nair household for any woman inhabitant in its traditional form was one that gravitated around one's natal family, with a fringe of spouses immediately surrounding it, and where all arrangements to meet life's necessities, except the provision of sexual needs, were already available within this homestead, the film's depiction of matriliny does not necessarily explore creatively the implications of such long term matrilocality for women residents nor does it study the implications of homosocialities produced by traditional gender-segregation. While sexual needs would be met by means of visiting male spouses, this may have guaranteed a modicum of freedom to the female partner, but at the same time, one must note that the procreative function is still central to the Nair household. The woman must have children to carry on the line; matriliny is invested in carrying out certain heteronormative functions just the same as patriliny. Matriliny's possibilities for relative feminine autonomy are displaced and foreclosed here by depicting the matrilineal household as headed by a heterosexual nuclear couple. Kiran's inheritance then is not matriliny, but a modern nuclear family, a relatively recent historical arrival in Kerala, despite the film's normalization of it as the structure of functioning for Malayali households. In this sense, then, Kiran's mother, a Nair is as heteronormative as are Delilah's people, who are Christians.

Sancharam, while unyoking femininity from heterosexual desire or desire for a masculine object, does not necessarily examine the historical processes of producing heterosexual conjugality or patrilineage in Kerala to understand the processes of heteronormativity as they exist here. Instead, characters voice a variety of prescriptions that dovetail into normativizing femininity—for example, women should wear a lot of jewellery and stay at home instead of playing sport, says one character who is not contradicted thereafter; a place like this would have been a useful one to assert the real authority of the *tharavattamma* rather than leave untouched the compliance of the *veettamma*'. While real female authority is not necessarily a challenge to heterodominance, after all, much of Kiran's tragedy is produced by the real lack of social power for all women, including (un)familiar ones.

This lack of social space can be seen in the scarce public resources available to women for the sustenance of a non-normative relationship in Kerala (see V. N. Deepa in Narrain and Bhan 2005). *Sancharam* can be viewed as an exemplum—a moral story for how life should have been for these two girls, but how it turned out to be ; but despite its garb of near universality, or perhaps because of its need to appear universal, the film does not take into account how the specific difficulties of sustaining a lesbian relationship in Kerala also stem from the near total subordination of women to patriarchy demanded in Kerala's modern public sphere. As V. N. Deepa of Sahayatrika notes in her powerful piece in *Because I Have a Voice* (2005), men and women have different perceptions of their entitlement to the resources available to the individual for personal emotional sustenance. Men were the more frequent callers to the state's first designated lesbian helpline; women callers, on the other hand, few, and far between as they were, were more hesitant to make claim to a space designated specifically as theirs. Their caution and their sense of being undeserving of such autonomy which acted, as Deepa notes, as a barrier to many women initially in using the helpline, are particularly characteristic of how femininity has come to be shaped and perceived in this state. While Pullapally's film is concerned about making itself intelligible under the sign 'lesbian' with the result that the film is intelligible to anyone who watches it as a love story pure and simple, of two girls separated in love; the reduction of the problems of this relationship as a problem of 'homosexuality' rather than as a problem of female subservience, connected in turn to socio-economic structures, this film relies on the narrative of decontextualized lyricism.

In making itself intelligible as a thwarted romance, the film endorses rather uncritically Kiran's upper-caste position. Kiran's Nair ancestry, humanized with the help of the love-story of an ancestress who left it all behind for the love of a foot-soldier and journeyman, explains, for example, her endurance. Once ousted, Kiran tells her mother she will resist staunchly everyone's effort to quell her since she has blue blood, the blood of princes, running in her veins. Why must upper-class, feudal rank be deployed to help tell what is typically the story of economically and socially backward-caste young girls ending their lives when confronted with a heterosexual future? To the outsider, perhaps, Kiran's regal Nair identity might be necessarily exotic, fascinating and even endearing; perhaps the regality confers nobility of character in turn, but within the Kerala context, this invocation is more than problematic. As V. N. Deepa notes in her essay (2005), women from the lower castes and classes seem to be more prominently represented among those who have committed suicide rather than enter compulsory heterosexuality. While Deepa adds as corollary that higher castes, with greater access to social and financial privilege, are also more equipped to keep such data about their womenfolk from entering the records, the fact remains that in the public imaginary, the story of young girls killing themselves has been the story of the subaltern Malayali rather than the upper-caste one.

Pullapally's invocation of the Nair sub-caste's claims to martial and psychological superiority to tell their story is problematic to say the least. Both of *Sancharam*'s heroines are in positions of relative privilege, but in using Kiran's Nair ancestry as guarantee for her seriousness of intent restricts the scope of the presumably empowering gesture that Kiran's character is making for other such embattled lesbian women. Historically, the Nairs' access to social, economic and cultural privilege gave them ascendancy in Malayali life that arguably continues today and is the focal point of much social discontent in the state still. The character of Kiran, who happily allows herself to be addressed as *thambratti*, princess, a conventional greeting to upper-caste women, thus when translated for viewers of another social strata, sadly and irresponsibly routinizes lesbianism as an upper-caste phenomenon.

While many spaces in the film uncritically echo caste-privilege, Pullapally's use of the bathing enclosure in a film about lesbian love must be placed in a more favourable context. As a space for erotic encounter, the bathing pond had been a staple in most Malayali films till the 1990s; the hero and heroine invariably met for a secret liaison at the bathing pond, which being gender segregated, was a space that the opposite gender must necessarily literally penetrate in order to get an audience with their beloveds. In this film however, the depiction of love for one's likeness rather than for one's other, means the film-maker has an opportunity to queer one of Malayalam cinema's most resolutely heterosexual and male homosocial spaces. Friendships between men are frequent, in fact the norm for Malayalam cinema's circuits of desire, as T. Muraleedharan (2010) argues very persuasively. Perhaps unsurprisingly then, friendships between women are not; femininity is marked by not only its subordination to masculine preoccupations.

Femininity is also marked by its isolation from its own gender, especially in the last three decades of Malayalam cinema, which has seen a gradual diminishment in the roles given to female protagonists, a diminishment that may be said to have begun in the 1970s. Through the last three decades in particular, Malayalam cinema has proved to be stringently conservative in its representations of femininity, belying its reputation for radicalism among regional cinemas. Female homosociality that is physically demonstrative is not suspicious or marked as sexual in most traditional Indian conceptions of desire that cannot be allowed; indeed that place is occupied most often by heterosexual love, often deemed impermissible because of incommensurability in caste standing or intentions, as some of the protagonists' schoolmates find out. Kiran, identified with the life of the mind, is the 'teacher's pet,' while Delilah is presented as natural and sensuous. Kiran is also carefully placed as quintessentially Malayali in seeking to contribute creatively to the language she aspires to be a writer in, and indeed a poem of hers titled, with emotional portent, 'The Awakening'—suggesting Kate Chopin's novel about sexual coming of age at the same time—is published in an important Malayalam literary journal.

The link between creativity and survival, between being able to represent non-heterosexuality and being able to thus find resources within such representations for survival are part of the film's structuring. For example, the sexual charge between the two girls first finds expression through ventriloquism, in the form of an impromptu shadow-puppet play where Kiran is able to voice undying faithfulness and love to the 'woman' she addresses; later, the film subversively replaces the male poet who sings in the romantic lyric mode with the female poet, Kiran, whose writing and reading inscribes this (un) familiar love with a poetry that would normatively be the preserve of heterosexuality. Kiran's later reading, in the classroom, of 'Krishna you seem to have abandoned me' by famous Malayali woman poet, Sugatha Kumari, unshackles devotional love and the mystic experience of union with god/beloved this love can bring about from the traditional conception of the lover/beloved pair as cross-sexual, as the film shows Kiran's mature exegesis as drawn from her own still unconscious love and longing for Delilah.

(Un)familiar love is also generated as equal to heterosexual love within the film's plot, where Kiran and Delilah are surrounded by many successful and unhappy narratives of heterosexual fulfilment or its thwarting. Kiran's great-grandmother had abandoned her great family for the love of a poor soldier; his first gift to her was a glass bangle which was Kiran's mother's most prized inheritance amongst all the ancestral goods she inherits. Delilah's grandmother has loving memories of her dead husband, with whom she awaits reunion in death, though still joyful in life through her relationship with her beloved grand-daughter. However, a sense of how love is normatively valued and constructed also emerges through a set of other stories— two classmates of different faiths—one Hindu and one Muslim, elope from school only to be apprehended amid great scandal and public castigation. Heterosexual love is also revealed to have more tragic consequences for women than it does for men in the story of another female classmate who had been impregnated by a man she believed had loved her; however, he betrays her and she is forced to have an abortion.

For Kiran and Delilah, however, the impediment of heterosexual love is partly comedic, arriving in the persona of their classmate Rajan, who develops an immense crush on the beautiful Delilah, but Kiran has already occupied his 'natural' position as admirer of a beautiful girl. Through its appropriation of the solo dance scene in a saree that reminds one at the same time, of both the Shiv-tandav and the sight of innumerable Bollywood heroines in big blockbusters—Sridevi in *Chandni* (dir. Yash Chopra, 1989), Madhuri Dixit in *Beta* (dir. Indra Kumar, 1992), Juhi Chawla in *Darr*, Urmila Matondkar in *Rangeela* (dir. Ram Gopal Verma, 1995) to name only some of the most iconic, *Sancharam* subverts the visual referencing of such renditions of hyperbolic femininity by having Delilah perform just such a dance in a bright red saree in a dark smoky room with no other contours. The dance is entirely in Kiran's imagination, and it is a revelation to her and the audience that such a hyperbolic femininity can be appraised by a female gaze as much as it can be by the expected male gaze. Kiran is the homospectatorial audience then, whose desire for the leading lady is unmistakable and can be equated with the desires expressed by the male hero for the person of the heroine. Unlike the male hero, however, our protagonist cannot insinuate herself into such a dance scene by imagining it to be her due; she is tormented by nightmares in which Delilah dances like Shiv would on the burial ground. Pullapally's use of a respectably heterosexual convention to convey the sexual power of a desiring female gaze, loving a female body, is in keeping with such introjections of queer desire into familiar heterosexual locations and conventions by other directors like Pratibha Parmar in *Khush* (1991) and *Nina's Heavenly Delights* (2006), or more intrepidly by Deepa Mehta's use of old Hindi film songs as the stimulus for an impromptu fancy-dress dance at home in *Fire*. In all these cases, an open form, usually interpreted as heterosexual, can be appropriated by viewers of any persuasion to produce sites of immense pleasure.

At the same time, the film's static representation of Kerala as an unchanging domain brings with it a variety of problems. Setting such a story in a 'land steeped in tradition' does reify lesbian love. Love for a lesbian familiar when itself set in an unchanging realm congeals the meaning of lesbianism in much the same way as Judith Butler (1990) points out—continuous acts of performance makes gender congeal around particular bodies. Here, the effect is to valorize a particular romantic version of lesbian love, untainted by the contaminations of compromises such as marriage or poly-amory, besides reifying feudal, class and caste privilege. *Sancharam* encodes its lesbian love story in ways that would not be immediately obvious as classist or casteist to the non-Malayali viewer, who is the default viewer, given the film's distribution strategy. The film, out on Wolfe Video, a relatively main-stream US gay-and-lesbian distribution node, is one that is more eas-ily available for a dollar price on amazon.com than it is at any Indian outlet. Slotted as a 'lesbian' film, it was very favourably reviewed by peers in the gay and lesbian circuit and won a number of awards at film festivals, but is yet to have a non-festival large-screen release in Kerala, though promotional material such as trailers and music videos initially and later, the film itself, aired on various Malayalam cable channels. Given its international film-festival record and its touring chart which covers more western metropolises than Indian ones, *Sancharam*'s reception history is very different from *Fire*'s. *Sancharam* performs another kind of re-orientalization of the east. The film's DVD blurb locates the lesbian romance 'in a land steeped in tradition,' presenting same-sex love as necessarily making a break with tradition; however, as we have seen, (un)familiar love need not necessarily do this, and all breaks with tradition need not be subversive either. *Sancharam* ends with Kiran divesting herself of a symbol of her femininity—her hair. For one, this trimming suggests also the taking of religious vows, espe-cially since it comes after her having decided to wear white clothes, which she buys after pawning the minimal jewellery she wears. It is true that Pullapally does not shave off Kiran's head, but nevertheless, the plot up to that point suggests that Kiran will head in the non-marital direction, opposite to the one Delilah has taken.

The Nair home, which Kiran does not unequivocally renounce, may still be changed when it is headed by a Kiran who refuses to marry and continue the illustrious lineage. What looks like Kiran's asceticism might also be interpreted as Kiran's possible adoption of a butch identity, as Kishore Kumar suggests (Interview with Pullapally in the DVD); but her truncation of her own femininity is in either instance so as to undertake erotic responsibility for her (un)familiar love while at the same time not giving up claims to home. While it is a rare, invaluable instance of characterizations of autonomous femininity in Malayalam cinema which is so lacking in such depictions, the film's adherence to a theory of lesbian representation that is prior to the narrative impedes its artistic development. *Sancharam* cries out for these complexities to be part of the lives of those who resist compulsory heterosexuality. Pullapally arguably achieves what she sets out to when Kiran does not jump off the cliff. Her voiceover on the DVD states that Kiran was to have died as per the original plan. In 'saving' Kiran, Pullapally is indeed making a very strong case for survival at all costs, continuity and endurance rather than naive idealism. Where there are hardly any positive representations of lesbians, each film that does not kill its lesbians counts for a great deal. We must thus credit Pullapally for what she does achieve—in producing credible protagonists, making a powerful interruption in the politics of visibility by creating very visible and very dignified protagonists who are treated with compassion by their maker. The many homophobic castigations Pullapally received at various film screenings in Kerala, as also the various stratagems employed during filming, such as not telling people that this was to be a lesbian film, all illustrate amply the personal courage required to make these interventions (DVD features of the movie).

In stopping just short of pushing Kiran into this real world in which we so desire to take her measure, the film is indeed resorting to catharsis—upon the formation of a lesbian subject as a substitute for political reflection. When Kiran is outraged by Delilah's pragmatic offer of a secret relationship on the fringes of her marriage to Sebastian, *Sancharam* slights the compromises many women who love other women must make in marrying, marginalizing bisexual subjectivity completely further. The film-maker is clearly with Kiran's high romantic refusal of such a ploy; heteronormativity itself may offer spaces for the enactment of female same-sex love and desire, as the case of *Fire* proves. The film's answer to Delilah's question of how they will survive in the harsh world beyond their homes without graduating from school is a very depressing one. While the film shows its protagonist as successfully making the 'exit from heterosexuality' (to twist Bonnie Zimmerman's hypothesis [1983] that an 'exit from patriarchy' was the basis of lesbian desire), this however imbricates it in constructions of lesbianism that are themselves exclusivist in a number of constricting ways.

Privileging Kiran's emancipatory, utopian lesbianism rather than Delilah's pragmatic lesbianism, if such we may call it, the film refuses to consider the subversive potentials of strategies that may at first appear compromised or diluted in comparison to homogenous, totalizing, 'positive' characterisations of sexual subjectivity. However, these interventions in the form of direct gay and lesbian political work, especially the generation of positive representations, are often hampered by their translation of often western forms of sexual subjectivity into 'indigenous' locations. Pullapally too does confine herself to the emergence of lesbian desire as desire rather than also as a political tool for feminist liberation. Esther Saxey's complains that one effect the coming-out genre has had on the 'love that dare not speak its name' is that it 'frequently becomes compelled to speak only its name (Saxey 2008: 143), with the result that sexuality becomes the overpowering facet of identity rather than one constituent facet of individual identity.

Feminist, Queer, (Un)Familiar

But if Kiran lives, where does she go to? What are the intersections of the women's movement in India with its queer faction? The point at which sexuality becomes visible as an issue on its own is after the HIV-AIDS crisis of the 1980s, with funds coming primarily for medical welfare, such as disease prevention and palliative care. Lesbian women were perceived as a low-risk group, in comparison to high risk groups like Men-who-have-sex-with-Men (MSMs) and sex workers, it is disputable whether lesbian and bisexual women benefited from the upsurge in activity on sexuality related issues in the social arena, though it may have resulted in some marginal increase in visibility.

Among the pioneering organizations to claim a space for lesbian women, for example, was the Delhi Group, which started to meet in 1989, followed by 'Red Rose' meetings, again in Delhi, but these are only a few instances from among almost a dozen other organizations and groups that did not survive long. The genuine breakthrough was the formation in 1991 of Sakhi which became the 'first openly lesbian group involved in networking, research and documentation of lesbian images and history in South Asia,' with an archive of personal narratives beginning to flow in from all over India (*Humjinisi* 183). A year later, Sakhi calls for its inclusion among the databases of women's organizations published by two important organizations: Jagori and Kali for Women. Stree Sangam followed much later in 1995, in Mumbai; thirty women, mostly urban, attend their 'First National Gathering of Women who Love Women'. Stree Sangam still survives; today it is called LABIA, because its members decided to 'not [be] hidden any more under innocuous sounding names like 'Stree Sangam' but [to be] in the open, stating who we are,' as founder member Chayanika Shah notes in Narrain and Bhan (2005: 150).

Today newer organizations include Sappho for Women in Kolkata, Sahayatrika in Kerala, Sangini Humjinisi and Caleri in Delhi. The interventions of various such organizations have helped complicate Indian feminism's otherwise uncomplicated affiliation with heteronormativity. Feminists who wanted to mount a critique of heteronormativity came to be branded the 'radical feminists,' in keeping with Western nomenclature, as Chayanika Shah notes, though they self-identified as the real Marxist feminists (Narrain and Bhan 2005: 144). Till the emergence of this non-heterosexual critique, Indian feminism by and large has worked with defintions of family and marriage that, for instance, do not query their heterosexual assumptions; the patriarchal, procreative family has remained the threshold upon which all battles for women's empowerment have been fought. Be it property or reproductive rights for women, Indian feminist organizations have by and large taken normative gendered and sexual positions for granted. Further, sexuality was more or less deemed to be a 'private' question of preference and regard rather than a 'public' question in which consciousness could be raised or mobilized to change things or secure rights. In fact, as Maya Sharma puts it, the women's movement for decades held on to the position that sexuality, read homosexuality, was a threat to the movement's unity. As Sharma trenchantly observes, the women's movement by and large has put off politicization of lesbian issues on the grounds that 'such politicisation should be postponed for a later time, presumably when there is a greater level of societal awareness and acceptance of homosexuality' (Sharma 2006: 22), but the irony is also that it is the responsibility of just such movements to produce the spaces within which sexually minoritized women can dialogue with the rest. However, this 'paternalistic' dismissal of lesbian issues by 'mainstream' feminism points us in the direction of the split between gender-based oppression, and sex-based oppression; lesbian women are oppressed not simply because they are women, but because they are 'perverts' too. As Shah notes, 'we recognised that we were one of those oppressed minorities who had been invisiblised by the larger women's movements' (Narrain and Bhan 2005: 147) an insight that provides us, thus, with yet another inflection for 'coming out,' beyond the personal sense of coming out to one's immediate community. The questions of desire and pleasure that lesbian subjectivities raise have taken the subject 'woman' beyond the discourse of reproductive rights or victimhood that Indian feminism has most often addressed. This is a very important plank for protest; lesbian rights, in this argument, 'by their very nature foreground women as autonomous sexual beings imbued with selfhood, reason and desire, thus do not confine the issue to a particular sexuality or identity category, but open up possibilities for an overall redefinition of women, women's rights and human rights' (Sharma 2006: 27). The appearance of the sexually active woman in her own right has also been made possible by the lesbian feminist interrogation of mainstream, largely Marxist Indian feminism. Becoming visible and claiming spaces, especially public ones, become the most important agendas of this incipient queer feminist critique of feminism, an agenda that often was at odds with the mainstream 'women's movement.' For instance, questions about who should join Women's Day Parades would often elicit such demurrals as 'our women will not be able to identify with groups whose names contain words like Lesbian and so we cannot march with them for 8th March,' or 'there are no lesbian women amongst the women that we work with;' still others would argue that the very invisibility afforded to lesbians because of public ignorance should not be shattered by consciousness-raising or staking claims for space. Yet others would claim that lesbianism was only an urban phenomenon (Shah in Narrain and Bhan 2005: 147).

Of course a single forum would not be capacious enough for the various kinds of subjectivities and problems that needed to be addressed. Elavarthi Manohar one of the founder-members of Sabrang notes, most organizations do not provide a space for bisexuality; and organizations for gay men are not above the sexism and misogyny of heterosexual males, meaning lesbian women within such organizations were made uncomfortable and invisible (Narrain and Bhan 2005: 110). Where would lesbian women meet other lesbian women? Manohar provides statistics—more than fifty cruising sites for men existed in Mumbai in the 1980s, and none for women. Lesbian women are among the most invisible and the most resource strapped, spatially, economically, sexually and culturally, of the many sexual minority groups that have registered on the radar.

Reading Texts, Finding Lesbians

Same Sex Love in India, edited by Ruth Vanita and Saleem Kidwai (2000), provides short critical introductions to pieces, either in translation or in English, provides a model for exploring expressions of same-sex love that are emotionally primary and central to the actors involved. Vanita's and Kidwai's anthology is but a beginning, indicating that there are a number of directions new scholarship on the subject can take. For instance, their compilation does not anthologize much Indian Writing in English, as a result of which Suniti Namjoshi is not discussed at all; nor are writers like Kamala Das, Shobha De, Manju Kapur or Divakaruni, to name but a few who have dealt with female-female bonding, homoerotica or homosexuality in their works. At the same time, this anthology is a very important contribution to queer/gay/lesbian studies the world over because it breaks with what we might call a Foucauldian orthodoxy. Foucault's statement that the homosexual became a species in the year 1870 elides a number of facts. As another of Vanita's books shows, Foucault's *History of Sexuality* neither takes into account traditions of female homosexuality, nor does Foucault provide any justifications for the massive leap of several decades that he makes between the ancient and the modern periods: Vanita (1996) conclusively demonstrates that the medieval period was a rich source of writings and representations for both male and female homosexuality that would certainly not bear out any sweeping generalizations about how 'the sodomite had been a temporary aberration; the homosexual was now a species' (Foucault

1978: 43). Vanita's and Kidwai's anthology collects evidence to say that the 'homosexual role,' as Mary McIntosh (1996) calls it in another groundbreaking essay that preceded Foucault's 'invention' of homosexuality, did ante-date the late nineteenth century. As much other evidence shows, the medicalization of homosexuality did exist in other cultures in other ages; Zwilling and Leonard (1996) make this point for Indian heterodoxical approaches like Jainism and the third sex, the '*tritiya prakriti*'.

Giti Thadani, whose work *Sakhiyani: Lesbian Desire in Ancient and Modern India* (1996), is acknowledged by Vanita and Kidwai as an important contribution to the field, is relegated to a footnote in their anthology, but at the level of providing a theory speculating about the origins and antecedents of lesbianism in India, Thadani's is a groundbreaking effort. *MoebiusTrip* (2003) is another of Thadani's works which belongs in the genre of the travelogue, and which argues that the Feminine Principle has been systematically erased out of the Indian temple-architectural sphere, queering through its very premise several notions of sexuality as also philosophical, cultural and spiritual concepts that we take to be normative. *Facing the Mirror* (1999) is an anthology of autobiographical pieces along with shorter-length academically backed essays by writers including Thadani and Vanita. Edited by activist and lawyer Ashwini Sukhthankar this anthology is important in the diversity of material it assembles; organizing itself into thematic sections like 'home,' 'passages,' 'differences,' 'love,' and the like, it is significant if only for the range of specificities and milieus within which it locates the 'Indian lesbian.' It clearly belongs within the genre of autobiographical writing that as Biddy Martin puts it, wishes to generate identification and build community; as such, it collects pieces in a language that is not 'scholarly' so much as accessible and has a number of first-time contributors, ostensibly lesbians, writing under pseudonyms. All the same, *Facing the Mirror* carries a number of pieces on 'contentious' and 'controversial' aspects of lesbianism like sado-masochism, pornography, physical abuse and bisexuality. While not as 'damaging' as similarly-located Western collections like Joan Nestle's *The Persistent Desire* (1992), which featured, among other things, anal sex between lesbians, *Facing the Mirror* manages to claim a spectacular degree of sexual specificity and heterogeneity for lesbians/lesbian-friendly readers. Rather than settle for a politically correct collection where a self-censoring 'feminist' lesbianism alone is represented, it is an impressively heterogenous collection of what a lesbian might be in India. *A Lotus of Another Colour* edited by Rakesh Ratti (1993) collects diaspora-centric narratives of lesbianism; *The Very Inside* (1994) edited by Sharon Lim-Hing brings together some occasional writings by South-Asian-Pacific lesbian/bisexual women; however, this anthology for one does not collect major prose writers/novelists, and among major Indic writers, only features a few poems by Suniti Namjoshi.

Critical literature like *Queering India* (2003) is a collection of several essays that challenge the interpretative heteronormativity of most scholarship on different areas, be they readings of film, or of Urdu homoerotic poetry. Scholarship in a number of other areas, such as sociology, medicine, law, economics, architecture, religion and so on are of use, but only tangentially, in that none of them is centred around evaluating the textual manifestations of what may be called 'lesbianism' in India. *The Phobic and the Erotic* (2007) is another collection of critical essays that attempts to provide a prolegomena for the study of non-normative structures of desire, which, the editors Brinda Bose and Subhabrata Bhattacharya argue, attract responses that fall between the structures of phobia and of eros. Nivedita Menon's *Sexualities* (2007) carries forward the project of ending the silence on homosexuality that characterized an earlier collection edited by Mary John and Janaki Nair, called *A Question of Silence* (1998), subtitled *The Sexual Economies of Modern India*. While *Sexualities* does carry one insightful essay, by Georgina Maddox on the construction of modern lesbian sensibilities in India, this collection does not engage with textual representations of female homosexuality as such. *Because I Have a Voice*, edited by Gautam Bhan and Arvind Narrain, both of whom are activists, is a powerful collection of campaign documents from the ground, with a number of seasoned activists from various regions of India providing a genuinely diversified view of what it means to do political work in the area of sexuality in India. Lay perceptions of the 'lesbian' feature her as a westernized individual whose 'difference' is not merely sexual, but cultural; Maya Sharma's *Loving Women: Being Lesbian in Underprivileged India* (2006) corrects this bias by presenting a critical autobiographical anthology of lower-class lesbian women. However, as of now there is yet no full-length study of how lesbian sexuality and its literary depictions have queered the normativeness of heterosexuality. Further, a study of the nature of this 'lesbian' textual subject, ascertaining whether this lesbian subjectivity is a homogeneous one, or if not, how its own heterogeneities affect it, how the lesbian is contextualized vis-à-vis constructions of normative homosexuality, and whether it is transgressive of the bounds this normativeness imposes, or whether it stays 'straight'-jacketed within these, is still due.

Thus, there is a need for analysis of how lesbianism in India has constructed itself in literary narratives, a need this project hopes to fulfil. Scholars like Thadani, Vanita and Kidwai and Sukhthankar have indeed made lesbianism familiar by collecting immensely important empirical and textual evidences that attest to the plenitude of female same-sex love within Indic cultures. These scholars have domesticated lesbianism in the larger sense by demonstrating through their works that a lesbian tradition, in terms of textual production and cultural visibility, exists/used to exist in India, and that it was not a foreign import. Their pioneering contributions to the construction of a topography of the narrative construction of female, and specifically lesbian desire has to be supplemented by a study of contemporary textual productions, which this book proposes to do. Interrogating the public politics of visibility that dominates the contemporary politicization of sexuality studies, I study just how (un)familiar renditions of femininity have decanonized desire.

Sexuality is not purely corporeal, as Grosz notes: 'The body image cannot be simply and unequivocally identified with the sensations provided by a purely anatomical body. The body is as much a function of the subject's psychology and sociohistorical context as its anatomy' (Grosz 1994: 79). The realm of the sexual will thus include not only 'physical' space, but also the corporeal body. Chapter 1, which I call 'Gender Insubordination' after Judith Butler's watershed essay of the same name, studies the production of masculinity as it is evidenced on female bodies. Using texts by three writers—Shobha De, Abha Dawesar and Amruta Patil—I explore the (un)familiar butch body, but not within the ghetto of same-sex living-arrangements such as Esther Newton (1993) describes in her sexual ethnography of 'Cherry Grove,' but as permeating everyday urban Indian spaces, 'dubbing' and hybridizing and thus de-essentializing masculinity as exclusively male through their gender presentations of female masculinities. Chapter 2 deals with (un)familiar life scripts for lesbians: a new design for living is possible for many as depicted by a set of 'multiplex' films featuring protagonists of Indian descent: *The World Unseen, Bend It Like Beckham, Chutney Popcorn, Nina's Heavenly Delights,* and *I Can't Think Straight.* The diaspora as home is also a realm of contest within which the female subject is imbricated in a discourse of stasis that keeps the diasporically dispersed—and thus dynamic—male subject, and his investments in patriarchy intact. Analysing multiple diasporic texts, from the old diasporas of the time of indenture capital in other colonies, to new diasporas of transnational movements of global capital, I ask whether the nature of the (un)familiar female subjectivity must necessarily replicate 'modern' notions of visibility and 'progress,' or whether other templates are available. While the latter two films are typically fairytale narratives in their explorations of what a lesbian subject in a First World environment would be doing, the others permit the articulation of difficult questions within realist conventions. Placing under the banner 'homonormativity' the overt politics of sexual identities as 'coming out' of the home of tradition to enter the emancipated realm of the public sphere, I argue that many of these films re-claim female reproductive work within the home as necessary for re-housing the (un)familiar feminine, who is one of conventional 'family's outlaws.' The home that is re-made and revalidated by these protagonists is also explicitly the 'home' of the nation; as diasporic subjects, these protagonists are participants in a relay of desire, identification and pleasure between discourses that seek to heteronormativize nation/diaspora, and discourses that queer such hegemonic formulations.

The 'femme film' as many commentators have defined it, converts the space of the women's picture—the school, the home, the brothel, the prison—into a space where femininity does not have to automatically couple with masculinity. The same proposition can be explored with respect to a number of literary texts; in Chapter 3, I study how some literary texts convert what appear to be the stock-in-trade of female homosociality into tropes of female homoeroticism, that is, how the lesbian (un)familiar materializes in a number of female homosocial relationships like sisterhood, motherhood, and relationships with the underclasses—often domestic servants.

Here, I argue that the space and the context of the home itself, while it appears rigidly heteronormative, enables the emergence of (un) familiar desire. The texts that I reflect on, eroticize, for instance, the bonds between sisters to suggest a redefinition of family in which the male spouse is secondary to the sisterhood, companionship and erotic interest that the 'sister,' whether literal or figurative, provides. The production of (un)familiar bonds between members of different social classes allows the eroticization of the differences in power that lie between members of these classes; but where such an erotics of power exists, opportunities for abuse also do, as evidenced in some of the texts we study here; is (un)familiar love doomed in relationships that function across major differences in age, social or economic power, or beauty. The final strand this chapter will explore is whether the 'femme' woman can attain the interiority and the autonomy—in terms of both personal and social space—for generating art, given that in many social circumstances women are the last to have a room of their own. This section explores the function of the (un)familiar lover as artist. Such an artist is invested with the major responsibility of producing an archive for (un)familiar love out of the ever changing vestiges of the home in which this love is generated. This part of the chapter considers if such an artistic project may leave a lasting legacy.

Chapters 4 analyses Ismat Chughtai's *Terhi Lakeer* as (un)famil-iarity's engagement with the discourse of modernity for both indi-vidual and the colonized nation; I argue that Chughtai's protagonist, Shamman, queers Indian late-colonial and anti-colonial modernity through her singleness. Chughtai's parthenogenetic (un)familiar delinks female desire, pregnancy and childbirth from masculinity's presence altogether, creating a template for how to resist patriar-chy and heterodominance. The latter part of this chapter assesses a segment in Anita Nair's *Ladies Coupe* (2004) which articulates a life-story for the queer lower-class/caste feminine, allowing a com-parative understanding of the genre of the novel of growth. Assessing available models of the bildungsroman, this chapter posits that the (un)familiar feminine's coming of age is attained through unbecom-ing womanhood, unlearning conventional meanings of home-work, care-work and motherhood. Arguing with, stretching, subverting normative femininity, the (un)familiar feminine is not one identity, but a series of events, subjectivities, small acts of resistance that allow the re-imagining of familiar realms of homophobia and dimorphic gendering.

Notes

1. A brief study of a few well-known illustrations from Western literature will further clarify these difficulties. Vita Sackville-West was certainly 'lesbian' and pursued a number of affairs in the cognizance of and often, with active help of her husband, Harold Nicholson. But are Vita Sackville-West's conventionally-stylized novels more lesbian than Virginia Woof's *Orlando* (1928)? The eponymous Orlando of the novel is a transparent tribute to Sackville-West's protean, almost changeling personality, but Woolf, by her own admission and as per the endorsement of biographers, lesbian-friendly and otherwise, never did much sexually, lesbian or otherwise. So how does one bracket or hierarchize the works of these two authors? Woolf's novel, in its sheer androgyny has a narrative depth, lesbian and otherwise, that far outclasses Sackville-West's orthodox 'lesbian' fictions. So who is the more lesbian of the two? And if that wasn't mortifying enough, Djuna Barnes, whose *Under Nightwood* (1936), another lesbian classic, assiduously rejected the label 'lesbian',' though this novel draws from Barnes' own affair with the painter Thelma Wood, with whom she lived for almost a decade in Paris. Barnes preferred to say that 'I just loved Thelma' (Castle 2003: 4) rather than be labelled 'lesbian', however satisfying that label might have proved to her vast legions of lesbian admirers. And finally, to go a bit further back, Emily Dickinson, who seems never to have acted on a single sexual impulse, heterosexual or otherwise, certainly did love a number of woman, and as a number of her poems show, this love was emotionally primary and central to her love. But if she did not do it, then how are we to call her lesbian or anything else sexual for that matter? But at the same time, are we to ignore the same-sex eros that is so sharply evident in poems like 'Going-to-her' and 'Her sweet Weight on my Heart a Night'? How, then, to study the literature of lesbianism if one is not sure who the lesbians are. And the above examples have been enlisted simply to show how one can never be sure.

2. Mehta, Deepa. 'I Can't Understand the Stereotyping of Women'. Interview with Suparn Verma. Rediff on the Net. October 24, 1997. Accessed on 19 July 2008.

3. Retrieved from http://ibnlive.in.com/news/lesbian-marriage-falls-apart-in-punjab-one-booked/44151-3.html. The television footage showed the latter woman in a state of extreme distress, crying aloud and having

to be held back by people as she tried to commit suicide in protest against the separation.

4. The programme 'Lesbians Forced to Live in Anonymity' featured sympathetic interviews with a variety of lesbians, including many of the people who spoke about their own life-experiences at the LesBiT inaugural. http://www.ndtv.com/convergence/ndtv/story. aspx?id=newen20080048221

References

Brooke-Rose, Christine. 1981. *A Rhetoric of the Unreal: Studies in Narrative and Structure, Especially of the Fantastic*. New York: Cambridge University Press.

Butler, Judith. 1990. 'Performative Acts and Gender Constitution: An Essay in Phenomenology and Feminist Theory', in Sue-Ellen Case (ed.), *Performing Feminisms: Feminist Critical Theory and Practice*. pp. 270–282. Baltimore: The Johns Hopkins University Press.

Castle, Terry. 2003. *The Literature of Lesbianism*. New York: Columbia University Press.

de Certau, Michel. 1984. *The Practice of Everyday Life*. Berkley, California: California University Press.

Chatterjee, Partha. 1989. 'The Nationalist Resolution to the Woman's Question', in Kumkum Sangari and Sudesh Vaid (eds), *Recasting Women: Essays in Colonial History*. New Delhi: Kali for Women.

Das, Kamala. 1988. *My Story*. Kottayam: DC Books.

Deepa V.N. 2005. 'Reflections on Sahayatrika', in Narrain, Arvind und Gautam Bhan *Because I Have a Voice. Queer Politics in India*. Delhi: Yoda Press.

Dawesar, Abha. 2005. *Babyji*. New Delhi: Penguin Books.

———. 2007. *That Summer in Paris*. Knopf Doubleday Publishing Group.

Fernandez, Bina and N. B. Gomathy. 2003. *The Nature of Violence Faced by Lesbian Women in India*. TISS, Mumbai: Research Centre on Violence against Women.

Gopinath, Gayatri. 2005. *Impossible Desires: Queer Diasporas and South Asian Public Cultures*. Duke University Press.

Grosz, Elizabeth, A. 1994. *Volatile Bodies: Toward a Corporeal Feminism*. Allen and Unwin.

Hall, Radclyffe. 1982/1928. *The Well of Loneliness*. First published in 1928. London: Virago.

Halperin, David. 1989. 'Pederasty, Politics, and Power in Classical Athens', in M. B. Duberman, M. Vicinus and G. Chauncey (eds), *Hidden from History: Reclaiming the Gay and Lesbian Past*.

Hume, Kathryn. 1984. *Fantasy and Mimesis: Responses to Reality in Western Literature*. Metheun.

Liang, A. C. 1997. 'Creating Coherence in Coming-out Stories', in Anna Livia and Kira Hall (eds.), *Queerly Phrased*. New York: Oxford University Press, pp. 287–309.

Lispector, Clarice. 2012. *The Passion According to G. H.* New Directions Paperbook.

Mcintosh. Mary. 1996. 'The Homosexual Role', first published in Social Problems, 16/2 (1968). Reprinted in Steven Seidman (Ed.), *Queer Theory/Sociology*. Blackwill Publishers: Cambridge/Mass.; Oxford, pp. 33–40.

Muraleedharan, T. (2010) 'Women's Friendship in Malayalam Cinema', in M. Pillai (ed.) *Women in Malayalam Cinema: Naturalising Gender Hierarchies*. Hyderabad: Orient Blackswan, pp. 154–177.

Munoz, José Esteban. 1996. 'Ephemera as Evidence: Introductory Notes to Queer Acts', *Women and Performance: A Journal of Feminist Theory*.

Namjoshi, Suniti. 1998. *St Suniti and the Dragon*. Melbourne: Spinifex Press.

Narrain, Arvind and Gautam Bhan (eds). 2005. *Because I Have a Voice: Queer Politics in India*. New Delhi: Yoda.

Nestle, Joan. 1992. *The Persistent Desire: A Femme-Butch Reader*. Alyson Publications.

Newton, Esther. 1993. *Cherry Grove, Fire Island: Sixty Years in America's First Gay and Lesbian Town*. Boston: Beacon Press.

Niranjana, Tejaswini. 1998, 'Left to the Imagination: Indian Nationalisms and Female Sexuality in Trinidad' in *A Question of Silence? The Sexual Economies of Modern India*. Mary John and Janaki Nair (eds). New Delhi: Kali for Women.

Niranjana, Seemanthini. 2001. *Gender and Space: Femininity, Sexualisation, and the Female Body*. New Delhi: Sage Publications.

Phadke, Shilpa, Sameera Khan and Shilpa Ranade. 2011. *Why Loiter? Women and Risk on Mumbai Streets*. New Delhi: Penguin.

Roof, Judith. 1996. *Come, as You are: Sexuality and Narrative*. Columbia University Press.

Saxey, Esther. 2008. *Homoplot: The Coming-Out Story and Gay, Lesbian and Bisexual Identity*. Peter Lang.

Sedgwick, E.K. 1991. *Epistemology of the Closet*. Hemel Hempstead: Harvester Wheatsheaf.

Sharma, Maya. 2006. *Loving Women: Being Lesbian in Underprivileged India*. New Delhi: Yoda.

Sukthankar, Ashiwini. 1999. *Facing the Mirror: Lesbian Writing from New India*. Penguin Books.

Thadani, Giti. 1996. *Sakhiyani: Lesbian Desire in Ancient and Modern India*. Casell.

———. 2003. *Moebius Trip*. Spinifex Press.

Todorov, Tzevetan. 1975. *The Fantastic: A Structural Approach to a Literary Genre*. Ithaca: Cornell University Press.

Vanita, Ruth and Saleem Kidwai. 2000. *Same-Sex Love in India*. New York.: St. Martin's Press.

Winterson, Jeannette. 1991. *Oranges are Not the Only Fruit*. London: Vintage.

Wittig, Monique. 1992. 'One Is Not Born a Woman', *Feminist Issues I: The Straight Mind and Other Essays*. Boston: Beacon.

Zimmerman, Bonnie. 1983. 'Exiting from Patriarchy: The Lesbian Novel of Development', in *The Voyages in Fictions of Female Development*, ed. Elizabeth Abel, Elizabeth Langland, and Marianne Hirsch. University Press of New England, pp. 244–257.

Zwilling, Leonard and Michael J. Sweet. 1996. '"Like a City Ablaze": The Third Sex and the Creation of Sexuality in Jain Religious Liteature', *Journal of the History of Sexuality*, 6(3): 359–384.

1

Gender Insubordination
(Un)Familiar Butch Desire

'They wonder to which sex I belong,' said Rosa Bonheur, the French painter, to her sister in 1884, about the puzzlement her androgynous appearance elicited from the provincial gentry at Nice, where she had gone in 'her usual smock and trousers' to sketch, and where the most common description the ageing Bonheur elicited was the 'little old man' (Vicinus 1993: 285). Martha Vicinus' scholarly account of the different forms 'lesbianism' has inhabited begins with this striking mention of a woman who looks like a man, and does not seem to be too unhappy to look like one, and who indeed in the contemporary world is the shorthand for lesbianism, the 'lesbian vernacular' (Rubin 2006: 472). 'Butch is the recognisable public form of lesbianism ... inevitably interpreted as the true revelation of female homosexuality. Butch is the signifying space of lesbianism; when a butch walks into a room, that space becomes queer' (Munt 1998: 54). Munt's placement of butchness as queering a 'room' allows us further to ask, how are bodies shaped by the spaces they are in? How are spaces in turn shaped by the bodies that inhabit them or pass through them? The figure of the flâneur, the idle stroller, is our optic for understanding how this (un)familiar is created, for we follow the 'butch' body through the space of the modern Indian metropolis to ask whether and how the 'mythic mannish lesbian,' following Esther Newton's rubric, is able to refashion spaces and in the process is herself figured and created (Newton 1984: 560).

The befuddlement of the holiday-makers at the sight of Rosa Bonheur can be theorized as mystification at gender displays that are at odds with normative expectations of gendering: Bonheur's gender presentation is at odds with biologically determinist understandings of who she should be. Femininity and masculinity are theorized both as practices—gender displays, how people 'do' their genders—and as discourses—assumptions and norms about how people should do their genders. Normative constructions of masculinity tend to privilege heteropatriarchal masculinity as dominant to both femininities and masculinities that depart from ideologies of male dominance/gendered inequality (Connell 1995). However, if one theorizes masculinity and femininity as practices and discourses available to all genders (Halberstam 1998 on 'female masculinity'; Pacoe 2007), transgressive gender-displays can be seen precisely as that—engagements, challenges, subversions of heteronormative gendering. The current chapter examines masculinity as extending beyond male bodies. Studying the physical presentation of gender by lesbian women who style what Halberstam (1998) calls 'female masculinity', I treat the self as 'a certain kind of gendered norm through dress, cosmetics, adornments, and permanent and reversible body marks' (Lorber 1994: 31). These 'body marks' may include gender presentation and gender display through not only clothing, but also through hairstyle, body language, gait, ways of talking, etc., all of which can come together or independently signal and articulate the gender of female-sexed bodies as 'masculine.' Female masculinity in particular is viewed as culturally disruptive, ignored and at the same time generative of great anxiety: the pathologization of butch lesbians owes a great deal to this cultural anxiety, for example (Halberstam 1998: 9). Female deployments of masculinity can be viewed as contaminating the appropriate relationship between femininity and masculinity, leading to the stigmatization of such gender presentations as 'pariah femininity' (Schippers 2007). Our analytic for such stigmatized 'pariah' femininities will be that of the (un)familiar, to emphasize the intersectional aspect of gender with race, caste, class and space (see Introduction). Social science research has shown in many western contexts that the presentation of female masculinity is often the most visible gender presentation of lesbian identity (Kennedy and Davis 1993; Moore 2006), pushing towards theorizing a connection between spatialization and (sexed) identity. An intersectional approach for studying how caste, race, class, gender, sexuality, and geography are simultaneously articulated and constructed (see Hill Collins 1990; Bettie 2003; Nagel 2003; Wilkins 2004) will be most useful here, as all three texts are indeed located within an urban space. However, as (Maya Sharma 2006) shows, the presence of female masculinities within urban spaces can also be, in the Indian context, not so much visible presentation of identity as much as hiding in plain sight.

There is the risk of assuming that all such extensions of masculinity beyond female bodies are culturally disruptive and transgressive (Halberstam 1998; Schippers 2007; Shapiro 2007), but as I shall show further, not all such gender presentations disrupt normativities of gendering. Some kinds of female masculinity are acceptable, even lauded, as in the case of successful female sportswomen (Pascoe 2007: 120). But these are not gender displays that necessarily challenge the gender order. In other words, it will be useful and necessary to distinguish between those gender presentations that explicitly critique gendered and sexual norms from the masculinity practices of women whose use of masculinity helps keep gender-bias in place.

The (Un)Familiar as the New Woman

The arrival of the person of the 'mythic mannish lesbian' or the 'butch' in the middle of the nineteenth century is for several scholars a watershed moment (see for example, Vicinus 1993); this moment is the point at which women who desire other women, whose primary commitments are to other women, are no longer hidden under the seeming asexuality of romantic companionship, nor under the usurpation of male masculinity by women 'passing' as men. In other words, butchness of this kind is an identity and not merely a behaviour, though as Martha Vicinus points out (1993), Bonheur's own description of her androgyny 'revel[s] in her gender freedom rather than her specific sexual identity,' which would be accounted for as 'lesbian' today as Bonheur lived all her adult life, in male dress, with her female partner Nathalie Micas. Vicinus identifies 'two major paradigmatic forms of lesbian behaviour, namely romantic friendships and butch/femme roles' (Vicinus 1993: 288), tracing a geneology for gender-transgressive appropriations of masculinity by women, placing the emergence of the 'cross-dressed masculine woman (the mannish lesbian)' at the beginning of the nineteenth century (Vicinus 1993: 244) and identifies her as the forerunner of the twentieth-century 'butch' identity. This gender-transgressive figure of the female 'invert' whose deviation from the prescribed norms for femininity ruptures the otherwise seamless normative relay of desire as always already heterosexual, besides undermining the fixing of masculinity to biological maleness and femininity to femaleness, further serves at that point also, as an alternative to the asexuality of the romantic friendship paradigm (Newton 1984: 567–68). Women like Rosa Bonheur, whose appearance today would fall under the rubric of 'butch,' and 'lesbian', made legible with their sartorial difference a difference in their choice of object of desire as well. In these genealogies of the 'lesbian,' the figure of the 'mannish woman' whose 'primary emotional and probably also sexual commitment was to women' (Vicinus 1993: 289) was a category different from that of women who 'passed' as men. It was like the cross-dressing 'military maids' from the seventeenth century who may originally have been licensed to dress like men, or the 'female husbands' who cheated their female spouses by pretending to be male.

This 'troublesome' category is that of the woman who does not pass as male, but whose sex nevertheless is a source of much discussion simply because of her difference from the normative codes for self-presentation. The difference is visibly signalled through her appropriation of masculinity/masculine devices and is identified by scholars as emerging from women's entry into modern professional spaces in the early nineteenth century. This precursor to the 'New Woman' is also drawn to the city, be it Paris or San Francisco or Chicago, attracted by the subcultures there that allowed them to explore their sexuality.[1] But these 'sexual migrations' do not guarantee liberty from heteropatriarchal discourses about femaleness and femininity. Where the mythic mannish lesbian may have been asexual in the nineteenth-century articulation of the type, in the twentieth, as cited in Hall (1982/1928) the 'invert's' body is invoked not only as a space of gender difference, but as a terrain for female personal liberty.

Where the figure of the 'lesbian' before this idea is muted, and 'only when [such] a woman seemed to contravene directly masculine priorities and privileges was she punished,' sometimes with death, that too only when 'sexual deviancy ... [was] compounded by a trespassing upon the male preserves of religion or politics' (Case 1993: 439), the 'mythic mannish lesbian' that Radclyffe Hall wrote into being was immediately recognized as transgressive to heteropatriarchal status quos. The banning of Hall's own novel, *The Well of Loneliness* thus is a reflection of its radical potentials. Its characterization of the doomed Stephen persists through to the 1950s in the image of the 'femme damnee'—the lesbian as doomed to permanent loneliness and suffering—as well as in the dominant idea of the lesbian as 'mannish.'

With feminism's mainstreaming thereafter, the focus comes to be the imagining of 'woman's body outside male discourse' (Vicinus 1993: 304), and the 'mythic mannish lesbian' is now the dyke, or the butch, and so on. Till date, in the popular imagination, the figure of the butch lesbian is the paradigm of (un)familiar difference, but where 'butch' within lesbian culture is used to signify the assumption of masculinity by a woman, it has in popular parlance often been a derogatory term to describe a woman whose femininity has gone wrong, that is, it has become far more masculine than it should be. At the same time, as Lilian Faderman points out, it is butch styles that translate in a watered-down way 'via feminist PC dress codes, *the* feminist style and the symbol for the authentic, non-male-identified woman' (Calhoun 1994: 578–96, 1996: 26, emphasis in original). Following through Esther Newton's idea that Radclyffe Hall's Stephen Gordon represented 'the New Woman's rebellion against the male order' (Newton 1984: 570), Cheshire Calhoun argues that this meant the gender-deviant strategies used here could be appropriated by heterosexual feminists against patriarchy to the exclusion of lesbian difference. Calhoun argues that the 'lesbian' thus disappears under the sign 'woman,' with 'gender' operating within feminism as a 'lesbian closet' (Calhoun 1996: 29), subsuming non-heteronormative revisions of hegemonic sexual codes and deflecting anti-heterosexist struggles into an apparently utopic universe where all hierarchies between sexualities can be addressed merely by the redressal of patriarchal oppression. The 'mythic mannish lesbian' in this account is thus not only the woman whose sex is ambiguous, but also the repressed other within feminist narratives of the struggle against patriarchy. This account of mainly Western history is useful in our encounter with Indian narratives of the idea of the lesbian as a 'mannish' woman whose failed femininity is censured as a function and product of her un-Indianness.

The butch lesbian is, as far as this book is concerned, an (un)familiar among (un)familiars. The bulk of the texts that deal with lesbianism in the contemporary Indian scene feature femmes; despite this preponderance, as we shall see, the concept of the 'femme' is relatively under-theorized in comparison to the butch. The womanly woman is for western theoretical literature what the butch is for this thesis: a barely there sign. The mythic mannish lesbian who so haunts the western literary imagination is not the most frequent presence in Indian literature, though it is indeed the figure in which some of the most pestilential homophobia and misogyny has been encoded. The butch lesbian as a sign of visible difference, however, renders the (un)familiar as an intelligible sign, though all the significations of the sign are possibly not fixable. In the treatments of Shobha De, Abha Dawesar, and Amruta Patil, we shall see the figure of the (un)familiar become that of the butch, but in different ways. De's butch is clearly misogynistic and homophobic; an examination of this misogyny and homophobia, however, is essential for an understanding of what reverse-discourse might be made to it. Dawesar's *Babyji* (2005), the protagonist of the eponymously titled novel, is just such a literal reverse discourse, while Amruta Patil's *Kari* (2008) updates the figure of the 'butch' to accommodate some more mainstream versions of femininity such as parcelled into video games and films in the fig-ure of Lara Croft. In what follows, I try to place these (un)familiar figures within contemporary India to provide a history, a 'network of desires' for the modern 'mannish lesbian' that many would argue does not exist in India. In some ways this is a just observation; two of the texts I write about have themselves been written within the last decade and globalization is thus one factor in the origins of at least two of the occupants of the points of the isoceles triangle these three texts together make. In all three cases, the butchness of these women is gender insubordination in more than one sense—not only do they usurp masculinity at a corporeal level, they further dispense with the masquerade of having been castrated that is essential to the production of 'successful' femininity. In having done away with the pretence of powerlessness, butch femininities trouble more than just the appearance allocated to bodies—they also renegotiate the balance of power between genders. Patil and Dawesar try to accommodate their (un)familiar protagonists through compensations that make their butch a literal familiar, gifted beyond ordinary people, while De goes all out to decapitate any vision of the butch as the better man.

The figure of the flâneur, idling, strolling through the city, looking at everything, is the hero of modernity (Munt 1998: 31). The figure of the flâneur, strolling and botanizing the streets and arcades of Paris, is at the heart of modernity's self-fashioning as both consumer of new capitalist spectacles as well as author of the experience of the city. Modernity's characteristic experiences have centred around big urban centres which have been home alike to the industrious and the idler, the homeless and the propertied, the rich and the poor, the consumer and the creator. The heterogeneities of the great cities have also generated anxieties about this very heterogeneity; cries to evict the migrant, the one unlike 'us' have echoed in every major city from time to time in periodic outbursts of xenophobia. Just as there is no flâneur without a city, every city will have a flâneur, looking at it, strolling through it, leisured enough to disrupt the city's maddening flow of purposefulness by virtue of his/her difference. The use of pronoun here is worth commenting on—the flâneur within dominant narratives of modernity is usually thought of as male and assumed of white raciality. This 'hero' of modernity is a patriarchal one, with the liberty to wander the streets at will, itself identified as an exclusively male liberty. The only women who routinely entered the public sphere were by default imagined as prostitutes and working-class women, who were never imagined as equals by the male flâneur who botanizes them (Wolff 1990: 35). A female flâneur, or flaneuse, seeing, strolling and authoring the city was thus unimaginable within the hegemonic narrative of modernity, though there exist a number of narratives from where one can build a very strong case (see Wilson 1992). What happens if we imagine the flâneur as female, queer and non-white?

In this chapter, I ask if it is possible to imagine the flâneur as not only female, but also as queer female, investigating her existence and her presence in urban spaces. Rather than imagining femininity as always peripheralized in relation to the discourse of the city, this chapter sees the (un)familiar feminine as both inhabiting and arguing with normative and hegemonic visions of city spaces. A female flaneuse does not have the same liberties as a male flâneur because women are positioned as objects and commodities within the heteropatriarchal visual economy that shapes this hegemonic discourse. Is it possible to imagine subversive possibilities rather than only containment in the dialogue between femininity and this hegemonic discourse? The discourse of women's safety has often pre-empted other ways of thinking about femininity in public spaces. The women's movement has generated important scholarship on different explicit forms of gender based violence, such as sati, dowry, wife-beating, rape, honour killings, besides legal reform and general sensitization (see Agnes 1992; Dave 2006; Kannabiran 2006; Kumar 1993), but theorizations of pleasure are fewer. This chapter pays attention to flânerie as an activity through which to think through the revisions of normativity that (un)familiar femininities occasion in the process of loitering and lingering in and thus inhabiting spaces beyond the private space of the home, rather than only purposefully moving through these areas. Using an intersectional analysis of gender, sexuality, class and geography, I show that the queer flâneuse rewrites the position of women in consumer society. Shobha De's *Strange Obsession* presents us an opportunity to explore normative discourses of femininity as object/commodity, which I follow with an examination of two revisions of this discourse that imagine femininity as (un)familiar, agent/subject rather than object/commodity in Abha Dawesar's *Babyji* and Amruta Patil's *Kari*. My interest here is in picking apart some of the gendered polarities of active/passive and mobile/immobile as they are produced in cultural representations of (un)familiar femininity.

Homophobia and Queerness: Shobha De's *Strange Obsession*

The women in my books are definitely not doormats. They are not willing to be kicked around. (Interview, *Asia Week*)

I write with a great deal of empathy towards women. Without raising a feminist flag, I feel very strongly about the woman's situation. (*Hindustan Times* 1995)

De has made a success out of the Indian market for popular 'romances' (to use this term in a broad sense) like no one else has. Her success, it might be argued, issues from her contextualization of the genre of the romance, as typified by the Mills and Boon or Harlequin titles for example, and adapting it to Indian conditions. De's novels, after the fashion typical of most bestselling romances written with a largely female audience in mind, centre on the thoughts, activities, and social coming-of-age of a female protagonist. The course of this action generally culminates in the creation of an ideal couple; in the process, this protagonist and her reader are both socialized into an understanding of what is expected of them romantically and emotionally, schooled into becoming successful middle-class urban women. De updates some stock elements of the romance—her women characters are edgy, many have 'balls that clang when [they] walk' (*Snapshots* 2006) many have already had some sexual experience, and most of them are in a position of relative economic independence if not dominance over their immediate surroundings. De adapts the otherwise homogeneously Western-inflected genre to incorporate details that structure romantic and conjugal relationships in an Indian context, such as arranged marriages, husbands who do no housework, wives who don't expect husbands to do anything at all, and the like. Initially, De's novels appear to avoid an overt endorsement of a heteronormative status quo by issuing what seems to be a spirited challenge, in the form of a recalcitrant female lead, to this status quo. But in most cases, this protagonist is schooled, implicitly, into not only accepting, but actively seeking her appointed place within the heteronormativity that she is initially resistant to. On the one hand then, De's novels reflect the anxiety of middle-class Indian women; her novels being written in English, one may assume that they are read by this class primarily, given Indian educational patterns within a transforming economic order, which in turn effects changes on the cultural order, changes that require presence of mind on the part of both the women readers and the women protagonists. On the other hand, De's novels neither subvert existing ideologies, nor offer a sustained critique of these ideologies, deflecting the very anxieties they reflect by devising conclusions where the women in question attain success in terms of the society within which their roles are changing. De's annexation of an implicit feminism in the quote above, however, is very questionable, as her novels would rather glamourize the few women who play by the rules of the rarefied worlds they are placed in, than consider any alternatives to the structuring principles of this world. Anything (un)familiar is, indeed, summarily banished from the pages of the average De novel.

Strange Obsession is one such work, with lesbianism, as per De's definition of it, constituting the central obstacle to the heroine's self-realization via heterosexual bliss. It is a strange novel indeed in how carefully it places a particular kind of female masculinity, which it identifies as the only form of lesbianism, beyond the pale of both womanhood or empathy. In another De novel, *Starry Nights* (1991), the heroine has lesbian experiences in the course of her career as child star of pornographic films before she escapes from this life by eloping to achieve heterosexual matrimony. *Snapshots* (1995) is the story of the reunion, one afternoon, of high school friends after two decades of no contact; all manner of stories come out, and lesbianism features, predictably, among a kilter of non-kosher activities such as incestuous and pre- and extra-marital relationships. It so happens that two of the characters whose 'snapshots' are being sought are still in a lesbian relationship that began in school, and that has, over the years, come to accrue increasingly pathological levels of dependence, guilt, and shame as per De's version. De seems to think lesbianism is best suited in the world of criminality, pornography, incest, or as an unsavoury aperitif before or an interlude between heterosexual courses. The wide readership of her novels— De is a bestselling author—however, necessitates that we look at these novels closely in order to fathom how the readers of popular fiction conceive of lesbianism. Though De's characters are nothing more than perfunctorily sketched, and her writing is densely packed with every cliché possible, her novels are as good a place as any other to begin an examination of the representation of the contemporary lesbian because De, if nothing else, has captured with an uncanny precision almost every misunderstanding of the 'lesbian' that exists in contemporary public cultures in India.

Shobha De's *Strange Obsession* is set in the world of fashion, at the heart of the production of the spectacle of consumption wherein women are eternally the object and a scopophilic predatory masculinity is constantly courted as the ideal consumer of this object. In placing a supposedly lesbian relationship at the centre of this novel that retains its pace through her obviously good knowledge of this world, De serves as our 'guide' to its mysteries. Departing from the bulk of the gossip industry's reportage of this world's relatively 'straight' transgressions, De's novel carefully purports to give the reader an ostensibly inside view of the 'real' doings of the stars we love, or at least love to follow. *Strange Obsession*, then, fulfills the requirements of the good bestseller—we become 'supertourists', to use Susan Sontag's phrase, who will be given an ethnographic tour of a strange realm, bring back 'news of exotic doings and strange gear' (Sontag 1973: 42), and as far as the obvious logic of the piece goes, we are to return to our less sparkling worlds comforted and elevated by the re-affirmation our superior sense of morality has received by what it has seen in the new world.

The contemporary city is itself a grand consumerist spectacle; if spectacle is 'a social relationship between people that is mediated by images,' the flâneur is the ultimate connoisseur of spectacle (Debord 1994: 2). The contemporary mega-city, such as Mumbai, is a metropolis quite different from the Parisian arcades of a Baudelaire, but the flâneur in this world is still a consumer of spectacle, particularly spectacle and image generated by mass media. In such a postmodern space, the flâneur is 'a vicarious conqueror, self-confirmed in his mastery of the empire of the gaze while losing his own self in the commodified network of popular imperialism' (Shields in Tester (ed.) 1994: 78). Within this economy where the gazer is the (implicitly male) flâneur, the city itself is often personified as a 'she'—Paris the city is always gendered female, and her charms are after all what the (male) flâneur and 'embodiment of the male gaze' lavishes on himself whilst he takes 'visual possession of the city' (Wilson 1992: 98). The underlying economy of exchange of gazes here then is directed between flâneur and the female city, whose gender thus becomes extendable to the objects the flâneur gazes at in the course of his/her adventures—a number of these objects are also feminized, and in the contemporary universe, woman as object appears not necessarily in the form of the grisettes and the coquettes of the Parisian flâneurs adventure, but as the spectacle (and image) of commoditized woman that is used to sustain the consumption activity that femininity, in another gendered polarity, is thought to be characteristically invested in. In other words, the image of woman is used to promote through consumer capitalism the idea that objecthood is for woman and subjectivity for men. What happens when a narrative makes a non-male masculinity the originator of this predatory, consuming gaze directed onto a feminine woman?

In De's novel our own standing as consumers, supertourists, voyeurs even, is mirrored in the behaviour of the villain of the piece, the 'mythic mannish lesbian,' the (un)familiar queer of the story. Minx's entry, immediately after Amrita's introduction, is as an evil familiar buying a cigarette across the street that Amrita, only shortly arrived in Mumbai, is clumsily trying to navigate, giving Minx occasion to come across and help her after berating the crowd of lusty onlookers who have gathered to behold the 'Shampoo *walli ladki*' (De 1992: 4) whose 'pretty pink panties' (De 1992: 5) as Minx notes later, only serve to collect more curious spectators. Amrita is depicted as lushly beautiful, in the tradition of both thoughtless potboilers and ancient classical texts, but unlike the heroines of the latter, Amrita is not shown to work towards self-realization that transcends the accident of her physical beauty. Thus, while very aware of the effect of her beauty on 'people' (De 1992: 3)—both on men and women, Amrita is the ultimate male fantasy—endlessly beautiful, but all body, all commodity, all consumption. Meenakshi/Minx, the incurable lesbian of this plot, with her masculinity gone wrong is the 'wrong' kind of male gaze; her scopophila is unacceptable coming from another woman but the same kind of gaze from biological males is legitimized as Amrita's due share of appreciation in the narrative. Meenakshi, as we shall see, provides an excellent example of heterosexist, homophobic understandings of what it means to be a lesbian; this means that she is very 'butch,' and thus, very dangerous. To carry the idea of familiars further, she is hardly ever referred to as 'Meenakshi,' barring a few occasions, one of which is in the newspaper obituary that informs the world of her death. Whether De does this consciously or no, 'minx,' with its sixteenth-century origins mired in the history of witchcraft, is a very evocative appellation for someone whose lesbianism is depicted as identical with a panoply of obsessive behaviours that seem to give her powers beyond the reach of ordinary mortals. Minx, suggestive of an evil sprite at large, is the lodestone of lesbian dysfunction for the purpose of the plot of *Strange Obsession*.

Two things strike one about the scene in which Amrita and Minx meet. The first is the virilization of the character who will shortly be revealed to be a card-carrying lesbian: Minx's confidence, which the novel ties to her butchness, to the fact of her being lacking in conventionally defined femininity, is in striking contrast with Amrita's lack of it, which in turn is presented as femininity. Second, Minx's casual confidence and knowledge of the city of Mumbai; Minx is everywhere, knows everyone—she is a kind of evil omniscience in Amrita's life, bestowing unwanted attentions on the new girl in town like she has on other similar girls she has predatorily consumed already. In other words, Minx is the flâneur as stalker, queer and evil, whose homosexuality as excess is the vehicle the narrative uses to externalize and make intelligible the multiple forms of violence women face in scopophilic urban spaces. However, the homophobic nature of this manoeuvre misrepresents heteropatriarchal violence itself as homosexual excess. Minx's persona is a curious mix of masculinity and misogyny even as it seeks to make love to other women, other women, the chosen erotic object to which the butch persona vitally stakes its claim to in the first place. Minx's butchness seen in this sense of taking 'erotic responsibility' for nonheteronormative affect is therefore not authentic in the world of *Strange Obsession*, as she is not innocently a production of masculinity on a female body. What Halberstam (1998) calls 'female masculinity' is here grafted onto violent, abusive, predatory consumptive behaviour, producing a scenario where Minx externalizes the idea of the male gaze as the 'vicarious conquerer' of femininity.

In housing this predatory consumption in another woman rather than in the more likely person of normative male masculinity, this novel under-represents the power of the male gaze to commoditize, surveille, and produce hierarchies which disempower the feminine. Pretending thus, the novel legitimizes the problem of gender-based violence is at worst a female collective hallucination and at best a female fantasy. The concept of butchness, as Esther Newton reads it, is not a mimicry of heterosexual masculinity, but is a subversion of the seamless transposition of masculinity onto heteronormativity by making the masculinity of a non-male body signify to other women (Newton 1984). That is, butchness makes masculinity unfamiliar in that this non-male body subverts heteronormative masculine gendering in order to make it intelligible within a homosexual/homoerotic continuum. As Esther Newton puts (1984) it, butches are not men, but are masculine lesbians who would like to make love to women. The butch's willingness to take 'erotic responsibility' even at the expense of exposing her subversion of gender to visibility and thus homophobia, thus, characterizes butchness in many readings.

However, Minx's desire to make love to women attains a level of erotic and material power that the 'ordinary,' or normative butch on the street would not have because she herself is a woman, deprived of many kinds of power within a patriarchal world. Because of constant gender-harassment, butches have to be 'tough' but Minx's butchness goes beyond 'toughness' to enter the realm of downright pathological disorder. Minx's butchness is indeed delineated by way of what would be reckoned as masculine activities and behaviours, but De goes beyond this in making her also the carrier of a hyper-masculinity, an exaggerated masculinity that the average male would find difficult to embody. Minx stands around on street corners smoking like the average man; she idles, but in the process also has friends in unsavoury places. Her career as 'fixer' is built on these connexions created through the communal idling that men feel empowered to perform in a way women both singly and in groups are not encouraged to do in most cultures.

The street as public space is not available to the 'woman' as *Strange Obsession* repeatedly shows, even as it is available to the perverted masculinity of Minx as it is to other kinds of criminalized or abnormalized normative masculinities in this novel. Minx is, in short, a *goonda*, which I argue, is as close to a familiar as one can get in the world of secular literature. The goonda, in both Hindi films and sundry Indian literary texts, is the one character-type who, by virtue of his occupation, is able to both gratify middle-class longings, as also rupture them. The goonda, located as he is just outside the pale of middle-class morality, is also the one character in Hindi films who seems to have a lot more fun than anybody else. He also seems to have a lot more rage, Amitabh Bachchan's angry young man persona through the 1970s and 1980s being a case in point. I use the male pronoun advisedly—female goondas are rare, and usually on a much smaller scale in terms of power. The crimes they commit are also pettier, as is their potential for vengeful vigilante redressals. Also, they do not seem to stay very long on the wrong side of the law—a (heterosexual) redeemer is not very far away; romance brings them back onto the path of the straight and the narrow. De creates an anomaly however—her female goonda is no *tapori* (the Marathi equivalent for flâneur but with connotations of lower-class and possibly abnormalized social position in relation to the law). Instead Minx is far more powerful than most of the men in the narrative to the extent even the law and order machinery stops working when she is on the scene. The (un)familiar as goonda or tapori is the opposite of the loiterer, as Shilpa Phadke theorizes her (Phadke *et al.* 2011); as voyeur, the female (un)familiar on the street is part of the threat, the risks that other females entering the street, the space of the public sphere, in *Strange Obsession* will encounter and be worsted by.

V. N. Deepa in her account of the short career of Sahayatrika, a Kerala-based lesbian help-group, notes, based on the nature of calls the group's helpline received, the general public seemed to think a lesbian was a woman who would have sex with anyone (Deepa, V.N., in Narrain and Gautam Bhan [ed.]. 2005). De takes this further by placing before us under the sign 'lesbian' a woman who will not baulk at anything in order to get another woman to have sex with her and with her alone. Minx's father is an Inspector General of police, so Amrita cannot go to the police to get her off her tail. Neither can she run away to Delhi—Minx has already made friends with her family and what is more, is an honoured guest at Amrita's house. Minx also gets the police, or hired killers, to damage Amrita's male lovers—a male boyfriend who is also conveniently bisexual, is tortured in jail following a police bust into cruising areas along the Mumbai waterfront; lover-to-be Partha has an accident along a deserted roadway immediately after a meal with Amrita during the course of which she briefs him about her 'unnatural' relationship with Minx, begging him to save her; a male photographer admirer is edged out similarly; a female competitor has acid thrown on her face and her insides ripped out with a blade to end her budding modelling career Several other episodes later, Amrita is literally taken prisoner by Minx, who keeps Amrita under lock and key, hardly letting her out of sight, escorting her everywhere, including to photo-shoots.

Amrita's enslavement is problematic, however. Initially, Amrita is mercenary enough to think that Minx's showing up uncannily at shoots without being invited wasn't a bad thing because 'Quickly, she calculated that, thanks to Minx's efficient transport arrangements, she would be able to save fifty bucks worth of cab fare' (De 1992: 12). Later, after Minx has already socially isolated her from all possible companions, Amrita is still able to think 'Minx ... a big asset as far as Amrita's contracts and schedules were concerned. She handled both with enviable efficiency' (De 1992: 130), while Amrita, defined as she is entirely by physical attributes, is glad to leave it all to Minx because 'In any case, she didn't really have a head for money and it was a relief to have someone handle hers' (De 1992: 131). She even strangely elects not to tell her family till they find out from someone else the extent of her entrapment, though this exit is offered to her at several points in the novel. Where Minx has the flâneur's super-mobility, Amrita has only the object's fixity, paralysis and immobility, again, a stasis that is gendered female and feminine even as De's strategy in *Strange Obsession* is to produce a situation wherein we feel sympathy towards a woman who is stalked, trapped and exploited by an intimate partner. The partner's sexual orientation or gender need not even be considered for one to recognize the situation is one of intimate partner violence indeed; instead, in De's homophobic narrative world, it is this sort of intimate partner abuse that becomes equal to lesbianism, whose abnormality is over determined to such an extent that though one is reminded of the *deewane* ('mad') lovers of Hindi poetry and cinema, one fails to remember that this sort of violence may also be staged in relationships with men. Minx, the stalker par excellence may be seen for example in Mumbai films of the time such as *Darr* (1993) and *Anjaam* (1994). Does this mean then, that unhealthy heterosexual behaviours are akin to homosexuality? Homosexuality, here, is an unhealthy manifestation of desire; where films like *Darr* offer a healthy heterosexual 'cleanser' in the form of Kiran's fiancée, essayed by the 'macho' Sunny Deol, Minx's excesses may not be similarly be offset by a healthy homosexual passion. In fact, the only homosexualities one sees in the movie are disease-laden and transgressive—Amrita's one-time one-night-stand partner Rover is revealed to be a bisexual who goes cruising at night picking up truck-drivers. De's conflation of homosexuality with drugs, thuggery, promiscuity, and deceit leave one in no doubt about either the provenance of homosexuality or its social consequences.

Minx's self-fashioning of herself as a child who went, as a result of abuse, 'from being the daughter, the only child, to a ghost or shadow' (De 1992: 47) is one of a piece with several other instances in the novel where either one of the characters or the narrator describes hers, uncannily, with precisely words like shadow or ghost; weirdo, freak, creep, abnormal and demoness are also part of the repertoire. Shobha De makes sure the reader has enough cues about what moral position to take vis-à-vis the distasteful 'lesbian' Amrita finds stalking her, leaving Cartier diamonds and Armani cologne in her wake. Amrita is able to see Minx clearly only in her nightmares, when Amrita realizes how ugly she really was. Amrita could not put her finger on it—was it the flaky, mottled skin that gave Minx a reptilian appearance? Or the close set, grey-green eyes that never seem to blink? Was it the lank, cropped hair that looked listless and dull, or the mouth set in a severe line, like a gash carved by a blunt knife? (De 1992: 30).

This bestial description of Minx shows that De clearly locates lesbianism in a species outside either femininity or humanity; Minx cannot be 'normal' by any definition of the term if her appearance is so ghoulish. Some way into the story however, Amrita finally capitulates, after Minx returns from an uncharacteristic period of absence to tell Amrita she has had a painful breast reduction surgery for Amrita's aesthetic and tactile pleasure. Amrita is repulsed but 'she felt pity too, and perversely, for the first time, a feeling of sympathy for the wretched woman before her' (De 1992: 93). Comfort sex, graphically described by De, follows. Amrita sees herself in a 'dream-like state,' unresisting of Minx's caresses, finding 'her legs open almost voluntarily' to Minx's probing. De tells us 'Amrita had never known anything like this … never' (De 1992: 94), tellingly different from Amrita's first heterosexual encounter, with the narcissistic Rover with whom she 'had not experienced any pleasure. Just a dull pain, which had receded into the background as curiosity took over. She recalled thinking 'So, this is what it's all about. How disappointing.' (De 1992: 35). Lesbian love making then gives pleasure, but this pleasure is steadfastly made out to be different from the desultory but awakening experience of heterosexuality. De makes sure that lesbian sex with Minx covers the entire gamut from voyeurism to bondage to rape, leaving the reader in no doubt, once again, as to the censure with which we are to read these practices. But the graphic nature of these passages has, I argue, a dual effect. Even as the plot says 'no' to each of these activities by way of authorial disapproval, the effect the mimetic representation of transgressive sexualities has is to make visible what it proscribes. Even as the rituals of what is ostensibly the normative lesbian sexual repertoire are played out, with Amrita represented as blocking out Minx's image with that of other lovers, her body all the same goes 'begging for more and more' (De 1992: 108). The sex passages in achieving their object of titillating the reader also implicitly raise the question of the nature of desire. Amrita's ostensibly resistant heterosexual body is aroused by the obstinately homoerotic Minx; Minx's expert lovemaking is figured as a temptation that Amrita tries to resist but succumbs to each time, begging the question: is the sexing of desire and its fulfillments as homosexual or heterosexual an adequate conceptualization of desire? But De is, after all, not producing great literature to explore this question with any degree of sincerity. On the one hand Minx's distaste of her breasts, her desire to undergo gender reassignment surgery and her general refusal to remain 'female' in any fashion, bodily or psychic, signals butchness, De's reading of this gender difference, and the sexuality that this gender carries is such as to present it not as butchness, but as a particular form of dangerous pathology that is narcissistic at best, and only regressive in development. A conversion narrative for the 'femme' as Amrita appears to be in Minx's eyes at least, is in order.

In the romance narrative, the woman lover is shown as holding out till the man woos her the way she wants to; this deferral of the ultimate marriage plot till the ideal man expresses himself through the right signs is read by readers as the heroine's triumph rather than solely as the hero's assertion of patriarchal primacy (Radway 1983). Janice Radway unpacks the 'heroine's triumph' as part conservative strategizing with the romance—after all the hero triumphs—and as part critical resistance, allowing women readers an outlet for otherwise repressed anger at their subordination to masculine social registers. In *Strange Obsession*, given that the 'proper' romance can only happen when the butch (un)familiar is put down, the heroine does not need to show any anger towards patriarchal dominance at all. She is a ready convert to heterodominance already. The proselytiser is Rakesh Bhatia, the man chosen for Amrita by her mother. Rakesh is eager and willing but there remains the small matter of Minx's revenge when she finds out Amrita has been trying to fashion an escape to New York with the help of marriage to this man. A gruesome rape follows:

> Without a warning, she forced her legs apart with her knees and Amrita experienced a sharp, searing pain as something hard and long was shoved into her. 'Enjoy, enjoy, enjoy,' Minx laughed pushing the object in and out. 'Think of him. That's how it would have felt, come on, show me how much you like it, I got it specially for you ...' (De 1992: 147).

Amrita's abjection leads to her being saved by Rakesh finally drafting Amrita's family to rescue her; her escape is so easy one does not understand why Amrita did not attempt this earlier. The logic De's plot enfolds, however, is obvious—now that Amrita has had a taste finally, of how 'unnatural' love can damage her, she is 'ready' to be saved. Approaching lesbian rape this way, De does provide one of the very few examples of this in literature. A documentary on lesbian rape *She Stole My Voice* (Director: Chang and Kane 2007) became extremely controversial because lesbian community groups found the idea of documenting the rape of women of any sexual persuasion by lesbians as akin to promoting pernicious views about lesbians and lesbianism. Among the few representations of lesbian rape in films is that in *Jaded* (Director: Caryn Krooth 1996), a very low-budget independent film where a young woman who is not a lesbian, is raped on an evening out in the town with two young proclaimed lesbians. *Jaded* has contributions and lessons to offer, but nevertheless, *Jaded*'s construction of lesbian desire itself as a pathology in at least one of these lesbians is as troubling as De's pathologization of Minx's possessiveness as lesbian in origin.

De effects the correct conversion of Amrita to heterosexual desiring, even as Amrita notes, with barely any surprise, 'how easily she had fallen into a pattern' (De 1992: 130)—the pattern of homoerotic desire, coming to 'accept the love-making as part of the strange, twilit life she led now' (De 1992: 133). The reversal is complete when, later, during sex with a man, she still has to block off images of Minx, wondering, despite the trauma of rape at Minx's hands if Minx 'had ... spoiled her for everyone else—particularly men? Would she ever feel the same with another person—a less adoring, less worshipful, less awestruck partner?' (De 1992: 158). This is key to the argument that despite its obvious reinforcement of heteronormativity, a careful reader of even a text as reactionary as *Strange Obsession* can see that the normative is inflected with the proscribed, even defined by it; (un)familiar pleasures are so delicious that disturbing as they are, they cannot be disowned. Amrita must teach herself, though, 'not to expect smooth hands caressing her breasts or a soft face nestling between her legs' (De 1992: 159), and that there is 'only you and me from now on—just us' (De 1992: 160): the plot's engine must quickly take us to the destination of Amrita's happy exorcism of the lesbian familiar, especially since we are almost at the end of the allocated two-hundred-page span Shobha De allows her novels, in keeping with the short attention spans of her chosen readership.

So a magnificent bodied woman being made love to by a woman has engrossed female readers—does not the reading itself become lesbian by default? *Strange Obsession*'s location in the world of fashion photography permits us to look at the location of the reader, presumably straight, within this enterprise of educating the heroine into heterosexuality. The industry of fashion photography is one of the few in which women may look at other women without being accused of 'lesbianism' because the premise of fashion photography is that it educates women into what they should be like. That is, the woman is told what to consume in order to become like the woman/women represented as desirable in the photographs of attractive models who are the 'faces' of various brands. In other words, women are encouraged to want to be like the women in the photograph, while at the same time steering clear of wanting these very women themselves. As Diana Fuss notes in 'Fashion and the Homospectatorial Look,' the fashion industry provides 'a socially sanctioned structure in which women are encouraged to 'consume', in vouyeuristic if not vampiristic fashion, the images of other women, frequently represented in classically exhibitionist and sexually provocative poses. To look straight *at* women, straight women, it appears, must look *as* lesbians' (Fuss 1992: 713–714). Diana Fuss' account (1992) offers us very valuable points of entry into the scopic pleasures of a text like De's. I would argue that Minx looks at Amrita *as* a lesbian; however, in having looked at her as a lesbian, and having wanted her, Minx has transgressed the line between identification and desire that keeps homosexual desire outside the pale. Minx is made to pay for her consumption by being treated in a bestial fashion, with many animal and sub-human metaphors being marshalled throughout by the text to keep alive the notion that a butch lesbian like Minx cannot after all remain either female, or human. Minx herself is the vampire, the two-faced evil twin who must be excised for having sought a deeper transaction than the visual. Minx's punishments, then, are consequent upon her border crossing. The homospectatorial look, once converted into action, takes Minx's desire out of the repressed unconscious lesbianism of the look and places it within the realm of deed; where the homospectatorial look can be understood to be a necessary part of the shaping of the modern urban woman, the punishments De retributively brings to bear upon Minx seem to serve as a reminder of what will happen to the same modern urban viewer/reader of these fictions if they seek to make them any more real.

These scopic pleasures then, seem to run contra to what Laura Mulvey would posit; the viewing position, the gaze, need not be automatically (heterosexual) male (1990). The female reader of *Strange Obsession* could appreciate De's descriptions of Amrita's body *as a woman* rather than as a man, and further, the queer reader can desire the same body instead of merely identifying with it. That Minx must be tortured for what the male characters are rewarded for points to the differential power positions invested in the male and female viewing locations. Male desiring looks are legitimate, but female desiring looks are not, *Strange Obsession* suggests. After Amrita's escape, Minx tries to commit suicide, in keeping with the sado-masochistic, passive-aggressive behaviour she exhibits in her relationship with Amrita, but Amrita decides to go ahead and marry Rakesh all the same, though she 'had not been able to overcome her shame and guilt quite as easily ... wondering how she had allowed herself to fall into such an obvious trap' (De 1992: 157). Amrita's conversion narrative is troubled by misgivings and the onrush of doubts that bring us back to the premise that the disturbing love, though repressed, will remain 'a part of her consciousness' (De 1992: 166). Minx appears in Amrita's dreams, sometimes as 'a benevolent figure, at other times, a psychotic despot' (De 1992: 166)—Amrita's consciousness indeed continues to be seared by guilt and shame, or is it something deeper? De's novel functions within the Oedipal imaginary, where lesbian love is posited as the consequence of an imperfect or impartial Oedipalization of the female subject. In placing at the centre of correct socialization desire for the father, who is to be acquired by displacing the mother by becoming like her, the Oedipal model brushes aside female–female trajectories of desire. Most psychoanalytical theorizations centre around this Oedipal discourse where femininity is a lack, and the desire for the mother—for the same sex in the case of the daughter—is located within the realm of the psychotic, the abject, in the pre-Oedipal, and therefore pre-Symbolic ego. Her reasons for her lesbianism is her alleged sexual abuse as a child by her father, and her rendition of this story transforms her into a child: 'the woman whimpering helplessly as she leant against the door frame was not the Minx she knew. This person was speaking in a child's voice, lisping …' (De 1992: 45). Amrita maternally lifts up this child, providing her with the solace her own mother supposedly did not provide Minx with through the years of abuse: 'Spontaneously, Amrita hugged her. Minx settled into her arms like a grateful child, and Amrita began to rock her gently' (De 1992: 46). Amrita's wanting to mother Minx is located within the realm of female homosociality, but Minx plays upon this maternal impulse to coax Amrita into loving her. Finally, their first love-making comes about under the gruesome auspices of Minx having had her breasts surgically lopped off; Minx once again breaks down, and Amrita is 'felt pity too, and perversely, for the first time, a feeling of sympathy for the wretched woman before her' (De 1992: 93). Their roles reverse while they make love—Amrita lies 'inertly' against the pillows, in 'a dream-like state,' struggling 'not to lose herself entirely to what was happening to her' for though she had had sex before (with Rover), she has never had pleasure like Minx was giving her (De 1992: 94). The removal of the breasts permits Amrita to succumb to Minx's physical ministrations finally—now there are not two pairs of breasts, it appears lovemaking with Minx is less offensive; Amrita though repulsed succumbs, it seems, to the misguided logic. That Minx must place herself in the position of a child in order to solicit Amrita's desire is telling: while on the one hand the maternal returns the women presumably to a foundational subjectivity, at the same time, this self is also regressive. Therefore this desire, which masquerades as the maternal but is not, must also be regressive and thus dangerous for the fully formed individual. Minx's own distaste for conventional heterosexual relations, ostensibly because of abuse by her father, must be evaluated anew in the light of her desire for the same sex. It may be that her desire for women makes Minx identify heterosex as a violative tax, a corvee placed upon women for their daily bread (Wittig 1992). Minx's desire for women is posited as downright dangerous. Even before Amrita comes onto the scene, Minx had been associated with another gorgeous female model, whose sudden disappearance from life, it is assumed, was Minx's doing. De does not take any chances in establishing this psychotic aspect. Minx's mother is presumably also mentally ill, and in all likelihood, Minx is walking down the familiar path of madness: 'Poor Meenakshi,' says her father, 'I wish I'd realised earlier just how sick she really was. Maybe I would have been able to save her the fate that befell her mother' (De 1992: 203). De's location of this desire in the realm of the psychotic, the pathological and the violent, makes lesbian desire function not as a positively valued form of desire, but as the psychotic excess, the abject supplement, the remnant of the pre-Oedipal, which is where (hetero)normative discourses like conventional psychoanalysis would also place it. In the heterosexual imaginary then, lesbian desire is psychotic, abject, repellent, as is borne out by Minx's repeated actions. Yet, their first love-making takes place in Amrita's house, to which Minx has gained access by feigning 'normal' female homosociality. This violation of the home by the (un)familiar evil lesbian sprite foregrounds the nature of the evil that is lesbianism: like a familiar, it comes in many guises, changing shapes and affiliations at will, taking over even the strongholds of the heterosexual family.

On the one hand, the constant description of Amrita on every page as beautiful serves to make the reader identify with her. In presenting Amrita as someone who is to be identified with and who at the same time, albeit unconsciously, may awaken desire in individual 'lookers', (De 1992) is giving a certain amount of play, again unconsciously, to the idea that heterosexual love is to be carefully policed. Minx's desire for Amrita must be counterposed with Rakesh's 'healthy' desire to be with her, even as the psychic costs of identification and desire for a beloved object of the same sex as one are externalized through Minx's many lies, delusions and constant abuse of power. Rakesh functions as the fully Oedipalized male who may release women from regressive confinements by supplying them with the opposite of psychosis—a healthy family life with motherhood. Yet, the (un)familiar threatens to remain right in Amrita's system despite expurgation. Amrita after a sojourn in the West with her husband, and now pregnant, possibly with twins, 'felt herself shiver involuntarily' at her freedom when she finds Minx's obituary note in the newspapers upon returning home. Why should she shiver when 'free at last' we wonder; Minx's astrological sign was Gemini, the twins in Amrita's belly suggest an eerie new lease of life *within Amrita* for the now-good-twin now-bad-twin that Minx herself seemed to be. As Diana Fuss (1992) would say, fashion photography permits homospectatorial looks that allow the desire for the mother to intrude into the Symbolic space of the Oedipal subject—that is, into the realm of the social as we know it. At the same time, the look, insofar as it remains a look, cannot disrupt the system despite the discomfort it produces due to the unconscious memories it stirs up. Similarly, memories of an earlier same-sex love erupt into the heterosexual family unit 'involuntarily' despite Amrita's and De's disavowals.

This narrative culminates in Minx's setting fire to the isolated wood-shack they are in, amidst her filming Rakesh's and Amrita's copulation at gunpoint. Rakesh magnanimously rushes in to save Minx from the fire after having saved his wife, thus symbolically reprising the role of the fully Oedipal male in 'rescuing' the butch lesbian from her truncated, unfulfilling, impotent existence as lesbian. *Strange Obsession* then, plays upon most conventional fantasies of the 'lesbian', particularly the butch lesbian, as a familiar, that is, as a creature in possession of strange powers, fantasies where the lesbian is also a gender outlaw who will cross sartorial barriers alongside of other barriers of decorum in sexual, professional or psychic aspiration. At the same time, De's 'other lesbian', Amrita, refutes just such unfamiliarities being so familiar herself—conventionally feminine, she is nevertheless susceptible to the homosexual love that would otherwise have remained the preserve of the 'strange' Minx. While Amrita cannot be described as 'femme' as the novel at least explicitly denies that she is attracted to Minx at all, her 'conversion' into heterosexuality suggests precisely lesbian fears about how femme women are likely to cross over to the other side because they do look normatively feminine. The 'lesbian' is thus both disconcertingly familiar and unfamiliar;

further, some are born lesbian while others are 'fully convertible', able to revert to heterosexuality when the opportunity presents itself. Amrita, in turn, is given the real thing, male masculinity instead of the masculinity Minx had grafted onto her own female body, which she modifies, lops off and arrays in ways that enable performances of masculinity that De refutes as 'unreal'. Only the real thing is good enough for a heroine as beautiful as Amrita, De implies. At the same time, Amrita herself is that other real thing—the real woman. *Strange Obsession*'s overpowering intent to locate Amrita within the discourse of 'real' femininity which precludes anything lesbian, paradoxically also makes Amrita available to the (female) reader's (queer) gaze as that one thing we both want to be, and might just want to have. De's novel, in a sense, re-validates and normalizes 'heterosexuality'. But not before heterosexuality reveals itself to be both troubled and modified by crossings that happen at the osmotic border between what is permitted and what one must learn to repress. The sheer magnitude of the troubles the plot has to design and resolve before the vision of homosexuality is barely exiled provides a foothold from where to gain a greater understanding of how heterosexuality itself is only learned behaviour. The behaviour of the characters in *Strange Obsession* suggests that, given enough opportunity, anyone could 'go native'—taken out of familiar worlds, we adapt to the (un)familiar as if a previous, normatively defined code for 'normal' sexual behaviour never did exist.

Roaring Girls: Abha Dawesar's *Babyji*

The boundaries between 'polite' treatments of lesbianism and relatively more pornographic ones reveal themselves to be artificial because of the often impenetrable difficulties of telling them apart in practical terms—witness *Strange Obesssion* as also several selections in *Facing the Mirror*. More importantly, perhaps, there is no reason to try to tell the two apart as the apparent distinction only hinders our understanding of readers and their reception of texts. The pornographic belongs to such a shadow realm of Indian culture that there is hardly any 'polite' academic study of the area. Pornography as a genre also suffers from the misapprehension that only men read smut, when women might be as avid consumers of pornographic titles, though their reading of the same texts might be different from their male counterparts. An analysis of the consumption of pornography, especially lesbian pornography, fascinating as it may be, is unfortunately far beyond the scope of this book. However, 'an honest critic should be prepared to acknowledge that pornographic texts ... have contributed in significant ways to the overall cultural assimilation of the lesbian idea' (Castle 2003: 26).

Linda Williams suggests that pornography's significance in queer lives is that it makes 'sexuality visible, and sexual visibility has personal and political importance for sexual minorities who are under-represented in mainstream commercial media' (Williams cited in Lipton 2012: 198). William's argument is about pornography as film, but the point holds in general, and is specifically important from the point of view of lesbian interlocutors. While Castle essentially makes her argument based on Western authors of repute—whether Martial or Chorier or Cleland or Diderot or Sade—or the more humble pornographic smut purveyed in the common marketplace, the same argument holds for Indic literatures. Rekhti poetry, the low-brow version of the high Urdu genre of Rekhti, is a case in point. Though some scholars like Carla Petievich have argued that Rekhti cannot be seen as a 'lesbian' genre because Rekhti essentially has male poets masquerading as women in love with other women (Petievich 2002). I follow Ruth Vanita and Saleem Kidwai in reading Rekhti as 'lesbian' indeed because regardless of the gender of the author, Rekhti poetry makes available lesbian experience in all its corporeality and tangibility (Vanita and Kidwai 2000). Rekhti poetry, as Kidwai and Vanita have noted elsewhere, may also be 'lesbian' in that the male poets often drew their understanding of lesbianism from women involved in lesbian relationships. Veena Talwar Oldenberg, for the lifestyle arrangements of the courtesans of Lucknow, uses the phrase 'lifestyles of resistance' in their economic and sexual autonomy of men and conjugality (Oldenburg 1990). The sexual autonomy of the Lucknow courtesans often also translated into intimate sexual relationships with other women, often in the same *kotha*. The kotha was the favourite haunt of the Urdu poet of the nineteenth century, and the Rekhti poetry of the century is often a reflection, clear or exoticized, of the lifestyles of these women. Just as the sexual indiscretions and unorthodoxies of Marie Antoinette were available to the very interested public of England and France in the form of graphic toxic pamphlets in the 1780s and 1790s, Rekhti poetry made available to generations of Urdu poetry-readers the possibility of relationships that were not heterosexual. Heather Butler suggests that lesbian pornography provides alternatives to women 'taking it and faking it,' besides upsetting the heteronormative temporalities of the penis-focussed money shot and male orgasm (Butler in Williams [ed.]. 2004). Williams reads the earlier generation of 1970s female-centered lesbian porn's presentation of lesbian sexuality as nurturing and gentle as influenced by mainstream feminist readings of all confrontational/violent activity as masculine. Terming this 'lesbian' porn, Williams suggests that the 'sex-positive' 1980s saw a shift towards a more 'dyke' version of porn, with role-play, sado-masochistic practices, alternative gender presentations, etc. getting representational space.

Abha Dawesar's *Babyji* performs a similar function in the twenty-first century for readers of Indian writing in English, but unlike the genre of Rekhti, written by men masquerading as women, Dawesar's photograph on the cover reveals her to be a woman writing a sexual autobiography of the eponymous Baby-ji of the title. The physical evidence of Dawesar as writer of the text preserves the novel from what is often the chilling anonymity of the pornographic genre, and also seems to guarantee the authenticity of the experiences the text delineates. Dawesar's identity then functions like the Rekhti poets' pseudonyms did; male poets would take up female pen-names to perform the masquerade of 'authenticity' of knowledge for their readers. But at the same time, none of the material released either by the author or her publishers offers any clues about the author's own sexual preferences or orientations, making it impossible for the general reader to tell whether she herself is 'authentically' lesbian or no, perhaps an authorial strategy at distancing herself from too close an identification with the sexual practices in this romp, for Dawesar's *Babyji* is hardly the kind of novel one would expect a well-educated Indian woman novelist to write. *Babyji* provides a bracing dose of the bawdy that has been much missed in the Indian English scene—an unapologetic and fun female character has long been awaited. Further, Babyji's location within the educational system, where 'appropriate' knowledge is defined, imparted and evaluated, permits us the opportunity to see just how normative knowledge about sexualities are also defined, imparted and evaluated. *Babyji*'s escapist fantasy turns institutionalized school learning upside down by placing at its centre a lesbian Babyji. At the same time, the novel succumbs to the pressures and contradictions inherent within the reverse discourse of (un)familiar escapes from heterosexuality that it is writing by collapsing the discourse of utopian escape from heterosexuality as a utopian exit from India at the same time: the lesbian super-heroine, Babyji, cannot, it appears, survive in India for reasons we shall study further.

Babyji, the precocious teenager at the centre of the novel, is a sort of Roaring Girl, like Moll but untroubled by any worries about sexual performance or responsibility. Babyji's real name is Anamika—literally, the un-nameable—but this novel is a playful exercise in naming and making visible this Indian vision of unremorseful female carnal enjoyment, untouched by either the nineteenth-century's pieties, or the twentieth-century's medicalized monsters of AIDS or venereal diseases. Quite the reverse of Minx's troubled butchness, Anamika's 'baby dyke' as one butch character calls another in Nisha Ganatra's *Chutney Popcorn* (2000), is growing up happily free of the prescribed Oedipal traumas of fear of regression, infantilism or non-belonging. Cannily parking itself at the intersections of a very important junction in contemporary Indian history, the turn from the older self-contained closed-economy model of the socialist state to the neo-globalizing Western-model state, the novel is able to, however peripherally, locate the sexual autobiography of Anamika Sharma within a variety of discourses that seem to underwrite the arrival of freedoms analogous to presumed Western ones, among which is sexual freedom. Anamika's young life, in the space of less than a year, witnesses many watershed moments, from that of the caste-based reservations crisis generated by V. P. Singh's government deciding to act on the Mandal Commission Report, to the movement of Indian intellectual capital to the assumed meritocracy of the West, to the emergence of a sub-culture, as it were, of the newly divorced. This novel has its eager teenager explore these via Delhi, the 'undercover' city that 'churns slowly, secretively' (Dawesar 2005: 1) with an urgency hitherto more characteristic of the young hormonally motored teenaged male protagonist.

Babyji cheekily reverses the gender of the characters of the literature of contemporary sexual churn—instead of the eager young male lover climbing up 'sewage pipes to consort with their neighbours' wives' the eager young flaneuse walks in through open doors to go down on quite a number of women (Dawesar 2005: 1). The nectar this secular *manthan* yields is not sperm; the pleasure it is 'seeking is the pleasure in that way by which Venus outwits Venus' as the comically virginal Octavia in Nicholas Chorier's *Dialogues* puts it. Chorier's *Dialogues on the Arcana of Love and Venus by Luisa Sigea Toletana* is a series of dialogues on sex by one recently married Roman matron, the initiate Tullia, to her virginal fifteen year old cousin Octavia. These dialogues are pornographic after the fashion of an instruction manual, and were wildly popular in seventeenth century France. Dialogue 2, on lesbianism, yields a pragmatic defence of female homosexuality, 'it will not make you pregnant' as well as a chic one 'all the sophisticated ancients and moderns practiced some form of it', says the experienced mentor to her disciple (Castle 2003: 153). *Babyji's* very energetic heroine is uninitiated all right, like Chorier's Octavia, but in the absence of any instructrix, is eager enough to train herself. This she does via discourse, rather than the more usual masturbatory training that lesbian smut relies on, by deciding to memorize the *Kama Sutra* in anticipation of future needs.:

> My knowledge of the facts of life was based entirely on books, and clean ones at that. I read nineteenth century classics by George Eliot and Emily Bronte. These books never went into any details. To remedy this, I decided to read the Kamasutra. I had to do this while standing in the scooter garage, which had been converted into a storeroom. I would sneak out with a flashlight after my parents had gone to sleep. The Kamasutra I forcefed myself seemed completely of another world, alien and absurd. (Dawesar 2005: 1–2)

'And no sooner does she read it than "magical" things started to happen. In particular I met a *woman*' (Dawesar 2005: 2, emphasis mine).

If Babyji is reading the *Kama Sutra* on the first page of the novel, on the second it is evident that the uses she will put the *Kama Sutra* to will be far from heterosexual. *Babyji* perforates the boundary between the polite and the pornographic considerably with Dawesar's eponymous protagonist turning out to be a nonchalantly rambunctious proto-lesbian teenager, and whose biggest dilemma in the book is not about her lesbianism, but about her relationship with a man who seems to be drawn to her. This world is poles away from that of the lesbian topos constructed by most of the other texts this thesis studies. Gender insubordination in Anamika's case does not produce merely an empty replication of male behaviour, nor is it an effort to claim male social privilege, but, to use the Foucauldian phrase, is an effort to produce a space within which sexual love and desire may be directed towards women. Claiming autonomy from male stipulations in thus directing desire towards women, *Babyji* staunchly resists any feminist logic of women identification, positing instead the existence of autonomous sexual and erotic desire between women within the otherwise closed spaces of the middle-class residential locality and school. However, Babyji's own (un)familiarity as a young girl often mistaken for a boy follows certain normative trajectories that makes Dawesar's butch heroine not so much a real character as a template for presumed homosexual prowess, which has limitations when it comes to creating characters that go beyond 'flat' qualities. Babyji also tops school as a matter of routine, plays hard, and to boot, sleeps with both her maidservant and the attractive-older-woman-next-door. Both these *affairs de coeur* are neat reversals of mandatory male rites of passage in schoolboy novels. *Babyji*, in fact, makes lesbian sex look natural, besides depicting it as happening all the time, especially in boring places immediately around you, even in a dull, drab, pre-liberalization city.

Dawesar represents Anamika as a familiar in terms of her academic prowess and her achievements as a veritable lesbian Casanova in obtaining no less than three conquests in one school year. Completely impervious to male charms, whether adolescent or mature, Anamika has, in addition to her scholastic brilliance, a keen eye for women; constantly checking women out at any available opportunity, Anamika's materials for actual action have been limited till she meets, on the very second page, the older woman she calls 'India'. Anamika is thus possessor of a gaze directed erotically towards femininity and her territory as flâneur is 'India.' *Babyji's* deployment of (un)familiar female desire to this end equates sexual coming of age with freedom—Anamika feels that 'Squeezing India's rear violated every rule of veneration. It transformed her from an elder to a sexual being, an equal. It made me an adult' (Dawesar 2005: 27). India—the country—seems, from this passage, to have suddenly opened up in front of Anamika the (un)familiar flâneur. Dawesar's use of India thus, as a nickname suggesting nation as also Anamika's older girlfriend, clearly suggests possibilities that mean to make the image of Bharat-mata very different from the normative discourse of heteropatriarchally oriented, exclusively maternal femininity that most nationalist discourses wish to fix on 'her'. At parties she is forced to go with her parents, Anamika productively spends her time looking at the women: 'They were all wearing saris, their ample midriffs gathering around the folds of their waists, the shapelessness of their backs clearly visible. I visualised them minus their small, tight blouses' (Dawesar 2005: 5). Separating the sexually attractive 'aunties' from the ones she finds merely dumpy, Anamika is able to put her forced attendance at social gatherings to a use her parents would find shocking; as Anamika goes around thinking about what lies beneath the blouses of the various women she meets in social contexts, the roving female eye, and the inbuilt and invisible possibilities of female–female desire are revealed in a map of a possible queer nation, also called India.

If the relationship with India permits Anamika to cross the age-divide, then her other parallel relationship with her maid Rani—whom Anamika is instrumental in rescuing from the hands of her wife-beating and alcoholic husband—signifies Anamika's ability to penetrate the class barrier. Rani's subalternity places her at Anamika's feet literally, as disciple: Anamika teaches her to read and write English, and 'uplifts' her by giving her a home away from her battering, drinking husband. Anamika also gets her better clothes and more elbow room in the family by negotiating with her parents, but all the same, India is Anamika's interlocutor about aspects of life Anamika cannot discuss with her parents. Rani is, thus, relegated to the position of lower-class (and lower-caste, as we find out at the end) concubine, albeit one living in relative material comfort. Anamika has yet another relationship, but not entirely sexual this time; with a girl of her age, her own classmate though of a higher social class, Sheela. Sheela's presence combines the beauty of Rani with the style of India, but Sheela also signifies the closest to a sustainable relationship Anamika is depicted as having, in that Anamika worries about wooing Sheela the right way, quite unlike her far less sensitive dealings with the other two women. India, Rani and Sheela, though all of them described as exceedingly beautiful types of women for their ages, typify three kinds of femininities available to Anamika to be duly consumed.

Unlike Amrita in De's *Strange Obsession*, these three women are very attracted to Anamika's budding butchness. With her 'boys' shirt and jeans' 'black boys' shoes' and Old Spice from her father's toilette, Anamika is often mistaken for a boy, and delighted to be mistaken for one, in contrast to Anamika's mother, who would much prefer a 'lighter skinned, heavier set and more domestically inclined' daughter, but as far as Anamika is concerned, if her mother 'really wanted one of those girls I could always bring one home' (Dawesar 2005: 34). 'Replacing the Lacanian slash with a lesbian bar' (Case in Abelove *et al.* (eds) 1993: 295) that is the bar between the words butch and femme in the butch/femme pair, Babyji scripts a reversal of the femme damnée, the tormented ill-fated lesbian who is oppressed and erased by heteronormative narrative. At the same time, a set of binaries similar to male/female dichotomies flourishes here too—Anamika, the butch girl or baby-dyke, is the active wooer, while India, Sheela and Rani are willing to be wooed. However, at least one of them—the partner that Anamika most seeks—is shown to be actively taking up positions of agency within her relationship with Anamika; Sheela refuses Anamika's fervent attentions till Anamika devises a milder wooing technology; refusing Anamika's use of force, Sheela is able to set the pace within their butch/femme unit, though this also, paradoxically, leads to there being no more sexual contact between the two of them. Nevertheless, in seizing agency within the relationship, Sheela's character refuses to feel victimized by Anamika's literal probing of her body, a contrast to her feelings of having been violated when a man masturbates on her body in a particularly disturbing and graphic depiction of 'eve-teasing' on a DTC bus. Memorable because of its verisimilitude, this episode has Anamika fighting and struggling against the men who are groping her, while Sheela is passively in tears, unable to resist except masochistically. Anamika's presence of mind and desire to protect Sheela sees to it that they get off the bus and reach home via more safe means. Sheela's abjection in this scene is different from Anamika's. Upon seeing Sheela's face wet with tears, unable to push off the man who is fingering her, Anamika lets out a 'blood-curdling howl' that frees her of her own groper, permitting her thus to attack Sheela's: 'I … brought my right hand down on his head with all the strength I could muster. He jerked backwards and clutched at the railing. His eyes opened. He looked vicious and dirty. He was a bit off balance, so I lifted my foot a few inches off the ground and kicked it in his direction. It missed him' (Dawesar 2005: 87). Having failed once, Anamika still tries though: 'I brought my foot up to the level of his fly and kicked with all my might. Sheela had turned her face and was watching me' (Dawesar 2005: 87). Identifying the situation correctly as 'borderline rape' Anamika's disgust at their fellow passengers' indifference does lead to tears when Anamika comes home to Rani after having seen Sheela home; the sense of violation that she herself feels is compounded when Rani's sympathy is directed to Anamika's being a child. Refusing this child-like status, Anamika in her turn has rough sex with Sheela, in which both of them have a powerful orgasm apiece for the first time. Anamika's inability to protect Sheela is however, produced by the novel in terms of her refusal of the powerlessness of childhood; with no economic or sexual independence, Anamika and Sheela had to resort to stratagems to stay back together at school, missing the school bus on purpose. Taking public transport had been the only way they would earn some time with one another, but after what happens on the bus, Anamika is able to recognize the consequences of her powerlessness all the more clearly. Recognizing that it comes from being seen as a child, not a bona-fide adult though she is almost seventeen, Anamika realizes that 'Money would be the key to my life with Sheela. If you had money you could be in control. Otherwise you'd have to compromise and do what everyone else was doing: conform' (Dawesar 2005: 303). Thus, Dawesar sets out the necessaries for a successful lesbian lifestyle—financial independence. With money comes the ability to buy the privileges of a ride in an autorickshaw, which is what Anamika and Sheela take after getting off the bus—once in it, they are free of the dangers of the street. The space of the city becomes a 'queerscape' to borrow Ingram's term; sexual, political or verbal 'accidents' within the everyday space of the city become a way in which the (un)familiar manifests herself.

Anamika's invisibility as (un)familiar, dyke-girl is evident from her own vulnerability to sexual violence upon being identified as female in a bus: she is groped too; but her refusal of sexual violence queers the narrative of sexual harassment; it is her initiative of helping Sheela that is paramount in Anamika's consciousness at the time. Unlike in *Strange Obsession*, *Babyji* presents the female flâneur as herself vulnerable to gender-based violence as a woman as much as to homophobic violence; however, *Babyji's* refusal to allow this violence against her female person to scar her present inflects this violence differently for her subjectivity than it does for the other non-butch women in the narrative.

Babyji is important in naturalizing for the reader the fact that girls as young as seventeen have sex, and what is more, want to have sex, a sharp contrast to the public sphere discourse, most evident on All India Radio's and Doordarshan's public broadcasts, that girls below the age of eighteen are not physically *ready* yet for sex. While *Babyji's* lightness of texture, thinness of character perception and facile insights into the nature of life in general might make some argue against reading it as serious literature, *Babyji* is still among the better- written of the best-selling popular novels by Indians. *Babyji* belongs to the genre of *Five Point Someone* (2004) or *One Night at the Call Centre* (2007) by Chetan Bhagat—these deal with the young new globalizing India, have young protagonists whose lives are shaped by the movements of transnational capital, and while the merits of these novels as literature in the long run might not be great, they depict the world as India's cable-TV generation see it; these novels are a log of the vital statistics of this post-socialist, post-state-television Indian generation. But *Babyji* twists our expectations of this genre in locating at the centre of its plot a lesbian Babyji, where the 'good' hero or heroine of the popular novel has to have sex with the opposite sex, even if it is in the backseat of a car (as in *One Night at the Call Centre*).

The construction, within the larger urban Indian imaginary, of the child and adolescent as completely sexless, is taken apart by Anamika's rigorous love-life. However, within the institutionalized educational arrangement, sexuality of any kind, least of all queer sexuality, has little space. While heterosexuality is imparted in the form of the motherliness of some teachers, or in textbooks that represent fulfilling heterosexual partnerships, all literally performative encouragements with sex are completely invisibilized. However, student sexual-exploration continues despite adult obliviousness; students like Anamika's classmate Chakra Dev are having sex with prostitutes even as Anamika herself is engaged in almost three same-sex affairs; both of them, independent of one another, are also fantasising about their pretty and female maths teacher. The principal of the school is forced finally to notice the discrepancies caused by the 'huge generation gap': 'Your classmates are thinking about intercourse with their teachers while your school counsellor thinks a joint sex-ed class is a scandal' (Dawesar 2005: 219). The sex-ed class is a transparent site of struggle where universities and schools perform their roles as boundary police in ratifying and maintaining heterosexuality. The contrast between the establishment that denies the student any performance of sexual desire, and the counter-culture that students develop to this policing may be seen quite clearly through *Babyji* where the effects of this invisibilization of sexuality literally explodes in the form of a literal cracker in the text, as we shall see later. The well-intentioned visiting doctor is certainly less hidebound, but only marginally than Mrs Shah the school counsellor who thinks the sex-ed class should not discuss homosexuality at all. The doctor's description of male homosexuality as 'not natural for men to have sex with each other' because 'sex was biologically designed for procreation' is telling. Despite the doctor's desire to convey the existence of homosexual encounters, the language of promiscuity and AIDS, along with that of procreation, are her parameters for discussing homosexuality. The pleasure of sex figures only marginally, and any discussion of the emotional content of sexual encounters is also beyond the pale. Institutionalized sex-education at least in the Western world seems marked by this lack. In the Indian context, sex education is mostly not a part of school curricula; however, teenage pregnancies, a constant preoccupation and worry for those in charge of education in the West, have a different social context in India. Sex education in India by and large is forgone in educational systems and replaced with elementary reproductive health guidelines for young women within the category of 'public health' advertising which today also enfolds anti-AIDS campaigns. The doctor's identification of male homosexuality with Western promiscuity is also in keeping with grassroots perceptions of the spread of homosexuality in India. Anamika wonders what the doctor's own views on the matter are; yet the disconnect between personal views and publically espoused views constitutes a gap where the boundary between the healthy and the unhealthy (read the non-normative) is placed. Lesbian sexuality only features very briefly in a discussion dominated by AIDS-linked homosexual male contact, bestiality, transvestites and hijras. Anamika's friend Sheela only half-raises her hand but fortuitously, the doctor sees her, and lesbian sexuality is acknowledged for a brief moment but almost instantly, the school counsellor tries to wrap up the discussion. That lesbian sexuality should only be a momentary flash in a room full of young girls is perhaps a telling rendition of normative expectations of sexual passivity and 'innocence' on the part of young girls. Rather than identify structures of compulsory homosexuality, as Adrienne Rich would put it, sex-education in Anamika's school, and in most other schools, focuses on a narrow definition of 'sexuality' where the word means deviant sexualities. Thus, ironically or otherwise, the sex-ed class episode in *Babyji* locates the school within the locus of contested territory. Heterosexuality must be shored up by the definition of homosexuality as an excess because it does not facilitate procreation and a danger. Anamika herself is sexually active; the sex-ed class does not talk about safe sex, hetero or otherwise; a student like Anamika would never be informed via an official medium that lesbian-sex has a very low risk of HIV transmission due to physiological reasons. Thus, within institutional arrangements, 'knowledge' may be filtered or distorted in ways that align with normative societal definitions, producing homosexual love as 'impossible.'

Anamika's methods for wooing Sheela are summarized by this overturning of Kipling's 'If' that occurs to her when she initiates Sheela into horse-riding, again in school—'If you can make twenty miles an hour on a horse and be in control, you can make a few inches a minute with a lady and be in control, I thought to myself' (Dawesar 2005: 51). The pleasures of horse-riding, of course, signal pleasures that will be had elsewhere, but these are first honed on Rani and India. While Anamika sees Sheela as 'someone more or less my equal,' Rani and India are in various ways members of incompatible psychological castes in a novel that is preoccupied with the place of merit in a society structured by what Dawesar sees as caste-based appeasements. Nevertheless, as far as Anamika is concerned, three lovers at the same time is all right if managed properly: 'As long as I saw all three of them equally, it would be fine,' and this principle of sharing is based on Draupadi's equal sharing by the Pandavas on Kunti's orders: 'They laid down rules on how to share. They would all have her equally, and she was not to be disturbed if she was to be with one of them' (Dawesar 2005: 56). While *Babyji* offers a representation of lesbianism beyond monogamy, the novel is pulled down by its curious lack of specificity and erotic power in its description of lovemaking between the women, which often seems to be no better than male pornographers' wonderment at and subsequent (bad) fabrication of what they think women do in bed. At the same time, the flatness of these various love affairs precludes any serious examination of the lesbian (un)familiar: Anamika simply seems to be a female version of the roving male eye (and hand). Dawesar's novel also suffers from a pornographic inattention to emotion; Anamika undertakes no emotional responsibility towards two women who are emotionally attached to her and polyamory here becomes merely casual sex, much as Minx's was pathologized.

Despite Anamika's own sexual immaturity, India, Sheela and Rani offer her a measure of sustenance and nourishment that heterosexuality does not seem capable of providing. In all of the instances in which masculinity is seen in clearly sexual contexts, masturbation, voyeurism, and violence are foregrounded as male fantasies that violate women. Though Anamika is very good friends with her classmate Vidur, and later with his father Adit who develops a very strong crush on her and calls her lesbianism a 'phase,' the novel's overall mise-en-scene serves to locate male masculinity as dangerous and volatile, and emotionally confounding. Within the school, lack of heterosexual performance avenues like the prom in American narratives, or societies and sororities and the like in college mean that adolescent male heterosexuality is necessarily routed through violent exhibitions of sexual desire. Sexuality further serves as a control mechanism wherein you can be thought of as 'not normal' if within the co-educational establishment, prominent displays of conquests of the opposite sex are not made. For boys, within this novel, being a 'sissy' is the most fearsome aberration, which they try to correct by compulsively engaging in a sexual discourse wherein masculinity is attested by the number of times per day one can masturbate, as Chakra Dev, Anamika's roughest classmate, is shown to do. Despite sex education classes, heterosexual sex is presaged as a space of violence, which pervades the whole of society, as evident from the 'cheapads' chapter where Anamika and Sheela are molested on the DTC bus home from school. There is no meeting ground between the requirements of male masculinity—which Anamika tries to negotiate with by trying to reform the out of control Chakra Dev—and Anamika's or the other women's sexual, emotional or economic requirements. This together with the disconnect between the emotional and the physical components of the (un)familiar lesbian relationships surfaces within the novel in the form of nightmares. Adit's description of Sheela as 'not the smartest, but cute. Beddable' (Dawesar 2005: 299) awakens deep nausea in Anamika: 'The idea of Adit staring at Sheela's pouty pink lips or smelling her hair, or touching her breasts made me want to heave. I couldn't stand the idea of anyone within two feet of Sheela's body' (Dawesar 2005: 299). Further, Anamika's own feelings are uncomprehended by the otherwise understanding Adit, who has by this time recast himself in the role of non-familial elder mentor to Anamika once he finds that she is unwilling to be Lolita to his Humbert. Adit's thoughts generate a 'whirl of sewage' in Anamika's head, and the realm of the (un)familiar, defiled by both Anamika's adoption of 'borderline rape' in order to make love to Sheela, and Adit's representatively rampant heterosexual masculinity push Anamika's unconscious mind into a dreamscape like that in a Hieronymous Bosch painting—

A cacophony of real and imagined lovers filled my head. They were screaming, shouting, accusing me of treachery and betrayal, infidelity and disloyalty ... all grievously claimed injury and showed me the damage I had done. Love in my dream was not a many-shaded thing but a single blinding light. Everyone bathed in it together, without distinctions, all balanced precariously on the edge of an abyss. The compartments of my brain were erased, compassion and maternal affection paraded naked with desire, lust conjoined with admiration.... I saw amputated limbs, hearts outside their bodies, thighs cut open like meat, knees swinging out of their sockets, and eyes, disembodied and bleeding eyes, watching me from everywhere. (Dawesar 2005: 289)

This externalization of the untenability of being a 'happy queer' in India is something this novel is unable to deal with except by way of transparently invoking caste privilege through Anamika's pet project of remaking Chakra Dev, to whom Anamika is a 'chutiya Brahmin.' Chakra Dev—an OBC, as Dawesar makes sure to specify—who sets off bombs at the water-cooler in order to injure Anamika, leaves used condoms on Sheela's desk because he fancies her and so wants to defile her, and masturbates at the two girls whenever he has an opportunity, morphs suddenly into the novel's metaphor for the (un)familiar Anamika's survival in India. Being of the problematic lower-castes to whom reservations have been extended within the Mandal Commission's framework, Chakra Dev is not only a frantic attack on Anamika's sense of autonomous, lesbian selfhood, but also on Anamika's suddenly awakened caste-solidarities. Realizing she is a brahmin, Anamika feels that she too should join the bandwagon of youth who immolated themselves in protest against the Mandal rulings—

> Schools in Delhi were still closed. North India burned like a large funeral pyre. The smell of kerosene and young upper caste flesh invaded villages where the reservation policy made no difference because there were no schools, no colleges, no drinking water. I wanted to make the same kind of heroic statement. I wanted to burn, too. I wanted to sacrifice myself for the right thing, for justice, for my pure Brahmin genes, and for India. It almost didn't matter what the cause was.' (Dawesar 2005: 284)

Initially, Anamika's response to the anti-Mandal agitations offered her a correlative for her own intolerable 'borderline rape' of Sheela. Modelling her own sexual solicitation of Sheela on heterosexual male examples like Howard Roark in *The Fountainhead*, Anamika finds that heterosexual rape that leads to a love affair in books does not quite work like that here. Her triumphant 'I just fucked you,' after getting on top of Sheela one afternoon when Sheela's parents are away and fingering her with 'all the force I could muster' because 'I was afraid if I was too gentle she would use it to move away' (Dawesar 2005: 237), Anamika finds Sheela's reaction quite different from what her limited reading of (mostly male) literature had prepared her to expect. Sheela sees Anamika's digital invasion as the equivalent of 'those *cheapads* on the bus,' and mortified, Anamika can only run away. Confiding later in Adit, Anamika says 'I raped a girl today,' which Adit says is impossible, structuring penetrative sex as entirely male. The logic of the book however, shows us that Anamika's act is rape indeed, as it is this penetrative violence that is followed in the novel by the virtual shutdown of Delhi under the impact of the Mandal crisis. Strange reflections hound Anamika; shame for the Sikh riots of 1984, strange because Anamika cannot have been over ten at that time, within the novel's chronology. 'Feelings of shame at being a Hindu in 1984 mixed with feelings of shame at having forced myself on Sheela' (Dawesar 2005: 244), followed by a loss of will to live, akin to a nervous breakdown. However, the shame of having become a rapist—at least in intent if not in action—has to be displaced by Dawesar onto the body politic so that Anamika can find there is a strange correspondence between herself and Chakra Dev, united as they are by violence. From here, however, the dystopia takes over once the novel identifies sexual violence as available alike to male and female masculinity; nightmarish images float around Anamika's reform project because reforming him would also mean she deserves a second chance too but he rejects all this violently. Uneasily juxtaposing Chakra Dev's recalcitrance with the inefficacy of reservations for what in *Babyji*'s narrator's view is an academically unmotivated and thus undeserving set of lower classes, *Babyji* proceeds towards its heterotopic exit, not from heterosexuality, but from heteronormative India. 'If I didn't want to commit sati, I would have to win,' thinks Anamika; this image unites the Brahmin dyke and the Yadav misogynist into what appears to be heterosexual marriage, but of course self-immolation is not an option for Anamika, only successful reform and upliftment of the lower castes is. In denying subjectivity to these lower castes—earlier represented by Rani and now by Chakra Dev—Dawesar's novel reifies and automatically confers upon Anamika a caste privilege that makes Anamika's (un)familiar sexual escapades also seem, in retrospect, to be available as a coherent narrative only to a member of the upper castes. Belonging to the brahmin group, Anamika has an exit option—to go abroad and study, and once abroad, her sexual life can attain an openness and visibility that India recognises as being unavailable to them in India. Chakra Dev—or bondage to inferiority and truculence—remains confined to an India—the nation—that can be left behind in the pursuit of interiority. However, in invoking caste privilege as a route to attaining the position of subject, *Babyji* demonizes the lower-caste other most damnably. Anamika at the end of the novel is given her dreams, the holo-caust in her mind replaced with visions of a meritocratic utopia waiting for her in the USA, to which she has won a scholarship: 'meritas' Anamika's modification of the word 'veritas' that appears on a school-motto, is the last vision Anamika has, quite a contrast from the blinding dreams earlier. Shopping for the party, she sees a white gay male couple with a child eating cosily as a couple at the bakers'. Leaving Rani, India, and Sheela behind, the novel pushes Anamika into a new world where she will not have to sneak away from under the eyes of watchful but unsuspecting parents in order to conduct her love affairs. Sexual freedom will go along with freedom from anti-casteism it appears. However, in moving from loving three women to focussing exclusively on getting out as the last sections of the novel do, one cannot but see Dawesar's authorial vision failing. The depiction of Anamika's lesbianism is completely displaced by the question of what a young upper-caste girl should do—the 'right thing' for her is to get out of India. Why not, then, a novel about caste in the first place rather than this? The selling power of sex seems to account at least partly for Dawesar's use of the lesbian (un)familiar in *Babyji*. But despite its sometimes inadequate or sketchy treatment, Dawesar's novel opens up a space within which to think of sexuality as more than individual identity. Sexuality cannot be seen on its own, artificially extricated from other social differences—caste, age, educa-tional aspiration, as can be seen from Anamika's entanglements with women of different social or educational backgrounds, or even ages.

Babyji is an escapist fantasy where Anamika is able to fashion a way out of the many oppressive invisibilities thrust upon the lesbian, writ-ing a 'happy queer' (Ahmed 2010: 118). In writing a 'happy' reverse discourse that seeks to overturn existing homophobic perceptions, much complexity and productive artistic ambivalence are given up in the effort to make Anamika a consumable that can provide some alterity in the world of heteronormative sexual romps. At the same time, Anamika is literally a familiar in her access to relative power of self-determination conferred upon her through her scholastic achievements—she can indeed apply for a scholarship to go abroad to study, and presumably, break out of compulsory heterosexuality.

That academic achievement enables sexual expression makes *Babyji* superficially at least a tremendous literary role model for those otherwise exposed only to pathological narratives of lesbianism within educational systems, where invariably pathologization is a concomitant of victimization. Anamika's alignment of herself within an active sexuality and also within an accomplished scholastic locus makes her a poster-girl for lesbian sex. The value of such a literary icon should not be underestimated, given that a disproportionate number of suicides are of young people who cannot accommodate themselves within heteronormativities. Lesbianism, as located in the persona of the school-topper, head-girl and over-achiever permits lesbian subjectivity to be seen as something other than a subaltern choice. At the same time, even as Anamika's love affairs and her queering of her educational contexts also point to changing definitions of 'adolescence' and female sexual subjectivity, these are established on the untenable but unchallenged foundation of caste privilege and superiority. Sexual difference, thus, is also about power over other beings, thus showing how a narrative of lesbian desire need not be necessarily empowering or transgressive. Sexuality is read, created, produced and resisted through power relations as is implicit in Anamika's relationship with Rani the servant, and Anamika's inability to force a similar surrender in her social equal, Sheela. Anamika's relationship with India—Tripta Adhikari is a divorcee—signals a changing society wherein marriage is not forever, contrary to what Anamika's own parents attest. The final image of freedom remains that of the white gay men at the bakery; with Rock Hudson's good looks, these Americans with their hands 'interlocked. Not in the usual way that people may casually hold hands, but with each finger interlaced' (Dawesar 2005: 364). Introducing herself to them, Anamika tells them of America: 'I hear it's free' (Dawesar 2005: 364). The men's response should mitigate somewhat Anamika's eager and uncritical reading of their partnership, but overall, within the logic of *Babyji*, the only place for Anamika's quests is also free America, not India.

'I Will Not Die'—Amruta Patil's *Kari*

Kari, the twenty-year-old protagonist of the graphic novel bridges the gap between Minx and Babyji. Visual artist and writer Amruta

Patil is able to convincingly imagine an androgynous butchness for her eponymous protagonist that does not involve either menacing evil, nor empty reversal of stereotype, while at the same time permitting her androgynous protagonist to remain in India. Like Minx and Babyji, Kari enters the novel with short hair, but this shortens even further into a buzz-cut that enables her androgynous body to trespass the lines that separate maleness from femaleness. The clear line between the realistic and the counter-realistic is collapsed most imaginatively by *Kari's* creator Amruta Patil's plot and treatment of her lesbian protagonists familiar, yet unfamiliar life in one of the best popular books, for the many reasons we shall examine further, to deal with lesbian experience. *Kari* is most likely to develop into a series, as the open-ended finish of the first volume promises and may well offer one of the most inventive, imaginative, tender and beautifully whimsical studies of character available in popular fiction today in India. *Kari's* range of reference—to other literary texts as to popular culture—places it in a league of its own, the messiness of its frame of reference a richer and more rewarding experience than that offered by the often more ectopic styles favoured by most other writers, serious or otherwise.

Amruta Patil's use of the (un)familiar through *Kari* challenges notions of a unitary reality in real, active, dynamic ways, resisting a static location of the text within conventional categories of realistic and counter-realistic. In challenging an easy separation of real from un-real, familiar from (un)familiar, Patil's text has the effect of disrupting the normative conventions that script social life. Many moments of rupture in this graphic novel wilfully disorient the reader's attempts at fixing narrative sequence, verisimilitude or clock time. In moving thus in the ambiguous space between the familiar and the dextrously (un)familiar, *Kari* makes the reader investigate the scripted, constructed nature of the 'real' itself. Kari herself dyke-in-formation is a snippet of a bildungsroman that permits us to see sexuality itself being shaped by 'time and incident' (Patil 2008: 69) rather than by clear intent. Instead of high romantic declamations that move towards an immobile fixing of identity entirely with sexual choice, *Kari* anchors its protagonist within a variety of life-worlds, revealing a subject whose sexuality is one negotiation amidst a number of other existential preoccupations, the chief of which is to put an end to loneliness and to find fulfilment. Thus, love, bonding and spiritual connect are, perhaps paradoxically, the objects of Kari's quest in a Mumbai where distance and psychic isolation are her daily diet. The graphic novel, with antecedents in both the comic book and pulp fiction, permits the exploration, often 'graphically' of areas that would not be of interest in the 'normal' adventure story that comics depict. The protagonist's psychological interiority, backgrounds, existential dilemmas, etc, are only glancingly mentioned in the mainstream comic-book, and often the reader must glean such information from years of perusal of the series. Sometimes, as a longer, more adult version of the comic-book, the graphic novel can venture beyond the purely plot-inspired machinations of the comic book hero/heroine's life and depredations to venture into a tongue-in-cheek biography of the psyches of these characters. *Kari* as a graphic novel is informed both by the adventure strip's intrepidity and the novel's psychological probing. Kari our protagonist undertakes new travels much like a conventional comic book heroine would; however, like a conventional novelist's heroine, Kari also acknowledges her life is mostly conducted in armchairs: 'The circus isn't in my life. It's in my head' (Patil 2008: 79). This acknowledgement, prefaced as it is by her admission that she is more 'armchair straight, armchair gay' rather than 'like, a proper lesbian,' brings the world of the comic-book ninja turtle into the quondam universe of ordinary people, even when these people are lesbians, armchair or otherwise. That lesbianism may be part of the quotidian rather than only of daring moments of high living is one of *Kari*'s greater achievements. Yet, in defamiliarizing the operations of 'love laws,' this graphic novel opens up a third space between fantasy and reality, where the uncanny potentials of everyday are harnessed within the parameters of a popular mode—that of the graphic novel. Further, the graphic component permits Patil to represent a holistic androgyny or butchness that language, with its dimorphic gendering, often finds impossible to achieve. Where Monique Witting uses the bar between the two alphabets that represent 'I' in French, Kari achieves its own equivalent of 'j/e' by pictorially, graphically permitting Kari to move in a world that refuses the reality of her gender. The visible evidence of Kari's presence in this world thus queers this same world, revealing slippages within which Kari might be housed, instead of having to ship her off to America or death as De and Dawesar have had to do.

Todorov's remarks on the fantastic are useful in the consideration of this novel. At the beginning of the essay, Todorov outlines the characteristic modalities of the fantastic, one such characteristic being the literal use of figurative elements through the text (Todorov 1975). Kari opens with 'The Double Suicide'—Kari and Ruth commit suicide, filmi-style, by jumping off their respective buildings; both survive their falls. Mysteriously, Kari survives because she falls into the sewer; Ruth, fortune's favourite even otherwise we find, lives in a building with a safety net, which catches her. Another similar safety net, we suspect, dispatches Ruth to a far away country. Thus safely removed, Ruth leaves behind Kari who must continue to live after pulling herself out of the cess-pit she finds herself in. Located within a globalizing Mumbai, Kari's style is not only 'indigenous' not only Western, but rather a 'dubbed' style that intermittently, fragmentarily and superficially sometimes picks up elements of Western cultures, but hybridizes them to produce authentically national styles elsewhere, here butchness (see Boellstroff 2005). Located as the story is within an English-speaking aspirational middle-class and almost entirely female world, Kari's lesbian style rings true. The novel represents Kari in the style of a biker-babe, albeit with no feminine markers like long hair, in black-based clothes and eyes heavily lined. Kari's is recognizably Goth-girl style, a movement from the older all-butch look of the 1950s through the 1970s, to the more toned-down styles thereafter wherein everyone became butch with androgyny becoming the homonormative paradigm within Western feminism as much as within lesbianism (see Calhoun 1994). Ruth on the other hand signifies the femininity of the femme that was displaced and driven under by the androgyny this same lesbianism demanded, a disappearance enacted also in Ruth's disappearance from Kari's life. Ruth is feminine in clothing, appearance and demeanour, with lush hair, tender and doe-eyed, again in possession of a fairytale-style femininity.

Kari is unambiguous about the nature of their bond—the opening page of this graphic novel features Kari and Ruth, sitting hand in hand on a bench in a fashion very similar to Frida Kahlo's 1939 painting 'Two Fridas'. A pair of scissors in Ruth's hand appears to have just cut her vein; the caption reads 'There are two of us, not one. Despite a slipshod surgical procedure, we are joined still.' The Kahlo painting can be read as Frida post-divorce, sectioning off her colonially compliant self from an unruly 'Mexican' Frida; 'Two Fridas' in this reading is about one woman sectioned into two as a result of the demands of heterocompliance. But the first line of a novel named after one protagonist so insistently, even anxiously, insists echoing this very image, 'there are two of us, not one.' The opening lines, then, make literal the phrase 'two bodies, one heart' with the accompanying illustration showing Ruth's and Kari's hearts connected by a blood vessel. Ruth, looking rather wan, has just cut this blood vessel which ends at her pulse. The other end, via their hearts, entwines Kari's left arm, ending at her wrist. 'Two, joined by one heart' here is, thus, literally realized. An everyday metaphoric staple from love-literature, this literalization of the phrase here places *Kari* within the realm of the fantastic, the (un)familiar as we have defined it. Two other modalities that Todorov outlines are the presence of phrases that syntactically cast doubts on 'reality,' or at least constantly call attention to its constructedness—phrases such as 'it seemed,' 'as if,' and the like. The other is the presence of hyperbole or exaggeration; on this count, *Kari* does not qualify, as it relies more on understatement rather than on exaggeration; yet, at the larger thematic level, its literalization of many romantic clichés may be taken to serve as exaggerations of tropes that are otherwise invisible so as to make them evident. Together, their presence in a text necessitates a 'hesitation' between multiple explanations of phenomena. Something may have really happened or maybe not; it may have a rational or a non-rational explanation. Forcing the reader to choose between these many possibilities has the effect of questioning the real itself; as we shall see in *Kari*, our hesitation between the nature of the explanations we must adduce for Kari's tales has a variety of effects on both the story, and the reader's own desires. For instance, still later, we realize, Ruth could just as well be someone only we the readers see; no other character in the book ever encounters her. As Todorov puts it:

> In a world which is indeed our world, the one we know ... there occurs an event which cannot be explained by the laws of this same

familiar world. The person who experiences the event must opt for one of two possible solutions: either he is a victim of an illusion of the senses, of a product of the imagination—and the laws of the world remain what they are; or else the event has taken place, it is an integral part of reality—but then this reality is controlled by laws unknown to us. (Todorov 1975: 25)

Seen in this light, the invisibility of this lesbian lover of Kari's can also be read as a potent signifier by the 'don't show, don't be punished' mentality that governs societal responses to most same-sex relationships. *Kari* thus shows us a reality 'controlled by laws unknown to us' is indeed a reality controlled by laws unrecognised by normative scripts of sexuality. As we shall see further, Amruta Patil's text navigates the very terrains of the familiar we delineated earlier. Kari is a familiar—spirit with special powers to see and feel what no others can because of her lesbianism. At the same time, as her caution—'Make no mistake—there is no such thing as a straight woman' (Patil 2008: 58)—places the reader herself in a quandary; so am I a straight woman or no? The reading experience that Kari provides renders (un) familiar many familiar experiences that occur in familiar spaces; yet focalized through Kari's specific difference as lesbian from the 'rest of us' the rest of us are also changed by the things that seem otherwise to carry no burden of sexuality.

Kari's failed suicide attempt lands her in a sewer, from where she climbs out to work in a cubicle only as large as an airing-cupboard for her muck-soaked clothes. The world at work in an advertising agency does not see Kari's grief, it can only smell her clothes. Loss, bereavement or grief that results from a same-sex relationship is not only unfamiliar to most of Kari's familiars, but also unwelcome. Her deprivation is something she alone sees and must cure or cauterize; where the fellow-inhabitants of her world are indifferent, the reader on the other hand, is pushed into the experience of the fantastic: 'The fantastic is that hesitation experienced by a person who knows only the laws of nature, confronting an apparently supernatural event' (Todorov 1975: 25). Kari's fall into and re-emergence from the sewer belongs within the realm of the fantastic, as do her later journeys as 'boatman' into this Mumbai's sewerage. Todorov sees the fantastic as the duration of the hesitation between supernatural and natural explanations—he terms them respectively the marvellous and the uncanny. To qualify for treatment within the fantastic, the events within the text must be treated as real events among living people by the reader. Further, the reader's hesitation between explanations may be mirrored by the hesitations of a character within the text between the natural and supernatural explanations of the same events; the hesitation the reader feels must have a mirror in the form of a character or characters within the work; the hesitation itself becomes 'one of the themes of the work' (Todorov 1975: 33). The reader may hesitate, as Todorov shows, between the real and the illusory, and the real and the imaginary. In the first case, one is sure that the events in question have indeed taken place, but one doubts one's construction or understanding of them; in the second case, one doubts whether one has imagined it all after all (Todorov 1975: 36–37). In the case of *Kari*, our hesitation about accepting Ruth's reality are indeed mirrored by Angel's and Lazarus's doubts about her existence, compounded further by others complete ignorance of her. We hesitate, with Angel and Lazarus, wondering if Ruth exists and if she does, why she does not appear before anyone else even within the flashback sequences. Ruth, apparently, exists on another, more unfamiliar plane of reality; *Kari* thus qualifies for a supernatural or marvellous explanation but the many natural explanations for Ruth's being incognito provide us with the 'experience of limits' that constitutes the uncanny, the socially impossible, the unfamiliar that is excluded from the purview of the reassuringly familiar.

On the one hand, Ruth may indeed be a product of Kari's hyperactive imagination; on the other hand, Ruth's actual presence may have been misinterpreted by Kari—perhaps she was not a lover after all even if she did exist. But this begs the obvious question—why did Ruth disappear finally? This question is one that the reader must answer with the help of her knowledge of the consensus realities that make female same-sex love difficult if not impossible. The reader is forced to enter Kari's mental process and provide the answer; Kari's life wrecks a number of consensus realities inventively but Ruth may have been unable to carry on doing this in the face of overt or covert homophobia and being rendered 'family's outlaws' as Cheshire Calhoun puts it (Calhoun 1996). *Kari* invites the reader to identify with the narrator with the use of the pronoun 'I' which places the reader in a presumably positive affiliation with the narrator while at the same time requiring the reader to make choices between the real and the fantastic, between natural and supernatural explanations for the various events this 'I' takes her through. As Todorov would put it, hesitation and uncertainty are part of the narrative itself in such cases. The first-person narration forces the reader herself to confront the 'consensus reality' to use Kathryn Hume's phrase, that makes homosexuality impossible (Hume 1984). Since the fantastic is usually present only for a duration, for the period of hesitation, this unstable genre is usually 'resolved' into the more stable modes of the marvellous or the uncanny. *Kari* mostly permits natural explanations for how things turn out, placing itself, thus, within the mode of the uncanny. The uncanny for Todorov provides an avenue for the entry of 'rational' yet 'incredible, extraordinary, shocking, singular, disturbing or unexpected' debris of reality that would otherwise be normalized or routinized (Todorov 1975: 46). Kari's life's many events—whether downright fantastic such as a sewer serving as both safety-net and navigable body for her (perhaps metaphoric, perhaps literal, night-time) boat, Ruth's particular relationship (or not) with Kari, Kari's defamiliarizing encounters with the city of Mumbai itself—all take us into the third space between the realist and the fantasy narrative; uncanny elements sneak into renditions of the most mundane familiar things as we shall see further.

Kari's grief, as it turns out, gives her the creative satisfaction of being able to produce an advertising campaign that takes her out of the '*chaddi-baniyan* mode' where she and her friend Lazarus, apprentice copywriter and art-director respectively, have been festering for no one knows how long. Patil thus brings up two incongruent, yet true aspects of (un)familiar existence. Kari's grief goes unrecognized; yet this grief is the source of creativity and thence, career advancement. The lesbian here is a familiar—her special powers of 'paging [the] inner fox' of creativity originate in her love for Ruth (Patil 2008: 11). *Kari* thus locates same-sex relationships within the space of love and joy in creativity as directors like Ligy Pullapally, Nisha Ganatra, and Shamim Sarif, and writers like Manju Kapur and Suniti Namjoshi will, in the chapters to come, rather than purely within the space of desire or negative emotion as Shobha De had. However, unlike in most of the above-mentioned texts with the exception of Kapur's

Delhi-based characters, Kari lives and breathes the same air as the millions that inhabit Mumbai, that El Dorado among Indian cities for many. Unlike, say, Pullapally's characters in *Sancharam* who live in tharawads that are still shrines of caste privilege and walk in fields where no other people but them are ever seen, Kari is in possession of an enviable mobility, rubbing shoulders with men and women in what Raj Rao describes as 'soul city.' Intrepidly she walks all over Mumbai, discovering fresh 'tender offshoot[s] to the tar' (Patil 2008: 43) that shoot off seemingly exhausted terrain, her discoveries providing a cartographic metaphor for a narrative of lesbian sexuality that must find (un)familiar ways of doing familiar things due to sheer necessity. The space of the city is heterogeneous—it has within it many kinds of mini-spaces that have to be negotiated differently. The (un)familiar is not living within a ghetto as much as living within the larger space of the city itself. Kari shows the spaces of the city— building terraces, railway stations, parties, nightclubs, all as sites for (un)familiar femininities to explore and inhabit. The queer flâneur thus serves as our guide to the queer city, irrespective of whether he/ she is used with homophobic ends.

Names are evocative. Kari is not given a surname in the book. While her butchness prevents her from successfully passing as Ruth is able to with her more conventional feminine good looks, the author's non-conferment of a surname suggests Kari's 'type' holds true for a larger terrain than that of Mumbai. It is hardly possible to 'place' Kari within a particular Indian state or region; she could be from anywhere. Neither can we make out from her salwar-kameez-clad mother or moustachioed father's appearance where they hail from. 'Kari' could come from just about anywhere. Her parents are indeed located within an emotional specificity—they love their daughter, give her good advice, she misses them, but as is true for almost all 'successfully' socialized children, she must leave the homestead to make her own way in the world, emotionally and economically. The name 'Kari' with mock-playful similarities with nicknames that are also endearments, suggests an individual whose identity itself is playfully and at the same time vexingly mobile; our inability to reference particular geographical locations makes the name at once refer to an infinite number of local habitations and possibilities. Ruth's name on the other hand has vivid 'lesbian' overtones, invoking the story of

Ruth and Naomi from the Bible. Ruth's devotion to Naomi, whom she follows leaving behind the land of her parents and her youth, despite her marriage of convenience to Naomi's kinsman Boaz, is a story that lesbian-friendly readers have interpreted and invested with positive significance for female same-sex love, as Terry Castle's many examples in *The Literature of Lesbianism* (2003) show. Ruth's leaving behind home and memories, the realm of the familiar, in fact, in order to be with her mother-in-law even after the death of her husband, Naomi's son, bespeaks a devotion to the elder woman greater than the duties of filiality warrant. Ruth's steadfastness and Naomi's intrepidity and presence of mind make it possible for these women to choose and retain one another as primary emotional and physical presences in their lives. Ruth in this novel, however, is not half as kind. Kari does not show us why Ruth wishes to die; Kari's non-judgemental reception of this attempt at suicide and Ruth's departure and disappearance after it, however, suggest that ideas of non-reciprocality in love are not are not all that old-fashioned after all. Kari's love for Ruth continues unabated, despite the lack of mutuality that Ruth's absence ensures. In fact, the closest positive analogue for the relationship comes from the lexicon of male-bonding in Hindi cinema: Kari is like Mohan in *Dosti* (Director: Satyen Bose 1964), that wonderful paean to male same-sex friendship and love; Mohan, though blind, puts his friend Ramu through school. Ramu is trapped by a teacher-benefactor into leaving Mohan for a better life, ostensibly, and events transpire such that he cannot speak to Mohan or explain matters. Mohan's love sees Ramu is devoted and in need still of love: '*chahoonga tujhko shaam savere/phir bhi tere naam ko/aawaaz mein na doonga*' (I will love you night and day, yet, I will not speak your name out any more) sings the discarded Mohan. While the song might at first hearing be mistaken for the voice of a wounded ego, the narrative of the film places Mohan as the seer, endowed with *drishti* (vision) despite lacking sight via eyes. Mohan's perceptiveness enables him to see other's sufferings and to respond with an immediate love and compassion; his friendship and his love, as another song goes, that quietly lights up each step of a difficult way. *Kari* is too worldly-wise a book to unselfconsciously devote itself to the radiant, ego-effacing, transcendent power of selfless love, but all the same, Kari's forbearance towards Ruth merits comparison with the mutual devotion of these boy-heroes from a 1960s mainstream film, the conventions of which are all loaded towards the achievement and valorization of the *karuna rasa*, because *Kari* as a graphic novel enters the realm of public culture in a rather wider arc than does the average printed book.

At the same time, *Kari* is edgier, her voice more wry, ironic and self-depreciating; yet, Kari's love for Ruth is a constant, mounting defences for Ruth left, right and centre, whenever occasion demands it, which is quite often; Angel for instance finds Ruth a 'gasbag' (Patil 2008: 50) while Lazarus takes the beast by the horns, saying 'I'm not sure the Ruth bitch ever existed' (Patil 2008: 79). Ruth, then, is no devoted daughter-in-law; but why does Ruth try to die? *Kari* does not tell us, and we can well supply the reason. In the familiar world of the everyday when to appear to conform sexually if not psychically, in appearance if not content, is only one of the fracturing demands made on the self, people like Kari and Ruth are among the first to find out that the sexual is indeed not very separate from the psychical, that while (un)familiar desires may be acted out, desires when they fructify into love must be allowed the room that the conventional outlines of family, domesticity and public affirmation supply to the heterosexual couple. Ruth, with her looks, can 'pass'—she does not trouble conventional expectations visually or sartorially. Depicted most times in a skirt, or in clothing that displays enough feminine contours, Ruth is a far cry from the angular, almost breastless, shorn-headed Kari. Kari would be unable to 'pass;' with time, her tomboyishness would have settled into the acknowledged contours of butchness without the accessories of a suitably reassuring male partner. In the frame where Kari 'falls into' Ruth—literally— the walls of the railway station bear a set of posters of the film *Dilwale Dulhaniya Le Jayenge* (DDLJ) (Director: Aditya Chopra 1995). This film has an iconic status in Indian public culture, with the characters essayed by leads Shah Rukh Khan and Kajol having almost become the romantic pair everyone desires to be; in fact, the domesticity and partnership the two promise one another is a de-masculinized, less hypertrophied one than the ones projected by earlier star onscreen couples. Shah Rukh Khan's relatively less 'masculine' masculinity, coupled with Kajol's scrappy, almost dishevelled femininity redefined the normative spouses that filmgoers at least of this generation have been trained to expect or desire. However, despite the relatively more equitable arrangements between the warring genders promised by DDLJ and similar films following that focussed more and more on romantic and comic engagements and less and less on vigilante-justice based action films which in Bollywood tend to centre around the person of the hero, the focus of these films is still the ideal and idealized heterosexual unit (Ghosh 2002). The untidy paradoxes that Ruth and Kari fall into when they break the 'love laws' are thus nailed by Patil with her placement of the DDLJ posters in the background, but at very centre of the frame where Kari 'fell into' Ruth.

Kari takes the train every day to work, something that most Hindi film-heroines even today don't do much, or at least not in a way that consciously marks them out as labouring creatures. Kari's presence there is not offset by the arrival of a suitably dashing hero who will remove her from the scene of her 'implied' drudgeries; instead, she meets another woman in a space that like most Indian public spaces, belong to women only during the day, in particular instrumental ways. The hero at the railway station waiting for the belated heroine to arrive is another commonplace in Bollywood cinema, as are stories of love blossoming right there between strangers on the way to somewhere. That the hero here is a butch woman getting besotted with a femme heroine renders (un)familiar most of the planks of the conventional heterosexual family drama of romance that must ensue. Where the formation of a heterosexual pair could have been invested with love, radicality and many songs in the hands of even an incompetent director, Kari's story produces instead a cul-de-sac. Since the formation of the idealized heterosexual unit can at best be imitated without success, at worst be parodied, a suitable exit must be devized; of course, there are no honourable exits within the 'femme damnee' script. One of them must die. Kari decides both of them could just as well die, since she cannot live without Ruth.

Not being able to live without Ruth, she discovers, is another romantic cliché. The content, one sees, is the same as that which underlies the tender devotions of a heterosexual pair; the forms are similar, but prohibited. Ruth and Kari perform that other great gesture allowed to doomed lovers in Hindi cinema till recently—the double suicide that places the lovers beyond the reach of mortal laws. Iconic heterosexual couples like those essayed most recently by Rati Agnihotri and Kamal Hassan in *Ek Duje ke Liye* (Director: K.

Balachander 1981), or Aamir Khan and Juhi Chawla in *Qayamat se Qayamat Tak* (Director: Mansoor Khan 1988), could stage their joint deaths as protests against and defiance of this unjust world's cruel laws; however, in the last two decades, the double suicide has lost its place as a high romantic tour-de-force in Indian cinema. Ironic reviews of the situation have existed alongside its deployment, *Sholay* (Director: Ramesh Sippy 1975) having a particularly memorable satire on the tendencies of lovers to kill themselves. An obvious recent example is *Saathiya* (Director: Shaad Ali 2002) where the hero tells the heroine that he wants to live with his love rather than jump out of running trains out of devotion, while the protagonist of *Munnabhai MBBS* (Director: Rajkumar Hirani 2003) takes more obvious potshots at the genre of dying for love. *Kari* also enters this revision of one of the most resonant high romantic conventions in popular, public cultures; neither participant in the joint-suicide dies, or is visibly injured. The latter means they are spared of both public disparagement and police cases, but at the same time are also deprived of the space for public mourning and grief that a failed suicide attempt invariably secures. As Kari says, someone who has tried to commit suicide is scary, and 'a failed sucide is death still' signalling as it does the death of innocence about life (Patil 2008: 10). An act of closure thus paradoxically begins the narrative; as is obvious, a failed suicide cannot provide closure, and Kari spills her guts to us much as the city of Mumbai spills itself into its intestines, the sewers Kari services nightly. Patil is unable to organically mesh the metaphors she sets ringing with the simpler narrative of Kari's own life thereafter, but the potentials may well be taken up in later books in the series.

The postlapsarian narrative lands Kari in what appears to be the foul wastes of a poisoned body—failed female same-sex love. The choice of a sewer as a landing place for Kari makes it impossible to miss the associations Patil's narrative makes of lesbian desire with waste, though, however, she does not cast Kari's contact with waste as polluting Kari; rather, the encounter with the 'other' to the self is a site of (un)familiar discoveries that enables Kari to go back to life. Rejected by the body, the various wastes that we produce everyday—hair, excreta, dead skin, bodily fluids—must all find their way into the sewers of the cities we live in, moment after moment. The smell of the bog, however, is something most cities are able to confine to the unfortunates who work in them. How has Kari gained the same access to this cesspit that its scavengers, who still perform manually tasks that have been mechanised in less-barbaric nations? Love for the familiar has placed her in the middle of the sewer, in a boat, but she will not resist taint for long, as the sewer's fluid media are corrosive. This sewer can be both Kari's unloved state—she loves Ruth, truly and without fuss, but like Mohan in *Dosti*, cannot help feeling abandoned—as also the status given to same-sex love, particularly female same-sex love. Kari herself is Ruth's waste now, and by extension the waste of the world at large, being unable, with her androgyny, to belong within the narratives of heterosexual privilege, however (heterosexual) feminist or emancipated. Yet, as boatman and implicitly, scavenger, Kari is also in a powerful position. The relief she as scavenger provides is what keeps the city afloat; it would be unable to breath, its gut would burst if the excreta were not allowed an exit-passage. Amruta Patil's text allows one to imagine lesbian love, love for the similar as an exit valve that permits patriarchy to stay afloat. The subterranean world that Kari as Minx in Shobha De's novel *Strange Obsession* would have been able to inhabit is not considered here; *Kari's* preoccupation is with waste itself, not with the glamours of being in the underbelly. Desire for the same-sex places Kari in precarious positions in dangerous places; she sometimes goes diving, at other times rows immediately back to the safety of plain land. Yet, these spaces so (un)familiar to the rest of us are just underneath the drain cover in the bathroom; 'the mother-bog' of love for similar beings is just underneath the clean surfaces of heteronormativity then. Kari is able to travel back and forth, but her amphibiousness is suspect; at times it appears she will be drowned by the undertow of self-loathing and sheer desire for love. The sewer of (un)familiar desire in Kari disrupts consensus reality with the smell of various rejections that it brings to the dinner table. The abject nature of this waste allows the reader to examine the status given to female same-sex love while at the same time to mull on its powers—this love, this desire gurgles just underneath the everyday, and like a familiar, is powerful enough to emerge unsuspected from sundry corners to turn life upside down if not suitably pacified.

After the fall, Ruth is saved; the Christian narrative of redemption by proxy is not available to Kari who must make her own way, surrounded by characters with sufficiently resonant Christian names like Lazarus and Angel. Kari herself reveals to Angel, halfway into the book, a tattoo of wings that takes up most of the space on her back. As an angel with shorn wings, Kari was bound to come plummeting to the ground every time she tries to fly; being with the angelic Ruth—who literally flies away to safety—was flying too high for Kari. Angel her friend, is in the final stages of cancer; as a terminal patient, she does not care about Kari's romantic woes. This presence of an unchosen death tethers Kari to life, and in a sense, Kari is saved by proxy, not by Christ the redeemer, but by a bald woman called Angel. Angel is a reluctant intercessor between death and Kari; yet, her sassiness—we are to assume wisdom—and her nearness to death invariably fascinates Kari. Angel's presence as an older and thus sadder mentor places her within both the Sapphic and Marian traditions, as Ruth Vanita defines them, in lesbian or female homophilic writing (Vanita 1996). The Sapphic tradition, as Vanita (1996) places it, derives from death-wish the poet from Lesbos sustains after the departure of her beloved; the Marian tradition is more life-giving, if erotically also less explicit, focussing on female celibacy and autonomy primarily. Kari is a devoted follower after Sappho, actively desiring death; yet, with Angel, in the presence of a suitable teacher, Kari learns to devote herself to life. Angel, like Mother Mary, offers Kari hope for a better tomorrow despite her many sins. With Ruth absent, Kari is an unstable presence; with Angel, Kari enters a dyad that offers both women sustenance though it does not substitute, and indeed, does not seek to substitute for the previous relationship. Kari and Angel share a tender though superficially brusque solicitude for one another very much like the sisterhood Kari is never able to achieve with her heterosexually mated housemates Delna and Billo. Because of their autonomy, Kari and Angel have time for one another, as indeed Delna and Billo have for Kari when their boyfriends are not around. Autonomous feminine companionship on such evenings as a sorority, in fact, makes Kari say 'There is no such thing as a straight woman' in a frame that stretches across two pages and in which the girls are seated at table as they would be if they had been posing for the painting of Da Vinci's 'Last Supper' (Patil 2008: 58).

But an autonomous femininity must be short-lived; your female best friends will want to marry, your housemates' boyfriends return, and Angel dies of the cancer. The Marian plot scheme only goes so far within a Sapphic plot of doom, which however Patil overturns by harnessing Kari's energies to her work instead of to her spiritual existence. Her 'Fairytale Hair' ad-campaign, which reinforces the notions of homospectatoriality in fashion photography that we considered earlier in this chapter, wins her awards and enables her to think of a life in a 'lotus pad' beyond the one she leads in her present 'snakepit' (Patil 2008: 24), with 'ambiguous sexual affiliations' et al (Patil 2008: 109). The Sapphic seeking of closure through suicide is stood on its head with Kari realizing with each new step that she must live, whether Ruth is present with her or not. This postlapsarian life does not all travel through the vale or tears any more than the prelapsarian one must have been all Edenic. Kari's friend Lazarus is both revivified and reborn—after an AIDS scare, an imaginative enough updating of the death and rebirth story of Lazarus from the Bible—but his rebirth is a severance of the umbilical cord for Kari because it comes via Lazarus' attachment to another woman; Kari must indeed go through it alone. Sitting on the roof the morning after having received 'the campaign of the year' award for her Ruth-inspired 'Fairytale Hair' campaign with Lazarus, Kari finds herself completely companionless. Marguerite Yourcenar (1903–1987) provides an unlikely correspondence when a story of hers, 'Sappho or Suicide' from the collection *Fires* (1936) ends similarly with her protagonist, a modern-day circus artist as the tawdry namesake of the great poetess, thinking of suicide, and deciding against it. 'I will not kill myself. The dead are so quickly forgotten' (Castle 2003: 945). For the Sappho of that story, 'It's not a question of suicide. It's only a question of beating a record' (Castle 2003: 945). Standing on the roof of her high building, watching gulls fly by in a passage that eerily Yourcenar's story as well, places her on the terrace, a classic in-between space characteristic of the flâneur, Kari, watching her doppelganger, the 'bird girl' who feeds the gulls breakfast every day, step off the opposite building and die, finds that: '1) I feel no bird urge. 2) I want to step back, not step off. 3) I still love Ruthie more than anyone else in the world, but I won't be jumping off ledges for anyone any more' (Patil 2008: 115). Yourcenar's Sappho falls into the circus' safety net for the high-flying trapeze artists, and thinks, 'One can only raise happiness on a foundation of despair. I think I will be able to start building' (Castle 2003: 945). Similarly Kari sees that 'this PVC suit itches' (Patil 2008: 115): acquired, together with her boatman-hood upon her own attempted suicide at the beginning of the novel, this suit was what permitted her to go wandering amongst the sewers in the dreams that appeared as real as her twilit wanderings within the city. Now, having decided to live, the novel concludes on a strange note of re-connection, with the last line saying 'In a faraway city where the palette was pure and bright, Ruth stirred in her sleep, and smiled' (Patil 2008: 116). Broad pencil strokes mar this frame with undiminished greys and blacks that immediately suggest that apart from Ruth feeling anything, it is Kari who is able to assimilate Ruth into herself. Her compassion for herself finally ignited, Kari is able to love herself along with Ruth, transforming despair into a foundation for life and happiness rather than for death.

Coda

All three writers locate their (un)familiar mannish lesbians within urban contexts. Babyji is a 'baby dyke' as Nisha Ganatra's *Chutney Popcorn* (see Chapter 2) would name her. Kari as the sanest, deepest treatment, and Minx as the most troubled, most troubling figuration of who a butch lesbian is and why she becomes that way. But within Indian English fiction the urban space, with economic independence, seems to suggest the only possible way of living for the butch lesbian. In contrast, *Loving Women: Being Lesbian in Underprivileged India*, a compilation of autobiographical narratives from interviews with mostly non-urban, non-English speaking lesbian couples shows how butchness can be transcultural as well as integrate itself into the mofussil or rural milieu just as well as it can insinuate itself into the relatively more anonymous space of the city (Sharma 2006). The strategies of visibility and intelligibility are different, however. As anthologist and interviewer Maya Sharma observes, neither the English word 'lesbian' nor the Sanskrit-derived *sanglaingik* were used by the women in question to define their relationships, which had often been long-term ones. Within the English texts that I have considered, the word 'lesbian' is very much available and employed, though its gendered adjective, butchness, is relatively more invisible and implicit. In Sharma's collection, the feature that jumps out as being common to all the narratives she collects is the physical lack of space. It is possible to posit that this is the real distinction between the English-language texts we have read in this chapter and the transcriptions of interviews in Indian languages that Sharma presents. De, Dawesar, and Patil present lesbian (un)familiars with access to economic resources that provide them with autonomous spatial arrangements. The realm of the (un)familiar in most of these spaces is crucial to the actualization of the individualized 'lesbian' identity—I place the word lesbian here in quotes in order to signify its often non-indigenous roster of suggestive possibilities, such as interiority, self-actualization and autonomy, suggestions that are authored as much by material resources as much as they are by intent. While in the texts above Minx, Kari and Anamika can with relative liberty move into and out of relationships on the sly or openly, the women Sharma studies are relatively more confined in terms of partnership possibilities: marriage and their female companion's shifting residence to her husband's house are common interruptions, which as the three novels we study here show, are not necessarily part of the urban butch lesbian's life-narrative.

In all, the figure of the lesbian as butch/dyke, however, is important for signalling that gender difference here relates to sexual difference. When this interruption of the seamless connections between gender and bodily sex is successfully made, the definition of the body changes along with the use of public spaces, the world itself—the realm made anew. To employ Eve Sedgwick's notion of minoritizing and universalizing discourses, De's novel sees Minx's butch lesbianism as Minx's private psychological disorder that has unfortunate consequences, but that can be managed by Minx's excision from a narrative that happens almost entirely in private. Babyji's movement through the spaces of homes, middle-class parties and schools renders lesbianism more accessible, less unfamiliar than De's location of the lesbian within high-fashion does. Queering Delhi by making it available to Anamika's amatory excesses, Dawesar is able to place the modern city as not a bad place for the 'baby dyke' albeit with the proviso that she goes abroad in order to grow up and become truly free. Kari represents to my mind the true success in making possible an authentic butch urban Indian sensibility; identifying with KD Lang whom she sees on MTV, and working in an ad-agency, Kari has more in common with the western lesbian than she does with the 'indigenous' non-English speaking Indian one. But nevertheless, in placing Kari's adventures in Mumbai, Amruta Patil makes Kari's butchness and her love for Ruth signify in a universalizing way—if the Indian realm has room for Kari, then it cannot be as homophobic as the traditionalism presumed by most top-down queer theories from Western centres used to presume was the case for the non-West. In all, butch gender insubordination permits a visible theatre of sexual difference. In contrast to the 'homosexuality' that makes straight theorists see lesbian desire as necessarily and essentially masculine in function, a less biologically determinist conception of homosexuality permits the representation of intra-female desire that is autonomous of phallic constructions that locate the phallus itself within male physicality and biology (Abelove 1993: 142). Transcending the requirements of this male body, the butch's appropriation of masculinity permits, in Teresa de Lauretis' convincing borrowing from Luce Irigary—homosexuality to be replaced by the 'homosexuality' of same-sex desire as desire that is not identical with women-identified bonding, and is not the same as heterosexual desire (Case 1993: 142). Joan Riviere's identification of femininity itself as masquerade is very useful in order to understand the (un)familiar that these three texts write into being. Riviere argues that heterosexual femininity is a masquerade wherein women take possession of the phallus, but so as not to awaken castration anxiety in men, pretend that they do not possess it. Riviere's important formulation stems from her own role as analyst to an intellectual heterosexual woman who confessed to feelings of extreme anxiety and near-hysteria upon flirting with men after concluding important public academic work (Riviere 1929/1966: 213). Riviere theorizes upon this near-neurotic oscillation women perforce have to make between 'wearing the pants,' and necessarily having to be seen as not in pants. Sue-Ellen Case in 'The Butch/ Femme Aesthetic' argues that while heterosexual women masquerade and show off their castration in order to hide their possession of the phallus, butch women, in not relating to heterosexual masculinity in the same way as straight women, 'foreground' their possession of the symbolic phallus that enables them to desire women. Within a heteronormative paradigm, butch freedom from having to masquerade enables them to 'openly' appropriate masculinity, and it is the guises of masculinity transgressively employed that heighten butch/femme attraction, as Case argues (1993: 294–305). In the three texts that we have considered, the butch/femme pairing either does not exist, or dissolves, or is itself a fiction, but all the same, the charade of masquerade as castrated objects is precisely what is refused by all three protagonists. Minx, Babyji, and Kari are indifferent to male machinations to draw their sexual energies, and instead, pursue women with varying degrees of consent involved in these pursuits. But in all cases, these three butch/lesbians are able to make (un)familiar both maleness and masculinity, as also female agency and powerlessness or its opposite through the script of re-gendering the masculine via (un)familiar desire for women. Butch desire, in giving agential subjectivity to women who love women in an immediate fashion through the rehousing of gender norms, invades the realm of public space, thus respatializing (un)familiar desire. In their inability to pass, butch lesbians present a spectacle of (un)familiarity that is in your face, forcing an interrogation of normative rules of gendering, sexing and desiring. In its invasion of public space, it foregrounds questions of visibility, the gaze, identity and intelligibility to the beholder that are not so immediately available in non-butch desires, which we shall explore in the succeeding chapter.

Note

1. See Benstock (2010), for example, for a discussion of the lesbian subculture in Paris.

References

Agnes, Flavia. 1992. 'Protecting Women against Violence: Review of a Decade of Legislation, 1980-89'. *Economic and Political Weekly*, XXVII: 17.
Anjaam. Dir. Rahul Rawail. Perf. Shah Rukh Khan, Madhuri Dixit. 1994.
Ahmed, Sara. 2010. 'Unhappy Queers', *The Promise of Happiness*. Duke University Press.
Bettie, Julie. 2003. *Women without Class*. Berkeley: University of California Press.
Benstock, Shari. 1986/2010. *Women of the Left Bank: Paris 1900–1940*. University of Texas Press.
Boellstorff, Tony. 2005. *The Gay Archipelago: Sexuality and Nation in Indonesia*. Princeton and Oxford, Princeton University Press.

Butler, Heather. 2004. 'What do you Call a Lesbian with Long Fingers', *Porn Studies* (ed.) Linda Williams, p. 167.

Connell, R. W. 1995. *Masculinities.* Berkeley: University of California Press.

Calhoun, Cheshire. 1994. 'Separating Lesbian Theory from Feminist Theory', *Ethics* 104(3): 558–581.

———. 1996. 'The Gender Closet: Lesbian Disappearance under the Sign 'Women', *Feminist Studies*, 2.1: 7–34.

Castle, Terry. 2003. *The Literature of Lesbianism.* New York: Columbia University Press.

Case, Sue-Ellen. 1993. 'Towards a Butch Femme Aesthetic', *Lesbian and Gay Studies Reader* (eds.) Henry Abelove *et al.* London: Routledge.

Dave, Anjali. 2006. 'Feminist Social Work Intervention: Special Cells for Women and Children', (ed.) Kalpana Kannabiran, *The Violence of Normal Times: Essays on Women's Lived Realities.* New Delhi: Women Unlimited.

De, Shobha. 1992. *Strange Obsession.* Penguin India.

Debord, G. 1994. *The Society of the Spectacle.* New York: Zone.

Deepa, V. N. 2005. Narrain, Arvind and Gautam Bhan (eds.) *Because I Have a Voice: Queer Politics in India.* New Delhi: Yoda.

Darr. Dir. Yash Chopra. Perf. Sunny Deol, Shah Rukh Khan, Juhi Chawla. 1993.

Dosti. Dir. Satyen Bose. Perf. Sudhir Kumar, Sushil Kumar, Sanjay Khan. 1964.

Doty, Alexander. 1993. *Making Things Perfectly Queer: Interpreting Mass Culture.* Minneapolis: Minnesota University Press.

Dilwale Dulhaniya Le Jayenge. Dir. Aditya Chopra. Perf. Shah Rukh Khan, Kajol, Amrish Puri. 1995.

Ek Duje ke Liye. Dir. K. Balachander. Perf. Kamal Hassan, Rati Agnihotri. 1981.

Fuss, Diana. 1992. 'Fashion and the Homospectatorial Look', *Critical Inquiry, Identities*, 18 (4): 713–737.

Ghosh, Shohini. 2002. 'Queer Pleasures for Queer People : Film, Television, and Queer Sexuality in India', in *Queering India* (ed.) Ruth Vanita. New York and London : Routledge.

Halberstam, Judith. 1998. *Female Masculinity.* Durham, NC: Duke University Press.

Hill Collins, Patricia. 1990. *Black Feminist Theory: Knowledge, Consciousness, and the Politics of Empowerment.* New York: Routledge.

Hall, Radclyffe. 1982/1928. *The Well of Loneliness.* First published in 1928. London: Virago.

Shields, R. 1994. 'Fancy Footwork: Walter Benjamin's Notes on Flânerie', in K Tester (ed), *The Flâneur*, pp. 61–80. London/New York: Routledge.

Kennedy, E., and M. Davis. 1993. Boots of Leather, Slippers of Gold: The History of a Lesbian Community. New York: Penguin Books.

Kannabiran, Kalpana. 2006. *The Violence of Normal Times: Essays on Women's Lived Realities.* New Delhi: Women Unlimited.

Kidwai, Saleem. 2000. 'Introduction: Medieval Materials in the Perso–Urdu Traditions.' in *Same-Sex Love in India: Readings from History and Literature.* Ruth Vanita and Saleem Kidwai (eds), New York: St. Martin's Press.

Kumar Radha. 1993. *The History of Doing: An Illustrated Account of Movements for Women's Rights and Feminism in India 1800–1990*, New Delhi: Kali for Women.

Lipton, Shawna. 2012. 'Trouble Ahead: Pleasure, Possibility, and the Future of Queer Porn', *Journal of Contemporary Cinema*, 10(2–3): 198.

Lorber, Judith. 1994. *Paradoxes of Gender*. New Haven, CT: Yale University Press.

Lauretis, Teresa de. 1993. 'Sexual Indifference and Lesbian Representation', *Lesbian and Gay Studies Reader* (ed.) Henry Abelove et al. London: Routledge.

Munt, Sally. 1998. *Heroic Desire: Lesbian Identity and Cultural Space*. p.54. New York University Press.

Moore, Mignon. 2006. 'Lipstick or Timberlands? Meanings of Gender Presentation in Black Lesbian Communities', *Signs: Journal of Women in Culture and Society* 32:113–29.

Mulvey, Laura. 1990. 'Visual Pleasure and Narrative Cinema', in *Issues in Feminist Film Criticism*, (ed.). Patricia Erens. Bloomington: Indiana University Press.

Munnabhai MBBS. Dir. Rajkumar Hirani. Perf. Sanjay Dutt, Arshad Warsi. 2003.

Newton, Esther. 1984. 'The Mythic Mannish Lesbian: Radclyffe Hall and the New Woman', Signs, 9(4).

Oldenburg, Veena Talwar. 2002. *Dowry Murder : The Imperial Origins of a Cultural Crime*. Oxford; New York: Oxford University Press.

Pascoe, C. J. 2007. *Dude you're a Fag: Masculinity and Sexuality in High School*. Berkeley: University of California Press.

Phadke, Shilpa, Sameera Khan and Shilpa Ranade. 2011. *Why Loiter? Women and Risk on Mumbai Streets*. New Delhi: Penguin.

Patil, Amruta. 2008. *Kari*. New Delhi: HarperCollins.

Petievich, Carla. 2002. 'Doganas and Zanakhis: The Invention and Subsequent Erasure of Urdu Poetry's "Lesbian' Voice"' in *Queering India*. (ed.) Ruth Vanita. New York and London: Routledge.

Radway, Janice. 1983. 'Women Read the Romance: The Intersection of Text and Context', *Feminist Studies*, 9: 1: 53–78.

Riviere, Joan. 1929. 'Womanliness as a Masquerade', *International Journal of Psycho-Analysis*, 10: 303–13.

Rubin, Gayle. 2006. 'Of Catamites and Kings: Reflections on Butch, Gender, and Boundaries.' *The Transgender Studies Reader*, (eds) Susan Stryker and Stephen Whittle. pp. 471–481. London and New York: Routledge.

Schippers, Mimi. 2002. *Rockin' Out of the Box: Gender Maneuvering in Alternative Hard Rock*. New Brunswick: Rutgers University Press.

———. 2007. 'Recovering the Feminine Other: Masculinity, Femininity, and Gender Hegemony', *Sociological Theory* 36:85-102.

Sharma, Maya. 2006. *Loving Women: Being Lesbian in Underprivileged India*. New Delhi: Yoda.

Sontag, Susan. 1973. *On Photography*. New York: Rosetta Books.

She Stole My Voice. Dir. Justine Chang and Armand Kaye. 2007.

Saathiya. Dir. Shaad Ali. Perf. Vivek Oberoi, Rani Mukherjee. 2002.

Sholay. Dir. Ramesh Sippy. Perf. Amitabh Bachchan, Dharmendra, Hema Malini. 1975.

Todorov, Tzevetan. 1975. *The Fantastic: A Structural Approach to a Literary Genre*. p. 41. Ithaca: Cornell University Press.

Vicinus, Martha. 1993. '"They Wonder to Which Sex I Belong?" The Historical Roots of the Modern Lesbian Identity', in *The Lesbian and Gay Studies Reader*, eds. Henry Abelove, Michèle Barale, and David M. Halperin. New York: Routledge, pp. 432–452.

Vanita, Ruth and Saleem Kidwai. 2000. *Same-Sex Love in India*. New York.: St. Martin's Press.

Vanita, Ruth. 1996. 'Sappho and the Virgin Mary', *Same-Sex Love and the English Literary Imagination*. New York: Columbia University Press.

Wilkins, Amy C. 2004. 'Puerto Rican Wannabes: Sexual Spectacle and the Marking of Race, Class, and Gender Boundaries', *Gender & Society*, 18(1): 103–21.

Wilson, E. 1992. 'The Invisible Flâneur', *New Left Review*, 191: 90–110.

Wittig, Monique. 1992. 'One Is Not Born a Woman', *Feminist Issues I: The Straight Mind and Other Essays*. Boston: Beacon.

Wolff, Janet. 1990. *Feminine Sentences*. Berkeley: University of California Press.

2

Lesbians in the House!

Cinema and Queer Female Desire

> Mother, just because I wear trackies and play sport does not make
> me a lesbian! Me and Jess were fighting because we both fancied our
> coach, Joe!
>
> What, a man, Joe?
>
> Yes, as in male—Joe! Joe, our coach! Joe, man, Joe! Anyway, being a
> lesbian is not that big a deal.
>
> Oh no, sweetheart, of course it isn't. No, I mean, I've got nothing against
> it. I was cheering for Martina Navratilova as much as the next person.
>
> *Bend It Like Beckham* (Director: Gurinder Chadha 2002)

The (un)familiar woman as butch lesbian remains apparently more
at home within the public space of the city than she is at home.
What happens if 'family's outlaw' engages with conventional family? Through analysis of transnational films, *Nina's Heavenly Delights*
(Pratibha Parmar 2006), *I Can't Think Straight* (Shamim Sarif 2008),
The World Unseen (Shamim Sarif 2007), *Bend It Like Beckham* and
Chutney Popcorn (Nisha Ganatra 1999), I examine the exchange
between female homosexuality and cultural reproduction within
three ethnic-Indian contexts, one in South Africa, one in New York,
one in the UK. All these films have been made by second- and

third-generation diasporic Indians, are located broadly within the genre of comedy, and examine the question by opposed strategies, as it were, of what it means to be non-heterosexual within the space of the 'Indian' home. I examine how these films document emerging homosexual 'identities' but how, at the same time, cinematic images of homosexuality can also lend themselves to unfortunate homonormativities, even making themselves available to the homophobic gaze whilst they establish the presence of the homosexual. The chapter also shows that rather than the emergence of a politics of enablement for non-heteronormative subjectivities, oftentimes, diegetic resolutions can go in the direction of the personally therapeutic, with the consequences of transformative action becoming entirely personal or remaining within the private sphere. While films like *Nina's Heavenly Delights* and *I Can't Think Straight* absorb the (un)familiar outlaw rather easily into existing family structures, I study how *The World Unseen* and *Bend It Like Beckham* along with *Chutney Popcorn* imagine the space of the home—as family, diaspora, nation—as one that can be inhabited by the non-heterosexual or non-heteronormative female subject.

Queering India without Homecoming Queens and Daydream Believers

The title of this section draws from an exuberant song in Pratibha Parmar's *Nina's Heavenly Delights* where Parmar shows the love-story of a closeted South Asian Scottish lesbian, the eponymous Nina, as enabling her to find her way back to her family and patrimony. *Nina's Heavenly Delights* (NHD hereafter) answers to Roof's summary (see Introduction) of the coming-out story's plot almost word for word and is vulnerable to every criticism levied against the genre. Any material that might make Nina's transformation from closeted to out lesbian interesting is transformed instead to facile kitsch, by the extreme readiness everyone in the film has to welcome female homosexuality, even perhaps denying altogether that homophobia or discrimination exist at all. 'Welcome to Scotland' says a poster at the airport where a very ebullient but relatively underdone queen goes to receive his homecoming friend, the prodigal Nina, to take her to her father's funeral. Nina Shah is the daughter of Mohan Shan, the owner of the New Taj in Glasgow. Nina ran away from her own wedding three years ago because she did not want to marry Sanjay, her father's friend's son and heir to competitor and neighbouring restaurant 'The Jewel in the Crown,' and become one half of a 'power cooking-couple' with him. Nina is shocked to find her father had planned to sell the restaurant; cooking was his passion and she thinks it impossible that he should go against his heart. She convinces Lisa, now owner of the half-share Nina's father sold, to not sell the restaurant till the 'Best of the West Curry Competition' goes through, Nina's and her dad had already won it twice and are on a hat-trick chance. Winning it, Nina thinks, will restore her to her father's faith and reunite her to the family she ran away from. In the process, she falls in love with Lisa, and surprisingly, the 'victorious final assertion' of her lesbianism is not made only by the protagonist, but also by her unanimously unstintingly supportive South Asian diasporic family. Nina had remained closeted for the greater part of the film because she is unable to imagine such a reaction, of course, but this is forgotten in the fairy-tale settlement of loose-ends.

NHD suffers from this fairytale, tourist picture-postcard treatment of the South Asian presence in Glasgow. Avowedly, director Pratibha Parmar did not want to make a 'gritty, realist drama' (DVD features) but given the paucity of lesbian representations that have Indian material, the viewer and the critic cannot but sigh at the lost opportunity. Indians form one of the largest ethnic communities in Scotland, with histories dating from the post-World-War labour shortages and the expulsions of Indians from various parts of Africa from the 1960s, a history that resonates with the larger history of Indian presence in Britain . NHD completely decontextualizes these histories of origin to produce a romance that supposedly speaks universally to all lovers, or at least to all lesbian lovers. This begs a question about the coming-out story: where does race figure in it? In NHD's hurry to recognize and validate the lesbianism of a South Asian woman, the viewer loses sight of the fact that the very word 'lesbian' is often taken to auto-refer to whiteness; the film's desire to produce successfully a non-white lesbian undercuts its ability to racialize whiteness. In other words, the discourse of successful de-closeting predominates over and forecloses other questions where visibility equals privilege. NHD facilely buys into the teleology of diaspora as a place where lesbian and feminist agendas might be achieved without demur from society, whether one's own coloured one at home or the mainstream majority white world one has been living in. While it might seem unfair to castigate one film for stripping its love affairs of context, these missing contexts might have saved the film from lapsing into exoticizing the diasporic Indian family and its female subjects, presenting them for mindless consumption in the manner of the food that Nina cooks, consumes or throws away through the film.

Dealing exclusively with Nina's emotional dilemma about coming out, NHD may well have been about people of any ethnicity or accent with no hybridization involved. Parmar apparently chose to set the film in Glasgow upon a whim because she found the Indian-Scots accent delightful. The film's most memorable role, however, is that of the 'homecoming queen' not Nina, but her male cross-dressing friend Bobbi, who runs the other ubiquitous Indian business—the video store that provides the cultural material that links the diasporic Indian to the land s/he has left behind, in the manner described by Ziauddin Sardar in 'Dilip Kumar Made Me Do It' (Sardar 1998: 19–20). While Bobby might also be seen as that predictable character now, Bobby has a vitality the lead characters lack. 'With my dress sense, deceit is not an option,' says Bobby, when Nina remarks on his openly gay lifestyle and wishes she were like him too, offering the viewer an opportunity to think of how 'coming out' might pertain to those who cross-dress or are transgendered. For Bobby, staying in the closet is not an option because he is so 'out' in so many other ways; the valorization of the victorious assertion of a lesbian identity once and for all is thus not available to Bobby, since he has always carried this very visible identity. Bobby's assumption of male femininity, if one may turn Halberstam's phrase upside-down, comes with its own quantum of struggles, one imagines, in a world where normative masculinities have such hegemonic strength that homophobic violence against men who depart from norms is as probable as patriarchal violence against women who disobey is. In the film however, Bobby is also untroubled, and happy to offer the benign shelter under which Nina conducts her love affair with Lisa. This affair culminates in their running the restaurant jointly; at the film's end, all smiles and with arms around one another, they are shown gleefully entering their full restaurant, apparently blissfully together. Nina has not, by the end of the film, become as interesting as Bobby, whose cameo does indeed carry the film away, but nevertheless remains the boring lesbian subject we must study as best as we can before we decide to do without her altogether.

Despite its many shortcomings, NHD carries the trademark that made Parmar's *Khush* (1991) such an interesting text. Cutting familiar Bollywood songs such that the viewing position was occupied by a woman where in the original text it was an implied or an explicit male position, *Khush* offers a revisioning of the politics and the erotics of the gaze. Instead of a normative heterosexual male gazing, *Khush* presented the possibility that the gaze could be the vehicle of erotic and not only aesthetic pleasure to the female viewer as well. The hyperbolic femininity of the Hindi film heroine, for instance, can be enjoyed as much by a woman watching any Hindi film-song, as it can be by a man. In making the gaze thus homoerotic and endowing it with lesbian potentialities, Parmar breaks new theoretical and creative ground. NHD normalizes and indeed relishes this female gaze all round, but in such a stoically straight way that deprives the viewer the pleasures of unpredictability or curiosity. The queer gaze, however, returns in the shape of Bobby's many adventures with fashioning himself—as the lead dancer and choreographer of a motley crew of non-professional dancers who want to break into Bollywood films, Bobby's cinematic desires are often more inspiring and at any rate more energetic than Nina's. Bobby's dancing, his cross-dressing and his affair with the hunky white plumber, place along with his video shop where he performs to a pre-adolescent audience of boys and girls who marvel at his many transformations of himself, inhabit a realm of reality that defamiliarizes the meanings of normative sexualities in a way Nina's love-story does not. Thus the (un)familiar as a place of hesitation between consensus reality and challenges to it in the form of madness, eros, violence, etc., is a space occupied here not by the protagonist of the coming-out story, but by a side character whose very arrival onscreen challenges different normativities—of clothing, of gait, of labour—through his gender-presentation. One wonders then if the coming-out story may not have unintended consequences wherein the boredom of Nina's attainment of lesbian identity on television—no less—allows us paradoxically to reflect on how coming-out also serves her as one more event in the culmination of the modernization process of Nina's ethnic group. NHD's representation of the Glasgow South Asian diaspora as progressive is produced through its equation of the group's positive/neutral response to 'outness' with its similar response to female agency (an older widow's desire for romance and new love; her younger daughter's creativity in claiming her right to practice a Scottish art/sport) and inter-racial coupling (Nina's brother secretly marries a white woman; at the end, everyone's happy about this too). Coming out then, is placed within the larger frame narrative of diasporic modernity, but in such a way that the corollary is also a necessary supplement of the first articulation—for a people-group to be regarded as modern, it must be possible for them to accept 'out' homosexuality.

Thus, the South Asian diaspora of Glasgow in NHD is emancipated enough to go beyond discourses of racialized, gendered and sexualized purity and authenticity: Nina's coupling with the white Lisa is on par in the narrative with her brother's clandestine marriage to a white woman. These couplings are legitimized under the benign rule of Nina's newly widowed mother, suggesting that the end of patriarchy in terms of the symbolic removal of the authoritative father is necessary for the diaspora to move on. However, Nina's mother is also courting another authoritative patriarchal figure, so the film's choice of using the interim in which she is a free woman to change the structure of the acceptable diasporic family must be noticed. At the same time, all the happy changes seem to remain within the family. Bobby's presentation by the narrative as someone outside the sphere of influence of family—an idea strengthened by the frequent reference shots to his beautifully decorated truck as a space for gender-transformation, clothing-changes and love, romantic and friendly, as a space that allows him to serve as Nina's chosen family—suggests there is much more to diaspora than family, but disturbingly, it is the gender-congruent Nina who gets to go home to her biological family. Bobby's own serendipitous romance with a white man only just grazes the edges of the film's frame as its major preoccupation is the lesbian track, not the queer one. These two men provide much of the broad and fine comedy, as well as the high kitsch of the film, but as Bobby is not a member of the Shah family, he is merely just one more presence, an outsider still in the diasporic celebration of biological inheritances restored to kin. The gender-insubordinate Bobby seems to not have a South Asian family of his own to negotiate with. NHD may be about the lesbian coming out and coming back home to her South Asian family, but it is also about queerness like Bobby's represented as unhoused or in exilic relationship to the diasporic home as Gayatri Gopinath has shown is the case with many diasporic narratives (2005: 79). Bobby's persistent queerness, however, prevents easy daydream versions of cultural hybridity, and homophobia-free utopias from clouding our eyes.

I Can't Think Straight (ICTS hereafter) complicates this celebration through the love-affair it tells of, between a Christian Palestinian Arab woman and a second generation British–Indian Muslim woman. The former, Tala, has already dumped four fiancés at the eleventh hour, echoing the runaway Nina's own history at the heterosexual altar. The latter, Leyla, is an aspiring writer and daughter of an insurance salesman who has made it good and will leave his two girls a successful business. The two women come together after they are introduced by the man Leyla is seeing at that point. Later, after a short-lived idyll with Tala where Leyla finally understands she cannot click with Ali because she likes women not men, Leyla dumps this man, tells her parents that she is 'gay' moves out, has another girlfriend, and publishes the book she has been writing all along. Tala meanwhile finally tells Hani he is not the man for her either, and later still, after a meeting with Leyla set up by Leyla's sister and Ali—on the verge of becoming a couple themselves—decides to break the news to her parents. With this coming out, Leyla feels she can now be with Tala, and the movie ends with them on a park bench, admiring children and planning their own. While many of the things the characters do necessitate social and economic privilege of a high degree—Tala plays polo, for instance, and her mother can come to England from Jordan within hours of hearing that her daughter might be much too interested in another woman; or luck; Leyla is able to write and publish her novel with a speed that might not be possible in real life on the strength solely of great talent. The film nevertheless manages to establish a new paradigm for the family that surrounds those who come out. Both women have supportive fathers, while the mothers are depicted as more deeply conditioned by society—Leyla's mother comes around before long though Tala's mother is left fuming at the end. However, in all, both these films signal an acceptance by the diasporic South Asian family of the central lesbian relationship. One must remark on how the accepting families are portrayed though; Nina's and Leyla's families have now been in the UK for two generations; the UK is home even as they are still vestigially Indian in food habits and occasional family 'values.' The mothers in ICTS are more resistant all-round than the fathers are; Leyla's mother curses Leyla with burning eternally in hell for being a homosexual while her father deadpans 'It's time we got you that flat you've been talking about,' in his benign intervention to rescue his daughter from her mother's ire. Tala's mother is against Israel and homosexuality almost equally and the film's comic comeuppance of her is its closing high point, with even the imported subaltern Indian domestic help being able to gloat finally and fully on the fallen grand lady.

ICTS ends with Tala marching off to tell her parents; the music is victorious, attaining a crescendo at the point Tala steps into the room her parents are seated in. We are in no doubt at all about how the narrative feels about this final moment. The preceding action sets up the reason for celebration as Tala's liberation from imprisonment by both convention and her own duplicity; thus, coming out of the closet is indeed liberating for Tala after her many misadventures with men, with trying to conform to normative sexuality. Tala's family, still located in Jordan, in the East, is more recalcitrant, given their position in a society where the word 'lesbian' triggers off a joke reminiscent of a similar scene in *Bend It Like Beckham*—at the end of the movie, when word of Tala's lesbianism has got abroad, two women sit at one of Tala's parents' parties talking. One tells the other: 'Lebanese? She's become Lebanese? But some of my best friends are Lebanese!' Mistaking 'lesbian' for the aurally somewhat similar 'Lebanese' this uninformed Jordanian signifies those peoples of the East who are still far from knowing about visible gay and lesbian identities. The speaker is wife to Ramzi, an old 'uncle' of the family who makes very evident eyes at all the good-looking men whenever he is on screen, but Ramzi's happy marriage to his much younger showpiece wife provides Ramzi with cover that is not available to Tala. As Tala's father puts it, 'Men have options, especially in the Middle East; but a daughter needs a helping hand,' when consoling his daughter after she has finally broken her fourth engagement. Tala's options in Jordan are to be mistaken for being 'Lebanese' and or living like

Ramzi but probably finding out in the process that it is much harder for her than for him to sustain a marriage of convenience. Tala's dilemmas resonate with the viewer; after a night with Leyla, Tala overwhelmed by changes she will have to engineer in her life if she is to steer clear of deceiving her family and friends as Leyla says she should, says of the possible freedom that may come to her from the honest approach, 'No one lives like this! Not where I come from.' Tala's puzzlement about how to achieve sexual autonomy even within a loving family that unfortunately does not see anything other than normative heterosexuality as a real design for loving, rings bells in a way that Leyla's easy existence does not. A few tears and recriminations later, Leyla's mother comes around to Leyla's lesbianism quite easily, while her father and sister are more than tolerant to begin with. Tala's dilemmas communicate better because Sarif supplies a social context within which to read them; yet, the relative wealth and the relative personal success of individual characters makes any real struggle mostly unnecessary in these lesbian fairy-tales of acceptance and cultural mutuality.

Leyla's own lesbianism matches Roof's summary of 'she pretends to be straight, … feigns an interest in boys,' and experiences discomfort at the clash between 'the known heterosexual part' of her identity and 'an unknown, but intuited, correct identity,' which the film shows her sister as diagnosing about her from the objects in her room, such as the biographies of other known homosexuals, the music of KD Lang, etc. Leyla's identity as femme lesbian is quickly consolidated after her confrontation with her parents. Having moved out of home into the flat her father buys her, she quickly gets a girlfriend too, and the bad blood between her mother and herself is completely wiped out of the film's narrative. Again, but for one confrontation that turns out to be worse in the protagonist's imagination that it is in reality, the declaration of homosexuality does not upset that much. ICTS frames lesbian desire as part of consensus reality, but again, this is more wish-fulfilment achieved by selectively framing the coming-out experience as happening in an accepting environment. Why are these films reluctant to make a realistic assessment of the experience of living as (un)familiars in a sometimes very homophobic world? The attractions of a feel-good story of course are self-explanatory, but perhaps more importantly, these films themselves are in a sense evangelizing the act of coming out. If one follows this line of argument, it is then true also that the coming out story is heavily invested in one cathartic coming out moment, rather than in studying coming out as a process articulated over several events, as Eve Sedgwick shows it to be:

> ...every encounter with a new class full of students, to say nothing of a new boss, social worker, loan officer, landlord, doctor, erects new closets whose fraught and characteristic laws of optics and physics exact from at least gay people new surveys, new calculations, new draughts and requisitions of secrecy or disclosure. Even an out gay person deals daily with interlocutors about whom she doesn't know whether they know or not. (Sedgwick 1990: 68)

If these films present coming-out as a sanitized one-act exit from homophobic clandestinity into lesbian utopia, they also present the coming-out process as entirely a personal choice. There are no pressures on Tala, or Leyla, or Nina to come out. They do not seem to be at risk at work, or with their landlords, or even in social situations; once they come out, again, this information does not seem to have to be relayed to any other than the very few characters who already fill the screen. The spare nature of the social in these films can be read as an externalization of this privatization of the question of the sexual. ICTS and NHD present their female protagonists' ideas of who they are erotically as shaped entirely through processes of interiority, through self-realisatory epiphanies that conclude all investigations into the question of the sexual/erotic once the protagonist 'comes out.' As such, any potential the narrative may have to seriously challenge heterosexual systems is diffused or foreclosed. ICTS does this in idiosyncratic, interesting ways: Tala's vegetarian sister is creeped out by her meat-eating family's preoccupation with finding her a man; vegetarianism here is a form of anti-heteropatriarchality for this character, marking her difference from her other sisters whose normative inscriptions of femininity make them uncritically consumptive of not only meat, but also of other kinds of practices such as compliance to heterosexuality. Tala's mother's handmaid is an Indian woman from India, who is shown subverting Tala's mother's attempts at total dominance over her labouring person by spitting in her drinks, through theft of time, or by eavesdropping, and so on. The film makes visible the first generation Indian female migrant in a way rarely seen in Indian cinematic oeuvres, but unfortunately, only the viewer seems to be aware of her ethnicity as akin to Leyla's. The two characters never once are shown interacting with one another even though they are in the same frame a few times. Tala's mother's attempts to monopolize the person and labour for her Abigail are shown rather badly, no connection is made between these subversions and Leyla's attempts at trying to loosen her hold on Tala. The maidservant's resistance to her oppression as domestic-labourer and care-worker is presented as completely isolated from the emotional labours Leyla must perform against Tala's mother's overpowering efforts to will her daughter into heterosexuality. The running time of the film shows Tala's mother as constantly at work to secure her daughter's marriage; in other words, Tala's mother is heterosexuality itself at work. Insulating Leyla's life fully away from the work of the maidservant in maintaining the apparatus through which Tala's mother operates, ICTS separates one kind of reproductive labour—housework—traditionally consigned to women, from the heterosexual reproductive labours of marrying and keeping up appearances that both Tala and Leyla feel overpowered by initially—enjoined upon women by heteronormativity.

Splitting the labouring female body from loving/eroticized female bodies, ICTS represents the (un)familiar as a non-menial, non-subaltern feminine. ICTS thus also isolates the UK-based diasporic Indian's lot completely from that of the migrant working Indian woman abroad, thus identifying Leyla as defined entirely in terms of sexuality (lesbian soon), location (Westernized diasporic) and class (same kind as Tala's) rather than also in terms of race (the casting at least makes Tala's family appear to be whiter to the naked eye than Leyla's Bangladeshi family). In not exploring the cross-racial potential that a pairing like Leyla's and Tala's has, in which white and black/brown are not the terms relating to one another, but two kinds of culturally othered 'oriental' races, the film mis-translates the coming-out narrative from a possibly racialized encounter into a universalized one in which cultural difference does not very much change the progress of the coming-out story despite Tala's demurrals. Leyla is so fully hybridized and Tala's personal courage and relative privilege will find her a way out of Jordan; the two women only need to be in London for the coming out to culminate in monogamous perpetual coupling with hybridized children (who will also then look like their parents, hinting again at uninterrupted biological transfer of lineage, albeit through a lesbian couple). On the one hand, the film normalizes the lesbian as a woman of colour and routinizes the coming-out story as available to women of colour, not only to 'white' couples. On the other hand, in casting international looking model-like actresses for the parts, the film also materializes the non-Western lesbian as exotically beautiful, slender and rather femme, a manoeuvre similar to NHD's. However, both films are able to place the (un)familiar such as she is within the space of the family; in refusing the abdicate relationships to roots, these films are making a strong political case for seeing homosexuality not as exiled from diasporic familial inheritances, but as very much part of them. While this goes against evidence that diaspora is heavily invested in heteronormativity (Gopinath 2005), the refusal to give up the space of home is made possible by marrying techniques used in mainstream Indian cinematic melodrama to narratives apparently using realist conventions. Insofar as these films use the conventions of the mainstream genre, the coming-out narrative is often reduced to becoming only another version of heterosexual romance—the celebration of a monogamous romantic pair is the culmination of the film—but if one does not focus exclusively on the linear romantic for- mula's resolution, these films are able to use the coming-out narrative to showcase the exploration of alternatives to heterosexual coupling. Thus, unyoking femininity from heterosexuality through their use of 'femme' heroines, these films make possible an imagination of (un) familiar love that goes beyond the elisions of anxious ridicule or misogyny or inevitable heterosexuality. This section has shown that 'the status of women and the whole question of arrangements is deeply and inescapably inscribed even in the structure of even relationships that seem to exclude women—even in male homosocial/homosexual relationships' (Sedgwick (ed.). 1985: 25). In the following section, I examine the implications of replacing the visible vernacular figure of the 'butch' woman with a 'femme' visual aesthetic.

Lost in Translation

In the year 1893, Mohandas Karamchand Gandhi was thrown out of a train from Durban to Pretoria where he was going in the capacity of legal counsel to his Muslim employer in Durban. Being thrown out of this train was to be a shaping force in transforming Gandhi from 'an Indian nonentity' to one of the most powerful leaders of people of all time (Gandhi 1927 (reprint 2007): 111–12). Shivering at the Peitermaritzberg station where he had been offloaded from the train for refusing to travel in the van compartment when he had a ticket entitling him to travel in the first class, Gandhi says, 'I began to think of my duty.' Was it to remain and 'root out the disease of colour prejudice' in South Africa or was it to be insulted and to return to India? He decided 'to take the next available train to Pretoria,' and his activities thereon in South Africa are as well-known as this incident— rooting out the 'superficial' symptoms of colour prejudice, Gandhi was convinced, was necessary to attest the fundamental equality of all human beings. Gandhi's struggles in South Africa were conducted on a variety of fronts, and one of the most important effects of these was to draw international attention to the system of indenture in the various British colonies, besides raising critical questions about the ethics of racial discrimination.

In the year 1892, two years before Gandhi, Begum the grand-mother of one of the central characters in Shamim Sarif's *The World Unseen* makes a journey in the reverse direction from Gandhi's. Where Gandhi is able to stand up and decide to fight colour prejudice in South Africa, Begum is being 'returned' to India in disgrace for hav-ing been raped by a black man. The logic of colour prejudice here also operates in the opposite direction from how it does in Gandhi's case, emanating as it does here from non-whites, directed against the Blacks. Begum is on the train from Pretoria to Durban, from where she must board a ship back to Bombay, to her own natal family. Once the child conceived by this rape is born and its non-Indian genes make themselves evident, Begum's in-laws beat her badly, disabling her for life as her punishment for having 'allowed' herself to be defiled. They decide that neither she nor her children can stay in their community any more. It does not matter to this small community of Indians in Pretoria in the 1890s that Begum was 'raped' by a black man and is thus herself a victim and a survivor, and deserving of love and minis-tration. The diaspora's patriarchal logic of lineage from father to son is made further obvious in the latter half of this episode, when Begum's marital family refuses to let her son—also the firstborn—go with her.

Begum however, refuses to leave without both the children and the threat of her presence continuing to defile them is enough to make the family agree. It turns out this is for appearance's sake only; as the train is pulling out, her husband requests her to hold their son out of the train's window so he can say a final goodbye. Begum agrees, thinking 'he has feelings after all,' despite his willingness to part with his wife. Her husband however, simply seizes the child from his wife's frailer grasp as the train picks up speed, leaving Begum screaming and empty-handed as the train quickens out of the station. Having abducted his child thus, her husband and his family 'did not linger for very long in the station, but moved hurriedly to return home, because they, and everyone else who remained in the station could hear the screams of the woman on board the train even after it was long out of sight' (Sarif 2001: 144). Deprived thus of her first-born, Begum, then only nineteen years old, is banished to India where she brings up this miscegenated daughter, Amina's mother. Begum insists to this daughter, her son-in-law and her granddaughter Amina that they never return to South Africa, the land that humiliated and deprived her so entirely, but upon Begum's death, her family does migrate once again back to this country.

Life in the multi-racial British and Afrikaner colonies of southern Africa was organized along a carefully monitored system of privilege and deprivation guaranteed by race. This racial ranking system, which David Horowitz calls 'positional psychology' arranges blacks, coloureds, and whites on an ascending cline. Traditional blacks were at the bottom of the pile, Westernized blacks a mite above, coloureds further above, followed by Indians, followed by whites, themselves sorted out into various degrees of privilege. In addition to Indian indentured labour in South Africa, there was also a relatively better-off class of immigrants called the 'Free Passenger Indians' because they had paid their own passages to provide trading services in South Africa, unlike the indentured labourers whose passages were paid by those who imported this labour to work in the mines and plantations. The majority of the Passenger Indians were Muslims, and generally of a higher social class than the indentured Indian labourers in South Africa. They were also given citizenship rights, and were not subject to the same level of humiliation and deprivations the poorer, mostly Hindu indentured labourers who had been arriving in South Africa from the 1860s on were exposed to. By about 1911, about 30,000 of them were settled in most cities and towns over South Africa (Thiara 2001: 129). Indian indentured labour had primarily settled in the Cape province and KwaZulu–Natal where the Indian population by the turn of the century exceeded the white settler population, arousing much anxiety amongst the British, who then sought to contain the enterprise and mobility of this Indian population through discriminatory methods that sought to clearly place the Indian as a 'coolie' a 'scab' whose existence was defined only by his ability to provide labour. Repressive and humiliating systems of taxation, repatriation and confinement were introduced. For one, the British administration of these provinces sought to restrict Indians to specific areas within these provinces, and any kind of travel outside them was possible only through the acquisition of passes that were hard to obtain. Indentured labour was outlawed altogether by the 1920s to altogether stop Indian immigration as the Indian population by that time exceeded the British population in Natal, which was where Gandhi started the campaign that successfully fought against many of these discriminatory provisions.

Sarif's location of her story in the 1950s, with much of the backstory occupying the previous decade, is significant because in this decade, many of these very provisions became South African Law. In 1946, when Amina and Miriam come separately to what to them was a land of opportunity, was the year the Asiatic Land Tenure Bill, also called the Ghetto Act, which altogether prevented the sale of land to Indians, was passed. Further, two years later, Apartheid was introduced in 1948 causing immense upheavals within South African society. The Group Areas Act of 1950 was a further such instance of racial positioning, literally demarcating areas where different populations might live. Initially confining the Indian populations to particular areas and designed to confine them to servicing just their own ethnic group, this policy served as the groundwork for Apartheid:

> Expropriation, forced removals, and disempowerment were just some of the historical hurdles that the South African Indian community faced under Apartheid as racist stereotyping designated Indians as unscrupulous business people, who posed a threat to white-owned commerce. This stereotype motivated government response and reinforced the divisions between groups. (Fainman-Frenkel 2004: 60)

The Group Areas Act of 1950 banished Indians to 'Asiatic Bazaars' where facilities were poor, though often better than in black areas; on the one hand, it forced Indians and blacks together in that they were both very much below any kind of white in the 'positionality' charts the whites devised, but at the same time, the Indians neverthe-less believed they were far above the blacks and in many ways did have it better than them. Only in 1961 when South Africa became a republic did the view that the Indian population was an integral part of the South African republic and not a group of lowly 'scabs' to be wrung dry and repatriated gain currency (Rastogi 2008: 10).

Fighting to alleviate the racial oppression Indians in South Africa were subjected to by the whites, Gandhi's campaigns primarily drew participation from middle-class Indian men. In 1913, however, when the South African government passed a law that nullified all mar-riages except those registered as Christian, Gandhi called for women to participate in large numbers as the case directly affected them and this mass mobilization contributed directly to the concessions the Indians were able to secure from the South African colonial govern-ment of the time. The rights of Indian women in the South African diaspora to personal autonomy outside of the family, however, were secured much later by the visible participation of a number of women like Amina—one of the two female protagonists—much later in the joint struggle by Indians and blacks both against white racism. The personal histories of the women characters, primarily Amina and Miriam, with the figure of Begum serving as both a gloss and a her-ald, placed against these larger historical events in their country of adoption allows a comprehension of their larger, political significance to the story of the Indian diaspora. Admitting a queer feminine sub-jectivity to the account of diaspora enables the book to transform the often patriarchal, heteronormative, Oedipal and biological logic of diaspora, as we shall see further.

Shamim Sarif's novel traces the fictional lives of three genera-tions of the Muslim trading community settled within the Afrikaner region of Transvaal. Starting in the 1870s the Free Passenger Indians, mostly Gujarati in origin, had established successful trading units in the Transvaal, particularly Pretoria and Johannesburg, to which a tiny Indian 'coolie' population of less than a thousand had migrated before laws prevented such relocations within the colony. Soon, stringent policing of these communities in various ways became the norm, especially once their trading hegemony became evident; one such regulation was the 1885 Transvaal law to segregate Indians. Sarif's titling her work *The World Unseen* (2001) is quite resonant because the history of this small diasporic group is not very prominently narrativized. One of the few texts that exists is Imraan Coovadia's *The Wedding* (2002), where the story of the Passenger Indian's arrival in South Africa in the 1870s is fictionalized. Sarif's fictionalization of this history, however, follows not the traders, but their womenfolk; her fictional foci are the lives of Amina and Miriam, both born in India, but whose families have brought them to South Africa. Unlike *The Wedding*, set almost entirely in India and dealing with the how and why of Muslim merchant migration from the west coast of India to South Africa, *The World Unseen* is set in the as yet unexplored South Africa for these descendants of the Passenger Indians.

Amina Harjan's father runs a gas station in the town of Springs, near Pretoria, while she herself runs a cafe in Pretoria, an unusual occupational choice for a young woman of her ethnicity when most other Indian women were housebound as a rule. Miriam helps her husband Omar run his all-purpose store in Delhof, out in the boondocks of the huge veldt. Amina's life-story reveals the difference in the social worlds the passenger 'Indians' inhabited, in comparison to those of the indentured Indian; the former had both the freedom and the wherewithal to return to their homelands whether to stay or to find spouses, unlike the latter. Miriam herself is one such chosen spouse, chosen by Omar on a visit to family in Bombay, where he is 'feted,' a celebratory homecoming that resembles that of later such diasporic homecoming heroes like Shah Rukh Khan's characters in *Pardes* (Director; Subhash Ghai 1997) and *Swades* (Director: Ashutosh Gowarikar 2004), to name only two such characters. The notion of exploration that a title like 'the world unseen' communicates, however, is very different from the relatively more stable dialectical coordinates offered by *Swades* and *Pardes*. This sense of movement—familial and individual—helps interrogate familiar notions of place and self and produce a narrative different from the often patriarchal logics that films like the above-mentioned ones, along with other Shah Rukh Khan vehicles like *Dilwale Dulhaniya Le Jaayenge* (Director: Aditya Chopra 1995 and *Kabhi Khushi, Kabhi*

Gham, Director: Karan Johar 2001). *The World Unseen* allows an older diaspora, now forgotten in the clamour of newer, first-world diasporas, to provide a position of interrogation of the Oedipal logic of normative diaspora: (un)familiar desire interrupts the placement of women as static placeholders and load-bearers for tradition. Through its articulation of (un)familiar desire between Amina and Miriam, *The World Unseen* allows a different cartography of diaspora, as we shall see.

Amina is very much her own woman while Miriam is the lowly and subservient household drudge to her husband's family; her sister-in-law, Farah, with whom it soon turns out her husband Omar is having an affair, plays the role of surrogate mother-in-law to the hilt, making Miriam work so hard in their household in Springs that Miriam is more than glad to leave for Delhof. Delhof's isolation is analogous to Miriam's own isolation; cut off from the more urbanized towns of Pretoria and Springs due to lack of her own conveyance, Miriam's mobility or its lack plays an important part in the novel. Learning to drive the car, which would bridge the gap between rural seclusion and urban autonomy is something she very much wants to do but which Omar feels threatened by. In the final parts of the book, when Amina has offered Miriam a job as part-time cook at her cafe, Miriam's driving lessons place her in a position where she makes a choice not only between remaining forgotten in Delhof, but also forgotten by Omar, and attaining a selfhood where she has mobility, independence, and resources of her own—a choice between being herself or becoming more like Amina, it would seem.

The home that Miriam marries into is emblematic of many of the complications the novel produces of the idea of the nation and the diaspora. Omar and Sadru are South Africans; born and brought up there, they see South Africa as home. However, what is home for the two male children is not quite home for their sisters Jehan and Rehmat. Hegemonic articulations of both nation and diaspora rely on the symbol of the uncorrupted, pure woman. Sarif's story reveals the heavy investment in the figure of the sexually and emotionally chaste woman for the diaspora, and the violent, often noxious energies that are required for its impossible preservation. Jehan is mentally retarded and syphillitic. Farah, in a moment of rare revelation, tells Miriam that 'Omar and Sadru only prefer to think that Jehan had been raped' when in fact the origin of her syphillis was a consensual sexual relationship with her boyfriend (Sarif 2001: 41). Jehan's consequent madness following the onset of syphillis functions as a sign of both resistance to being 'set to order' by her brothers and fathers and 'the men in the family who ... almost beat the life' out of her boyfriend, finally driving him away from her (Sarif 2001: 41). Now isolated totally by madness, Jehan with her cackling laughter and endless flow of nonsensical utterances is a cipher to Miriam at first; thinking syphillis to be a strange African disease, Miriam prays she may not contract it. Miriam's innocence is ruptured soon enough, when she goes through days on end without a smile watching and learning from the conversations family members and their friends have, which perforce do not include her. Unlike the laughing but insane Jehan, the silent and efficient Miriam finds herself marked by servitude to heterosexual patriarchy. Jehan's sister Rehmat however, ran away from this home when she falls in love with a white South African and now lives in Paris. A law that prohibited mixed marriages came into force from 1948, making Rehmat and her husband James vulnerable to police persecution when they come home in 1952 for a short visit to see James' dying father. Rehmat is betrayed to the police by her sister-in-law Farah in a characteristic fit of jealousy at Rehmat's sophistication and success. Rehmat's life is intended by Sarif to be a signal critique of much of what was wrong with South African Indians as much as with Apartheid. One of the most potent stories in a novel choc-a-bloc with stories is the story of Rehmat's flight from home one cold April morning eight years ago, 'with heavy bruises leaching out across her arms and legs, bruises that her father had given her ... for he had finally heard the rumours about James and herself' (Sarif 2001: 98). Remaining at home after these beatings, which resonate with the story told later about Begum sixty years earlier, would have meant Rehmat's being palmed off on some cousin or stranger. Flight, however, would also mean pursuit:

> They had needed to get out of reach of the group of thugs, all of them her relatives, that had spread out at once across Pretoria, trying to locate her by means of rumours, sightings and whispers. James's at the university had been broken into and searched by men carrying knives and sticks. If she had been found within a day, she would have been

dragged home alive but beaten. After two or three days, they might have simply brought her home dead, for by then it would have been too late to pretend that she had never left; the damage to her reputation would already have been done. On the boat out of Cape Town she had had plenty of time to consider this, and to wonder whether her own brothers and father had been amongst those searching for her. (Sarif 2001: 99)

Rehmat's flight takes her to Europe, where she is able to live a life of dignity and autonomy with James, without recriminations about how she had corrupted her race dodging her at every step. Begum's life-story and Rehmat's are curiously similar, though separated by about sixty years; the diaspora appears to be fixed within a narrative of non-progress, of feudal subjugation of women with no quarter given to their rights as individuals. But South Africa's white government further complicates the story of honour killings and vendetta within the diaspora with Apartheid regulations that themselves are a product of white fears of being assimilated within a burgeoning black/brown matrix. In equating the settler colonialists' policies designed to avoid racial contamination with the Indian diaspora's own desire to avoid such mixing, Sarif's novel makes it very difficult, if not impossible to valorize the diaspora itself as a counterculture of modernity, a phrase Paul Gilroy uses for black-derived diasporas on both sides of the Atlantic (Gilroy 1993). Gilroy sees these diasporas as constituting a genuine form of resistance to the movements of capital that structure (the repressions of) the modern nation-state, a formulation that others have extended to include all diasporas. Sarif's novel problematizes such a de-materialized conception of diaspora through its focus on the movements in which all these women—Begum, Amina, Miriam, Rehmat—are involved. Moving back and forth along the Indian Ocean, the South African Indian diaspora constitutes, it appears, not a counterculture to modernity, but an underbelly shaped by the very movements of capital Gilroy's formulation claims black diasporas resist (Gilroy 1993: 16). This diaspora's preoccupation with maintaining an always-already fictional purity has violent consequences for its women, who invariably become the symbolic receptacles wherein this purity is placed and sought to be maintained. Rather than a counterculture—and thus a critique and an alternative to modernity—this

Indian diaspora is vehemently pre-modern in its cultural attitudes to women even as it is Anglophilic in matters that suit its economic interests; dress and language are obvious examples of the Passenger Indian community's willingness to abandon the ways of the old world for pragmatically achieving success in the world unseen.

The World Unseen complicates the normative account of the diaspora as characterized by a longing for the land of origin with the backward and forward movements of its characters both between the 'home' of India, and South Africa, and within the South African host itself. Both nations are both homes and prisons to various characters at various times, with the result that the nostalgia for home is queered in significant ways. These homes reveal themselves to be places of violence, dishonour and fear for their various women inhabitants; at the same time, some of these homes provide spaces of opportunity within which autonomy can be sought, and new desires fashioned and fulfilled. Amina herself, described as 'fucking queer' by an infuriated policeman, finds in South Africa new life, and the energy to fight what she does not like. Starting a business in South Africa is easier for her than it would be to do so in India, placing the diaspora thus as a place where the female subject also has room for manoeuvre, to become modern in ways not permitted in the home country. Amina's queerness itself, displaying itself the way it does, in trousers, manual labour and car-driving, would perhaps have never found expression in the home nation, while South Africa's dramatic racial heterogeneities offer Amina a number of traditions to model herself on. (Un) familiar female desire thus signified by Amina offers an alternative, hybridized model to the conformist patriarchal model adopted by the male members of this same diaspora. Amina's life is organized not around undercutting black people or treating them as invisible and non-existent—as Omar does when they come to his shop—but around making common cause with the 'other' races. Amina's liminal position as a quarter-part black herself makes her stand at a tangent, literally, to the narratives of racial purity and sexual probity that both the Indian subaltern diasporas in South Africa, and the white, dominant settler diasporas wanted to believe in. Amina's invention as (un) familiar butch woman is also an attempt by Sarif to find a history for female homosexuality outside exclusively white butch/femme couples/narrativizations.

The novel starts in April 1952, the year in which passes have been made compulsory for all coloureds including women, in South Africa. A major prong in the Apartheid arrangements ensuring separateness in all social transactions between whites and non-whites, these passes involved the classification of one's race first through extremely complex and arbitrary methods. In fact, members of the same family could find themselves classified under different heads depending on which petty official did the testing. Whites and non-whites were supposed to live in demarcated, separate areas and all told, the whites had access to the best facilities, while everyone else was given what was left over. Indians, confined to the Asiatic bazaars of South African townships, had a better deal than the coloureds and blacks, whose livelihoods were jeopardized almost totally by the Pass system. Passes for work would be issued only to those with government approved work, which directly plunged the unorganized sector, which depended on non-structured avenues and opportunities for employment, deeper into poverty, affecting the quality of life of the majority of South Africa's non-white population.

Further, the Pass laws separated families too—black men working in the mines would not be able to live with their families as they were not mine employees themselves. The Pass system enforced from the 1950s sought to carefully monitor women's access to urbanization and employment; black women at the heads of households found themselves under a new system of colonization whereby they would not be permitted to seek employment as their presence in urban areas as a free labour force, in contrast to the contractual male labourers in the mines and other primary sector industries, would defeat the structures of separateness the Apartheid policy sought to enforce. Though women's groups in the previous years had resisted strongly the introduction of this system, by the end of the 1950s, it was as Winnie Mandela put it, impossible even to die without a pass. With this context in place, Sarif's beginning her story in 1952 enables a link between the presence of autonomous female labour and resistance to racial hegemonies that underwrite both nation and diaspora, white South Africa and 'passenger' India. Amina reveals herself at an unusual location—lying on the roof, repairing the tiles—for a woman in the 1950s surely, and the reader's assessment of this positioning is revealed to be accurate when we realize that she is also the owner of the business whose roof she is fixing. This business is a cafe, which she runs with a coloured man, Jacob; in the South Africa of the day, owning a business with someone of another race was itself punishable by law. Amina is a site of transgressions that leap out immediately at the reader.

The film version though, moderates these very transgressions. While the book clearly places Amina as 'lying on the roof,' the film begins with Amina delicately hammering at the nameplate of her cafe; though dressed in trousers; unusual again for Indian women in the 1950s, this Amina is a great deal more feminine than the book leads us to expect. Where the novel says Amina is tall, straight-limbed with 'long curls,' the Amina of the film is a very petite femme with rather long hair that may at best be described as simply uncombed. Amina's hair is a source of much fuss in both texts—being one-fourth part black as a result of her grandmother's rape sixty years ago, Amina is identified as not quite Indian by the other Indians of the Pretoria community. Amina's mother's curly hair had at birth led to the suspicions of miscegenation that finally led to her mother Begum's abuse and banishment from South Africa in the first instance.

The film's styling of its lead actress dilutes the potential her appearance has to communicate both racial and gendered/sexed appearance. Amina in the book clearly gives people pause—they wonder to what sex she belongs, to borrow from the title of Martha Vicinus' essay (1993), discussed in Chapter 1. Vicinus (1993) argues that the butch lesbian's appearance signals a disruption of gendered expectations. The butch lesbian's sartorial choices and mien is an interruption, Vicinus argues, to her being placed as a 'she.' Vicinus' essay uses examples from history, starting with the seventeenth century, of many women who had successfully passed as men, sometimes even marrying other women. She joins to this history the appearance of lesbian trendsetters of the late nineteenth and early twentieth century like Rosa Bonheur the French painter and Radclyffe Hall the writer, among others, to establish the importance of the persona that we today call 'butch,' to the construction of a visible lesbian identity. Sarif's coding of Amina—with trousers, hat and suspenders—seems to be clearly butch as far as the points of reference in the novel go; in the film, however, Amina's femme-ness seems to be a gendered crossing necessary for Sarif's film to garner as wide an audience as possible.

The femme film, where two women whose appearances conform to normative expectations of femininity are at the centre of the narrative, is a text that itself can 'pass' amongst heterosexual audiences as a film 'not' specifically lesbian or homoerotic. Femme films, as Christine Holmlund has pointed out, can suggest a friendship between the women to heterosexual audiences who do not wish to see any deeper than this even as queer-friendly audiences are able to read aspects of this very friendship as coding a more than friendly relationship (Holmlund 1991). Femme films, Holmlund further argues, function on the basis of an economy of looks and looking—the audience is disposed to look at the femmes a certain way even as the femmes are looking at one another in different ways. These exchanges of various looks between the women may or may not be suggestive to particular viewers, but because of the range of interpretations these looks allow, the film-maker is able to appeal to the mainstream rather than to just niche audiences. The cinematic text of *The World Unseen* is precisely such a discreet femme text, where the track of (un)familiar passions offers a selection that heterosexual and non-heterosexual spectators may explore.

The book is able to critique diasporic normativities at many points—the stories of Jehan, Rehmat and Begum pile on one another to produce a dissatisfaction early on with the promise of modernity that the move to South Africa suggests. The film on the other hand completely removes Jehan, thus occluding one of the strongest stories of racialized and sexualized feminine oppression and resistance that the novel tells. Rehmat's own story is indeed briefly told, but without the back-story that the characters' own meditations revealed by the third person narrator of the novel, the cinematic version of Rehmat becomes just a very chic Indo-African-Parisienne who appears and then disappears in the blink of an eye. In fact, in the film, Rehmat, once betrayed by Farah, comes running to Amina's cafe where a motley crowd of Indians in full fancy dress—the regalia of the sari and the kurta-pyjama that they have abandoned for everyday use—is dancing away to 'Pyar hua ikraar hua' (from Raj Kapoor's film *Shree 420*). In the book, Amina not only conceals Rehmat in a cupboard in her room in the back annexe of her cafe, but also drives her to safety with great intrepidity the next morning under the watchful eyes of the insidious white policemen out to enforce Apartheid with glee.

Amina's enviable mobility, in a beat-up pickup truck that travels long distances over flat endless plains points to her as indeed an unusual person for her times; more affluent than the average black woman, Amina has a car of her own to drive. But unlike the wives of the white men whose tenants Omar and Miriam are, this car does not convey a sense of racialized luxury and privilege, where these women have a driver to chauffer them to afternoon tea with Miriam, a drive that takes hours but whose diversion they can afford, Amina's driving gives her financial independence. Replacing all this with images of cardboard-faced extras dancing to a catchy old Hindi song (a sequence not in the book) has the effect of nullifying completely the resonances the novel allows between sexualized oppression and gendered oppressions and their connection in turn to patriarchal notions of lineage, descent, and inheritance.

Amina, unlike most other Indian women in the small Indian community in Pretoria, is both financially independent and self-confident almost to the point of being cocky. The odd jobs that she takes to support herself are distinctly uncharacteristic ones for the approved feminine roles the Indian community offers its women; she ferries passengers in cabs between the far-spaced towns of the South African veldt, one time going the distance of almost 1500 km between Pretoria and Cape Town; she also tills land to establish gardens for anyone interested in market-gardening. Amina's job portfolio places her in a truly liminal role; her mobility and the labours she undertakes for pay are not labours that Indians—men or women—performed yet in South Africa. Though her family is not affluent, as an Indian, her social and financial position place her at a level probably better off than the average Black or Indian woman; Amina's social relationships with the Blacks are considerable in comparison to the other Indians, and a great deal of her autonomy and free-spiritedness seems to come from her association with Black people, women in particular, whose lifestyles do not seem as constricting as those adopted and tenaciously adhered to by the Indians of this diaspora. While for her fellow-Indians her racial background is a scandal, for Amina and for those who like her, Amina's acceptance of her ancestry enables her to embrace a far less insular life than the ones the Indian diaspora of Pretoria permits its own. The film version, though, is careful not to overemphasize Amina's un-feminine job roles; arguably dressed 'like a man,' Amina in the film is more a business-like contemporary woman in khaki casuals rather than a woman whose 'queerness' is visibly recognizable to all who see her in the case of the book. Amina is seen dancing in her cafe in the film, a girlish manoeuvre that again puts her at a remove from the stately dignity that Amina in the novel possesses, despite her youth. Amina's self is predicated on her vehicle thus effectively marking her as different from Miriam in her mobility and autonomy. In showing Amina's truck only occasionally, rather than as a necessity to Amina's many 'jobs' delivering goods, making up land for market-gardening, as a cab she drives between Pretoria and Cape Town, the film version of *The World Unseen* renders illegible many aspects of Amina's identity that would on the one hand highlight her non-femininity as per the conventions of her day, and on the other hand, point to the very constructedness of femininity itself. Keeping Amina static places Amina outside what the audience would identify immediately as (un)familiar, as Amina's pick-up truck is the equivalent of a woman today driving a ten-ton truck; she simply would not be the girl next door if she did.

The reader's perception of Amina's difference from her ethnic group is more nuanced than the viewer's—the film unaccountably elides ethnic specificity to make Amina a rebel without context, making it harder to place Miriam's own later rebellion in a frame that is any more than individual. Amina's family lives apart from the Indian Muslims in Pretoria; as a result they are able to give their daughter free rein. Efforts are made by Amina's paternal grandmother, on a short visit from Bombay, to reintegrate Amina to the brotherhood of Indian Muslims in the town, but with tragicomic effects—Amina's many queernesses—of dress, occupation and mobility—come home to the grandmother giving her, literally, a heart attack, which she dies of. The novel is able to assess the tragic and the comic impact of this shock while the movie plays comic music all through Amina's 'bride-viewing,' and the crisis it soon precipitates through the conservative Ali family. Persuaded by the grandmother into thinking that Amina was reformed and made afresh in the mould of the conservative Muslim Indian woman, the Alis come to a meal where Amina is exhibited to her prospective suitor, much to both parties' shock. Amina, unregenerate as ever, is a modernity that the Alis refuse to have anything to do with. Amina is also not in possession of a suitable virginity; rumours abound of her involvement with women, many of them black. Further, Amina lives by herself in the cafe unsupervised by any 'elders,' and goes off by herself to do what she chooses. For the Alis, as for most South African Indian Muslim families, the sceptre of a woman like Amina destabilizes every tenet they hold dear about accepted Islamic and Indian values. In telling off Amina's grandmother, the Alis ratify Amina's otherness. But in killing off Amina's grandmother—herself an Indian from the old land—the film makes Amina's queerness a comic failure of the old lady's, when the novel unequivocally presents these episodes as benchmarks wherein Amina is recognized as the figure of the (un)familiar in society at large, and that Amina is a signifier of something shocking not only to the old lady, but to every Indian in their community. Cutting away the social milieus the novel painstakingly writes in, the film version makes of Amina herself a consumable when in the novel Amina displays a staunch resistance to being consumed and allocated to the labours of diasporic patriarchy.

Miriam's predicament, in her turn, is one that still echoes that of many brides to diasporic locations. With uncertain means to remain connected to her natal family, Miriam is literally all alone in a new world, making her journey from loneliness to confident exploration virtually unassisted except by Amina. Raised by her widowed and very poor mother in Bombay, Miriam's marriage to Omar is a godsend for her family, who consent to Omar's impulsive proposal without asking her. Meeting Amina for the first time in September 1951, at Amina's cafe, Miriam is most unwanted and lonely within Sadru's and Omar's noisy household where she is effectively dominated by the raging Farah. Amina is the first person to smile at Miriam in over ten days, the book's very first chapter makes clear, placing Amina's and Miriam's attraction to one another within a relationship of complementarity with warmth given and taken. The film, however, fails to build Miriam's isolation as resulting both from virilocal residence and individual coldness within a stratified diasporic society. Miriam as a young Indian bride is the last person to be fed, and sometimes goes hungry because the food runs out; Miriam is the one who does all the hard housework, the one who takes care of mad Jehan, the one who is left out of all the good things in life, including meaningful contact with her husband. In avoiding these contextualizing factors, the film version is unable to produce as powerfully as the novel does the meanings Miriam's journey towards independence have for both Miriam as a person and as a woman far away from the familiar, reassuring presence of India as both natal home and nation. Removing 'India' from the backdrop, Sarif's film with its cosmetic references to history and place, is very much a text of new diaspora, while her book, written only six years before the film, enables an investigation of the hegemonic and stratifying powers of diasporas that the film takes as normative.

In employing a uni-tonal English as the only language within the film, *The World Unseen*'s many dialogic movements between Gujarati-speaking Bombay Indian Muslims, and the different 'Englishes' employed by the whites, coloureds and blacks within South Africa are glossed over. For instance, Afrikaans in this region is very clearly marked as a white language, which English-speaking Omar is not allowed access to, even though he knows enough of the language to converse in it, while English is the tongue the whites use on everybody, including their black servants. Newness does not enter the film while the novel is able to make heterogeneity and racial difference palpable on virtually every page, where Miriam does not know how to speak with the blacks because her husband has told her they are only animals for labour, not people, and where the visits of her landlords, the Kaplans are 'redolent of a world which Miriam could hardly fathom' (Sarif 2001: 44), reminding the reader yet again of the low place these Indians occupy in South Africa. The blacks who come to shop at Omar's are very poor wage-labourers who look to Miriam for help with purchases, while Omar talks exclusively to their Afrikaans boss. The everyday impoverishment of these people that is evident when a penny or two less to the price of a dress makes all the difference between what a day-labourer can afford for his daughter, and what he cannot, is not part of the film, just as the luxurious life of the Kaplan's, with driver and long-play records in their car, are not. In not depicting these episodes with blacks and whites—Afrikaaners and English settlers—the film short-changes the viewer about the real nature of the world unseen. Miriam's gesture of helping a black man run over by a neighbouring Boer farmer is particularly important in underlining her sense of justice. However, in the novel, she cannot even see the black man in the intense dark that descends upon the veldt in the winter, let alone help him, though she tries her best and leaves water and blanket, while in the film, she is depicted as helping him out of a ditch even though he tries to fight her off. Miriam's being unable to see the injured man as he lies in the bush road serves as a trope for the years of negligence and separateness from the blacks that Indians in South Africa invested in, suggesting that this cannot be bridged through a few moments of an individual seeking to help; the film's treatment of this scene serves to highlight Miriam's personal courage and defiance of Omar's unspoken attitude to the blacks more than anything else. The film has the paradoxical effect of suggesting Miriam is able to help the black man despite his wishes, while the book in the same scene shows Miriam as shamed by the man's pride in refusing help; her Indianness is for the black man no different from the alienness and unconcern of the Boer farmer who ran him over and worried more about his broken car lights. While both texts suggest individual acts of courage have suggestive power and value, the film wants to play on the symbolic significance of this act of Miriam's—this is the only time a black and an Indian body are touching one another so much in the film, in contrast to other efforts to get closer to a racial other, such as Madeline's and Jacob's.

The novel revolves on the individual lives of Amina and Miriam primarily, and as it draws to a close, the focus is on their desire to make a shared life possible. The film however, gives equal billing to the budding relationship between Jacob and Madeline Smith, the postmaster who is also white. In Apartheid Africa, relationships between the races were prohibited by the law. In the book, the character of Madeline Smith makes a relatively late appearance, and leaves to our imagination the shy development of Jacob's and Miss Smith's relationship through the former's weekly visits to the post office she runs. The film chooses instead to introduce her in the very first scene; she is eating at a table in the cafe when the police arrive, wanting to check passes and more generally, make a nuisance of themselves. The Mixed Marriages Act of 1949 prohibited marriage between whites and other races, while the Immorality Act prevented any 'indecent behaviour' between these races. Further, the various regimes of economic segregation prevented non-whites from establishing businesses in white areas or employing white people; economic relationships between the other races were also restricted in similar ways. One of the chief mechanisms of enforcing 'petty Apartheid' was through prevention of any sharing of facilities among races; whites-only restaurants meant coloureds, blacks or Indians would not be allowed to enter. Sarif's film, in placing Madeline at the restaurant, strengthens the resistance to Apartheid that Madeline in the novel displays. Yet, in placing a heterosexual love-narrative of equal length parallel to Amina's and Miriam's growing attachment, the film version reveals its diffidence about being a lesbian film all the way. In fact, the casting of the Madeline–Jacob pair is better both in acting skill and attention to detail than the Miriam-Amina pair, which lends a greater authenticity to the former, while the latter pairing requires some imaginative suspension of disbelief at their accents, appearance and the like. Madeline and Jacob are affected by Apartheid, the novel and the film agree, while Miriam and Amina are affected, by metaphorical extension, by rules as silly as Apartheid; why should two women be kept apart if they love one another, asks Sarif, any more than two people of opposite gender should be kept apart by race? The general public marks Madeline's pleasant treatment of a coloured man and set about humiliating him—a boy a third his age calls Jacob 'boy,' ordering him to bring a glass of water; a policeman notices how smartly dressed both Madeline and Jacob are on the evening he was to take her out to dinner and to escape his censure, Madeline has to pretend Jacob is her driver, not her date. They do not have dinner together through the length of the text. While the film is able to depict the social existence of Apartheid through the public difficulties Madeline and Jacob face even before they are able to head out for a planned date in a strikingly evocative manner, the dilemma of Amina's and Miriam's (un)familiar love is progressively depicted as an increasingly privatized matter.

Miriam's and Amina's affair, however, despite obvious parallels with the Apartheid-separated couple, does not manage to explicitly attain the dimensions of a social problem in quite the same way as the former does in the film; the novel on the other hand, enables the reader to linger on the significance of the dates that Sarif marks different segments of the story with. This structuring of the novel as a diary of sorts, collated from the individual unwritten diaries of many of its characters, however, is hardly evident in the film, where the font that displays the month and the year vanishes almost the instant it appears into the yellow and brown tones Sarif uses to capture the vastness and flatness of the African prairie. However, even this cartography suggesting space and possibilities of mobility and thus freedom from constriction, are not available in the film as they are in the novel, where alternating claustrophobia and spatial liberty suggests connections between personal development and literal availability of space or territory. Not mistress of any territory of her own, Miriam's sense of self is meagre to begin with, and only gradually, after a couple of driving lessons, does Miriam decide to make use of the immense spaces of possibility, of the world unseen South Africa offers her. Meanwhile, upset at not being able to make headway with Miriam, Amina thinks of leaving Pretoria altogether for any other town; again, the liberty of space is hers to take, but the over-furnished bedroom assigned to Amina in the film, in contrast to the very spare room the Amina of the book sleeps in, scarcely suggests an undomesticated individual given to travelling at will. Amina's critique of constricting domesticity—which involves violence in the case of Miriam's with Omar—is embodied in her living arrangements, but again, the film version passes off a glossier, picture-book like South Africa for the spare lives of the passenger Indians in the decade immediately after the Second World War, when petty Apartheid, with its various segregation laws had indeed wrecked the hard-earned capital of many Indians, especially the ex-indentured labourers.

Amina's father, on a rare visit to his daughter's cafe, tells her that all the local gossip is indeed linking Miriam to her, whereupon Amina tells him that Miriam's husband hits her. Her father's response is unequivocal: 'then go and fetch her' (Sarif 2001: 331). In deflecting the conversation from the viability of lesbianism to domestic abuse, Sarif's text places us in the same unenviable quandary Deepa Mehta's did; is marital unhappiness the only genesis of lesbian love? Sarif's structuring of the conversation may also be read as a recognition of the true nature of marital bonds for those in love with an (un)familiar; heteronormative marriage bonds may well be abusive and violent for those in love with one of their own sex. However, Amina's emotional pain at her beloved's being battered by her husband is sufficient to persuade her decent father to, in turn, persuade his daughter to 'liberate' Miriam; the logic of lesbianism might be unpalatable for this honourable man, apparently, but not the logic of human dignity. The specificity of lesbian love and the specific nature of the social recognition it requires as also an erotic bond between two women is here occluded by lesbianism becoming a particular kind of problem within heterosexual marriage. Thus, while public resistance to the Madeline–Jacob affair is explicitly staged in both the film and the novel, showing the unreasonableness of Apartheid South Africa and at the same time making evident the social nature of couple-formation, the Amina–Miriam one, conducted largely in Miriam's household, is relegated thus to a 'private' set of acts—their affair does not convey in equal measure the social construction of heterosexual coupledom which it would have stood in contrast to.

Miriam and Amina get to know one another and recognize an emotional kinship when Amina is getting Miriam's husband's garden ready; the familiar space of the patriarchal home—though it is a nuclear diasporic one this time—provides them the vital site for exchange and sustenance. Amina eats Miriam's cooking and is struck, later, by the idea of starting an Indian menu at her cafe with Miriam as cook, pointing thus to a mutually contributory autonomous economy the two women can participate in, in contrast to the unpaid labour that Miriam must do for Omar. Miriam's road to financial autonomy is also, interestingly, the road to emotional reciprocity; the mutuality that Omar denies her, through a combination of coldness and being otherwise occupied by his affair with his sister-in-law Farah, had placed Miriam from the first in the space of an observer in her own life. Amina's offer of engagement is not only financial; it is also spiritually engaging for Miriam finally, to find that appreciation for the things that she can do is to be had. Miriam however does not want to take Amina up on her suggestion that they take the three children Miriam has with Omar and leave for Cape Town where Amina promises Miriam she can look after her. Miriam's refusal to flee shows her resistance—and the novelist's resistance—to placing this lesbian exit in the realm of the escapist. Miriam instead wants to make her own way. In focussing only on her wanting to cook two or three times a week instead of working every day unpaid as Omar's labour, Sarif calls attention to the poignant nature of her struggle; large gestures are not for the likes of Miriam. Miriam's road to liberation will only come three steps at a time. In the book, Miriam writes a letter of acceptance to Amina's offer of a place and plans to take a bus the next morning to work in Pretoria; in the film, Miriam somehow drives to Pretoria despite her unfinished driving lessons. Miriam's fantastic driving thus places the film's rendition of Miriam's victory also in the realm of what is at least partly magical while the book's resolution carefully places Miriam's victory as another mundane victory, all the more (un)familiar because real. In the film, Miriam and Amina meet in the last scene—Amina is proud that her beloved has managed to make it to the end of the journey, which, if it is not in her arms, is at least in her kitchen. The book avoids this utopic resolution; instead of seeing Amina and Miriam together in the final frame, we are left to think of how Miriam's morning will be. Will Omar try another time to beat her into submission? How will she dispose of the morning's housework? Will she get on the bus after all? The film's desire to end on a positive rather than an ambivalent, though still open note, is perhaps understandable given the lack of affirmative representations of lesbianism.

However, in translating Amina's persona into completely femme, and editing out several other stories and characters, Sarif's film privileges a certain kind of lesbianism as possible and blocks out others. Representing the figure of the mixed-race working-class butch woman more honestly onscreen would have effectively supplied a material link in the film for the interconnections in between national/racial authenticities and heterosexual purity. In rendering visible a woman of some black ancestry, with a great fondness for women and a love of many masculine activities, Sarif's film could have broadened the range of lesbian types beyond the 'femme,' or the Western/white butch/dyke. The novel suggests interconnections between non-white women that are built on joint labour, looking out for one another and sharing fun; however, these cross-racial homosocialities are sadly erased by miscasting in the film. Likewise, if it had generated less parodic Indian coordinates for the various characters when showing them at home, the film's critique of Indianness—in both its 'authentic' mainland version and its ghostly diasporic other—would have resonated differently, communicating Sarif's ambivalence about both, and opening up both thus to re-evaluation. At the same time, this would have perhaps made the film an (un)familiar text for much of its intended Western audience. In its current version, the film features strikingly good-looking women of South Asian origin in the lead parts; their good looks, along with their accents float decontextualized in a world of similarly good-looking women with, say, dark hair and dark eyes. However, the greatest loss sustained via this translation is in the biting interrogation of (heterodominant) diaspora the book makes possible; where Sarif's novel enables a critique of normative diasporic values of patriarchy, Oedipal lineal succession, and female subjection, the film displaces this interrogation with its privileging of the Amina–Miriam love-story as a romantic triumph over adversity. Where Amina and Miriam in the novel struggle to establish sites for (un)familiar love within the home and the workplace, the film reifies their love for one another as yet another timeless story that happens to be set in South Africa. Jacob's and Madeline's story in Sarif's film functions through the better known black/white dichotomy within Apartheid, as a result of which it does not necessarily lose when treated primarily as a tale of thwarted love because the reader/viewer is more attuned to the socio-cultural implications of forcing a dichotomous perspective on race relations. The cinematic version of Amina's and Miriam's love story, set as it is within the history of the little-documented diaspora of passenger Indians in South Africa, when decontextualized into an eternal story of lesbian triumph over heterosexual marital impediments, loses much of its impact as also an (un)familiar critique of the consensus realities of home, nation, diaspora, and colonialism.

Racial and Sexual Others

Bend It Like Beckham details the coming of age of the Indian diasporic community in England, with second- and third-generation ethnic Indians wanting lives very different from the lives imagined by those before them. The protagonist, Jasminder, or Jess, is a young woman with the unlikely hobby of playing football in the park with the local Indian boys between errands; she also speaks to 'that bald man' David Beckham's poster when she's alone in her room. Beckham, 'bald' and 'skinhead' respectively to Jess's father and mother, is to Jess a veritable god, but tellingly, Jess idolizes not the sexualized consumable that Beckham often is, but the great footballer. A chance encounter in the park with another girl-footballer leads to Jess being offered a place in the local girls' team. Jess has no theory of the game; when asked where she plays, her answer is 'In the park.' Further interrogation by the coach on her 'position' leads to the offer of the following answer 'Up front, right is best.' Jess is raw talent, it appears, and very little terminology; however, she can indeed bend the ball, having learnt from watching Beckham play on TV. Jess secretly plays with the club till an important match coincides with her sister's wedding; the truth comes out and Jess must admit she's been sneaking out all this while, not for a 'fella' but for football. Initially she is reluctant to fight her family for football; in the end, her decorum and willingness to put family ahead of football melts her father's heart and he 'allows' his daughter to play, sending her to the field with the benediction that she not have to make the same mistakes as he did in his time, choosing the safe life rather than the heartfelt one.

Chadha's fairy-tale about a successful amateur women's footballer became a surprise hit not only in the Indian diaspora, where it was located and made, but also in India. What is very rarely mentioned, outside of queer discussion circles, is that Chadha had originally planned to centre the film around a pair of lesbian female footballers (Warn 2003); however, the exigencies of film-distribution prompted a 'course-correction' transforming Jules and Jess, the two female protagonists, into heterosexual female footballers in consequence, with a male coach, Joe, serving as the focal point of a putative heterosexual triangle. Queer readings of the film are nevertheless possible. The 'mainstream femme film' defined by Christine Holmlund as a 'hybrid subgenre of the woman's film and the lesbian drama' (Holmlund 1991: 145) is a category within which *Bend It Like Beckham* fits, with its employment of very femme actors for the lead parts of boyish footballers. Yet, the nature of the sport is such that it destabilizes the seamless transfer of femininity to heterosexual pleasure by showing female bodies at labours that are non-reproductive, set to music that eroticizes victory on the sporting field rather than a romantic object. At a key moment in the film, when Jess has to take a penalty kick, which the film has earlier shown her to fail at, the soundtrack is 'Nessun Dorma', which might ring bells for the audience not only as a classic in the Western opera tradition, but which also was the opening song for the FIFA World Cup of 1990. Pavarotti's rendition of the words 'Vincerò' (I will win) spans the entire space of Jess's kicking the ball and its safe, bent flight into the goal; the choice of song reassures the viewer who knows the song that victory will result,

Jess will win the match for her team. The soundtrack continues as the visuals confirm the successful goal, followed by Jess being lifted atop team-mates shoulders in celebration; the visuals suddenly cut to Jess's brother-in-law hoisting her sister, his newly wedded spouse, suggesting two paths to fulfilment for feminine desire. Pinky's life-narrative reconciles the heteronormative path of marriage to a suitable boy with the diasporic celebratory narrative of finding that boy within one's own ethnic group. Jess' life-path is also, however, validated as no less and no better perhaps than Pinky's; Chadha's use of editing validates both their experiences of celebration as spiritually uplifting in context also of the sisters' religious Sikh identity, as Claudia May argues (2010: 268). While the heteronormative is not disturbed by Jess's choice of Joe as partner, *Bend It Like Beckham* is still a drama about one young woman's liberation from the strictures of her particular diaspora in enabling a path outside her ethnic group for sexual fulfilment. The (un)familiar potentials of the film however stop at admitting that the feminine body is available to creativities other than those of romantic heterosexualized pleasure or biological maternity, both embodied by Pinky; in not encoding this feminine body as also gender-bending the film is able to safely contain the powerful challenge of lesbianism, with its making over of the female body to the possibility of non-heterosexual desire. Thus, may the diasporic female subject be lesbian? The film's answer appears to be no.

The chimera of the (un)familiar diasporic female subject however is very clearly visible to Jess's partner Jules's mother, one of the speakers in the epigraph above. Mrs Paxton sees her gender-bending daughter turn lesbian practically before her very eyes with the kind of girl she thought free of the taint of the homosexual; *Bend It Like Beckham* is able to laugh at Mrs Paxton's homophobia even as it confirms that Mrs Paxton was right after all—good Indian girls cannot be lesbian, as the film's narrative proves in the end. Mrs Paxton fears through the film that her androgynous daughter Juliet, whose feminine name is used only once and generally referred to by her androgynous nickname, is having an affair with Jess. Mrs. Paxton is outnumbered at home by her cheerfully pot-bellied husband's support for Juliet's footballing; he's her first and most enthusiastic coach. Mrs Paxton's comic bamboozlement centres around the transgression involved in an Indian girl playing football; her patronizing attitude references the attitudes of a white majority towards ethnic minorities even as her shock vindicates the unlikeliness of someone like Jules/Jess being the norm for any girls anywhere; the validation of the unlikeliness of this resonates with Jess's response to Tony's being gay. Jess's family does not encourage her footballing either because it brings her in contact with men and therefore, places her femininity within the space of the un-chaste, having been already sullied by contact with men who are not traditionally sanctioned sexual partners. Mrs Paxton's homophobia is only one generation away from Jess's family's heteropatriarchality. *Bend It Like Beckham* is very successful in showing how much heteronormativity and homophobia share in terms of control and surveillance strategies, and how subjects trying to liberate themselves from these forms of control often choose similar strategies. Additionally, the film places the burden of homophobia on the female subject on this occasion as well—it is Mrs Paxton who is heterosexuality's policewoman. In the end, it is Jess' father, like Jules's right through, who decides to back his daughter, urging her to go play her big match even if it meant missing part of her sister's wedding party. While the film explicitly stages diasporic inheritance as being transferred from father to daughter, instead of through the Oedipalized conduit of son or son-in-law, the logic the film subscribes to all the same is the logic of normative femininities that look feminine, are decorous, await approval before running away, and that do not disrupt sanctioned flows of desire. The compulsory invisibilization of the possibility of (un)familiar desire also permits us to enquire into the nature of modernity insofar as it concerns female same-sex desire; how does queer or lesbian desire challenge, reify or stabilize conceptions of feminist transformation of structures of family, labour and identity?

While the homophobia of the epigraph is located within the comic, its output is recognizable in the dangerous practical consequences it could have had; perhaps, in the absence of a successful wedding celebration as backdrop to Mrs Paxton's allegations of lesbianism, Jess might have been incarcerated or worse for sexual deviance. That nobody notices is a relief, but as Tony's anxious response to Jess when she wonders how 'these tossers', the very macho young men Tony hangs out with, would respond to Tony's gayness, suggests, being out in an ethnic diaspora is not going to be entirely easy. The film is willing to disturb the normative gendering of sport as representatively male by investing in young female sporting champions on the make; yet, it is not willing to disturb how the femininity of this sporting cast is annexed into heteronormativity, displacing instead the burden of being queer onto Jess's 'mate,' Tony, a young Indian man who is willing to make a marriage of convenience with Jess to help her though he is gay. Unfortunately, while the removal of female homosexuality arguably permits the director to focus more entirely on issues of racism and female empowerment, the film as it stands suggests that sexual subversion is exclusively male territory. Jess' response to Tony's 'coming out' is a comically aghast 'You're Indian!' which can be read as a Jekyll and Hyde-like comment, self-awarely ironic for the film as a whole, but expressive of naïve shock for the character in question, on how Indian-ness and homosexuality may not go together. The twin effect of irony and naiveté retains focus on the body of the gay man as active doer, habiting a gay identity for South Asians/Indians in the diaspora, and on the diasporic Indian woman as passive spectator, comically thrown by the newness the man creates, even as the comedy of the moment focuses attention away from reflection on how 'gayness' is here gendered as only male by emphatically retaining the gendering of the 'sporty' female footballer as normatively feminine—after all Tony's revelation is made when Jess asks to go out with him.

Who is afraid of female homosociality?

Bend It Like Beckham is anxious to foreground its heterosexualization of the heroine; educating the young woman on her place in the normative order, it fits in the tradition of the romantic comedy, privileging heterosexual marriage, companionship, motherhood and related family roles. To borrow from Judith Butler, gender identity is thus 'a performative accomplishment compelled by social sanction and taboo' (Butler 1990: 270–271). The film is able to show the production of the correctly gendered female body as required by various ritual contexts. However, this production of the female body as feminine through the use of technologies for its aestheticization are almost entirely located in relation to heterosexualized 'functions' even as they happen within contexts that are largely exclusively female-only. The visual narrative does not challenge these often humorous moments with moments of equal narrative weight wherein female homosociality is available without reference to heteronormative work. Thus, the film does celebrate moments of athleticism within the sporting domain, but once outside it, the visualization is careful to contain suggestions that the labours of femininity can be retained within femininity as its rewards. In the locker room, for example, Jess's initial discomfiture seeing the captain, Mel, take off her t-shirt to reveal a lacy black bra is represented by a look that suggests not merely discomfiture, but also curiosity. Jess never acclimatizes enough to the locker room to take off her clothes in full view, a reference no doubt to her 'proper' Indian unbringing but also expressive of a (self-)consciousness about the potential availability of female bodies to female gazes and thence, shared (un)familiar pleasures. But in a later instance, the conversations in the locker room are about allowed (heterosexual) marriage possibilities according to the codes of Jess's ethnic group, and sex outside of marriage, with all of the exchanges being locked into the heterosexual. In a final instance, the entire team stands around Jess helping her tie her sari back on, playful and clumsy at the same time. Here, the homosocial is presented as an advantage, an asset for the female protagonist—teamwork and support are key to a woman's success in the world, the film suggests. Tony, her gay mate, drove Jess to the match; her straight team-mates, who by like token are uninterested in Jess, will help her return to her sister's wedding on time so her cover is not blown before the community. The space of female homosociality in the women's locker room thus mirrors the similarly sexless bonhomie of the women at Jess's home helping with marriage preparations, even as it seamlessly ties back with Jess's sexless cross-gendered friendship with Tony.

   Bend It Like Beckham's contribution lies, all the same, in the sensitivity and seriousness with which it approaches female homosociality and friendship between women. Jess and Pinky cover for one another routinely, thus documenting sisterhood's genuine political impact in easing the situation at home for many young women. Likewise, *Bend It Like Beckham* displaces the backward glance of diaspora with an ethnic group aware of its role in the present through showing how the girls' mother is also aware of how Pinky sneaks off to be with her lover, but lets it be, certifying for the viewer that theirs is a family that has come a long way from old mores even though she is represented as most liable to break into Punjabi dialogue and only ever seems to watch television programmes from the subcontinent. If one is willing to become a 'perverse spectator' as Janet Staiger puts it (Staiger 2000: 2), one can invest many of the images this friendship generates with queer valences—the language of looks, the music that accompanies many narrative episodes, etc. give premier space to the friendship between the two key female characters, even as the game of football shows female bodies engaged in labour beyond heterosexual or maternal reproduction. The spectacle of attraction to the female body, however, is encouraged at the level of film footage, though, with the fit footballers bouncing around the field in sports bras, a possible source of delectation to all audiences, not necessarily the normatively imagined male observers alone. An appropriative queer reading, as Katharina Lindner calls it, of the film permits just such moments to attain a fetishistic queer valence (Lindner 2011: 204). Jess's fight to play football, for the queer spectator, approximates the (lucky) homosexual individual's struggle to secure social validation and support. At the end of the film, Jess and Jules leave for the USA, football scholarships having permitted them to postpone for a while the requirements of domesticity, which are presented as natural—by de-routinizing Jess as the exception because of her talent—even while comically satirized by the excesses of Mrs Bhamra's and Mrs Paxton's performances of the role. *Bend It Like Beckham*, viewed in this light, is a film that permits an ostensibly feminist triumph but meticulously cleaves the feminist project from a possible lesbian one. For a film ostensibly about football, *Bend It Like Beckham* is ruthless in allowing very few subjectivities to emerge from within the surrounding team-mates outside of these moments. In denying narratival subjectivity to the other players on the team, the film does emphatically train the viewer's focus on the pair that is Jules and Jess. This focalization however valorizes them as highly gifted individuals at the expense of undercutting the premise that team sports work on—that the entire team contributes and plays as one. The argument I would like to make here then is that *Bend It Like Beckham* has the unfortunate effect of substituting female homosocial teamwork with the narrative of personal excellence that can ultimately feed into the narrative of the heroic, with all its de-gendering and therefore de-politicizing implications; the question of a young woman's personal liberties are rendered as a question for her family and her ethnic group rather than the body politic.

Yet their survival within the extended ethnic group is mediated by those 'traditional' older mores, within which racial purity and the fear of miscegenation are realities: Pinky's in-laws-to-be are able to veto her marriage to their son on the grounds that Jess was kissing a white boy at the bus-stop. The infinite corruptibility of daughters and their central role in family honour is something the film does not dispute; the family are shown apologetic, as the bride's family is expected to be within traditional norms. However the situation is defused somewhat when Jess swears on Guru Nanak's image that she has not been kissing any boys at all. Jess confirmation of being sexually unsullied is key to retaining her family's trust in her; Mrs Paxton's homophobic eye sees in Jess a potential lesbian, while Teetu's parents see in Jess a potentially sexually active woman. The confusions, serious for Pinky's and Jess's dreams of marriage and career respectively, and comic for the film's own denouement, these place the ethnic group and the larger community it is located within on par in revealing equal, albeit different blind spots. Jess is caught in the eye of the panopticon that is the larger diasporic family on the first occasion she is shown in the film to be going somewhere outside the immediate suburbs of her Hounslow neighbourhood; earlier scenes have documented her with her sister (performing 'ethnic' shopping, eating 'ethnic' food in an 'ethnic' neighbourhood), or the neighbourhood boys or bringing home the shopping, but now, Jess goes on her own errand, to get herself her first pair of football shoes, with Jules. They take the Tube into London proper, going to a mall and then a pub, where the girls sit down to admire their purchase, and Jules has a beer while Jess has a non-alcoholic iced drink. These scenes, the only ones in the film that are markedly not South Asian as well as off the football field, mark Jess's entry as national subject and independent consumer of non-ethnic goods, but these possessions predictably get her in trouble at home—the shoes are too expensive and of course not for the wedding; she is also accused of smoking, which would have been out of line given the Sikh-religious ethos at home. Not achieving the correct heteronormative function, the homosocial pleasure of hanging out with a non-diasporic girlfriend has also to be paid for with five laps around the football pitch, sanctioned by the coach, who in turn does not like the girls' talking during exercise. The film's placement of female homosociality as a challenge to the authority of the male coach is remarkable. Jess's refusal to share details of personal distress with a professional mentor, her coach, leads to punishment; later they bond over it, but insofar as it distracts attention from his authority as coach during exercise, the girls' relationship to one another is immediately censured by Joe, in contrast to his encouragement of it in the cause of passing to one another on the field during play or as a go-between for a romantic relationship between him and Jess. Immediately after this episode, Jess goes to Jules to get the requisite replacement pair of shoes secretly off Jules's mother when their encounter with Mrs. Paxton produces the usual laughs; the girls are laughing at her at the bus-stop where Teetu's in-laws mistake her for having been kissing a white boy. Consequent to the expression of female homosociality as a challenge to the requirements of authority, the film defuses its own subversiveness by showing how it is disciplined by yet another authority—the diasporic need for racial purity and chastity in its women.

Thus, while Mrs Paxton can visualize, even if homophobically, the figure of the (un)familiar South Asian woman, the Bhamras and their diaspora unfortunately cannot tell a lesbian from a Piscean or a Lebanese. *Bend It Like Beckham* produces the 'white' Mrs Paxton as an anomaly, as one headstrong but eventually comic and thus harmless mother, not as a structural expression of a larger whiteness, balancing her homophobic excesses with the stolidity and common-sensical warmth of her equally white husband. Concurrently, the tragic overtones the film supplies to Pinky's cancelled nuptials ratify the value it gives to the way the diaspora runs itself; the coach finds himself going to Jess's house to request parental consent for Jess's footballing, approving the idea that parents have absolute authority on a daughter who is almost adult (the film is set in the summer after Jess's final school exams; it is expected she will soon go to college) even though Joe tells Jess in private, parents are not always right. In the run up to the denouement, Mrs Paxton and Mr Paxton both think the girls are indeed a lesbian pair. Clearly both of them are wrong, but *Bend It Like Beckham* shows the usually genial Mr Paxton down at the mouth because his daughter, whom he is supportive of has just achieved a life-dream and is also lesbian, because he and his wife both believe the 'ocular proof' they have just received; news that they have both been given scholarships leads to a fleeting moment when the girls embrace and it appears from the distance that they have kissed briefly on the mouth. While Mrs Paxton's function as caricature enables some of the fear of female homosexuality to escape into comedy, Mr Paxton's unusual capitulation cannot be explained merely as his fear of scenes with the wife: he does stand up against her typically, but here he too fears she is not jumping to conclusions as her wont; she has for once rationally arrived at them. The threat of lesbianism thus leads even the good father to withdraw support (temporarily though, within the diegesis of the film) in one household. However, as Guido Rings recognizes, the film's 'transfer of homophobia' to white characters instead of the predictable Asian ones, 'helps the viewer to recognize British pre-Enlightenment thinking,' instead of uncritically admiring the 'Anglo-American lead culture' Britain thinks is its gift to its ethnic minorities (Rings 2011: 120–1).

Privatizing the question of feminism splits feminist work away from the work then, of freeing young women to follow their dreams. If the dreams of young women are sanitized and suitably safe, the family project, of course is adequate. However, what if these dreams do not fit within realms designated safe? The film circumvents this question by producing male characters who are themselves likeable; Jess's father is shown to be a sensitive and caring father rather than a distant patriarch, gentle with niece alike as with daughters, welcoming finally towards the partners, respectively brown and white, his daughters have chosen for themselves, clearly marking some other men—Tony's friends at the park and the young Sardar at the wedding—as macho and thus 'other' dangerous to the project of companionate marriage but comic in context here. Meanwhile, within the space of a largely female-centric romantic comedy, characters like Tony and the effeminate videographer later in the film (who says 'Don't smile; look sad; the Indian bride never smiles; You'll ruin the bloody video'), whose own gender-crossing strangely does not attract the community's attention or come in for reformatory containment, serve as benign all-male representatives of sexual and/or gendered crossings. Yet, their work is on the fringes; to offer support to the heroine as Tony does, even offering a marriage of convenience to his 'mate', or as documenters and thus non-participants of heterosexual rituals, as is the case with the videographer. However, the videographer is beaten up, in an unmarked comic interlude just before the bride leaves, for having recorded the indiscreet coupling frenzy of two guests at the wedding. Is this a suggestion of what might happen to those who record that which would be best off undocumented according to the community in question? *Bend It Like Beckham* also separates eroticism from female creative passion, Jess veritably dematerializes the palpable eroticism of Beckham's body itself, which Tony immediately emphatically restores in his statement of his own sexual identity. The erotic for the diasporic female subject can only belong in the confines of the safely monogamous heterosexual relationship while Tony's fancies may wander free still. At the end of the film, when Beckham has been glimpsed in the distance at the airport, everyone returns to what they were doing soon enough but Tony's gaze stays with Beckham the longest, free to desire, to wander, as a young, available, gay man. Thus, dreams that do not belong with the female protagonist can be displaced onto a male one; support across the barriers of gender, age, and authority-roles is presented as the norm rather than the exception.

Staying Put, But Bending Little

Jess's desire to take up her football scholarship in California leads to Tony offering her a marriage of convenience; in her 'coming out' moment, she speaks up fully and finally, talking back to her mother, not her father, identifying mother as centre of tradition and stasis, admitting that Tony is only helping her get away. Gayatri Gopinath argues in her reading of the film that by figuring the resolution as 'getting out' rather than 'staying put', the film in a sense concedes the space of the home as one of gender and racial fixity and oppression' (Gopinath 2005: 128). Contra this, I would argue instead that the film is careful to show that Jess does not wish to abdicate the space of the home. Her final act of speaking up is that moment that reconciles family with personal ambition; Jess is indeed paid back for being resourceful, through the film, she has indeed been shown as resistant, unhappy, regretful, vigilant for opportunities, and taking them. Yet, it often also shows her very compliant, incorporated very much within these ideologies of race and gender, unwilling to push very far. The film ends with a snapshot of Jess's new American team being put on the mantelpiece by her heavily pregnant sister. Their mother is solicitously knitting little baby booties, and outside the window, Joe, Tony and Mr Bhamra are playing a game of cricket. An ice-cream truck drives into these happy suburbs, which Jess and Jules still continue to inhabit in absentia, providing the frame for the integration of the diasporic family into the mainstream and for female ambition into the world at large. The film's ability to draw race into the question of the diasporic woman's feminine sexual pleasure and desire is also limited, with Joe's wholesomeness and Jess's very responsible attraction to him substituting any deep engagement with the tensions that such racialization sets up within diaspora, ignoring with the help of the romantic comedy framework most of the anxieties and complications of honour, familial, and national pride, not to mention racial pride, that such unions end up having to navigate. Closing in the happy suburbs, the film's 'originary narrative erases political and ethical considerations that mark history as a site of struggle ... (effacing) the everyday hardships and struggles of daily life in favour of a reformulated, faux progressive New Labour vision of gender, race and class relations' (Giardina 2003: 78).

The film displaces and ultimately contains female homosocial bonding by replacing the female–female dyad with the female–male–female triangle that is the explicit precursor of the potentially envisaged female–male dyad; a freeze-frame of the pair as they wave to family on leaving for the USA precedes the scene where the team photographs that confirm their successful California sojourn are memorialized in their respective homes. This freeze-frame pairs Jules with Jess, not Jess with Joe—the film thus gives space to female friendship and homosocial bonding, even interrupting the physical flow of the narrative medium of cinema to 'fix' this pair for the audience, only to displace it within images of undisturbed heteronormative continuities—pregnancy, new additions to family. One assumes Tony has still not 'come out' in any sense that remakes the space of the diasporic home for a queer politics, though he figures in the final scenes. The film thus runs the fulfilment of the female protagonist's dream in parallel to the creation of the heterosexual romantic pair, as if terrified of the threatening consequences of not containing female aspiration within the narrative of potential matrimony. Thus, sadly, while family is seen as part of the inheritance of the young female subject ('You're lucky…to have a family that cares that much about you. I can understand you don't want to mess with it,' says Joe despite Mr Bhamra keeping him away from Jess), the inheritance the spunky Jess in the final analysis refuses to forfeit is quite heteronormative.

Expressing female sporting excellence through carefully feminized bodies despite showing awareness of how female sports have always carried the 'taint' of lesbianism, with many sportswomen being automatically thought lesbian on account of the redrawing of bodily contours that constant physical training produces, and preferring to 'out' the audience's own doubts on the subject through Mrs Paxton's doubts about her daughter, Chadha erases and reduces what would have been the dangerous spectre of female homosexuality to the merely comic. Once the laughter track establishes the corresponding seriousness of the heterosexual angle, the film's recuperation of heterosexuality is complete. Further, the film contains the potential these femininities have of expressing themselves in homoerotic relationships with one another by placing the sporting story within the frame narrative of an ethnic wedding with its emphasis on correctly racialized couplings.

Thus the absent heroine, safely affianced to a loving and none too masculine Joe unlike the eponymous Beckham's own much more virile masculinity, can be absent from home as an ostensible mobile female protagonist without fears of her mobility disrupting this very desirable heterosexual coupledom. Chadha understands how, 'in order to present a palatable narrative of female fulfilment in sport, Jess and Jules have to be 'pretty' and feminine as well as athletic, and most of all, they have to be straight' (Treagus 2002: 2). Thus, *Bend It Like Beckham* is willing to go far in bending one category of gendering in its production of a sporty protagonist. But this 'sporty' prototype, bookended by the almost-anorexic, boyish-framed Keira Knightley who plays Jules in the film, and the wholesomely girlish Parminder Nagra who essays Jess, belongs more to the world of fashionably chic girls approved of as desirable in the contemporary world than to the more unfashionable type of female sporting champion signified by, say, Martina Navratilova or even Serena Williams or from a still earlier era, by Indian athletes like P.T. Usha. Navratilova's butchness, Usha's less than pretty appearance and Williams' muscularity all pose challenges to conventional femininity in a variety of ways; their 'difference' means that they interrupt the seamless visual transfer to the gender 'female' that Jess and Jules do not because of how conventionally feminine they are in many ways sanctioned by both contemporary Western and Indian tastes. *Bend It Like Beckham*, thus, for all its bending, shows itself to be quite straitlaced about how female sports-models should look and be, using as Jayne Caudwell puts it, 'signs of lesbianism … to expose heterosexuality as the more visible and viable version of the sporting heroine' (Caudwell 2009: 260). This role-model, the film suggests, will not rupture familiar expectations of gender in a fashion that is constantly visible and thus an interruption that will be remarked upon. In short, the film will make visible queerness, barrier-crossings, only insofar as these crossings themselves remain un-queer, reassuringly the same as everything else they come after and this familiarity is maintained through the disavowal and containment of the possibilities of female (un)familiar love and desire.

Chutney Popcorn: Dykes with Friends and Histories

Chutney Popcorn functions as a 'cinema of attractions' (Gunning 1984: 64) in that it is explicit about the continuum between female homo-sociality and female homoeroticism. Where *Bend It Like Beckham* is most circumspect about what women may do if they wish to when they are by themselves, *Chutney Popcorn* imagines at least some of these women as falling in love with one another, and carrying on with life. Exploring even the comic everyday failures of a (lesbian) sex-life in the process, *Chutney Popcorn* is able to establish a lesbian world in which the lesbian of Indian origin has a history, friends, memories and possibilities outside the space of the family that Jess is so careful not to upset, and that Jules and Joe constantly identify as reactionary and oppressively traditional, identifications the film does not explore, valorizing instead the narrative of Jess's intuitive understanding of what her 'tradition' means. *Chutney Popcorn*'s strength is that it does not disintegrate into ethnography, detailing the ways of life of a strange people inhabiting a strange place, or scopophilia, which 'can become fixated into a perversion, producing obsessive voyeurs and Peeping Toms whose only sexual satisfaction can come from watching, in an active controlling sense, an objectified other' (Mulvey 1991: 61).

Dealing with the life of a second-generation Indian–American, *Chutney Popcorn*'s depiction of desire does not have to follow the facile polarization of home versus society, nation versus the diaspora that *Bend It Like Beckham* rehearses, nor does it populate its canvas exclusively with conventionally feminine actresses to stay within the dynamic of the woman's film. In realistically representing both the challenges and the possibilities of lesbian community and family, *Chutney Popcorn* is also able to defamiliarize the meaning of 'family,' unhousing and making unhomely many familiar familial patterns to generate a structure within which to imagine an 'outlaw family' to twist Cheshire Calhoun's phrase (Calhoun 2000: 30).

Nisha Ganatra's first film is consciously an effort, like Chadha's, to write a script for Indian–Americans of the second generation, who are now no longer Indian, but who are not American in the same way as other assimilated ethnic minorities of Caucasian descent are. Placing ethnic difference parallel to sexual difference, Ganatra interrogates whether these heterogeneities can yield viable subject positions, challenging 'the construction of South Asian American identity as heterosexual and masculinist,' as Anupama Arora points out in her analysis of the film (2007: 41). The film opens with its protagonists, Reena and Lisa on a bike, with a gift-wrapped parcel in the back, Reena driving in a sari worn over a t-shirt and a biking helmet. They are headed to the wedding of Reena's sister, Sarita, to Mitch, who is white like Lisa. These two bi-racial relationships frame the film's engagement with the relationships the sisters and their mother share and are irked by; it is not coincidental that the frame narrative of the wedding is present in more than one diasporic film—the wedding is a marker of ethnic difference in this case, and if weddings are rites of passage (Hogan 2000; Van Gennep 1960), Sarita's wedding attests to how Reena and Lisa cannot participate in the ritual creation of a new couple; as family's outlaw, the lesbian woman of race must create new rituals. Symbolically, Reena and Lisa arrive late for the ceremony and stand at the fringes of the party thereafter looking on as others dance, foregrounding the many difficulties in the way of their full participation in such a ceremony. Though living with her girlfriend Lisa, who has just moved in with her, this new beginning in Reena's life cannot be marked according to the rituals her mother and by extension her larger community are in possession of, even as Sarita and Mitch are given a ceremonial spousal with all guests, white and non-white symbolically wearing Indian clothes. Reena's lesbianism is disguised by her mother with the statement, 'This is Lisa, Reena's old room-mate from ... college.' Prevaricating about the exact, erotic nature of her daughter's relationship with Lisa is for Meenu a strategy for continuing to keep the world the same even as Reena's everyday appearance signals important ruptures—'I feel like I'm in drag!' Reena says about the sari she is wearing, for Indian clothing is far from her set of everyday sartorial choices—the sombre jeans and t-shirt, with work-boots is a personal choice that sets her as sexually apart from the other women, just as her mother's clothing similarly performs heterosexualized femininity every day.

Lisa, for her part dressed in a salwar-kameez too, is very understanding about Reena's mother's need to 'closet' Lisa. Reena and Lisa are a model bi-racial relationship in their willingness to meet one another half way on the question of cultural difference in the face of Reena's mother's inhospitality and churlishness. As Lisa leaves, the background score of the scene, set initially to Punjabi wedding music '*dupatta tera sat rang kaa soniye*' changes to a western song, marking Reena's position as a conflicted other between two sets of accommodations literally with a musical correlative that is itself hybridized, just as Reena herself is, now, as a second-generation Indian-American in New York. The realm that *Chutney Popcorn* fashions is the de-routinizing one; that of an Indian lesbian living with friends but visiting her mother every weekend to set the lawn sprinklers right, trying to cook to earn approval, and fending off 'protective' gestures from horny Indian men who want to sleep with her good-looking, all-American Italian girlfriend, and finally, becomes a surrogate mother so her infertile sister can raise the family she so desires. The film seeks to show an Indian family reinventing itself as a result of a lesbian daughter becoming surrogate mother on her sister's behalf. This brief synopsis is suggestive of many problematics; to take just two questions—how does the film reconcile the lesbian protagonist's approval-seeking behaviour with dignified adulthood? Does the film not sanctify biological reproduction, even if by proxy, against possible reconceptualizations of family and inheritance?

Mehendi as Intersectional Language

The film's opening credits roll to the images of Reena putting mehendi (henna) on the bodies of women at the beauty-salon she works in. She also provides conventional beauty services like waxing and eyebrow definition, to clientele who appear mostly to be lesbians, suggesting connections between female homoeroticism and the labours of producing a femininity that is usually associated with heterosexuality. Reena takes pictures of the women whose bodies she has decorated with the green dye; these adorn the entire salon, making it look, her boss tells her, like a museum. Reena's camera should be read as her effort to organize an archive of cultural artefacts that literally defamiliarize and queer given notions of femininity. Reena's use of mehndi marks her designs with an ethnicity that tattooing ink onto the body does not have within Western culture. Instead of the permanence of the tattoo, mehndi offers the comfort of painless body-art that does not have to last forever or need expensive removal techniques. The use of mehndi in India at least invokes strong tropes of female homosociality; women putting henna in one another's hair is a quotidian hair-conditioning and maintenance activity for many women. Decorating one's palms and feet with mehndi on the other hand, evokes the spectacle of the Indian wedding in North India, and in a more mundane way, is an act imbued with aesthetic pleasure when performed outside the ambit of preparations for a wedding. *Chutney Popcorn* harnesses the tactile pleasures of mehndi application to convey a female homoeroticism that is far removed from the spectacles of heterosexuality that the Indian wedding conveys. The film's title credits roll alongside of Reena's adorning Lisa's body with mehndi designs; various parts of the body—cleavage, the back, arms, the belly-button, the thighs—are the recipients of Reena's artwork, but the pleasure is not merely aesthetic; Lisa's reason for not getting a permanent tattoo is that this way, she has 'an excuse for getting close to you all the time,' signally a forthright rendition of everyday sexual chemistry between long-term lovers. Reena's professional use of the dye also takes her away from the conventional parts of the body henna adorns in India—by not confining herself exclusively to the arms, hands and feet, but instead making a canvas of the whole female body. The potentials for homoerotic pleasure this supplies can well be imagined. Separating the female body thus from the heteronormative mechanism of the wedding party, *Chutney Popcorn* suggests many opportunities for making love to the female body. The body art of real artists is displayed in the film as Reena's mehndi designs on a number of women's bodies, some naked, some partly clad, but all adorned in ways that remove the humble mehndi far away from its demure traditional home on the modest extremities of female limbs. Further, Ganatra also queers the suggested consumerist heterosexual possibilities made available by the 'mehndi kits' as 'Indian body art' that Sunaina Maira documents as one of the tools to mark ethnicity by female South Asians in the Western club scene in the late nineties (Maira 1999: 32).

Reena's photographs of these bodies signal a female aesthetics that manages to sidestep the masculinist fragmentation of the female body into 'money shots' that focus on supposedly erotic places on this body. Instead, in photographing women such that their nakedness is not foregrounded, but the erotic potential of this design placed on them is, Reena's persona as a specifically lesbian artist calls for a re-evaluation of phallocentric art *and* provides an alternative to it, going beyond the split in cinematic gaze that attempts to make 'active/ male and passive/female' (Mulvey 1975: 9) looks. Her customers are not always sensible to this critique, for them, often, mehndi is an exotic dye, just as Reena is an exotic Oriental. 'Is this how it's done in India?' asks a woman who has just got her hands dyed with her friend. The tiny gap between the question and Reena's answer, coupled with a barely visible shrug reveals the 'oriental's' inability to combat being pigeonholed by the well-intentioned. Reena's artistry has been to remove mehndi from its old 'oriental' home to produce an art that starkly emphasizes the sexual potencies of the female body alongside of conveying erotic pleasure in this body, both on the part of the woman whose body it is, and of the viewer. Ganatra is able to frame this complex interchange of looks between artist, artist's model and art, even as she comments on the identifiably 'ethnic' provenance of this art. But what is art for Reena is 'nonsense' for her mother, who says, when told that her daughter's art might make the cover of a magazine, 'You don't even appear in these pictures. How will anyone know they are yours?' Showing Reena looking at the two women looking at her asking her if this was indeed part of the authentic

Indian ritual of applying mehndi to take a photograph at the end of it, the narrative of *Chutney Popcorn* looks at exchanges between being visible in one's artistic endeavours as an ethnic artist, being visible as one's own art, and being visible as a lesbian through one's art in a way that complicates many homonormative views about 'seeing' and being visible. In an excellent trope for the film's own self-reflexivity about its definitions of 'lesbian' 'woman' 'Indian' and 'tradition' a mirror behind them, meanwhile, reflects Reena looking at the two of them—Reena's art is framed on the one side by western expectations of 'Indianness,' and on the other by the mundane nature of this Indian-ness. Her own presence outside both these definitions of her is signalled by her perception of herself in the mirror; neither entirely Indian nor non-Indian, Reena's lesbianism is a border territory wherein cultural identity and personal identity negotiate; *Chutney Popcorn* answers calls to queer migrant narratives (Manalansan 2007: 229), illustrating alongside how American-Indian young people often negotiate various dissonant identities simultaneously (Agarwal 1991; Bacon 1996; Gibson 1988; Maira 1995, 1999; Wakil *et al.* 1981).

Lesbians Abroad, Out and Visible in the Urban Space

Chutney Popcorn is probably the only film with Indians in it that refers to casual lesbian dating, non-monogamous relationships or possible promiscuity among lesbians. In breaking from the mould of eternal lesbian love, *Chutney Popcorn* breaks new ground in not representing lesbianism as the more faithful version of heterosexuality, breaking away from what in some ways is a staple homonormativity about lesbianism. The lesbian is as vulnerable as the heterosexual to dating games, mind games and manipulation; Reena and Lisa inhabit a world populated by other lesbian friends, and ex-girlfriends, supportive parents and indifferent one-night-stands included. In giving the lesbian a history, friends and memories, the film is able to move beyond the victimology model.

A key moment in the film is when Becky and Reena make the street—the realm of the public—their own by 'scoping the street for dykes.' Reena and Becky are relaxing, trying to identify the dykes from the straight women, locating the essence of lesbianism even, 'it's the socks! No self-respecting dyke would wear those socks'. This lesbian radar is a direct reversal of gaze—sitting on the street occupying a traditionally male place the two women virtually see lesbians everywhere. Ganatra is able thus to suffuse the entire New York street with (un)familiar desire—all these women are made available to the queer gaze. A woman comes out from inside the salon, and hearing the 'dyke' word and says, 'That's great, why don't you just appropriate the culture of our oppressors!' The other women however confirm she is a dyke too, whether she likes it or not, confirming thus both that labels are powerful and that the queered gaze makes available all women to (un)familiar femininity. Becky, Reena, and Janis who joins them, see lesbians everywhere, all for the taking, and for them 'dyke' is a term they have already appropriated to signify a positive meaning when they use it with respect to their own lives. The film makes the realm of the public sphere its own in showing its characters inhabiting different spaces—the bar, the street itself, parks—where the world is around them; yet, their relatively 'leisured' positioning in many of these spaces also indicates that they stand at a tangent to capitalist America, unlike, say, Sarita's office-going husband.

Chutney Popcorn makes use of Sarita's inability to produce a family as a trope in reverse for Reena's own partial loss of family because of her lesbianism. Being lesbian, Reena is an outsider to a number of rituals that till the end of the film implicitly require heteronormative partnerships, her presence disruptive of the consensus reality of the Indian-American diasporic life their mother wishes to uphold. However, in the spirit of comedy, what begins as Reena's altruistic though approval-seeking motherhood culminates in the successful fashioning of a new kind of family where, in yet another of her mother's many pujas depicted in the film, her brother-in-law is the father while Lisa is, finally, acknowledged though as 'like the husband'. Sarita the elder sister is made to perform duty as her sister's brother, in the absence of one, and has to hold an umbrella unfurled to 'protect your sister'. The camera frames this motley crew of Reena, Lisa, Mitch, and Sarita standing where Meenu places them, to form a queer family photograph of sorts—two couples, one sitting, and the other standing, make up Meenu's family finally, in the eighth month of Reena's pregnancy. Paul Gilroy's concept of black diaspora as 'the changing same' (Gilroy 1993: 1) is useful here; while Meenu's rituals do not change, the instruments that perform them and the things that are made sacred or purified by them are in a constant process of self-definition or change. Earlier in the film, trying to bless Sarita's new house, Meenu is as puzzled as her two daughters are by the requirements of the ritual, where Reena's head is covered by a cap she runs to get since she does not have a scarf. Meenu's psychedelic idols and frail imitations of the 'real' thing, however, seem to do the job of sanctifying their lives quite well even as the aura of the ritual process is different with only three women performing them. While blessing Sarita's house and while setting afloat offerings in the river praying for a baby for Sarita, the three women belong quite clearly to a 'continuum' of women who look out for one another with the lack of male presence not being considered a negative.

Meenu is herself unconventional in the sense that she has long been divorced from her husband; conventional Asian male masculinity is totally debunked in the character of Raju, who cockily strolls into Reena's mother's yard to propose, secretly, to Reena that: 'I will get everybody off your back and pretend to go out with you if you hook me up with your fine-ass roommate, Lisa.' Reena can only tell him, 'she likes Indian chicks,' not Indian boys like him. Taken aback, he next suggests a threesome, relieved on the side that he wasn't being rejected for being brown, and leaves after his mandatory genuflections of devotion to 'auntie' Meenu. The Raju–Reena exchange comes after a sombre moment between Reena and Meenu where Reena pensively tells her mother that she never did have positive male role models, whereupon her mother surprisingly tells her with emphatic aplomb, 'you know, neither I did. Who cares?' Coming as it does after this moment of rejection of male masculinity as necessary to proper female development or happiness, Raju's comedic intervention only serves to highlight the autonomy of the women, lesbian or not, placing this autonomy both as a necessary survival strategy and as an alternative that already exists to patriarchal, objectifying males like Raju and to a smaller extent, supportive but still heterosexist ones like Mitch.

Reena's desire to attain some membership within her family however takes the film back to the standard script of the biologically defined family. A number of artificial insemination gags are played out through the film, but though there is an attempt at homoeroticizing the process of insemination, the cinematic imagery is strongest at suggesting a heterosexual fulfilment trajectory to Reena's final conception, coming as it does after an exchange wherein Mitch suggests since insemination is not something Lisa can do, perhaps someone who can do it right, meaning himself should be asked. The barely veiled pass at his wife's younger sister is couched by Mitch in entirely reproductive terms, but in light of their very combative relationship to this point, this exchange devalues and subverts Reena's labour as a lesbian, turning it to validating instead masculine patrilineal claims. At this point in the film, when Sarita is left out of the dialogue by the embarrassed Mitch and the shaken Reena, the question that floats uppermost is whether Reena's lesbian motherhood will be annexed entirely into the narrative of heteronormativity, with Reena and Mitch serving as the new dyad, with the lesbian sister supplanting the infertile Sarita. The imagery thereafter is disturbingly heteronormative—Mitch comes to Reena's to read to the baby in the belly; the visible pregnancy leads to lesbians on the street treating Reena as a renegade returned to heterosexuality; Lisa's frustrated departure from the apartment she shares with Reena parallels with Sarita's withdrawal from heterosexual marriage suggesting that neither motherhood for lesbians nor a non-procreative heterosexual relationship can survive. The film's intersectional analysis does reveal the existence of homonormativities within the dyke community Reena is part of, but its deployment of critique about traditional family is not as compelling, given that the protagonist's own desire for approval from her mother over-rides any other form of negotiation with the traditions the mother represents.

The pregnancy also leads to the entry of Reena as a sexualized subject into the diasporic public imaginary. Late into her pregnancy, Reena and Meenu share a joke sitting in the park in order to eat lunch in the first instance of genuine bonhomie between mother and daughter. Reena speculates about what life would be like if she had been in India, 'they'd kill you in India for being lesbian.' But at the same time, talking about Meenu's family, Reena asks Meenu, 'Have you ever thought your own mother, my grandmother could have been lesbian?' Meenu is greatly amused, saying, 'I never thought I'd see the day when I'd hear your grandmother was a lesbian!' Their laughter and pleasure at their whimsical exchanges about the history of their own family's sexuality, occurring out in the open, is an act similar to Reena's scoping out dykes on the street with her friends, but here gender and race commingle in two women's occupation of the space of the street where Reena becomes visible as a fertile, sexually active subject for once. Even as it opens up the space for the existence of lesbians, even in places where they might be 'killed' as Reena facetiously puts it, the scene invests South Asia with as much possibility for lesbian existence as it does the USA, and at the same time, in placing these conversations within the hearing of the *paan-walla* from whom the women order snacks whilst talking of their travails, the film penetrates the space of the diaspora with Reena's anomalous pregnancy status. The paan-walla, even if no one else knows it, knows the (un)familiar nature of Reena's pregnant self. Pregnancy is clearly an incitement to publicly discursivizing private dys/functions; at the same time, the South Asian viewer is alert to the fact that these conversations perhaps cannot happen in India in quite the same way because Reena's lesbianism might not be afforded a comic space within mundane considerations, but might be staged as a relatively more difficult, monstrous rite of passage. In these scenes, which happen mostly after visits to the obstetrician, the background score is the rich voice of Asha Bhonsle singing to a remixed background of club-music; the friendly neighbourhood petty-bunk-owners who know all the gossip places the scene's location as unmistakably within 'India' even if it is the 'little Indias' of Jackson Heights, New York. The 'changing same' of Indian diasporic experience in the USA makes space for both the buying of Indian clothes, spices and mehndi here, while at the same time enabling Reena's lesbianism scope for public recognition and validation; the paan-walla is probably the first person in the film's 'Indian' community to be subjected to the vicissitudes of having a lesbian daughter or sister who is also willing to carry her sister's baby for her. This public recognition of Reena's sexuality, however, is the first step towards the incorporation of this (un)familiar sexuality within the scheme of things Meenu well-intentionedly orders for her children.

The Lesbian at Home

Reena's pregnancy finally permits an interface between Reena's life with her more militant dyke friends and weekend visits to her mother's suburban home. Here, Reena seems most happy on the fringes—the yard where she does her mother's nails while they talk about male role models, or the basement where she fixes the sprinkler settings which her mother seems unable to not disrupt in the course of each week. Once inside the house, Reena is subject to censure and is unable to hold out against the expectations of suburban and middle-class stability, order and continuity that Sarita and Mitch, supported by Meenu, embody. Living in the city, not in the suburbs, Reena's lifestyle seems to the others to be hedonistic and unproductive even as Reena's photographs begin to appear on magazine covers. Between inside and outside, however, the liminal space of the yard, where Ganatra set most of her movie's outdoor scenes more due to budget constraints, offers Reena a Moebius-strip's worth of space within which to plant herself and retain her roots. Ganatra's construction of Reena's lesbianism thus as liminal might not have been intentional; her DVD track lists shooting in yards as one of the stratagems of getting a low-budget film made, but the film's development has consistency enough to merit the view that Reena, who would be stifled indoors by the requirements of 'convention' can retain her own family when in the meeting place between home and world. Her own family becomes more expansive once outdoors—Sarita and Meenu are both more patient and confiding, and Mitch is less oppressive when separated from the security blanket of American material prosperity. The great American middle-class values of having a suburban home with an immaculate lawn are employed by these Indians so as to make the lawn, the yard, signify as the place where 'home' is, even as the house—perhaps of America itself—is still not large enough to hold the many shapes of multicultural difference that come to it.

The house at the same time is also the stronghold of 'Indian' traditionalism, which unites here with similar American values; Reena's city apartment forms a subcultural space that this mainstream 'home' will not recognize easily, at least as far as the Indian diaspora is involved. In contrast is Lisa's Italian-American mother's supportive response to her daughter's lesbianism, though this is not to be read as dialectically opposite to Reena's mother's diffidence. While Meenu is able to accept Lisa, with her otherness, as a lesbian, she is still unable to give Reena due recognition for her orientation and emotional experiences in the course of an everyday life structured around relatively more heteronormative community structures. Lisa's mother, on the other hand, is represented as an individual whose Italian-American difference has long since assimilated into a larger 'American' culture. Never represented amongst other members of her own once-diasporic community, Lisa's mother is a more 'western' individual herself, dapper in denims and short hair, unlike Meenu with her strange pyjama-like outdoor trousers and her need to keep up her 'Indian-ness'. However, these differences or assimilations are not evaluated as negative by the text; presenting both as designs for living, Ganatra is able to inflect Meenu's traditionalism itself with an accommodatory power. Meenu is able to retain her non-Western roots and pass them onto her children, and later, possibly, her grandchild. These very roots are what Reena seeks, in the film's acknowledgement of her racial difference from the white Lisa's more comfortable blending into the surroundings of the largely white world the women move in. *Chutney Popcorn*'s lesbian pregnancy thus enables two worlds to meet along their margins such that osmotic exchanges are possible even as the core is not suddenly marred by change that no one is yet ready for. Reena's identity as an out lesbian is very much necessary for the text to produce its critique of the family, dismantling the heteronormativity characteristic of the diasporic version of the American dream. Further, Reena is neither the economic nor the social prototype for success this 'dream' mandates, being at best a resistant participant in the capitalistic life of the global city of New York, with her dyke-ness, her girlfriend, her lesbian pregnancy and her art, she is a very queer 'other' role model.

Chutney Popcorn must instead be read as a meditation on the meanings of the word 'lesbian'—as a dedicated lover of women who would also be a mother to her baby and daughter to her first-generation Indian mother, Reena symbolizes queer alternatives to heteronormativity that are not often visible within the Oedipalized logic of diaspora as depending on descent from the 'seed' of an implicitly male ancestor and in modern times, as the inauthentic other of the 'nation'. *Chutney Popcorn*'s repertoire includes a refreshing range of normal-looking women characters of various ages and persuasions who make life in a new country more than liveable. Meenu and Reena both re-world their new worlds—Meenu melds Indian with

American even as Reena's version of the mixing reveals to her yet another possibility for mixing, this time of 'lesbian' with 'family'. *Chutney Popcorn*'s sexualization of the narrative of cultural contact, conflict, acculturation and assimilation is a queer critique of otherwise normative narratives of heterosexual fulfilment attained by diasporic protagonists within a de-sexualized, racialized, diasporic environment where only marginal attention is paid to the normalization of heterosexual privilege in various forms. *Chutney Popcorn*'s successful re-accommodation of Reena within the household headed by her mother however, does gloss over a number of very specific questions; if Reena's mother had not come around, how long would Reena's resources have stretched, one wonders. Being in love with/desiring a same-sex partner is, even in Ganatra's 'emancipated' world, might not be as pleasant an experience without social infrastructure to match.

A Prolegomena as Conclusion

Indian cinematic traditions till the 1990s used the formulae of the mainstream film in inventive ways to express a broad range of relationships, mostly heterosexual and homosocial; the latter narratives, as compelling critical readings have shown, were amenable to the depiction of homoerotic themes too. This 'traditional homosocial formula' as Thomas Waugh describes it, in use till the turn of the century however, was soon replaced by a 'growing ambiguity and complexity, playfulness and boldness' (Waugh 2001: 285) within mainstream cinema in response no doubt, to the increasing visibility of a gay and lesbian discourse in the public realm in a big way in the wake of the medicalization of homosexuality following the AIDS-related public health crises of the 1990s. Where the male buddy–buddy film was indeed a constant implicit signifier on the mainstream screen, female bonding and female friendship still made for an unfamiliar spectacle, and few films dealt with these themes as centrally as they dealt with male homosociality and homoeroticism. Queer audiences can become 'perverse spectators' to borrow Janet Staiger's formulation, and fetishize even momentary appearances of the (un)familiar female desire (2000: 2) as Shohini Ghosh (2002) and Gayatri Gopinath have shown in brilliant readings of various Indian and transnational Indian cinematic texts, thus allowing 'impossible' female desires entry into public cultures (Gopinath 2000). Transnational films like Sarif's, Chadha's and Ganatra's however are referencing cinematic traditions that go beyond Indian ones in their production of diasporic Indian subjectivities. *The World Unseen* and *Bend It Like Beckham* for example unite the genre of the 'femme' film with that of the sports film while *Chutney Popcorn* pushes the logic of the 'femme film' as far as it will go by revealing all the femmes to be nothing by new-age lesbian dykes even as *The World Unseen* performs the opposite translation, converting the butch body into an onscreen femme one to perhaps make the film more marketable.

Chutney Popcorn and *Bend It Like Beckham* taken together, in their adherence to the conventions of comedy, take representations of the homosexual beyond the clines of victim or tragic hero. *The World Unseen* (the novel) attempts to historicize an older diaspora and in doing so extends the rarely narrativized history of the hybridized non-white butch woman backwards. As none of them is a coming-out narrative (though Miriam's story in *The World Unseen* may fit loosely into the parameters of the coming out genre), and deal with either those who are already 'out' or are not lesbian or gay and therefore do not need to be 'out,' these films allow exploration of the possibilities available to film-makers that are often not explored in the rush to make overtly positive images about queer South Asian subjects. Taken together, these films also enable examination of what it means to make or disable gay/lesbian community, membership with and cross-affiliations with other communities, including the heterosexual, and to consider the long-term implications of remaining 'out' and of never coming out, to evaluate the nature of the interventions these cinematic texts make to queer our notions of sexuality. Some questions that arise are—are viable visible identities for non-heterosexual subjects being produced? Does their visibility guarantee subversiveness and positive transgressions of the normative? Do these representations queer anything? Is the non-heteronormative articulated within this cinematic space by gender crossing as much as by gender normativity?

These films treat the space of the home (also extended into nation or diaspora) and the traditions it embodies as culturally valuable, and therefore not to be forfeited by the female protagonist; however, these spaces bring with them the architecture of the hegemonic and the heteropatriarchal. *Chutney Popcorn* is able to reimagine traditions to accommodate the 'family outlaw' that is the lesbian through the labours of the literal figure of the reproductive woman, while *Bend It Like Beckham* contains the subversive challenges posed by feminine labours on the sporting field and at home to enshrine normative femininities squarely within the renegotiated diasporic home even as the film version of *The World Unseen* displaces onto a fairy-tale conclusion the impossibilities of imagining (un)familiar femininity in the diaspora even though the novel the film originates from can imagine precisely this for us.

Chutney Popcorn's emplacement of the lesbian woman within the heart of family and ethnic community ultimately prevents it from describing the lesbian woman's specific outlaw status outside of her immediate community. The film thus bypasses the important problem of the creation of networks of support and sustenance for the lesbian beyond the 'virtual equality' available to some. All these films narrativize the female subject within diaspora. *Bend It Like Beckham* anxiously proscribes the possibilities of a queer female diasporic Indian subject even as *Chutney Popcorn* dialogically articulates precisely such a subjectivity; *The World Unseen* scripts a history for being butch/dyke that goes well beyond whiteness or Stonewall. Where films like NHD, ICTS, and *Sancharam* explicitly produce various forms of 'coming out' challenging and reinforcing homonormativities about what it means to be visible or invisible as a sexualized being, *Chutney Popcorn* provides a critique both of homonormativity in its many ironic and comic discussions of what it means to be not just lesbian, but also straight. In doing this, *Chutney Popcorn* queers the space of heterosexuality as much as it routinizes female–female love and desire even as it does not endorse monogamous devotion. However, it would be naïve to believe that even for a marriage-and-family-oriented ethnic group culture, that lesbians with babies would be automatically acceptable if the babies are not conceived from within the approved gene pool. *Chutney Popcorn* makes the lesbian quite visible, but only within the economies of biological family. At the same time, *Chutney Popcorn's* deployment of lesbian sexuality, in placing women within an 'actively sexual role' makes it impossible to re-place them back within a chaste, passive, de-eroticized femininity within which both diasporic and national modernities have sought to keep them, paradoxically expressed through films that express later-day diasporic idealisms, like *Bend It Like Beckham* and *The World Unseen*. In representing protagonists of Indian origin as challenging heteronormativity, these films allow the (un)familiar to enter public cultures, but even so, much care has to be exercised so as not to reify the female subject back into normative economies of family, tradition and diasporic honour.

References

Agarwal, Priya. 1991. *Passage from India: Post-1965 Indian Immigrants and Their Children: Conflicts, Concerns and Solutions.* Palos Verdes, CA: Yucati.

Arora, Anupama. 2007. 'Rituals of Queer Diaspora in Nisha Ganatra's Chutney Popcorn', *South Asian Popular Culture*, 5(1): 31–43.

Bacon, Jean. 1996. *Lifelines: Community, Family and Assimilation Among Asian Indian immigrants.* New York: Oxford University Press.

Bend It Like Beckham. Dir. Gurinder Chadha. UK, 2002. DVD, Fox Searchlight, 2007.

Butler, Judith. 1990. 'Performative Acts and Gender Constitution: An Essay in Phenomenology and Feminist Theory', in Sue-Ellen Case (ed.), *Performing Feminisms: Feminist Critical Theory and Practice.* pp. 270–82. Baltimore: The Johns Hopkins University Press.

Calhoun, Cheshire. 2000. *Feminism, the Family, and the Politics of the Closet: Lesbian and Gay Displacement.* USA: Oxford University Press.

Caudwell, Jayne. 2009. 'Girlfight and Bend it Like Beckham: Screening Women, Sport, and Sexuality', *Journal of Lesbian Studies*, 13:3: 255–271.

Chutney Popcorn. Dir. Nisha Ganatra. Nisha Ganatra, USA, 1999. DVD, Wolfe Video, 2000.

Dostana. Dir. Tarun Mansukhani. Perf. Priyanka Chopra, John Abraham, Abhishek Bachchan, 2008.

Fire. Dir. Deepa Mehta. Canada/India, 1996/1998. DVD, Eagle, 2008.

Fainman-Frenkel, R. 2004. 'Ordinary Secrets and the Bounds of Memory', *Research in African Literatures*, 35.4: 52–65.

Gandhi, M. K. 1927. *Autobiography/The Story of My Experiments with Truth.* Ahmedabad: Navjivan, 2007.

Giardina, M. D. 2003. 'Bending in like Beckham' in *The Global Popular: Stylish Hybridity, Performativity, and the Politics of Representation. Journal of Sport & Social Issues*, 27(1), 65–82.

Gibson, Margaret A. 1988. 'Accommodation without Assimilation: Sikh Immigrants in an American High School', *Ithaca*, New York: Cornell University Press.

Gilroy, Paul. 1993. *The Black Atlantic: Modernity and Double Consciousness.* New York and London: Verso.

Ghosh, Shohini. 2002. 'Queer Pleasures for Queer People: Film, Television, and Queer Sexuality in India', in *Queering India* (ed.) Ruth Vanita. New York and London: Routledge.

Gopinath, Gayatri. 2000. 'Queering Bollywood: Alternative Sexualities in Popular Indian Cinema', in Andrew Grossman (ed.) *Queer Asian Cinema: Shadows in the Shade*. New York: Haworth Press, pp. 283–297.

———. 2005. *Impossible Desires: Queer Diaspora and South Asian Public Cultures*. New Delhi: Seagull.

Gunning, Tom. 1984. 'The Cinema of Attraction[s]', *Wide Angle*, 8 (3–4): 64. Also published as 'The Cinema of Attractions', *Early Cinema: Space, Frame, Narrative*. 1990. (ed.) Thomas Elsaesser. London: British Film Institute.

Holmlund, Christine. 1991. 'When is a Lesbian not a Lesbian: The Lesbian Continuum and the Mainstream Femme Film', *Camera Obscura* (25–26): 145–78.

Hogan, D. P. 2000. 'Life cycle', in E. F. Borgatta and R. J. V. Montgomery (eds.), *Encyclopedia of Sociology*, pp. 1623–7. New York: Macmillan.

I Can't Think Straight. Dir. Shamim Sarif. 2007. DVD, Enlightenment Films, 2008.

Lindner, K. 2011. '"There is a reason why Sporty Spice is the only one of them without a fella..": The "Lesbian" Potential of Bend it Like Beckham', *New Review of Film & Television Studies* 9 (2): 204–23.

Mahn, Churnjeet. 'The Queer Limits of Pratibha Parmar's Nina's Heavenly Delights,' *Journal of Lesbian Studies*, 17(3–4): 317–28.

Maira, Sunaina. 1995. 'Making Room for a Hybrid Space: Reconsidering Second-Generation Identity', *Sanskriti*, 6 (1): 6.

———. 1999. 'Identity Dub: The Paradoxes of an Indian American Youth Subculture (New York mix)', *Cultural Anthropology*, 14(1): 29–60.

May, Claudia. 'What's love got to do with it?: (Un)bending identities and conventions in Gurinda Chadha's *Bend it Like Beckham*', *Culture and Religion: An Interdisciplinary Journal* , 11(3): 247–76.

Manalansan, Martin. 2007. 'Queer Intersections: Sexuality and Gender in Migration Studies', *International Migration Review*, 40(1): 224–49.

Mulvey, Laura. 1990. 'Visual Pleasure and Narrative Cinema', in Patricia Erens (ed.) *Issues in Feminist Film Criticism*. Bloomington: Indiana University Press.

———. 1975. 'Visual Pleasure and Narrative Cinema', *Screen*, 16(3): 6–18.

Nina's Heavenly Delights. Dir. Pratibha Parmar. 2006. DVD, Regent Films, 2006.

Rastogi, Pallavi. 2008. *Afrindian Fictions: Diaspora, Race and National in South Africa*. Ohio: Ohio State University Press.

Rao, Raja R. 2000. 'Memories Pierce the Heart: Homoeroticism, Bollywood-Style', in Andrew Grossman (ed.) *Queer Asian Cinema: Shadows in the Shade*. New York: Haworth Press.

Rings, Guido. 2011. 'Questions of Identity: Cultural Encounters in Gurinder Chadha's Bend It Like Beckham', *Journal of Popular Film and Television*, 01 (39): 114–123.

Sancharam. Dir. Ligy Pullapally. 2005. DVD, Wolfe Video, 2006.

Sarif, Shamim. 2001. *The World Unseen*. London: Headline Book Publishing.

The World Unseen. Dir. Shamim Sarif. 2007. Enlightenment Films, DVD, 2008.

'Think Hatke'. Virgin Mobile advertisement. 15 April 2009. www.virginmobile.in/tv_ads.php

Sardar, Ziauddin. 1998. 'Dilip Kumar Made Me Do It', in Ashish Nandy (ed.), *The Secret Politics of Our Desires*. London: Zed Press.

Sedgwick, Eve K. 1990. *Epistemology of the Closet*. Berkeley: California University Press.

―――. 1985. *Between Men: English Literature and Male Homosocial Desire*. New York: Columbia University Press.

Staiger, Janet. 2000. *Perverse Spectators: The Practices of Film Reception*. New York: New York University Press.

Thiara, Ravi K. 2001. 'Imagining? Ethnic Identity and Indians in South Africa', in Crispin Bates (ed.) *Community, Empire and Migration: South Asians in Diaspora*. Hampshire, UK: Palgrave.

Tinker, Hugh. 1996. *A New System of Slavery: The Export of Indian Labour Overseas 1830–1920*. 1974. Oxford: Oxford University Press.

Treagus, Mandy. 2002. 'Not Bent At All: Bend It Like Beckham, Girls' Sport and the Spectre of the Lesbian', *M/C: A Journal of Media and Culture*, 5(6).

Warn, Sarah. 2003. 'Dropping Lesbian Romance from Beckham the Right Decision', *After Ellen*. http://www.afterellen.com/archive/ellen/Movies/beckham.html

Wakil, S. Panvez, C.M. Siddique and F.A. Wakil. 1981. 'Between Two Cultures: A Study in Socialization of Children of Immigrants', *Journal of Marriage and the Family*, 43 (4): 929–40.

Waugh, Thomas. 2001. 'Queer Bollywood, or 'I'm the player, you're the naive one': Patterns of sexual subversion in recent Indian popular cinema', in M. Tinkcom and A. Villarejo (ed.) *Keyframes: Popular Cinema and Cultural Studies*. New York: Routledge.

Van Gennep, A. 1960 (Original in 1909). *The Rites of Passage*. London: Routledge & Kegan Paul.

Vicinus, Martha. 1993. '"They Wonder to Which Sex I Belong?" The Historical Roots of the Modern Lesbian Identity', in *The Lesbian and Gay Studies Reader*, eds. Henry Abelove, Michèle Barale, and David M. Halperin. New York: Routledge, pp. 432–52.

3

The (Un)Familiar in the Heart of the Family

Portraits of the Lesbian as a Married Woman

Unlike the butch lesbian, the womanly-woman, or the woman who does not defy the conventions of gender is more often to be found within her 'normal' environment, that of marriage, and within the family as a contributor to its upkeep by providing domestic, sexual and emotional labour and many times, contributing financially as well. Enmeshed, as it were, within compulsory heterosexuality, within marriage, child-rearing and heteronormative forms of sociality, these women might not have access to forms of lesbian community; often, it might even be that they desire women but have not acted upon these desires. Within literary scholarship, two dominant streams of thought emerge with respect to the woman-loving-woman who is feminine; one view describes 'female friendships' such as these as asexual and lacking in a genital erotic component, especially when these friendships are located in the centuries previous to ours (Faderman 1981). Lillian Faderman's *Surpassing the Love of Men* (1981) studies 'romantic friendships and love' between women in the Western tradition from the Renaissance to the present, while *Odd Girls and Twilight Lovers* examines different facets of identity creation and the emergence especially of butch and femme identities in the American context from the nineteenth century to the present. Faderman (1981) states that while erotic affinities between women might be primary, these need not ever have had a sexual component, but this view is contested by the other school of thought. At the same time, scholars like Vanita (2005) and Faderman (1981: 26–31) among others shows that 'friendship' might have been a cloak to deflect homophobic attention from what is a primary erotic and emotional relationship. Female friendships, as Vanita shows in *Sappho and the Virgin Mary*, might very well be sexual with asexuality or celibacy signalling that these women do not function or do not desire to function sexually within the heterosexual realm even as they aspire to erotic, emotional and sexual fulfilment within same-sex relationships (Vanita 1996). Martha Vicinus' term 'occasional lovers of women' might therefore be a more accurate description of women within the heterosexual libidinal economy, but looking for a place within an (un)familiar one (Vicinus 1993). As the texts in this chapter show, 'female friendship' or female bonding need not function so as to preclude female homoeroticism or female homosexuality. Instead, as we shall see, with one or two exceptions, most of the texts we study here do have women acting upon their erotic or sexual desires within an (un)familiar libidinal economy even as they desire freedom from heterosexual marital activities.

But as the title of this chapter suggests, if the women are already married women, their place within the familiar orders of heterosexual maritality must also perhaps be inflected by these female friendships? Castle's *The Apparitional Lesbian* uses the trope of 'ghosting', that is, the de-materialization of desires into non-corporeal forms like ghosts, apparitions and visions, to study how lesbian desire appears within what might otherwise be erroneously taken to be heteronormative sites of action. The lesbian 'visitations' that Castle studies suggests that while love between women is a real, spiritual, and, mystical experience for the women involved, its depth and validity might not be endorsed by the world around, leading to its becoming 'apparitional'. As we shall study further, this 'ghosting' of female same-sex love *within* a heterosexual economy, involving marriage and child-rearing within the marriage, literally makes familiars out of women-lovers; the women lovers of women move in and out of the marital home like ghosts because the primacy of their presence is never recognized, and when recognized, might be the occasion for terrible reparative violence. As might be seen in the story 'Home' in Ashwini Sukhthankar's anthology *Facing the Mirror* (1999), where once the (un)familiar love between Kanchana and Amba is suspected by their respective families, a number of violences, including forced electrocutions to brainwash lesbian love out of Amba's mind, lead to the destruction of any semblance of marital normalcy (Natarajan in Sukthankar 1999: 90–115). But Kanchana's earlier escape from her husband leads to the union of the two women almost a decade later, when Amba's similar escape can be arranged despite her still living in the panopticon of scrutiny by husband, children and community. Amba's and Kanchana's (un)familiar love for one another might not be intelligible within the sanctioned 'network of desires' permitted to heterosexuality, but they are very much legible when looked at from a non-heteronormative location. While lack of sexual subjectivity might initially seem to be a debilitating place within which to locate any lesbians, transgressive possibilities may also be recovered from an analysis of accounts of women who only occasionally love other women, or who do not act upon (un)familiar desires, that is women who are celibate or asexual because they have not found the right female partners because such accounts are resistant to easy recuperation within heterosexual marriage and conjugality. Offering alternatives to these, female same-sex love in the form of female friendship supplies a different framework for considering love, locating the most desired love-relationships not entirely within sexual prowess and its everyday verification in performance, but within the realms of companionship and emotional reciprocity that offer forms of sustenance that might be missing within cross-sexual bonds.

The category of 'femme' is a useful one in this analysis as it effectively suggests a femininity that displaces male masculinity as its only or central fulcrum of desire and subjectivity. Instead, femme-ness suggests femininities whose primary desire is for other women, but with one qualifier for the purpose of this book; the femme woman insofar as this book is concerned is not always a part of the butch–femme couple; rather, the femme woman, or the womanly-lesbian is in much of the lesbian fiction written in India today, the consort of other similarly feminine women. With the exception of the few texts we studied in Chapter 1, the butch–femme pair is not the norm whereas the femme–femme pair can be seen playing out across a range of texts. This chapter will analyse literary representations of the womanly-woman who loves other women in continuation of the ones studied earlier in previous chapters where 'femme films' as a tool for representing (un)familiar loves had been studied. Where a teleological movement is implicit or sometimes explicit in the logic of many of the texts in the previous chapter, with the (un)familiar 'subject' coming to solidify in the person of the 'lesbian' who must leave behind the traditional spaces of the home in order to attain subjectivity, the texts in this chapter operate in zones of slippage between homosexuality and heterosexuality. My use of the word (un)familiar to convey this slippage, to suggest that female same-sex love is part of a spectrum of sexualities, and dialogic in its relation to heterosexuality, thus, tries to find a way out of what we have called homonormativity—that is, solidified, often non-negotiable uni-directional assumptions about what 'modern gay and lesbian identities' should be. That the (un)familiar dialogues with more normative forms of sexuality and kinship arrangements is borne out by the various strategies of struggle, resistance, and sometimes, victory, as is evidenced in the texts analysed in this chapter. In almost all of them, female same-sex love is in a dialogue, however unequal, with heterosexual structures and requirements; in many instances, the (un)familiar emerges from rigid structures of heteronormativity, which however are revealed to be not as invulnerable as might be initially supposed. Thus, even though 'femme-ness' might appear to be a less radical subversion of the economies of sex and gender, the texts here show that femininity separated from its coupling to masculinity as the complementary other produces a radical reassessment of sexuality itself. While the butch lesbian's physical presence might indeed queer or destabilize the economy of gender, the femme lesbian's love for other women produces the less visible subversion of heteronormativity. In remaining invisibile, femme-ness need not be treated as the more regressive form of female same-sex love; rather, because it is unintelligible to the seeing eye, femme-lesbianism might well be more invulnerable to homophobia than its more visible counterparts. On the other hand, however, feminine lesbian women, 'passing' at least to the eye of the viewer as straight, might also find it that much harder to establish community or togetherness because the codes of femme-ness of femininity, that desires femininity instead of merely identifying with it, are so fluid. This chapter will study the implications of less communal forms of linkage and relationship than the more public ones that featured in the previous chapters, both at the level of personal performance and public politics. First we will study the eroticized mother–daughter bonding in Shani Mootoo's short story 'Wake Up,' set in a third-generation Indian diaspora in Trinidad, followed by an examination of similar sister–sister bondings in selected writings from Mootoo, Chitra Banerjee Divakaruni, Uma Parameswaran, and Kamala Das where the confirmed or possible incestuous bonds between sisters heightens the transgressiveness of these 'friendships,' and also suggests that the proscription of same-sex love has affinities with the proscription of 'incestuous' love for one's siblings. Lastly I follow some themes already suggested in Das's 'The Sandal Trees', through works by Manju Kapur and Mary Ann Mohanraj which figure lesbian desire as an entry into creativity and locate alienation and barrenness in heteronormativity. Taken together, these texts enable reflection on the invisibility of the 'femme' in public discourses, while simultaneously outlining theorizations of femininity that exist outside heteronormativity, suggesting that despite the diarticulations of invisibility, still there are spots of (un)familiar subversion and resistance.

A Portrait of the Lesbian as a Mother-Lover?

One very prominent theme in lesbian writing all over the world, that contemporary lesbian Indian writing also shares is that of love between sisters. The eroticization of the mother–daughter bond is not frequently seen, except in a couple of instances, where the protagonists are almost a generation younger than the women they fall in love with. One such instance is that of Anamika in Abha Dawesar's *Babyji* falling in love with 'India.' Another instance is Roma Bansal's *One Afternoon* (2008), where a college student, Ria, falls in love with her English teacher, Radha. Obviously older than the 'heroine,' this teacher's sexiness, articulateness and of course attraction towards her student enables the latter to come out from her relationship enriched, both academically and personally. The heroine makes a sacrifice of her own personal happiness to that of her lover's by reuniting her with the husband from whom she had unhappily separated a few years ago, even as she herself walks into the waiting arms of her male friend Manav, who both knows about her love for her teacher, and is himself in love with her all the same. The teacher–student bond is an eroticization and amplification of the possibilities inherent in the mother–daughter bond in that the older person cares for and nourishes the younger one much like a mother would. Further, the role of the teacher as a mentor also permits the younger protagonist's entry into a new, sometimes wonderful, sometimes threatening world. In Bansal's picture-perfect Ahmedabad, though, Ria Rathore only has to strut around like Veronica of *Archie'* Comics; nothing seems to be lacking in her world. In fact, the pretext for the book seems to be that Ria's banal existence must somehow be enlivened, and a lesbian episode seems perfectly in order to add colour to Ria's supposed 'feminism'. Thriving in stereotypes that do not bear much examination, the novel is marketed by its publisher, Rupa, as a light read; while the premise—that of a college girl falling in love with her teacher, and things falling apart as a consequence when the student goes away to other educational shores—is indeed an attractive one, Bansal is ill-equipped to do much with it. Indian Writing in English still awaits a serious representation of the lesbian equivalent of 'eros-eromenos,' to borrow Ruth Vanita's accurate identification in *Sappho and the Virgin Mary* of the intra-female teacher–student pair as also being a continuation of the Greek trope of cross-generational love between men. Glimpses can be had in Ismat Chughtai's *Terhi Lakeer, Lihaaf* etc (see Chapter 4), but here I read Shani Mootoo's short story 'Wake Up' from *Out on Main Street* as enabling an interrogation of the role of female (un)familiar subject's life through its focus on a literal mother–daughter pair's mingled love and hatred for one another.

Ancestors for colonized female subjects

In *Black Skin, White Masks*, Franz Fanon (1967) speculates upon the nature of a black man's identity, mining psychoanalytic formulations of the Oedipal complex to arrive at his theory of black masculinity. The shifting nature of identifications that constitute identity and how they are pinioned by the subject's location in metropolis or colony are a very important part of Fanon's construction of colonial masculinity: 'Attend showings of a Tarzan film in the Antilles and in Europe. In the Antilles, the young Negro identifies himself de facto with Tarzan against the Negroes. This is much more difficult for him in a European theatre, for the rest of the audience, which is white, automatically identifies him with the savages on screen' (Fanon 1967: 152–53). Fanon, however, does not have much to say about femininity in the colonies. What is a colonial femininity modelled on? Often, his constructions of white femininity is based on many of the same stereotypes that Fanon identifies as feminizing and sexualizing black men; the white woman is a neurotic hysteric. Of the black woman, Fanon concedes in perhaps the most damning indictment of his erasure, that 'As for the woman of colour, I know nothing of her' (Fanon 1967: 179–80). While I do not agree with the dismissal of Fanon as offering possibilities for a feminist assessment, Fanon's discussion does focus upon the family romance of the black man's identification and coming to manhood via the white 'father' not vis-à-vis desire for a black mother, but through the person of the white woman. The black woman's (or the coloured woman's) path to socalization is largely untouched in Fanon's account, and it is here that Shani Mootoo's work supplies an important set of narrativizations.

Mootoo's short stories, especially her short-stories where her protagonists are subjected to the pull and tug of alternately confirming and denying one or other identity as 'authentic' in order to 'belong'. However, Mootoo's work not only racializes the female subject, but also interrupts this subject's implied heterosexuality even as it permits us to meditate upon the subject-position of the post/colonial female subject of colour, generally ignored in the often exclusively black/white dichotomy that characterizes post/ colonial theory west of the Indian Ocean. In what follows, I assess how (un)familiar desire figures in the construction of femininity in the Indian diaspora, both the old diaspora of indenture in Trinidad and the new diaspora of transnational capitalism today, at third-remove, in Canada. The (un)familiarity of this desire has disturbing implications for home, diaspora and this diaspora's place in modern Trinidad. *Out on Main Street* (1993) is a collection of short stories that maps a spatial biography of the feminine subject; the younger, adolescent subject is mostly located within an un-named third-world Indian diaspora, which we can safely assume is Trinidad, while the adult woman is housed within a first-world diaspora, in Canada. In all of Mootoo's work, the figure of the female child is primary. In Trinidad, this child can be a trope for the Indian community's fledgling presence within the black–white binary structure of West Indian society. The child's gender is a clue to the social role occupied by women within this society; the infantilization of women in various ways hampers their development, stunting and literally maddening them spiritually and socially. Such a traumatization is presented in *Cereus Blooms at Night*, where the infantilization of the female subject follows the eruption of (un)familiar desire in the space of the colonial diasporic home (Mootoo 1996). In the text, the socially disruptive power of female homosexuality, with its non-reproductive, yet creative energies is particularly manifest though the 'lesbian track' of the story lasts only a few pages. However, the violence that the vengeful patriarch will unleash will fall not upon the lesbian lovers but on one, more precious to them, perhaps, than one another—their child. This child will, of course, not carry the blood of both the women, but is nevertheless theirs because they have raised it together, but have had to leave behind as a veritable hostage. In depicting this child's response to this brutalization, Mootoo tries to build an alternative to the traditional home; a home for (un)familiar desire where the destabilizing potential of female homosexuality need not be a liminal, hounded presence, but central to the architecture. The battered yet healing protagonist, Mala, from the very beginning shows compassion and tenderness towards the afflicted; rather than being the jealous spy from patriarchy, her way of maintaining the peace and the happiness of home is to remain watchful on behalf of her mother's happiness. Nevertheless, this new 'house' need not last forever but may need to be rebuilt every generation as is evident from *Valmiki's Daughter* and several stories in *Out on Main Street*. In comparison, the relationship between the adolescent narrator of 'Wake Up' who is a few years older than Mala, is locked in a relationship of love and hatred, feeling abjected by the image of the mother as monstrous while at the same time harbouring desire for the mother. While the child narrators in both cases do not feel equal desire for the mother, there are significant continuities in their desire to protect the mother from the violence the father can bring. While *Cereus Blooms* provides an alternative rendition of the Freudian Oedipal narrative in placing the little girl's fear of literal rape by the father at the centre of the narrative, 'Wake Up' also maps an alternative to the path to heterosexual socialization that the oedipal model discusses in greatest detail. In narrativizing young girls growing up, Mootoo permits (un)familiar desires to enter the world very early; figuring mother–daughter eros as entering through the trope of the dream, the story invokes not only the framework of the familiar this book has outlined, but also begs to be considered in light of mainstream imaginings of the mother–daughter story as part of our unconscious.

At first glance, 'Wake Up' seems to construct lesbianism as a way out of the subjugation of women by heterosexuality. Traditionally psychoanalytic understandings of identity formation, from Freud to Kristeva, have typically tended to split desire from identification in their study of the mother–child bond and the creation of femininity therefrom. Meaning, a subject's desire for one sex can only be obtained through the subject's concomitant identification with the other sex. Desire and identification are treated as mutually exclusive, with the successful attainment of one meaning that, correspondingly, the other is repressed. Critics have commented upon the circularity of this logic, pointing to places where, for instance, in Freud, identification itself is gendered masculine and male, identified with the father even as Freud is concerned with theorizing pre-oedipal desire, which by definition should be prior to gendering as Diana Fuss notes (Warner 2002: 54). While desire and identification may indeed be localized on separate individuals, there is no reason to assume that the two may not focus upon the same person; simply put, one might desire a person so much that one ends up becoming like that person. In the case of the female child as with the male, desire for the mother may add to the sense of identification the child is supposed to feel towards her. Desire and identification may indeed coincide, and the female subject's identity, as 'Wake Up' shows, may be formed by a complex set of identifications and 'disidentifications' with the mother which may be 'impossible' to imagine except through the vehicle of the dream or even the nightmare.

(Un)Familiar and Impossible Identifications with one's Mother

Within Freudian or Lacanian psychoanalysis what would be called a primary identification with the mother is a desiring/identifying recognition of the mother as one's love object; here, the mother is everything to the child. This is placed in the pre-oedipal stage in the Freudian system, and in the pre-mirror stage in the Lacanian one. If lesbian love theoretically at least, entails both desire for the mother and desire to be like her with respect at least to some parts of one's femininity, lesbian love for the mother then, in psychoanalytic terms, should predate subject formation, and would be located in what we can call a pre-subject relation with the mother. Psychoanalysis has been pillaged for identifying same-sex love as a return or a regression to the undifferentiated, pre-subject state and thus denying its existence within fully socialized or mature individuals. A strong critique of this reading may instead see lesbianism as contesting castration, as 'a restorative strategy which seeks to repair the losses, denigrations, thwartings that a patriarchal culture inflicts on the girl in her primary relation to the mother' (Fletcher in Shepherd *et al.* 1989: 105). Examining 'Wake Up' with this in mind, it is possible to see the story as presenting the story of the mother's castration, the daughter's recognition of castration as a threat, and thereon, her refusal to be castrated, that is, her refusal to become her mother. Desire for the mother complicates the fear of castration the daughter feels, while identification with the father is not total, as the daughter refuses to cognize a masculinity that is implicitly pain-giving, choosing instead to make an (un)familiar masculinity located on her person. In 'Wake Up,' the desiring subject sees her future in her mother, whom she desires erotically, albeit in a dream the exit from which is necessitated by the arrival of the 'monstrous' mother in real life. Not wishing to be like her suffering mother, she identifies with her father, but after first recognizing herself in her mother's image, that is, by refusing identification with the mother, but her refusal to identify itself indicates that some kinship, similarity and likeness—identity—exists. At the same time, the social coordinates of Angenie's awakening also implicate her within the 'negative Oedipal complex' which was Freud's term for the socialization path taken by the 'little girl' who is (mistakenly) attracted to her mother rather than to her father, as should have been; the word 'negative' implies an evaluation of lesbian desire that was, as this story shows, characteristic not only of Freud's times, but also of life on an insular island nation.

While love for the mother takes the female subject back to the very beginning of consciousness, this story's location of it within the dream-narrative of an adolescent girl enables a meditation on the criteria that determine our choice of our first conscious, self-chosen love-objects. Angenie, the adolescent dreamer and narrator of the story, is woken up most nights by her mother who knows her husband to be having an extra-marital affair. The loss of selfhood the mother feels at this is also an anguish shared by her four children; all of them sense this to be a betrayal by their father of their mother. Identification with the mother, thus, provides the children with an empathetic entry into her distraught condition in the many months over which this affair seems to have continued without any acknowledgement or revelation of it by the father to his family. Angenie is the oldest of the children, and perhaps the one whom, logically, the mother would choose for emotional reassurance. At fifteen, Angenie is also at the threshold of adulthood. Angenie is also at a border-crossing for another very important reason; this threshold also is one where the subject finds its sense of, self, challenged, penetrated and redefined by its encounters with the 'other' the desire for love if not for a lover. Adolescent longings may offer important portents for the future, Angenie's story suggests.

Angenie's mother awakens her at three o'clock in the morning, asking her where her father is, but implicitly asking Angenie do the stoic 'duty of the night nurse' and calm her mother down with assurances that are patently untrue, yet are calculated to cajole her into some comfort at her odious situation as virtually a grass widow. Angenie is both proud of the power of her situation, being the one whom her mother has chosen to give her comfort and aware of the abjectness of their roles in the scheme of things in their father's life. Their mother is insignificant to their father, plainly; Angenie's sense of self struggles against the fear that she herself will soon become insignificant to the father and to any man who places her in the same position as her mother is in now. Sensitive to the privilege of being the chosen comforter and aware subterraneously that this is a significant opportunity,

Angenie worries that her other siblings will suddenly awaken and 'jeopardize the coveted one-to-oneness I find myself afforded with my mother on these nights' (Mootoo 1993: 35). Her desire to monopolize her mother, if only momentarily, and to comfort her efficiently, balances out her concomitant disgust at her mother's lowly position in the world. Desire and disavowal battle it out, and the first line of the story suddenly offers a major clue: 'Angenie, Angenie, wake up,' opens the story. Coming back to this beginning after reading the whole story, Angenie having been almost awake, 'alighting on sleep the way a butterfly barely samples petals of flowers along its path' (Mootoo 1993: 33) becomes possessed with special significance. Angenie's mother only awakens a desire, a knowledge, a memory already within her daughter. Waking up to speculations on where her father is, Angenie must think and provide false defences for his absence, her loathing of the drunken state he will be in when he returns; subsiding when she realizes that alcohol would be better than the 'utter chaos' an affair means for them as a family tied to a philandering father's willingness to provide resources.

Angenie's own resourcefulness in consoling her mother notwithstanding, she feels inadequate because what her mother really wants is a grown young son to defend her against her demeaning husband. Mother and daughter share an undemonstrative relationship where for the daughter to touch the mother would be to do the unimaginable. Angenie can bridge this gulf only when she mentally models herself on the 'television images of cowboy heroes' she so admires (Mootoo 1993: 37). The gentleness offered by a hard male body outraged by the mother's humiliation by her husband would have best done the job of providing gentleness to her mother. In the absence of such a body, however, Angenie may not touch her mother, as no cues for such contact have been offered by the mother; even despite her distraughtness, everyday rules of behaviour and bodily contact are still in operation. Comfort for her heterosexual mother, is provided by a male body, even when that body occupies the desexualized position of a son; already, unbeknownst to Angenie, her sensitiveness to the nature of bodily desires reveals her intuitive foreknowledge of what kinds of touch between what genders would destabilize the already frail scheme of things she is part of. Mother and daughter must navigate physical touch much as strangers would; indeed the daughter's taking initiative to touch the mother would be harder given her conditioning in everyday physical aloofness. Mootoo's delineation of the uncomfortable physicality between a mother and daughter in dire distress underlines the sense of uncanniness, unfamiliarity that even immediate family members may awaken. The family as a body functions without such disturbing indicators of its underlying injunctions against close contact when members are performing ritualized quotidian tasks with one other. However, in a moment of crisis, the body of a parent whom one does not touch in these quondam tasks becomes a strange territory. The (un)familiar potential of this touch is highlighted all the more when one remembers that the mother would have been willing to be comforted by a son; it is comforting by a female body that would have been objectionable, humiliating.

The mother's injunction to wake up and come with her to her room is like 'a hand reaching into one's intestines and ripping out yard after yard, desperately searching for things it has not even defined' (Mootoo 1993). The mother's reaching into the daughter's innards reverses the process of childbirth, which itself might be reasonably characterized as a pain akin to scooping out the mother's innards in the endeavour to give birth. Reaching into the daughter's guts places the mother in the position of the child; once the mother, now her need for emotional solace places the daughter in the throes of a pain akin to the pain of parturition. In this sense, the mother is a monstrous object, as later, the daughter may not have the comfort of knowing a child will emerge; the object of the mother's search through the daughter/mother's innards is in search of an object as yet undefined, an anarchic, and mighty object whose emergence may well be a death blow to both or either. The eroticized comfort that a son might provide, on the other hand, is already structured within the paradigms of protection and safety which the vulnerable daughter cannot, presumably give. The son's presence guarantees wish-fulfilment, the daughter's threatens further abjection.

The daughter as narrator, meanwhile intercuts the text of the story with sequences from her dream, where she is a 'little girl with a frightened mother who may just as well be blind' in a rowboat tossed by storm-waves in a 'shoreless expanse of Atlantic seas' (Mootoo 1993: 35). The little girl performs a number of seemingly fantastic tasks—she comforts the mother, bails the leaking boat of the waters that pour in, gives her clothes to the mother to keep her warm, and rows the boat to safety. Outside the dream, similarly, she tells her mother that her father is only out drinking with buddies after a particularly hard day's work; each passing word progressively relaxes the mother back into a semblance of coping when suddenly she hears her husband's car. Guiltily telling her daughter to get back to bed because she does not want him 'catch us awake,' the mother restores order to this upside down world where mother has become daughter and daughter mother. At this point, the daughter's sympathies curdle into disgust, the mother's castration of herself and her daughter both being too much to take. The daughter, aghast at their having to behave furtively when their father is the culpable one, is nevertheless willing to keep the peace, knowing that her brief occupation of a role of any symbolic importance has come to an end. Pretending to sleep, she lies awake, wondering if her siblings are also keeping vigil like she is. Her parents settle into a uneasy quiet and she falls into another dream. Here, lying outdoors, in what appears to be a garden, between two others whom she knows to be female, she finds herself turning to one of her companions, the one she knows to be older than her. A man meanwhile paces up and down in the distance, at the window of a house. Angenie's dream persona 'gathers heat' from this other woman's body, and in the wish-fulfilment that dreams permit, finds herself alone with this woman, freed of that third body that lies in the same space as them (Mootoo 1993: 40). The man at the distant window is unaware that she momentarily kisses this woman. Longing for a longer embrace, she demands one but 'no amount of begging and tugging will bring her back,' and moments later, while wondering if that woman's stillness means she is dead, Angenie's dream-persona slowly recognizes that woman's face to be her mother's (Mootoo 1993: 40). Reassured by the familiarity of this face, Angenie demands 'with the power of an impetuous, desperate kiss that she not desert me' (Mootoo 1993: 40). In this part of the dream sequence, the daughter has morphed back into her role as recipient of the mother's confidences and attentions. However, the dream, portentously, ends before she can make her mother give her what she wants; it appears that even within the dream the mother is powerful and as giver has the power to refuse the daughter's demands, while the daughter when awake, cannot but subject her insides to the irresistible scrutiny of the mother's vulnerable quest for what she must not seek.

Waking up in the morning, the old defensive barriers that their night of shared misery somewhat erased are back on the map. The mother is able to occlude last night's levelling of their situations by addressing the daughter's adolescent incompetence; late for school, she is now the object of her mother's maternal worry and irritation rather than being the 'mother' substitute or resolute lover of her mother. Her mother's taciturnity in the morning effectively distances Angenie, who is unable even to conceive enjoying 'even the less odious act of hugging' her. 'Pleased that I do not have the remotest desire of hugging her,' Angenie goes about the day asking herself: 'Where do dreams come from? What inside of me could have created such a dream' (Mootoo 1993: 41).

While the rest of the narrative is unable to supply an answer to these questions, Angenie's daydreams point clearly to the validity of the castration complex as a hypothesis that helps understand femininity's dispossessions. Her own future as a girl looks 'grim, claustrophobic,' with only her forsaken, disregarded mother, as an available model of feminine aspiration. While Angenie's sympathies lie with her mother she does not want to identify with her mother in her role 'of excellent wife who stands behind her husband,' despising her mother's 'spinelessness,' her 'staying, for the way she allows herself to be hurt, for the way she accepts it' (Mootoo 1993: 42). The alternative, however, to 'being just like her is to be just like him … with modifications to the details, mind you' (Mootoo 1993: 42–43). Angenie realizes that no matter how sad she feels for her mother's plight, her father will always have the freedoms to philander, wander and come home undisturbed at four o'clock in the morning which seem 'more honourable than consenting to spend a lifetime trapped by the body of a female'. The contest, then, is between femininity's role as adjunct to masculinity and its necessary dependences versus the independence of the male:

> If I were afforded such independence I would see the world, ride a bicycle from Alaska to Tierra Del Fuego, hike in Bhutan, snorkel above the Great Barrier Reef, befriend Prince Charles, wrestle with him at polo, and then later that day talk with him about great world

architecture. I would make paintings like the one of Dorian Gray. I would write like Somerset Maugham. I would disguise myself as a boy and one would never know that I was a girl. (Mootoo 1993: 43)

Angenie's ideal is a femininity that is freed of the body of the female, housed within masculinity. This is a reformed, renegotiated masculinity, a queer masculinity, if you will, as is evident from her choice of Oscar Wilde and Somerset Maugham as male mentors. Angenie's dream of obtaining tutelage from an open homosexual and from another who was always suspected of homosexuality during his life, places her fantasized masculinity in a different kettle from her father's. Homosexual tutors like these signal that Angenie's masculinity, when she is able to engage in a successful mimicry, will not have as its high point what she nightmarishly fears: 'her father making love to a plethora of strange women' is precisely the possibility her chosen (homosexual) masculinity will negate. With her dreams of travelling to see the world, acquiring culture and intellectual growth, Angenie will certainly be a different 'man' from her father who at times 'never even tried to hide the lipstick on the collar of his crisp white shirts or on his white handkerchiefs' (Mootoo 1993: 37). This choice with its great freedom of movement contrasts dramatically with the claustrophobic stasis of the only role available to her mother—that of an 'infiltrator' within her husband's brain, able to second-guess every move of his, but unable to 'redirect him, reprogram him from the little niche she lives in inside his brain' (Mootoo 1993:37). Where her mother fills her with sadness, her father's 'boldness and bravery are intimidating,' and Angenie is 'cautious to loathe his actions, not him,' clearly choosing masculinity over femininity as the model upon which to shape herself.

Does the Freudian developmental model which posits that the female child must recognize her lack (of a penis) function here? It would seem it does. Paralysed by her mother's castration, Angenie desires to be a man for all intents and purposes, to range far and wide rather than be confined. On the surface of it, this seems to make lesbianism a developmental disorder of the psyche, a tendency of the subject to see itself as masculine when it should instead recognize its rightful feminine place. However, if we treat this as a descriptive account rather than as an evaluative one, Angenie's wish for masculinity also in effect queers masculinity as her version of the masculine is based on a self-exploration that does not violate others' emotional freedoms. Further, part of her desire to be male, her desire to see herself as a cowboy, 'bringing his wagon and putting the woman and her children in it and riding off with them to a sprawling homestead in the country, far away from other people' is also derived from her mother's wish for a first-born son instead of daughter (Mootoo 1993: 44). The daughter's successful self-fashioning then is interrupted by the mother's willing her to be something that she cannot be; the daughter's later desire to be that which she is not is itself a response to the mother's will. The daughter, as mentioned earlier, cannot refuse demands of the monstrous mother while the mother can castrate her by constantly presenting before her a vision of what femininity means. The mother's desire for a male child, rather than the female one she has, is further evidence of their impotence within patriarchy, which Angenie's (un)familiar desire for the mother seeks to counter, but cannot, given her the status of the dependent adolescent daughter.

The daughter's process of 'selving' is split by the mother's own castration; she would rather be male, but not so she can desire her mother, but so that she can be a son to him, in response to this mother's wish. Her further recognition of her father's liberty makes her desire to *be like* him, to be male so she too can be free. However, both processes are complicated by the (un)familiar reversals of relationships that her dreams produce. In her dream, she desires the mother whom she, awake, neither desires nor 'expect[s] to be able to please' (Mootoo 1993: 43). The desires of the dream, if expressed in a familiar daylight world would jeopardize her family just as badly as her father's adultery does, and even within the dream Angenie is aware that boundaries are being overstepped; the man policing the far distance of her dream-horizon is her internalization of the rules that govern normative distributions of love-objects. The desires of the dream once disavowed, can be displaced onto her need to be masculine to be free of the thraldom the mother is consciously under, with her sense of self itself destroyed by her enslavement. When her mother begins to cry, Angenie realizes her wail was 'more like a sound coming through her than from her … as if she were giving voice to all her female ancestors and they were all wailing at the same moment'

(Mootoo 1993: 36). This unindividuated femininity is very different from the suitably idiosyncratic characteristic attributes that characterize the male prototypes Angenie has chosen for herself. This is the point at which we may say Mootoo's story departs from the Freudian conundrum of what a woman who desires another woman must be. Angenie's desire for masculinity is a desire for selfhood, for individuation; further, this act of individuation is made possible, albeit at the realm of fantasy, only *after* she has dreamt of desiring her mother with a male figure pacing about the background, watchful, but unknowing of what is happening in his watch. Angenie's self-creation, then, in 'Wake Up' follows her desire for her mother. This female subject's entry into a self-chosen adult role is consequent to her desire for the mother. Desire, then, in this account, comes first; identification itself seems self-chosen, itself the consequence of a desire to do or be. But more importantly, this desire for the mother, both incestuous and homosexual, is also not disavowed by Angenie's identification with her father. If we locate Freud's concept of primary desire within the social rather than within the pre-social, within the subject rather than in the pre-subject, we can say, perhaps, that Angenie's primary desire is for her mother. In the Freudian account, if the child's primary desire is for her mother, then the taboo against incest, according to Freud, and more accurately, the taboo against homosexuality, as Judith Butler and Gayle Rubin argue, prevails and the child disavows this primary desire and instead identifies with this parent. In the process of identifying thus with the 'correct' parent, the 'little girl' gives up her impossible desire for this parent, introjecting that person into her ego instead through identification, thereby becoming 'feminine' in appearance and wants. Angenie's story, however, stalls this model, productively. Angenie's desire for the mother is not given up; arguing backwards within a strictly Freudian framework, to account for this desire, we would have to say that Angenie's primary desire before her entry into the Oedipal drama had been indeed for her father, whom she then identifies with through a literal process of incorporation, that is preserving on her body literally, as Angenie's desire to be masculine suggests. This enactment of the Freudian account is very much possible, but would break down if Angenie had instead chosen a 'femme' lesbianism rather than this modified masculinity wherein 'one would never know I was a girl' (Mootoo 1993: 43). In wanting to be male, masculine, Angenie might seem to be bowing to patriarchy, but in de-normalizing this masculinity onto her female body, Angenie is locating herself in a different 'network of desires' as Elizabeth Grosz would put it, seeking freedom in a way that is 'more honourable than consenting to spend a lifetime trapped by the body of a female' (Mootoo 1993: 43), as the only narrative available to the female seems to be an ancestral victimology.

Given the logic of dreams and the nature of their incursions onto the familiar, it would be fair to read Angenie's dream itself as a 'primary' desire that her conscious self suppresses, but which comes out anyway. Consequently, Angenie becomes 'masculine' in order to accommodate her desire for a likeness—her mother—so that she can prevent her father, or the distant man pacing up and down in her dream, from going on a rampage to restore heteronormative 'order'. Angenie's fear of becoming identical to her mother, which in turn signals her own refusal to be castrated by becoming like her mother, makes her identify with her father rather than with the mother she (un)familiarly desires. Rather than 'innate dispositions' that prevent identification and desire from coinciding, it appears the cultural marginalization of women determines the splitting of desire from identification, at least for the queer female subject. Mootoo's 'Wake Up' queers the familiar Oedipal family romance, standing it on its head to reimagine how women relate to their mothers, to accommodate (un)familiar desires where the mother is an important ancestor, tangibly present even if unpleasant and thus not to be dismissed, where fathers are shadowy and unreliable.

A Portrait of the Lesbian as a Sister

'Lemon Scent' is the only story in *Out on Main Street* set in the West Indies that features adult women. The story opens in the first person, where Anita is attracted to Kamini, the beautiful wife of a man she knows socially. Kamini offers Anita some hors d'oeuvres at a party:

> I look down at her offering—faintly wrinkled reddish black prunes. Careful not to linger to contemplate the shape of the hands, the impeccably manicured shiny-shell-pink fingernails, I concentrate, instead, on spaces between the scores of healthy-looking prunes slit

slightly and stuffed plump with peanut butter, the slits sealed over
with firm pink icing. The spaces between the prunes reveal a white,
linen-textured paper doily embossed with low relief paisleys. (Mootoo
1993: 24)

This passage is redolent with metaphors of the female genitalia,
ripe for eating, which at once draw notice to and subvert Kamini's
social role as hostess for her husband, purveyor of the food and
drink (he earns money to buy these) by presenting this edible as
available for a woman. Like the desire Angenie feels for her her as-
yet unrecognized mother in 'Wake Up', Kamini and Anita find a
'heat growing' above this very tray which presses against both their
stomachs, calling even more attention to the erotic, genital contact
that the latter half of this story describes (Mootoo 1993: 24). This
heat however, is destabilizing; a prelude to further eating, this very
erotic (un)familiar contact between the two women is ruptured in
the second part of the story by the depiction of Kamini's husband.
That he appears in the second part of the story strengthens Mootoo's
wish that we recognize Kamini's and Anita's pairing as primary and
Kamini's and her husband's ideal heterosexual couple as secondary,
but the more powerful socially. 'The gesture of deep concern' that her
husband offers is to ask Anita over to make sure he does not lose the
'prized exquisite accomplishment, envy of his men friends' that is his
wife, now 'huddled in a lifeless puddle on the bed' (Mootoo 1993:
26). However, in getting ready for Anita's arrival, Kamini betrays her
eagerness, 'He sees her chest flutter. Her breathing quickens notice-
ably' (Mootoo 1993: 26) but this is not for him. Watching her in
the mirror as she gets ready, he hopes that 'she will look over at his
pleading face', but 'without taking her eyes away from her face in the
mirror, she offers him a cup of tea before he leaves, but he can feel
that her intention to make it is weak and unwilling' (Mootoo 1993:
27). Kamini's not taking her eyes off her own face suggests that for
her, love for a familiar, a likeness such as one's mirror image is, is the
more emotionally and sexually fulfilling than anything she can feel
for husband, who is not given any physical description in the story.
He puts his hands into the back pockets of his blue jeans, looks
without seeing, threatens his wife against having any sexual contact
with Anita, but the reader does not get to find out how he looks,

suggesting, by extension, that his presence does not register upon Kamini or Anita at all, aesthetically or sexually. They do not 'see' him any more than he can see from his kitchen-window the 'miles and miles of undeveloped forest land—wild samaan, giant ferns, ginger lilies, bird-of-paradise bushes and palm trees, all meshed in suffocating philodendron vines—meeting the sea in the distance.' This 'undeveloped' forest land, yet to be tapped for economic value, is similar to his wife and her lover. Their erotic lives do not further his own sense of ownership of property, the sense of triumph he feels when 'those men he works with and parties with would like to have' Kamini (Mootoo 1993: 30). Unruly, wild and devoid at the moment of economic value, Anita and Kamini stand outside the circuit of power that his sexual possession of his wife enables him to enter. Their independent desire for one another, which not only leaves him out but renders him redundant, makes him threaten his wife with death.

Mootoo locates the women's desires in the yard that surrounds the house, on the fringes of the wilderness he cannot see though it is right in front of him, because 'one can only find this spot if one knows where to look' (Mootoo 1993: 28). Not knowing what it is that he is threatened by, but correctly suspecting an ambush, the potentially violent husband cannot imagine that his wife and her lover are making love within sight of his house, concealed from view by the ebullient foliage, chaperoned by 'hundreds of noisy parakeets' in the trees above them, lying on a blanket that is 'lime green, like the long thin leaves of the bird-of-paradise surrounding them', their clothes 'concealed in a straw bag a shade lighter than the earth' with the huge samaan fanning their sweaty bodies dry and cool. Having become very much part of the earth, the two women have indeed left behind the house, though Kamini (after making love ... 'always parts the branches and pensively looks over to the house' (Mootoo 1993: 29). Lesbian eroticism in Mootoo's hands becomes a return to the earth, where refuge from the house of heterosexuality may be sought and won. Kamini and Anita are one with the plants, the earth and the animals, including the tiny red ants that scurry around without biting them. Their peaceable belonging within this earth, Mootoo suggests, is possible awhile when they are in one another's arms. The house of nature supplies wants and makes amends for that which the colonizing, unseeing and brutal male could not discern or alleviate. Of course the bliss is short lived; the blue sky above them slowly curdles to a yellow akin to the lemons that make the scent Kamini wears when Anita realizes Kamini still has sex with her husband, an epiphany that comes in a pause in the women's lovemaking when Kamini tells Anita about her husband's intuitive discovery of the women's attraction to one another. Their lovemaking continues after the intrusion of the powerful spectre of possible male violence. Mootoo's location of the women's lovemaking in the yard, where the vegetation does not serve an economic or consciously organized aesthetic purpose may at first glance seem to idealize lesbian love as a return to an unrealized plenitude within the laboured economy of the organized garden or home. But in speaking about the presence of the husband in their midst even when he is far away, Mootoo instead places desire for the familiar instead as a faultline within the familiar space of the home. The home, threatened with disruption, cannot hold these (un)familiar women. Yet, it will return to haunt them even in their moment of greatest pleasure, truncating and exposing their most vulnerable moments to violence that will mar their beauty forever.

'Lemon Scent' connects the control of women within and through heterosexual matrimony with the enforcement of monogamy and chastity for women as well as with the exploitation of the earth. Mootoo is able to imagine the (un)familiar as both given a home by her unfamiliar desire (Kamini is limp till Anita appears at her husband's behest to help) as well as threatened with unspeakable violences in this very home by this same desire. Chitra Banerjee Divakaruni's novels, *Sister of My Heart* (2010) and *The Vine of Desire* (2013), Uma Parameswaran's 'What Was Always Hers' from her story collection of the same name, and Kamala Das' 'The Sandal Trees,' again from the eponymously titled collection of short stories, supplemented by sections from Mary Anne Mohanraj's *Bodies in Motion* allow us to engage in this section with the theme of sisterly eros. Sisterhood entangles other familial relationships, especially the relationships that the women have with their husbands. Partly, these books then reflect the suspicion of (feminist) sisterhood within most communities. To name but a few common cultural discourses and practices on women together; women getting together are always branded noisy, disorderly, wasteful; rituals and ceremonies with only women together are also viewed as subversive and regulated tightly; in the cultural conversation on women, women communicating with one another is after all stigmatized and dishonoured as 'gossip,' unlike similar communions between men. Female homosociality is at once taken for granted and feared not only as a tool for possible feminism, but as a tool against heterosexuality itself in its possibilities for sliding into female homoeros. The family in all these books is threatened, redefined and sometimes done away with when intra-female eros, in the form of (un)familiar love between sisters, refuses to yield the space of the home to normative exclusively heterosexual definitions of family.

Chitra Banerjee Divakaruni's fiction has mostly dealt with Indian-origin female characters in a strange world—the USA—where they come to selfhood largely within a romantic heterosexual narrative. Two exceptions to this heterosexualized diegesis are her novels *Sister of My Heart* and its companion piece and sequel, *The Vine of Desire*, which tell the story of Anju and Sudha. To my mind, these novels are telling a very (un)familiar tale in the nature of their focus on female bonding. Where, normatively, much diasporic fiction has depicted the coming-of-age within the diaspora of the *individual* female protagonist, who develops an interiority and selfhood even as she outgrows many relationships, particularly with significant men—fathers, husbands, boyfriends—these two novels represent what I shall show to be an (un)familiar selving, where Anju and Sudha retain, after travails of course, their sense of sisterhood that dates back to when they were born. Anju's and Sudha's uneasy 'male' interims do lead to loss of understanding and love between them, but the revival of their togetherness evaluates sisterhood, friendship, and companionate togetherness as more valuable than token heteronormative marital affiliations.

Divakaruni takes recourse to a literal form of the fantastic when she creates a domestic myth in *Sister of My Heart* and *The Vine of Desire* that will lead to Anju's and Sudha's being raised exclusively by women. The first part of the first novel opens in Calcutta, where retrospectively, we are made to piece together the family history, located partly within Bidish India a few years before Independence. Anju's mother Gouri Ma runs the bookshop her husband leaves behind when he goes missing; as the *karta* of the family, Gouri Ma finds herself hampered by a number of practices she cannot provide alternatives for. Chief among the symbols of these traditions that protect and at the same time wear the user out is the grand mansion in which all these characters live, whose upkeep is expensive, but necessary as it is the women's only link to the Chatterjee lineage that Gouri has married into. Nalini is the wife of the man, Gopal, who enters this household, before the girls are born to their respective mothers, claiming to be a long-lost Chatterjee scion fallen on hard times. Before long, maddened by the dishonour of living off lies, and spurred on by his nagging wife, Gopal comes home with reports of rubies of great price to be found in some secret cave in Bengal's coastal tide-lands. If a secret expedition is financed, Gopal will be able to finally repay Bijoy. Bijoy agrees to go with him, though both their wives are pregnant because, for him, 'the only son of the Chatterjees, trapped since birth in the cage of propriety, it was the one chance at a life of adventure. At a life which had seemed to him until now as remote and impossible' (Divakaruni 1999: 35). The expedition ends badly as may be expected; Gopal and Bijoy never return and are thought dead. Bijoy's wife finds herself bound now to her promise to bring up their child 'as befits a descendant of the Chatterjees' (Divakaruni 1999: 37) and runs the house as best as she can whilst Gopal, presumed dead and thus incognito, serves as chauffer to the girls. The fantastic story of the rubies in the cave, however, is also proven to be true—a ruby is indeed retrieved on the person of one of the dead bodies recovered from the waters where the men are killed. But this is merely the successful completion of a *deus ex machina* plot which serves two functions—placing the girls in an entirely female household, and two, serving to reify India—specifically Bengal—for an intended primary audience of westerners, as a place of great mystery and exotic adventures that lock one set of women so deep within tradition that they cannot escape it to fashion new lives till they are firmly settled within the same west about which Divakaruni writes.

It is also important to note that the girls' bond with one another is also located within this atmosphere of mystery: while *The Vine of Desire* is more circumspect, indeed forgetful of the girls' spiritual togetherness because of its own plot's requirements, *Sister of My Heart* provides enough background for their love. The two girls are born on the same day, a redoubt perhaps to time-worn melodramatic formulae for companionship that exceeds human boundaries. Nalini's is a difficult labour that does not end till the newborn Anju is laid on her belly; immediately Sudha responds from inside Nalini's womb, and emerges finally into the world. The girls feel they are twins, because as Sudha says, 'she called me out into the world' (Divakaruni 1999: 18), but all outsiders feel such attachment between two girls is dangerous. While Divakaruni never does suggest a sexual component, the depth of their bond is made evident by such statements; a component of erotic admiration is also evident from Anju's appreciation of Sudha's near-fantastic beauty. Relieved that Sudha's admirers cannot see her 'dressed only in her petticoat, her long hair spilling like black water over her bare breasts,' admiring the rain (Divakaruni 1999: 92), Anju reveals her desire for Sudha in not wanting this beauty for herself. In fact, moving away from common patriarchal wisdom about female same-sex jealousy, the two girls are at complete peace with their special gifts: Sudha loves Anju's intelligence and wants only the best for her, while Anju is proud of Sudha's beauty more than Sudha herself is. Now, in late adolescence, Anju's and Sudha's attachment to one another is legendary, a source of jealousy to all outsiders: 'What people hate is how happy Sudha and I are when we're together... [at] how we don't need anyone else' (Divakaruni 1999: 13). Divakaruni nowhere indicates that this togetherness at all has a sexual component, but all the same, their attachment is all-consuming: 'we found everything we needed in each other. As Pishi says, 'Why go to the lake to fetch water when you have a well in your own house already' (Divakaruni 1999: 15). But marriage is an exit from paradise, from homogeneity, entry into otherness: Sudha sees Ashok as the prince who is to carry her out of 'that dim green underwater light, those cool palace walls built of coral and sea-stone' (Divakaruni 1999: 93), into the world of light where she can finally perceive her beauty. Awakening to this 'magical universe of men—diamond light on sleek mango leaves, the kokils crying to their mates from the coconut trees,' this princess finds 'she would never be satisfied with the word-less songs of her serpent companions again' (Divakaruni 1999: 94). Grateful to the prince for having 'rescued her from sameness, too much safety', Sudha's 'inward-gazing smile' reveals to Anju that she is now indeed forgotten. When Sudha instead decides, in order to not jeopardize Anju's marriage prospects, to marry a man her family has found, she has 'a startling thought. If only Anju and I, like the wives of the heroes in the old tales, could marry the same man, our Arjun, our Krishna, who would love and treasure us both, and keep us both together' (Divakaruni 1999: 123), a desire that the novel acts on albeit in a convoluted way. Refusing the stereotype that co-wives will always be competitors, this utterance, which Sudha herself disavows moments later as 'a ridiculous wish, maybe even immoral,' shapes the structure of the novel.

Heterosexual desire predictably disrupts the girls' feelings for one another, gradually making their spiritual intimacy unintelligible to one another. At the wedding itself, at the auspicious moment when Anju's eyes 'are supposed to meet Sunil's … instead I crane my neck to look for Sudha' (Divakaruni 1999: 157), making the women around say, 'Here is her husband, right in front of her, and she is dreaming about someone else' (Divakaruni 1999: 158). These portents are unmistakeable, and Anju's hope that Sunil will sympathize with her feelings for Sudha are ironically realized when she finds out that Sunil too had fallen in love with Sudha when he first saw her. Anju requests Sunil to wait a few moments in the middle of the ceremony so she can watch Sudha's wedding rites being carried out, and unbeknownst to one another, both relish her beauty, enjoying it fully till suddenly Anju sees something amiss: 'So deeply in love myself, I recognize exactly what I'm seeing' in Sunil's face as she watches him watching Sudha (Divakaruni 1999: 159). Jealousy removes Anju from her trust and love of Sudha, and these marriages take one girl to Bardhaman and the other to the USA. Five years later, Sudha has run away from her marriage and Anju has had a miscarriage that makes her nearly suicidal. Sudha rouses Anju from her depressive stupor by telling her a story of a queen who is in grave difficulties and is homeless while pregnant; Anju, speechless several months now, finally shows willingness to speak, completing the tale saying the queen had a twin sister who both gives her a home and resolves her troubles. At the end of the novel, Sudha comes to the USA to help Anju out of her misery, her baby Dayita in her arms. Sunil is edged out of the narrative by the two women forming a couple with Dayita at the centre.

> If a passer-by who had the eyes to notice such things looked at us, she would see that we've formed a tableau, two women, their arms intertwined like lotus stalks, smiling down at the baby between them. Two women who have travelled the vale of sorrow and the baby who will save them, who has saved them already. Madonnas with child.
> (Divakaruni 1999: 340)

Divakaruni uncannily presents us with the Marian model of two mothers with child, where Anju is untroubled even by what she knows to be Sunil's now fully awakened love for Sudha. In the 'hesitant, holy light' of a beclouded evening, the baby, Dayita will not save Sunil's and Anju's already wrecked marriage, but rather, following the underlying logic of *Sister of My Heart*, restore Anju and Sudha to one another though only after Sunil and Sudha have had sex once, a betrayal that permits Sunil and Anju to finally leave one another. *The Vine of Desire* enables both women to establish a financial independence that years of tradition in India have prevented them from earning; Sudha becomes a sick-nurse to an old Indian man who lives half-heartedly in his wealthy son's mansion, while Anju gets on the dean's list in her college despite the meltdown of an excruciating divorce from Sunil.

The Vine of Desire, albeit timidly, challenges a number of stereotypes even as it writes in others. In one instance, Anju, having discovered Sudha's/Sunil's infidelity, has a conversation with him about it. Sunil presents a reading of *Pakeezah* in response—aligning himself as the man who seeks his love and wants her despite knowing her to be far from pure, Sunil's romantic recuperation of his own desire for Sudha, in addition to representing the latter as impure, altogether removes Anju from the narrative of his life, an erasure she refuses to take. Smashing all the breakables in her house, intending to walk on them, Anju's reprisal of a most famous moment in Bollywood cinema makes the masochism of this scene signify here not as a signifier of true love and willingness to walk over all obstacles including shards of glass, but as a signifier of closure. In order to leave her marriage, Anju must walk on glass, which she does. In an ironic comment on the nature of urban American living, the resident of the flat below Anju's objects to the noise, but once quiet is restored, is absolutely unaware that the woman above him has tried to walk on the shards.

Bleeding and about to lose consciousness, Anju's thoughts of suicide are replaced by her desire to live—calling a relative stranger, a woman from her writing-group, on the phone to help her, Anju is indeed able to walk over the threshold of marriage. She re-enters the narrative mended and well, but in her version of *Pakeezah* here, Divakaruni turns the libidinal economy of the courtesan story on its head. While Pakeezah's feet bleed for the loss, yet again, of the chance of heterosexual companionship because she is a courtesan, Anju's slow walk on the broken fragments of crockery and glassware is not the pain of true love that it is in *Pakeezah*, but a delayed bereavement for her still-born son, Prem. Literally reborn now, Anju learns, literally, to fly. At an earlier outing Sunil, Sudha, Anju and Dayita went on, the women had seen a hang-glider fly above the bay; Anju is enthralled, and Sudha sharing her enthusiasm, the recalcitrant Sunil helps them seek out the hang-gliders' base. The woman-instructor offers lessons, but Sunil 'suspicious of unrequired adventures' officiously hustles the women away, thinking the woman—and her woman lover—as 'Americans in the worst possible way,' that is, as unspokenly lesbian, a connection that occurs to Sudha only after they have left the scene (Divakaruni 2002: 44). Returning at the end of the novel to the steep hillside where the fliers take off, Sudha is afraid that Anju is about to kill them both 'going off the hillside together' (Divakaruni 1999: 368), but Anju has instead brought her to show her she can fly. In a meeting that truly wipes out the past, Anju flies over the same lake in her hang-glider, and upon touch-down, runs into Sudha's waiting arms. Without the man and without the child, Anju and Sudha finish the novel as the true pair whose companionableness is resistant to the pervasive unrest that heterosexual coupling has introduced between them. Though Divakaruni does not place an overt lesbian subjectivity up for our consumption, Anju's and Sudha's uncannily strong love for one another is a viable intra-female analogue for the many Hindi-film hero–hero pairs Indian viewers have been used to seeing. The heroine–heroine pairing, however, is that rarity that Divakaruni writes into a pair of novels that employ a number of mind-numbing clichés about Indians and America. Nevertheless, in locating the individual women's strength to look for economic and sexual independence within their sister–sister bond, Divakaruni is also queering the script of diaspora as a place for autonomous femininity. With her trans-national story of 'eros' within the sisterly bond, Divakaruni writes a continuum between female homosociality and female homoeroticism; Anju and Sudha are not lovers, but their relationship is the more valuable to them than marriages they work hard at. In untying femininity from heteronormative marriage and motherhood, Divakaruni produces an (un)familiar picture of self-hood as intersubjectively shared sisterly identity, rather than seflhood as self-contained interiority or isolation.

This sisterhood of common dreams and shared work is given corporeal erotic shape in Uma Parameswaran's 'What Was Always Hers,' the first story in Uma Parameswaran's collection of five stories that variously define and place diasporic Indians in Canada as claim-ants of Canadian citizenship in all senses of the world. In a collec-tion of the same name, this story stands apart from the rest of the volume in that it is the only one that does not feature the character of Maru, an Indian woman, now Canadian citizen, in her fifties, trying to be a writer and possessed of great good-humour, lively wit and much understanding. The title story stands as a unit on its own in its exploration of female bonding within, through and in spite of marriage while the other stories are about negotiations and comic tribulations within mostly equable heterosexual marriages. Parameswaran's writing places her characters within the Canadian milieu with a precision that Divakaruni often gives up for clichéd exotica; while Divakaruni's protagonists are also women whose eco-nomic autonomy is minimal if not non-existent when they migrate to America, their crises are located within the frame of reference of private heterosexually-generated family troubles. While Divakaruni does imagine erotic sisterhood as necessary, at the same time these novels stop short of allowing even the vaguest hybridizations for the protagonists from forming by exoticizing this sisterhood as essen-tially eastern, Indian, rather than trans-nationally feminist. Adhering to the concept of diaspora as always glancing backward to the past, the homeland, Divakaruni's female protagonists seem to be only Indian, never relating very much to the new culture around them. 'What Was Always Hers' claims a larger set of affiliations for (un) familiar love between women, placing its protagonist Veeru within a historically amaic narrative of diaspora—the Indian diasporic com-munity in Canada's fruit belt that Veeru's husband organizes is a very different one from the socially-isolated, much more assimilationist model signalled by Sunil, Anju's up-and-coming computer scientist husband. America is always described in a peripheral way, though difficulties with food and phone-calls home are mentioned; yet, the reader is not given a sense of the USA any more than about India; these backdrops may just as well have been anywhere else. 'What Was Always Hers' on the other hand studies in a beautifully nuanced way its protagonist Veeru's many roles within Canada and India, as wife, mother and individual, within the larger societies that she slowly ends up gaining stakes in. Individual and communal identities, in this long short-story, are carefully contextualized within the cultural geographies we find the characters in so that (un)familiar female desire can explore a network of affiliations that make it all the more threatening than a private affair of the heart as it becomes in the Divakaruni texts considered above, notwithstanding that Divakaruni's protagonists are also enabled to re-enter the diaspora as free labour on their own, without a paternal, masculine hand to steady them.

Parameswaran's short story opens with Veeru's waiting in bed for her husband to speak to her. Within the first paragraph, Veeru's disinclination 'for any intimacy' with her husband becomes evident, and within the first page, the reason for it. Niranjan's insistence on Veeru's having an abortion instead of a third child has complicated what has been the otherwise uneventfully happy marital bond, at least for Veeru, who however now, suddenly finds her sense of her own life sadly altered. Veeru has been a dutiful Indian daughter-in-law and wife, having come to Canada, yet a village-girl at heart, eight years ago to join her husband, student-agitator and labour-organizer Niranjan, years after he himself has settled into this new, very fertile and very large country where he had first come to do his PhD. She is the mother of two boys, but having always desired a girl child, she is dismayed to find that her excitement about this unexpected third pregnancy was not shared by Niranjan. The reason slowly emerges, retrospectively; Niranjan has been having an affair all through marriage with Jitin, fellow labour-organizer and second-in-command of the organization he establishes in Canada. The rest of the story follows Veeru's emergence from the marriage into an independent and self-reliant woman, with her becoming Jitin's lover at the end, once again disproving women's inability to share the same man for other (un)familiar ends.

Jitin is seen throughout by Veeru as a mentor rather than being identified as another contender for Niranjan's affections, 'Deedi, you are so much wiser than I am' (Parameswaran 1999: 19), Veeru says when they first meet, though Jitin tries to place the relationship on a less hierarchical footing, saying 'in this country everyone calls everyone else by just their first name' (Parameswaran 1999: 19). Veeru's only desire then had been to 'make herself his [Niranjan's] real helpmeet, his equal so that he could achieve his fullest potential, for she knew that he was made for greatness' (Parameswaran 1999: 11). From a peasant village girl a decade ago, Veerbala had 'set about educating herself' pouring heart and soul into becoming an indispensable part of the movement Niranjan spearheaded, into finally making "Veeru Deedi' … a household word in many an Indian cabin and home in the fruit belt' (Parameswaran 1999: 22). A decade ago, when Niranjan first meets Veeru to see if he can marry her, she likens his work as an organizer of farm labourers in the lumber mills and fruit orchards of British Columbia to that of Acharya Vinoba Bhave in India. Niranjan is taken aback by the young Veeru's awareness of Bhave three decades after Indian Independence, and decides that she is the wife he must marry, in preference to all the 'Girls who spoke English with a good Convent accent, girls who knew how to cook and sew, studying as they were towards a Home Science degree, recently named Home Economics' (Parameswaran 1999: 12) whom his family had thought he would want to marry, given his own wish to pursue higher education abroad. Veeru, Niranjan decides when she welcomes his 'vow of service to the community,' was 'a gem too precious to ignore' and he marries her (Parameswaran 1999: 14). Learning English and Punjabi at his home in New Delhi after they marry so she can be of use to him in this work, Veeru's desires are 'to grow so she could walk hand in hand with this giant mind who was her husband' (Parameswaran 1999: 11). It later emerges that Jitin and Niranjan had already been drawn to one another when they first meet in Canada; Niranjan, already married, was now also the father of three-year old Vikram, and his arranging for Veeru to spend a month with him in Canada was only, he later reveals, a failed effort to prise himself away from Jitin:

That is why I had you come over that summer, to break the endless cycle of frustration, of trying to break off and not being able to, and not being able to talk about it though each knew there could be no other. (No other? No other? What was I then? Sleeping with you every night for four months) And then after you left ...' he paused. (Oh my god, that was seven years ago, for seven years ...)(Parameswaran 1999: 24)

Veeru's thoughts, in the parentheses with no closing punctuations, inserted in Niranjan's self-righteous and insensitive presentation of his case for 'freedom' from his marriage of eight years with Veeru, refuse to cognize Niranjan's bracketing of her as the 'other' who is less than nothing in what he sees as his primary relationship with Jitin. Niranjan asks for 'freedom' also because 'it isn't fair to her (to her, she thought, to her, what am I?)... she has a right to her child, and to all that has been always hers...' (Parameswaran 1999: 24). Niranjan's desire to give Jitin a child whilst taking away from Veeru her right to hers immediately brings forth the cry,' Murderer, murderer,' along with 'a vicious anger [that] tore at her vitals' (Parameswaran 1999: 24) at the person who was responsible for the 'abortion of my beautiful baby at your hands' (Parameswaran 1999: 25), Veeru's response to Jitin when she next sees her after having found out about the affair is striking in its lack of anger—'Veeru left quietly, unable to bear the sight of the woman who seemed to have grown lovelier than ever before, and so far away, so far away' (Parameswaran 1999: 28), finding that the 'wild strangled stream of hatred that she alone could hear' (Parameswaran 1999: 25) is not directed towards Jitin at all. Instead, Veeru's desire is to confide in the same Jitin, wanting to embrace her when she sees how 'tired, lonely, utterly beautiful' Jitin herself looks through this period (Parameswaran 1999: 29). Even as Veeru tries to come to terms with Niranjan's surprising, life-changing act of betrayal, her real perplexity is about how to deal with the loss of Jitin she has suffered through Niranjan's infidelity:

Deedi, deedi. They were sisters. Could they not share one more thing? And be friends, sisters? No. Because they had shared it already, unbeknownst to Veeru. That was why they could not be friends. The hypocrisy of it all. But what could Jitin have done? Propose a ménage a trois? And how would Veeru have responded? How else could she respond now other than the way she was? Had she been the village girl she was when she first landed here, would things have been different? (Parameswaran 1999: 30)

As this meditation reveals, Veeru's real sense of betrayal comes in the loss of Jitin's friendship; sharing a husband seems a welcome relief, indeed, to the idea of losing Jitin's love. Wanting to 'just rest her head against Jitin's bosom and make time stand still' (Parameswaran 1999: 31), Veeru's musings reveal that she values friendship over marital reciprocity, her female friend and also her husband's lover over her (male) husband. The image of Jitin is desirable and inviting in a desexualized maternal and sisterly form upto this point, with Veeru's earlier memories of life long before her coming to Canada confirming the story's suggestions that in spirit, Veeru and Jitin have been united a long way before they ever met one another:

> Jitin was gone, vanished like the rainbow that arced across the horizon of her childhood. Always pining for lost worlds, pining in those early years for her aunts' arms, for the placid dewlaps of Amrita, Devika, Latika … cows she had named and fed and milked in those days which had vanished like the rainbows that arced across childhood horizons. (Parameswaran 1999: 30)

Veeru's memories of being nurtured and of nurturing animals in her turn suggest her kinship with Jitin goes deeper than theirs with Niranjan. 'Rage, jealousy and hatred washed over her again. But they could not wash away the ache of separation. Deedi, deedi' (Parameswaran 1999: 31), suggesting that the 'reflective solidarity' of having a sister to one's heart is deeper in one's selfhood than cross-gender spouses.

Two years after the divorce Niranjan dies suddenly; meanwhile, Veeru has successfully reinvented herself as a real estate business-woman, a far cry from the party-worker and labour-rights organizer she was when she was Niranjan's wife. 'The Party,' the exclusive theatre of all her earlier labour does not even call her to tell her of her ex-husband's death; she finds out instead from Niranjan's parents, who have been family to her regardless of the divorce. Veeru's everyday work does not seem to leave behind any legacy to be remembered, in contrast to the hagiographic attention bestowed on Niranjan throughout. Veeru can only think: 'She had never been part of their world then? Was that it? Like a stone ingested by some willy-nilly act of misplaced idealism, housed for a time, cast out along with other products the body did not need, the party did not need' (Parameswaran 1999: 40). Her sense of being unwanted, abjected to the level of excreta is only consoled by the thought that motherhood, '*her* sons, not his any more,' will speak for her value, her worth in the world in a way in which her work for Party and husband do not. At Niranjan's death, Veeru reaches out to Jitin, knowing intuitively perhaps that Jitin's own continuing work for the Party will leave her similarly dishonoured; where Veeru did not know what 'she had to do' after her divorce, now upon Niranjan's death, survived by Jitin and a baby girl, both unprovided for, Veeru finally does know (Parameswaran 1999: 52). In the interim between Veeru's finding out about Niranjan's death and the funeral, Veeru wants to comfort Jitin: 'Jitin, Jitin, she thought longingly, remembering the comfort of her arms which she could not now return to' (Parameswaran 1999:45) when Jitin needed ministering to. Where her son Vikram wants to hate Jitin, Veeru is able to convince him that blaming women comes naturally to many, especially the older generation, when it is often not the fault of the women; reminding Vikram never to hate a woman. Veeru is even able to sanction his temporary hatred of 'daddy' perhaps knowing that Vikram would claim his inheritance from his father as a man himself, which he does. Her own inheritance, 'what was always hers,' was to be Jitin herself, as Veeru decides one afternoon, going to meet Jitin in the one-room apartment where Niranjan and Veeru themselves had first started life in Canada.

Now comes the turn the story had been building up slowly, though disguised in the form of an asexual affection, which, however, now reveals itself to be also sexual, also bodily, besides being a desire to finally be together. For Veeru the years of marriage with Niranjan had been erased the day he sets up her abortion. Her separation from Jitin also starts from this point, as in the depression thereafter; Veeru had lived in isolation from everyone. It turns out Jitin never did know that Niranjan had had Veeru abort a baby, revealing yet another crack in Niranjan's commitment to 'service' at the expense of women's reproductive and emotional rights:

Then they clung to each other in a frenzy of need, hands, faces, mouths reaching out, the thirst of years seeking to be slaked. Jitin, Jitin, she moaned, and heard, love, love, my sweet love, and she did not know whether the voice she heard was real or in her head, his voice for surely the words were his or hers, but it didn't matter, at last at last they were together. (Parameswaran 1999: 59)

Their love for one another revealed to be mutual and suffused with desire for one another's bodies as much as with desire for togetherness, Veeru and Jitin enter a conversation in short sentences that occupies the rest of the story; a good tenth of the story consists of dialogue in which it is impossible, after three or four exchanges of sentences, to be sure who the speaker is. Veeru and Jitin speak as one in this conversation, unlike their own individual separate conversations with Niranjan which are sadly lacking in mutuality. Niranjan's interaction with Veeru through the story is in the form of memories of the past, or of negotiations for divorce in the present, while his life with Jitin happens off-stage, the author's third-person point-of-view focussing on Veeru's subjectivity all along. In contrast to the clipped nature of the exchanges with Niranjan all of which are subtle or unsubtle inequalities of power between the man who fights for the rights of the subalterns—immigrant Indians in Canada—and the wife he subalternizes in turn by forcing her, in various ways, to become his subsidiary—a helpmeet—the conversation Jitin and Veeru have traces the arcs of development the two of them have shared beginning with childhoods in which neither knew the other existed. Veeru's and Jitin's memories of games played, dreams dreamt and plans made are different from the bundles of 'plans, of which he had many and all very neatly tied and labelled' (Parameswaran 1999: 13–14) that their love for Niranjan makes them carry out. In this epiphanic conversation that suggests a pouring of soul into soul, of making one out of two bodies and beings we find a coupling absent throughout the story despite Niranjan's relationships with them; the women's coitus with one another is both literal and metaphoric. Their coming together is the only act of sexual coupling in a long short-story that begins with spouses in bed; in contrast to that sterile and murderous beginning is the end where the two women playfully nibble at one another's bodies as they lie together in the same couch that Niranjan bought the first time Veeru came to Canada. A full circle is attained when Niranjan is left out of this exchange: Veeru promises to help Jitin revive the Party, which has become centrist in the hands of leaders with aspirations far from the leftist political leanings that Niranjan, and Jitin so firmly adhered to.

Veeru and Jitin have doubts about whether they can be together, but realize they can, in this land of plenty. Jitin herself wants recognition as an individual with a sexual existence, though the puritanical Party 'pretended I was a virgin' even when she and Niranjan openly start living together (Parameswaran 1999: 63). Relinquishing her 'goddess' status for her place in Veeru's comforting arms, Jitin reveals her own desire all these years to have been 'holding [Veeru] just so when I've felt the ground was sinking under me' (Parameswaran 1999: 58). In the Marian model again, 'sisters' Veeru and Jitin can raise the two boys and Jitin's daughter Niranjana together in a land where male masculinity is finally extraneous for sustaining life.

'What Was Always Hers' locates same-sex love as love for one's sister, one's beloved likeness in whom one can delight and even share a husband with in contravention of the requirements of respectable heterosexual conjugality, a theme strikingly similar to Sudha's fleetingly desired resolution to the problem of separation from Anju in the Divakaruni novels discussed above. Parameswaran's long short-story also sees the economic coming of age of a woman protagonist whose sheltered existence did not require such autonomy earlier, though Parameswaran is able to avoid treating India—Veeru's carefully detailed natal home—as a space of regressive tradition, focussing instead on the enabling aspects of these traditions that empower Veeru into becoming what Niranjan and Canada require of her. In unfamiliar lands, though, the entity that sustains Veeru is not the husband she married in the familiar realms of home, but another kind of familiar, another woman whose protection, companionship and ability to provide and receive emotional nurture are to her a more compelling form of self-definition than is the presence of a husband she very much loves, even worships. In not having to worship Jitin—she is a sister, an equal, not a 'goddess'—Veeru is able to finally achieve a mutuality that was always missing in her relationship with her dead spouse. Veeru's and Jitin's union at the end of the story suggests a template for diaspora different from the patriarchal model

Niranjan's and his Leftist workers wittingly or unwittingly generate. In their intense lyricism and mutual contemplation of one another's beauty at the end of the story, Jitin and Veeru suggest emotional fulfilment as not an alternative but as a necessary supplement to the utilitarian political organization that Niranjan worked hard to build. Unrefined by this mutually sustaining ethic, Niranjan's more masculine legacy has come to nought. Suggestively, it is the women who must create anew what he fails to create; their biological productivity—their children—is not the defining attribute that Parameswaran ends the story with, but their identification of their history as lying within one another, in 'what was always hers,' in what was familiar. Reproductive, marital, spousal, and labour rights within the diaspora—often masked in introspections of individual subjectivities by diasporic Indian authors—are all quests that may be affiliated with Veeru's and Jitin's quest for what was always theirs, as is shown through their joint participation in struggles for the resolution of various kinds of parity through the organized movement. Unlike Divakaruni, then, Parameswaran is able to establish female same-sex love as a potent tool in re-worlding the world, enabling a critique of heteronormativity and political rhetoric in her protagonists' search for 'what was always hers', and therefore, only needing to be claimed.

Kamala Das's 'The Sandal Trees' shows how the legacy of the (un) familiar may go unclaimed till too late if lovers do not have 'the land of plenty' to feed on. 'The Sandal Trees' carries the transgressive and incestuous possibilities of sister–sister bonds further, explicitly sexualizing the attachment two half-sisters have to one another in the first half of their lives—showing that the etiology of lesbianism can be as much at home in the non-west as its more modern other, the west—together as sisters rather than at the tail end of their marital careers. Set partly in an ancestral Nair household in Kerala and partly in the modern city of Cochin a few decades after, 'The Sandal Trees' provides one of the few, and therefore invaluable accounts of the lesbian as an older woman. Das has been a remarkable fictional presence in the Malayalam short story, to say the very least. 'The Sandal Trees' is the first, and one could argue, the most compelling story in the collection *The Sandal Trees and Other Stories* (1995: the English version of *Chandanamarangal*, translated by V. C. Harris and C. K. Mohamed Ummer). The other stories of the collection engage once again with Das's most primary fictional material—the forest of the more normative man–woman relationships, their power relationships and filiations, negotiations and trade-offs, and as such 'Sandal Trees' is as much a critique of patriarchy as it is of heterodominance. Das in 'The Sandal Trees' filters through the prism of her protagonist's consciousness a set of disturbing realizations about the nature of love itself, complicated by the class equations generated by the feudal ecology that the protagonist and the amour she tries to disclaim.

Sheela, is the legitimate daughter of the Nair clan, who lives up to the decorum and piety that her name suggests. Sheela and Kalyani's story has its roots within the Nair clan. Sheela's monologic meditations yield the story of the present and the past, both hidden and in the open. 'The Sandal Trees' at least initially casts Kalyani as the evil familiar in a literal sense, 'an enemy who intensely hates me and all my relatives, dead and living' (Das 1995: 1), whose arrival from distant Australia on a vacation of a few weeks has wrecked many innocent lives, feels Sheela. Sheela's husband offers a taxonomy dividing women into two categories—harmless, asexual mothers and furies who 'can't help destroying everything' (Das 1995: 25). Placing Kalyani in the latter category, Sheela's husband tries to cheer up Sheela seeing how distraught she is at Kalyani's departure but as awhile earlier, driving to the airport to see Kalyani off, Sheela cannot see the 'Kalyanikutty who had turned into an avenging angel', instead seeing through teary eyes 'the old Kalyanikutty, my bosom friend who embraced me and dropped hot tears on my neck and shoulders...A girl whose skin had the colour of sandalwood' (Das 1995: 1–2).

The thought of Kalyani takes Sheela into the past where she is literally the fortunate one, and Kalyani the miserable charity-child supported by Sheela's family's largesse; 'the one who wore my old skirts and blouses and always accompanied me', and whose poverty meant the family kept her at arm's length literally, not giving her 'the right to enter my bedroom or dining room' (Das 1995: 2). Kalyani's socially prescribed role is 'to follow you as your shadow, as a maid to look after you', a familiar in more than one way, employed both as a menial and viewed as a false likeness, whose harsh tongue makes Sheela often accuse her of being an enemy rather than the beloved friend for whom Sheela fights with her family. The smell of sandalwood, intimately associated with Kalyani, is also the symbol for the silence that Sheela 'cultivated' between herself and her husband over the years of their loveless marriage, a tree 'giving...much happiness' to her (Das 1995: 13) who finds her wifely duties as exhilarating as 'eating leftovers, of eating leftovers over and over again' (Das 1995: 16). Silence permits her to 'awaken' from the spiritual death she experiences every day in the company of her husband—who in fact is for her a template for all men—but despite the beautiful silence the image of the sandal tree provides her, 'no relief was possible. I wandered in search of myself. At last, with drooping shoulders, I turned back and walked towards others' (Das 1995: 16) locked in the pain of never belonging to the woman who loves her and whom she loves too, unmistakably, in a fashion that is so primary as to remove all other considerations when the safety of this woman is endangered, as it is at one point during a botched abortion.

'The Sandal Trees' like most of Das's works, searches with chilling sangfroid 'a marriage that lasts for years, greying and rotting' (Das 1995: 12), a situation the protagonist Sheela notes, is, 'for civilised people, ... certainly impossible to bear' (Das 1995: 12). The husband, as usual, is much older than his wife—a twenty-one year gap between the spouses in this story—with his age serving to place them in different stages in the lifecycle prescribed by the Hindu shastras, which, despite not being explicitly mentioned, serve as spiritual and psychic signposts with which to create a workable cartography for life. But in 'The Sandal Trees' the husband's repulsiveness stands in contrast not to the clean virility of a younger male, but to the elegance of a woman of the same age as Sheela, Sheela's childhood friend and old lover, Kalyani. Attention to only the superficial devices of the plot would suggest that Kalyani is ironically named—Kalyani is a most inauspicious character indeed, managing in the space of a twenty-two-day vacation in Cochin to push the current wife of her ex-husband into attempting suicide upon finding that Kalyani had not only reunited sexually and emotionally with her husband of three decades ago, but was also planning to take the latter's daughter to Australia with her. The daughter emerges into open rebellion against her diabetic, always-ill mother, with the mother also claiming that there was something unnatural in the interest Kalyani took in the young girl. Kalyani's presence also succeeds in arousing Sheela's old husband into the wanting to commit adultery with her in his turn, though she spurns him—or so she tells Sheela.

The paradox, however, is that Kalyani's inauspiciousness is itself a function of Sheela herself being an embodiment of good conduct, as her name suggests. Sheela, 'born an aristocrat' (Das 1995: 11), cannot break away from the ostensibly natural-born ability of the aristocratic woman 'to live with such control' (Das 1995: 11) even as their fathers beget children like Kalyani on their poorer feudal dependents. Sheela's mother continues, perhaps in ignorance, perhaps in knowledge, Sheela's father's 'good works', sponsoring the education of Kalyani besides keeping an eye on the general welfare of her family. Kalyani is the more sharp-eyed one and even when they are children, one wonders why it is that she resembles Sheela though her genitor, at least socially, is Shekharan Master and not Sheela's father. Sheela, however, does not notice anything more than a well-brought-up girl should.

Kamala Das's figuring of lesbian desire in this context of miscegenation can be usefully read in the light of the notion of the familiar that defamiliarizes and makes strange—within the ecology of this story, with its bathing places where seductions happen, Kalyanikutty is a water sprite whose disappearance condemns Sheela to a barren existence with a husband who is very much like T. S. Eliot's 'Gerontion'. Kalyani's body radiates a glorious aroma as a result of her 'having swum and bathed in the pond for hours together, smelt and tasted of weeds and mosses, water lilies and medicinal herbs' (Das 1995: 26), striking in its healing connotations when observed against the malevolence radiated by the male body, with its genitalia described with surreal precision as 'hang[ing] loose and look[ing] unsewn', 'the figure of a rotten bitter-gourd' incapable of nothing other than mechanical oscillations (Das 1995: 15). Where the barren old man of 'Gerontion' is unstirred into fecundity even by mirrors infinitely replicating sexual fulfilment, Sheela's husband refuses to give Sheela children on ideological grounds—in a world soon to be decimated by nuclear stockpiles, what price are children? Kalyanikutty, on the other hand, wants Sheela's children, impossible as that is, and almost dies of a botched abortion to keep her womb free of any (male) other's children. Kalyanikutty is the perverse slippage in a feudal economy of desire where the female spouses only planted trees, while the males had the privilege of sowing wild oats in addition, but the fire in her belly is deliberately denied fuel by Sheela's almost moribund adaptations to her environment. Sheela almost strategically empties her life of the element of water, with its life-sustaining fluid connotations marking itself as different from the rigidities Sheela is forced to adopt every day in order to keep up the farce of marriage, taking herself farther and farther away from Kalyanikutty, only to find herself, at the end of the story, in 'the darkness that slowly spread in the car' (Das 1995: 26), old and empty, her ears sharp to the sound of Kalyanikutty's girlish laughter that seemed to rise from the dark waters of one of Cochin's numerous canals.

In 'The Old Playhouse', Das defines the wife thus: 'You called me wife,/ I was taught to break saccharine into your tea and/ To offer at the right moment the vitamins. Cowering/ Beneath your monstrous ego I ate the magic loaf and/ Became a dwarf.' At the end of 'The Sandal Trees', the opposite transformation takes place when Sheela finally realizes the value of the familiar that is Kalyani: 'Was it I, that woman with the glowing cheeks, hair clearly displaying its silver strands and the yet-to-be-effaced vermillion spot on the forehead? Never' (Das 1995: 26), finding herself transformed into a young girl, in the reverse of the process that seems to be transforming her still ageing 'very very old man' of a husband into a clown (Das 1995: 17). Trapped within heterosexual conjugality Sheela never did have a taste for, despite her best efforts to convince herself and Kalyani that it was what she sought, Sheela has become old enough to pass for Kalyani's mother even as Kalyani, free now of two marriages, looks so young no one can believe she is fifty-two, the same age as Sheela. Age and heterosexuality seem inter-linked in a causal relationship; even Kalyani when married to Sudhakaran is subject to the vicissitudes of ageing, appearing 'lean and haggard' in comparison to the 'healthy and handsome' Sudhakaran. Kalyani's haggard appearance has to do with an unwanted pregnancy, unwanted because it is Sheela's children she wishes to have, not the children of 'an ordinary *man*' like Sudhakaran (Das 1995: 7, emphasis mine); it is Sudhakaran's biology that makes him ordinary, not any personal attributes. Desiring only to love Sheela, to be with her and to give her pleasure, Kalyani's commitment is courageous just as Sheela's restraint is born of cowardice:

Still you chose for yourself the traditional path. The path to decadence … And now you have no one to call your own. No one cares for you. Of course certain people need you—to amputate suppurated diabetic limbs or to do a caesarean and pull out a baby. (Das 1995: 21)

Kalyani's characterization of Sheela's life as only instrumental to those in pain, and of no value or worth to the healthy and the living, least of all to herself is later ratified by Sheela when she finds Sudhakaran's daughter's questions about the naturalness or otherwise of Kalyani's love for her 'had fallen into my mind like a fishing hook in a lake' (Das 1995: 25). Unobtrusively reappearing at the end of the novel, this image of the self as a fish swimming in water, but flailing in air is completed when the smell of dried fish surfaces along the road Sheela and her husband are driving on homewards. The wind bears the smell of fish, but this is the smell finally of dead, dying fish, captured for sale and consumption; from the waters, Kalyani's girlish voice rises yet again, a reminder that Sheela has sacrificed herself in refusing to give and receive love from her sister, her likeness, her familiar, Kalyani. In between, Sheela's husband compares Kalyani and himself, saying, 'I was a mere drizzle arriving hesitantly, timidly, after a full storm' (Das 1995: 26); it is (un)familiar love that is presented throughout this story as the bread and the wine of life, while heterosexual love, for Sheela, is merely a transient drizzle, incapable of quenching her thirst and thus leaving her diseased, incapacitated, and in the pain of being unloved when love could have been had for the asking.

'I haven't betrayed you, and you haven't betrayed me. We have not slept apart for a single night' (Das 1995: 17) says Sheela when her husband asks her if they could possibly enter a contest for 'ideal couple'. While these parameters might suffice at least superficially to characterize ideal conjugality, Sheela's overwhelming everyday nausea at the sight of a companion who has become 'shameless' with old age, in contrast to the 'increasing sense of shame' women past a certain age feel at when the 'inelegances of their body start multiplying' (Das 1995: 14) makes very evident the nature of Sheela's preferences. Ascribing to all women a hatred of 'such ugly scenes' as can be witnessed when husbands take off their underwear and pace about naked, Sheela's description of their room as 'my room' calls attention to her husband's violation of her sense of space and self by the mere nature of his gender and its underlying exhibitionistic tendencies that mark it as different from the more dignified female body. In contrast to the gentle, refreshing odour of fresh linen, rain or sandalwood that marks Sheela's memories of Kalyani's body are Sheela's visions of heterosexual conjugality:

> To lie close to each other in the same bed and exchange the foul smell of sweat; to witness the excrement of your spouse who has forgotten to flush the toilet after use at sunrise; to feign sleep while slyly watching him masturbate, with his pretty fingers that seem to have been made for blessing others ... I don't want this much-praised *grihasthashram*. (Das 1995: 12–13)

In contrast to male selfishness in retaining pleasure for the male body is Kalyani's eagerness to give pleasure: 'I could not forget the way she had caressed me, pressed her fingers hard into me and satisfied me with her lips, all with the intention of giving me pleasure' (Das 1995: 5), smelling fresh and like nature itself in contrast to the stale, man-made odours of decay and dissipation that emerge from her husband's mouth. Twenty-six years later, when Kalyanikutty returns from Australia to see Sheela, each memory of the past is revived, carefully revisited and once again restored to their respective static places in the mind by Sheela who is unwilling to disturb 'that all too-familiar world of mine that comprised my house, the lovely objects on display there, my aged husbands, my patients' even though all she longs for is a positive answer to her heart-breaking question to herself: 'there is no other place for me to live ... and no one else to love me, is there?' as she returns home after dropping Kalyani at the airport. In 'The Sandal Trees', (un)familiar love plays out the dimensions of the lesbian lover as a mischievous familiar and at the level of same-sex love as a defamiliarizing medium through which to see the heart-breaking distortions heteronormativity produces on its craven adherents.

(Un)Familiar Femininity as Creativity

As analysed earlier, removal from one's sister, sometimes one's likeness or one's twin, is also a removal from one's natal home in favour of virilocal residence; the 'un-naturalness' of such a move is what is forcefully argued for by a number of texts in this section through their use of often disturbing—because the proscription against incest is so strong—tropes of love, erotic or otherwise, between those who have been marked as forbidden for one another. I now read Mary Anne Mohanraj's *Bodies in Motion* and Manju Kapur's *A Married Woman* as narrativizations of the exit from patriarchy as an entry into creative autonomy. Kapur's novel writes (un)familiar love between women into the cause of producing an Indian nation that is both secular and feminist; Mohanraj's examines the tension in binary discourses of diaspora as progressive and left-behind-nation/native place as regressive. The theme of narrativization that is implicit in the previous two sections is explicitly focalized in this section, as Kapur's and Mohanraj's protagonists' coming of age as an artist also coincides with her development of a personal theory of her own oppression as a woman by structures of family, marriage, child-rearing and domesticity. Alongside of her lesbianism, these protagonists achieve a measure of self-worth through their discovery of the artist in themselves, but this process is mediated in one text by a journey in search of community and belonging missing within prescribed, normative heterosexual structures and in the other by an elision of this life-journey itself to show only beginning and end. These novels like all the others we have seen so far in this book consciously or unconsciously makes use of and makes available the counterplotting of the male–male–female triangle of heterosexual fiction by replacing it with a female–female–male triangle where the primary erotic, psychic and even genital connections are made between women. That the complete realization of an autonomous female subjectivity is made possible by the removal of the male love interest from the triangle is noteworthy—taking off from Luce Irigaray (1985/1977) and Gayle Rubin (1975), we might say that the traffic of goods in the 'lesbian' novel occurs not between men, but between women; female–female eros subverts and re-defines the conventional erotic geometry of heterosexuality .

(Un)familiarity does not by definition only fail in the non-west, as Mary Anne Mohanraj's *Bodies in Motion* establishes. Three narratives out of almost two dozen centre around female same-sex love and desire, placed at two ends of this novel which is strung around a series of extended family snapshots of a Tamil and a Sinhala family apiece in Sri Lanka and in the global nations of the West, argue with the dictum that the non-west is a space where (un)familiar desires must be in exilic relationship with the home (Gopinath 2005: 166). The (un)familiar narrative I consider here is remarkable in its production of an aged lesbian subject, Mangai, whose story begins in the late-1940s. The first of Mangai's narratives is a tale in first person of her sudden sexual coming of age when she meets the beautiful Sushila, her brother Sunthar's newly-wed wife. Mangai is deemed too unattractive for the marriage-market, being 'too-short, too plump' with 'coarse hair and flat chest' and is thus, at the age of seventeen, already deemed an old maid (Mohanraj 2005: 24). In the week before the newly-weds leave for another home far away, Mangai and Sushila consummate their relationship; Mangai knows she has fallen in love, but Sushila is unwilling to 'lose caste, lose family, lose the future' in order to spend her lifetime with Mangai in deprivation, 'washing someone else's filthy clothes' as that seems to be the only possible avenue for earning a living that these two uneducated women will have apart from their families (Mohanraj 2005: 33). Sushila leaves after she and Mangai engage in the fitful secret space each night of the week in intricate love-making rituals that mark their bodies as one another's; the last line of the story, however, reads: 'the scar faded into nothing within a year' (Mohanraj 2005: 38). Mangai's sister-in-law can announce to Mangai before leaving that 'It's for the best, Mangai. You'll be married soon—try to be happy' (Mohanraj 2005: 33) but Mangai knows then that she 'would never marry' nor love anyone else the same way. At the end the narrative returns in 2002 to the same Jaffna village where in 1948 Sushila and Mangai had parted; Sushila is now safely in the Tamil diaspora in Canada with Mangai's brother, Sunthar, who has become, among other things, also a donor to the LTTE cause. Mangai, resistant to her brother's importuning her to live in safe America with them, has lived 'with her servant, Daya, for decades in a house with only one bed' (Mohanraj 2005: 273), not only confirming her own feelings about marriage from half a century ago but flaring up as an unusual kind of (un)familiar, resistant to heteronormativity, subverting hegemonic scripts for female desire despite the disarticulation and invisibility enjoined on her for the 'lack' of a discourse of queer sexual identity.

Mangai has evolved into an (un)familiar in more than one sense of the word this time; she enters this narrative as a wiry old woman in white who 'went out alone to the sea, every day, in her battered fishing boat' (Mohanraj 2005: 273). Fishing in order to support herself and her lover, Mangai's strangeness exceeds the merely sexual; the villagers 'let her fish' because they are also attuned to her 'madness' which has grown so old no one remarks on it any longer. But for the reader of the novel, who has now travelled through the many diasporic locations the other characters of the novel people, Mangai, in the home they all left behind, is the most wondrous thing our travels have yet shown us. Mangai's sexual identity would evidently require the word 'lesbian', given her life-long devotion to Daya, after whose death she takes to wearing widow's weeds. But the word 'lesbian' also, problematically, suggests a number of teleological narratives such as the ones suggested by *Fire* and *Sancharam*, where the nation as 'home sweet home' is viewed as the space of tradition that the queer female subject must escape from in order to attain a visible and intelligible identity. But as *Bodies in Motion* suggests, the space of the home as the (Sri Lankan) nation, in a forgotten Tamil village torn by the civil war between the LTTE and the Sri Lankan government, is far from closed, despite its impoverishment and its instability to the reach of (un)familiar desire. Far from being closed, this home compares favourably with another space in the First World: here, Leilani, the second-generation daughter of Sri Lankan Tamil immigrants in the USA, becomes a poet in defiance of the wishes of her mathematically ambitious family; she is also already lesbian, but unlike Mangai, the narrative leaves Leilani uncoupled after having informed us that in the course of her life, she will also have become bridesmaid to her lover. In this instance, Mangai's and Leilani's lives share a great deal despite their spatial and generational distance from one another. While Mangai never does have a 'lesbian' identity, having been branded 'strange' by the community she lives in, Leilani is visibly 'lesbian' though her family does not know this. Nevertheless, Leilani's lesbianism is camouflaged as celibacy and abstinence despite her being located in a presumably emancipated First World location. Within the diaspora, the premium upon female chastity is high enough for Leilani's mother to 'throw a pot of boiling crab curry at my head' which, while it misses the target, symbolically scars both mother and daughter (Mohanraj 2005: 103). Leilani and her mother are both bound within the conservative Tamil diaspora's expectations of its women while Mangai, within her Jaffna village, escapes from her own mother who never liked Mangai because Mangai was 'too clumsy, too fat' besides 'too dark' (Mohanraj 2005: 269). Setting up a home of her own, but among her own people, Mangai's (un) familiarity percolates the space of the nation in a way that Leilani's lesbianism cannot enter the space of the diaspora, while on the other hand, Leilani's non-Tamil peers know of her real emotional orientation. Mangai's (un)familiarity, thus, in contrast to Leilani's 'identity' can enter dialogue with her neighbours in which Mangai can stake her claim to live the way she wants and yet be part of the community, though 'one reason why Mangai can live in peace in this village [is that] she brings her neighbours as more pleasure as present scandal than she ever could as past expulsion' (Mohanraj 2005: 272). The scandal of Mangai's living with a woman all her life is told and retold, both 'what they know and what they guess' (Mohanraj 2005: 272). But as Mangai and Daya have always kept their own counsel, what the villagers 'guess' is more than what they 'know'. This epistemology of not knowing fully what a lesbian is, evidently, a great contrast to the dynamics of visibility, clarity, and consequent expulsion from the space of the home that films like *Fire* and *Sancharam* generate and wish to make paradigmatic. Mangai's story, on the other hand, in providing both a critique of the narrative of escape to the diaspora—from where Sushila sends her Teflon pans and other prize consumer goods—and a critique of the narrative of identity. In not making herself explicitly intelligible, Mangai's safety is assured, but years of uneasy coexistence precedes her current geriatric existence as a protected specimen on the fringes of life in the village.

Yet, the novel ends with Mangai cooking in plain view of all the village-belles intent on getting good husbands; Mangai's fame as a cook is so great that part of the unspoken bargain for her being left unmolested involves her letting generations of these village girls watch from outside her house as she cooks. Mangai's cooking is not an exhibition of skill, however, that will recuperate Mangai back into the economy of normative domesticity. Mohanraj on the other hand subverts the hearth by showing Mangai strip her withered septuagenarian body even as the food cooks. The novel ends with Mangai, now completely naked, leaning against the crumbling mud walls of her hut eating her splendid cooking after drinking from the same tin-cups she and Sushila drank water out of in their love-making fifty years ago: 'shuddering with pleasure, she eats' (Mohanraj 2005: 275). As the last words of this novel, these words make us reflect on the nature of sexual subjectivity; Mangai's love for Sushila, rekindled time and again in the marvellous spells of cooking that come upon her, attains a tangible presence even though we know Sushila herself has lived a chaste life with Sunthar all these years though Sunthar now knows without ever having been told that it is women she likes. Mangai's desire for rich food, cooked beautifully, is a metonym for her relationship with Sushila from long ago. While the psychic and social costs of choosing (un)familiar ways of living results in Mangai's having no opportunity for public affirmation of her grief for Daya, for instance, the aroma of Mangai's cooking does bring a circlet of village-girls around her to learn from her. Even these girls know that Mangai is what 'they will become in time' (Mohanraj 2005: 272), with the withering of the body in old age, the trappings of femininity will have worn away; the asexuality of Mangai's old age offers an analogue for her sexual unavailability to male masculinity through her youth. However, Mangai's desire in old age for rich 'food' suggests a full-blown critique of female imperviousness to desire; Mangai's asexuality is a critique not of femininity, but of heteronormativity. In fashioning a world for herself beyond heterosexual marriage, Mangai defies the normative. On a closing note, the word 'mangai' in Tamil means the ideal girl; it is a paradox that the girls of Mangai's village learn how to be a woman from a woman who has already stepped beyond the performance of femininity for the sake of masculine endorsement.

A Portrait of the Lesbian as an Artist

What happens however if the entire life in between must be imagined for Mangai as well? *A Married Woman* imagines the (un)familiar femme woman's life of self-discovery in parallel with her nation's moment of destruction—that of the Babri Masjid. Astha means 'faith', and Kapur's strategy of deploying such a name for her protagonist sets at rest any doubts one may have about the allegorical function of her narrative in contemporary India's attempt to resolve the role of religious belief in a secular state, though this state is underwritten by a peculiarly Indian re-casting of the secular signifier. In its counterpointing of personal history with social unravelment, this novel shares a great deal with R. Raj Rao's *The Boyfriend* (2010) and much of Shyam Selvadurai's work, where the gay male protagonists' articulations of gayness happens against a background of many non-sexual conflicts—with communal riots in Bombay and ethnic cleansing in Sri Lanka respectively. Homosexuality, then, in all these books, is not a universalized emotion that happens in a distinctly apolitical or unworldly space; the erotic is not a universalized, apolitical, other-worldly emotion, but one that is part of the re-worlding of the psychic and material spaces that the protagonists inhabit. Interestingly, *A Married Woman* also resonates with another lesbian novel from another time—Sylvia Townsend Warner's *Summer Will Shine*, where the wife and paramour of one (unfortunate?) man get together and become lovers, elliptically in the earlier book, graphically in Kapur's novel, like in Uma Parameswaran's story. *Summer Will Shine* has at its centre the French Revolution while *A Married Woman* returns time and again to the conflicted imaginings of 'Indianness' in the communalized public imaginary of India after the destruction of the Babri Masjid in 1991. Both novels share a common trajectory of female self-realization through same-sex erotic companionship, ironically made possible by heterosexual attractions that recede to the periphery. The 'powerfully physical relationship with a much younger woman' the blurb advertises materializes only when two-thirds of the book are already done, a placement that is remarkable if only in its difference from most other lesbian 'interludes', all of which invariably run their course in the first one-third of the narratives they appear in since lesbianism in most narratives is cast as penultimate to the 'real thing.' While most reviewers of the novel disapprovingly noted that Kapur's 'use' of a lesbian plot, if such it is, happens late in the day and seems adventitious to a novel titled 'a married woman', our reading below suggests that Kapur's delineation of 'a' married woman has the effect of suggesting that we reconsider 'marriage' itself: Kapur's novel at the very least contributes in providing a shift from the focus on marriage as largely heterosexual form of coupling at least in Indian society. At the same time, Astha's lesbian infidelity is not the only trouble her marriage has to go through.

Kapur's novel, located in the orthodox, conservative world of the New Delhi government elite and its underclasses, very accurately captures the changing yet static mindsets of this orthodoxy. This, I argue, only serves to routinize the lesbian within the humdrum throb of a patriarchy updating itself in accordance with the modernities of India in the 1990s—liberalization, globalization, and privatization. Locating itself in the centre of India's 'structural transformation' of its economy, *A Married Woman* queers domesticity, conjugality and contemporary historiography with its routinization of the lesbian in the realm of the familiar workings of everyday life. I argue that this patchwork quilt of social history and musings on one's own personal history may be read as an attempt to queer, to de-straighten the otherwise near-total heteronormativity of national and marital imaginings.

While 'Astha was brought up properly, as befits a woman, with large supplements of fear' in a house where her mother was always putting into 'a steel almirah another spoon, sheet, sari, piece of jewellery towards the girl's future' (Kapur 2002: 1), to marry and reproduce and be happy, *A Married Woman* is, in its totality, a carefully observed deflation of just such a heteronormative romantic fantasy. Astha's personal expectations of romance are typical of the romance-reading (heterosexual) girl. On the one hand, as important commentators have noted, romances give female readers both an opportunity to dream and an education in what is expected of them (see Radway 1983: 59). On the other hand, in masking the real-life impossibility of perfect conjugal harmony, they also produce in their readers anxieties when expectations are not met in reality. Girlhood crushes do not pay for the meal ticket in her humble family, and her only alternative is to 'drift into teaching' (Kapur 2002: 31) school students. The marks of 'confirmed adulthood' (Kapur 2002: 32) are a husband and children of her own, and soon Astha, and through the honeymoon, is 'too high to see the sludge that had gathered around the houseboat, too high to notice the slight smell that came from the stagnant edge' (Kapur 2002: 42). Once she settles into the aimless waiting that constitutes her prescribed dose of marital bliss in the home of her in-laws, largely ignored except at night by her businessman husband, the 'future seemed very pedestrian' (Kapur 2002: 47). On the one hand, because she has married into a family that has its pulse on the nation's growth in a way in which her own father, a less successful bureaucrat, did not, she is materially amongst the richest and most privileged top five percentile of Indians at that point in the eighties. On the other hand, because of this very prosperity, she finds that she serves best when she is a receptacle for children, preferably male children, and an adornment at parties. The in-laws are suitably emancipated in their desire that she work outside the home, but at a job that would not interfere with her wifely duties. Teaching it turned out, was 'good time-pass' that everyone approved of; it seemed as if 'all women were destined to be teachers or nothing' and Astha does indeed choose to teach rather than be a nothing. Astha becomes a traveller of sorts, between her affluent home and the (slightly) less privileged school she teaches at.

This is the moment of Astha's coming out. In sharp contrast to a homonormativity that presumes that the proclamation of one's (homo)sexual identity is the defining moment of one's coming of age, the evidence of most lesbian Indian texts reveals that one's voluntary revelation of one's sexual orientation is usually not the life-affirming moment for women in Indic characters. The moment of 'coming out' that permits characters like Astha to discover that 'the central thing in her life' (Kapur 2002: 51) does not have to be sex with their husbands. In a convincing manoeuvre, it takes a while before the narrative permits Astha to realize that she would rather engage with 'minds' rather than 'needs' all the time. Then follows another journey, one of looking into, around and at herself, in ways in which she had never been able to, or had mulishly refused at other times. The Astha who refuses to introspect—'I don't want to look inside myself' (Kapur 2002: 55), she tells her mother—becomes the Astha who is able to turn an unflinching gaze on herself and the world around her, to turn her experiences of it into art. Astha's movement from a very domesticated, romantic-brained girl is paralleled by the momentous restructuring of the Indian economy, first by delicensing, and then, through liberalization and globalization. While Kapur's novel does not explicitly make these parallels, the critical reader can see that Astha's emergence from the home, and her emergence into art are connected in at least some ways with the nation's emergence once again into the global economy. If Kapur wants the reader to focus on India's opening up to the world rather than to other events in its immediate history, then Astha's 'coming out' is validated in the same terms as the country's opening up—'gayness' and 'lesbianism' after all did enter the Indian public sphere as part of post-globalization discourses on AIDS, public health and whether government spending on public health was necessary in a market economy (Joseph 2005; Asthana and Oostvogels 2001).

Where it was earlier confined to the 'safe' heart of the densely urbanized older Delhi, the narrative gradually ventures out, with Astha's father-in-law's retirement, to their house in what was then South-West Delhi, into Vasant Vihar. The family move into the house that Astha's father-in-law had built on his lucky ticket in a cooperative housing society construction scheme, a pathetically sharp contrast to her own father's more unlucky draw of a 280-ft plot in a Trans-Yamuna jungle-plot. Vasant Vihar is both unmarked by the precedents that clutter Delhi's older conurbations, and affluent enough to be constricting in its own way for a woman who lived well in her husband's home, but had no idea of what the family's resources were. The novel also meanders South-East, with Hemant's business venture, into the now sufficiently urbanized 'NOIDA' sector, which at that time was 'Electronics City' only in governmental ambition. The Vasant Vihar that the senior Vadera draws is today the enclave of the very rich, those who have now come to be accepted as 'classily' so, while NOIDA remains the sector of Delhi that is motored by the dreams of a newly-liberalizing India, as opposed to the cluttered, older industrial areas of North Delhi. Hemant's business also takes him to consumerist-paradise:

> Four times a year Hemant travelled. The glamour of international references entered the house, as he flew to South Korea and Japan looking for the best deals. He always went alone, which he claimed he needed in order to establish personal contacts. He invariably came back in great good humour, with generous presents for everyone: perfume, chocolate, sweaters, jeans, toys, Japanese dolls, games for the children, underwear for Astha, toiletries, soaps, creams, shampoo [sic], kitchen and electronic equipment. Gradually their house acquired the gloss of a house with money. (Kapur 2002: 71)

This catalogue of acquisitions is an excellent illustration of the aspirations of pre-liberalization India. The austere self-sufficiency that the Nehruvian modernity aimed at through the 1950s and 1960s was gradually giving room now, in the 1980s, for desires for consumerist gratification. The capital, intellectual, creative and financial, locked up by previous investments was crying to be spent somewhere else. The gifts that come for Astha however reflect none of these socio-economic changes; they are after all fancy pieces that keep her in the old place of sexual commodity though she herself had 'changed from being a woman who only wanted love, to a woman who valued independence' (Kapur 2002: 72) though no one notices.

Another form of consumerist pleasure was being enacted in the communications revolution that in many ways was the precursor of the 1990s globalization of Indian media, especially with the entry of cable television. Astha's husband seizes these post-globalization opportunities, quitting a placid public-sector job to set up a colour-TV manufacturing unit. Innocuous as they looked, these colour televisions are heralds of a new order of things. The Asian Games of 1982, for the telecast of which the Indian government first sanctioned public broadcasting in colour, marks the turning of the tide though Astha sees none of this. The advent of cable television via satellite antennas was making it possible for sufficiently well-heeled Indians to watch in India programmes that would earlier be smuggled in on grainy VHS tapes. While on the surface it looks like the protagonist misses the boat, various episodes through the novel chronicle the small though revealing belittlements that the married woman undergoes in the course of her married career all of which might add up to kill her initiative and creativity even as it fosters her husband's entrepreneurship. This systematic counter-narrative to the romance novel brings us via Astha's growing disillusionment, pain and ennui, typified by her aggressive headaches, to yet another summer vacation. A theatre workshop at the school she teaches in brings her in contact with the left-leaning Aijaz Akhthar Khan, an agit-prop theatre ideologue who is also good looking and intelligent. Lest the guise fool us, Aijaz is not the sweet romantic hero making a rather late entry; Aijaz is sexually inviting, a far cry from the sexually disciplined ideal man of the romance genre, and appears to also not be above deception. But either way, the novel has Aijaz transform Astha not by resorting to the cliché of an extra-marital affair, but by drawing out her creativity, last manifested during her honeymoon, another period of intense sexual awareness that entangles with the monogamy Astha is expected to adhere to. Astha's second coming, however, takes her on a journey that is at best firmly tangential to the journeys good married women must make, such as journeys to places of pilgrimage, like Astha's widowed mother does. Aijaz is the thinly disguised fictional alter-ego of Safdar Hashmi, whose death marks a watershed in Kapur's chronology of modern Indian history. Aijaz, 'the voice of the underprivileged' (Kapur 2002: 102) speaks for those people and things the new media, the new consumer opportunities and the new culture of liberalization, globalization and privatization try to leave behind. Where Hemant can say with conviction 'we are not deprived Indians any longer' (Kapur 2002: 102) with justice about his upper-middle-class cohort, Astha is not sure it applies to her, or to women of the same upper-middle-class ilk, because despite an obvious affluence that sees to it that the husbands spend enough on the wives' 'clothing and jewellery that she always looked well turned out' (Kapur 2002: 72) these wives hardly had cash to dispose of as they desired. Astha's relative deprivation within patriarchal affluence gives her a point of entry into Aijaz's proclaimed aims: 'to create empathy, generate social awareness by having workshops that involve workers and students, bridge the class divide' (Kapur 2002: 103). Aijaz's entry permits Astha to evolve a conscious theory of protest against her gradual interpellation into subservience so insidious that it made her victimhood itself look dubious.

While Hemant is quick to spot a business opportunity in the television business, it is Astha who sees the transformations television-viewing wrought. The dangerous homogenization of representations is one of the novel's immediate concerns: the serialization of the Ramayan is an epochal moment in the history of the media in India, an event whose significance is not lost even upon children who grew up in the 1980s. Watching the Ramayan on Sunday mornings became a sacrosanct ritual, pan-Indian in the observance it elicited. Astha's house is no different:

Every Sunday morning, the family gathered upstairs before a ClearVision TV, twenty-inch screen, manufactured by the son of the house, and watched the story of the Ramayan. Week after week they agreed, this was the golden age of India, this is our noble heritage, now thoroughly debased, when justice flourished, when Hindus had pride, when a king showed responsibility towards his people, when a king showed responsibility towards his people, when duty, honour, devotion, truth and loyalty had a place in Ram Rajya. And today the birthplace of this king, our Lord, is occupied by a mosque, the shame of it, dismissing as nonsense the protest that it was not possible to really place the exact spot of a man's birthplace so many thousands of years ago. (Kapur 2002: 105)

Television mega-serials produce a script that in the novel Manju Kapur challenges with Astha's own script for the play that Aijaz's workshop will produce. Kitschy as it looks to the viewer revisiting it today, the characteristic feature of the Doordarshan production of the Ramayan was its un-self-conscious mimesis, its untroubled confidence about representing a myth of such emotive and religious significance. In contradistinction to this almost smug self-confidence is Astha's script-writing, anxious but thorough in its search for the truth. Religious conflict can be made to come to the boil better if participants are assured of the seeming timelessness of the conflict. Removing all elements of context from particular frictions, reducing them to what is seemingly their kernel of 'Hindus and Muslims have never, will never get along' is the formulation Kapur's exploration of Astha's creative process seeks to challenge.

Aijaz himself, the inspiration for Astha's art, is as seductive a (male) muse as 'Bharat Mata' is to the imaginers of the fundamentalist Indian nation. Astha's creativity has a distinctly erotic if not directly sexual edge, locating it as other to patriarchal feminine work. Devouring every inch of Aijaz's body with the ardour of a devotee though allowing herself only 'frequent covert glances' (Kapur 2002: 112), drinking in eyes, limbs, muscle- and skin-tone, gait, frame, energy and pearly white teeth, she finds 'the thought of not having anything to show Aijaz drove her on' (Kapur 2002: 108) to write, and then paint him. Astha sublimates her sexual desire into art, even as her husband identifies this artistic labour as labour alienated from his patriarchally sanctioned proprietary ownership of all her productive capabilities. The play is successfully performed, but within days, Aijaz is burnt to death in a gruesome act of politically motivated and sponsored arson along with the rest of his theatre group in one of the wilder parts of western Uttar Pradesh. Aijaz's death draws Astha out of her house for the first time, to walk with the massive crowd protesting his murder ever to do something other than the dignified 'time-pass' that her teaching career has been. The communalism that Astha recognizes as having its home in the retrospective homogeneous imaginings of an uncontaminated Ram Rajya in India free of Muslims has claimed the life of a theatre-artist because, as Hemant says with scarcely masked schadenfreude, 'he was a Muslim, he should have kept to the issues within his own religion' (Kapur 2002: 139).

Astha's act of mourning completes the coming out that her humble teaching career commenced. Art becomes an exit from an erotic monogamy, and Astha starts painting again, resuming a forgotten girlhood hobby and her canvases make tidy sums of money for the Sampradayikta Mukti Manch, a foundation set up by a female admirer to further Aijaz's legacy. Where sex with Hemant never enters Astha's subconscious, the trauma of the loss of Aijaz reinscribes Astha's erotic landscape. She dreams of Aijaz, the dream begins with Astha and Aijaz seated in an auto-rickshaw, kissing. More important than the kiss, however, is the fact that they are in the auto-rickshaw, the form of public transport Astha takes to get around Delhi; the auto-rickshaw gives Astha at least partial mobility, if not the absolute freedom conferred by that bulwark of individual liberty, the motor car. The auto-rickshaw is an unobtrusive signifier throughout the novel of Astha's status—as a woman of means, but no independence—and her efforts at broadening her curtailed strides. Aijaz himself is a vehicle, a humble one like the auto-rickshaw, for these dreams, but having been suppressed for so long, they must return only in dreams, prefaced by headaches so severe as to be pre-emptive punishments for the marital infidelity Astha is about to embark on. However, the moment of consummation within her dream is a moment of what in lesbian writing is a characteristic doubling of erotic possibilities. Aijaz suddenly metamorphoses into Reshana Singh, who in the interim has been acting as a sort of agent for Astha, exhibiting her work to best advantage and procuring good prices for it for the Manch's work. Where Aijaz was the muse, Reshana as the manager proxies in the role of sustainer that Astha plays vis-à-vis her family. Reshana does for Astha what only Astha's father had done so long ago—encourage her, however slightly, into entering herself as it were. Reshana's ends are not entirely altruistic, of course, and she makes a hasty exit once

Aijaz's widow Peepeelika enters Astha's life, but regardless, Reshana enters and successfully displaces Aijaz in what would otherwise have been Astha's only act of (emotional) infidelity with a man. Reshana's entry into the incipient Astha–Hemant–Aijaz triangle marks the moment of rupture of the male–male–female triangle by the more reactive female–female–male one. Astha is disturbed enough by Reshana's intrusion to immediately have sex with Hemant, but the physical act is not potent enough to push away the newly arrived (un)familiar homoerotic desire.

The uncanny dream provides Astha with the material for another painting, the one that confirms the first was no fluke and encourages in her thoughts of taking up art professionally:

> The disturbance lingered with Astha all next day, the vividness and strong emotions of her dream demanding some kind of recognition. Hesitantly she started making sketches. Two women faced each other in a scooter, their noses covered because of the pollution, only the eyes visible. The scooter-wallah was a dark Sardarji with a striking red turban. Perched next to him was a young man, taking a ride. Around the edges of the canvas, traffic, buildings, road, but at the centre the scooter with its passengers bent towards each other, the *devouring* eyes, the Sardarji and the young man. (Kapur 2002: 155, emphasis mine)

The desired but repressed genital contact with the familiar—the woman, Reshana—is here displaced to the realm of the visual; Astha makes a painting in which women's eyes devour other women. Sex with Hemant, and anticipated sex with Aijaz, then, were both red herrings; the real thing is here, with *devour* suggesting very accurately the performance of a lesbian sexual consummation that is markedly different from the pleasures of a penetrative heterosexual encounter. Painting becomes both means and an end: a means to creative and sexual autonomy, and an end in that *devouring* gives Astha pleasure that is valuable for its sake, food for the body transformed into food for the soul. 'Women Travelling' presages Astha's first real journey away from family. She takes a train, again another important signifier of a modernity that permits subversion of patriarchy and, sometimes, heteronormativity—as is the case in Kamala Das's *My Story*—to address a public meeting at Ayodhya on Reshana's insistence. In the months leading up to the destruction of the Babri Masjid, *kar sevaks*—marshalled from the common folk, not only from the card-carrying RSS/Hindu Mahasabha/BJP fold—had been gathering at Ayodhya for *Ram darshan*. Astha goes with the Sampradayakta Mukti Manch as one of the voices against this potentially mischievous mobilization of religious workers. It is here she meets Peepeelika Khan, Aijaz's widow, who has scrupulously kept away from Reshana Singh's activities so far because of her objections to the latter's commercialization and elitization of what she thinks are Aijaz's true legacies—his ability to appeal to the masses by the strategic use of a Brechtian rhetoric. Safdar Hashmi had, over the course of his theatre career, spoken of the need to re-fashion the structures of the traditional drama to create a medium capable of transmitting current realities. Hashmi, like his alter-ego Aijaz here, is aware of the interpellative power of artistic forms that artists have not made their own. Reshana Singh, working within the received wisdom of petitions, scholarly lectures and art exhibitions, takes Aijaz's legacy away from the subaltern classes he worked amongst, though he himself was an academic. Though Peepeelika is aware of this estrangement, it is Astha who fashions an artistic medium supple enough to both resist the snobbery of a verifiably 'high' culture, and the crassness of propaganda.

The seed for homoerotic desire has long lain buried within mourning for Aijaz, but with Peepeelika's long awaited arrival on the scene, the object of desire reveals itself to be not Reshana, but Peepeelika herself. Desire is recognized in incongruous moments: Peepeelika's arm tightens around Astha's in driving a monkey off Astha's back in Ayodhya; Astha feels cared for and worthy of love after a very long time. Our heroine finally has a series of dates with someone, albeit a woman, dates that do not involve the *in camera* performance of pioneering heterosexual caresses in the back-seat of a car. Instead, Peepeelika takes Astha here and there across Delhi on her motor scooter, which, much like the public transport that Astha has been taking all along, becomes another of modernity's liberating instruments. And unlike that early affair with a boyfriend, Astha is not afraid to be seen with Peepeelika. There is disapproval, but since Peepeelika is a woman, it does not look like the hymeneal barrier of conjugal fidelity can be breached here: 'Since Pipee was a woman, this disapproval was tinged with contempt and the assurance of no threat' (Kapur 2002: 218). The glorious irony is also that Astha herself feels liberated from the proscriptions of patriarchal organization of the female spouse's desires: 'indeed had Pipee been a man, Astha would have found it impossible to stray so far down the road of intimacy, or be so comfortable with it' (Kapur 2002: 218). Since female homoeroticism is so completely disregarded by heteronormativity to the point of absolute dis-recognition of any threat-potential, Astha is finally able to step out of an unrewarding monogamy. The 'mirror moment' of much homosexual writing is staged in Kapur's novel too.

> Are we going to do mirror, mirror on the wall / Who is the fairest one of all?' laughed Astha nervously....
>
> A modern version of it,' said Pipee putting on the light and pushing Astha's head gently forwards. 'Look.'
>
> Astha tried to turn away, 'I don't like looking at my face, especially so close.'
>
> Then she felt Pipee's hands in her hair, her clip undone, her hands framing the oval of her face. Lightly from behind she traced her eyebrows with her fingers, her nose, cheeks and mouth.
>
> The two women said nothing looking at their reflections in the small water-stained mirror. 'See?' whispered Pipee.
>
> Astha saw nothing, and abruptly left the bathroom. (Kapur 2002: 221)

Astha recognizes what is familiar, herself, but refuses to acknowledge it, to claim it and thus validate it. Astha's selfhood, fed only by the very rare acknowledgements of her family, is attenuated to the point of spectrality itself—'Astha saw nothing' when Pipeelika sees something. Astha herself has become a ghost, a spectre of herself, in following heteronormativity's rules so closely. To become visible in the mirror, to partake of the flesh, Astha has to be with someone who sees her, and not a wife. The infidelity that punctures most marriages, even successful ones, is literalized in the person of Pipeelika who kisses Astha's hands with the attention to detail Astha has not known in a while. The gender of the desired lover, however, is markedly different from the expectations raised by most romance or indeed, ordinary fiction. A woman helps Astha return to the world of embodied agency, selfhood and self-recognition, bringing her to be able to re-affirm her own existence instead of negating it. Thus, in *A Married Woman*, (un)familiar love enables Astha to find her way back to herself while heterosexual conjugality had merely displaced her from herself; queering the function of 'marriage' thus, Kapur is able to make Astha demand a more equal negotiation with hetero-normativity.

The disavowal of her selfhood is a cumulative corrosive procedure stretching over years of trying to maintain marital peace. Astha's avowal of selfhood, however, is a short flowering, short even in the space it occupies within the novel. Manju Kapur, writing in the twenty-first century, does not have to resort to the tropes of either silence or ellipsis in describing the coupling. Kapur also stages Pipeelika's first exploration of Astha on the martial bed for good measure, so that Hemant is paid back in kind: 'Women,' said the husband emphatically after a somewhat long phone conversation the wife had had with her friend, 'always mind-fucking' (Kapur 2002: 218). The joke is very much on Hemant when Astha realizes that 'mind-fucking,' far from 'lacking the excitement of the real thing ... [because] the organ penetrated the ears, the weapon of penetration, words,' was also liberating in the permission it offered for public performance of desire. 'Words, that left no mark but in the mind' permitted 'listening upon listening, fucking upon fucking. In full view' (Kapur 2002: 219), a fucking that Astha carries to its full physicality in a hurried afternoon meeting with Pipeelika. All these snatched moments permit a thorough cuckolding of Hemant that goes beyond the physical; the mind and the body both gratified alike, Astha realizes that she has found not only sex, but friendship: 'making love to a woman took getting used to ... And it also felt strange, making love to a friend instead of an adversary' (Kapur 2002: 231). The strangeness of this physicality however also mean that for 'an affair with a woman was not an easy thing for a husband to suspect' either (Kapur 2002: 232). Astha becomes capable of guile and strength, competently telling lies to further her amour, persuading her husband to buy her a car to further her mobility and thus, the range of her time with Pipeelika.

Unlike her non-monogamous husband, however, Astha is burdened by the operations of sexual guilt; her assigned care-work duties as a married woman mean that the sharpest burden is that of not being emotionally available for Pipeelika, and this, perhaps inevitably prises the two apart. Astha is unable to relate at a film festival to the coming-out on-screen, of 'the men and women ... speaking broad American about the discrimination they faced as gays' (Kapur 2002: 237). They all live in the 'open, none of them living a life of lies,' but the pure truth is another problematic category, its decontamination itself meaning that Astha must give up those things in her life she values at least as much as she does her lesbian love—her children and the home. Pipeelika, on the other hand, very much wants a life out in the open, but then, Pipeelika has definite assets, positive and negative—a home bought with among other things, the money due from her dead husband's life insurance, a supportive mother, unlike Astha's, no burdens in the form of children for the sake of whom fictions of happiness must be maintained, relative mobility in her life as a single woman free of in-laws, and so on. Astha's investment in the epistemology of partial disclosure is evident, but Pipeelika's desire for complete disclosure and presumed liberation is also presented as legitimate. Kapur's caution in endorsing the homonormativity that Pipeelika's desires embody in her quest for absolute 'openness' is noteworthy. This represents an important counter-narrative to mostly Euro-American prescriptions of a 'healthy' (sexual) existence. In the colonial period, the 'healthy' colonial functionary would be free of the contaminations of both 'tropical diseases,' and of sexual or erotic desire for the 'natives' that was only a prelude to the shame of miscegenation. A new queer imperialism, not unremarked by non-western critics, is slowly falling into place even in the non-west, with 'out'-ness being identified with modernity, and closetedness with a tradition always retrograde in its shaming of non-heteronormative sexual desire. Manju Kapur's novel understands that the interstitial spaces provided by patriarchy—but unsuspected of performing any such function—are capable of nourishing the roots of very strong and very fulfilling homoerotic desires, but at the same time, she does not valorize these possibilities. In a modernizing India, the spaces of the home are not uncontaminated by modernity—if indeed this ever was possible—nor are the protagonists themselves 'authentically' traditional by any stretch of the imagination. In a changing India, female homosexual desire itself is produced and marked by several modernities, orthodox and unorthodox. Astha does not walk in the path of western materialist feminism to reject the family altogether;

it is important enough to her to fashion a resistance that does not involve her leaving the space of the family altogether, which given her desire for it, would have been a capitulation, not a utopian celebration of autonomy. Astha cannot generalize on the nature of her desire either, for lack of sexual experience: so she does not know if she is a 'radical lesbian' who loves another woman for political reasons, or for personal ones. Indeed these are not the questions the novel poses. *A Married Woman* recognizes an overwhelmingly Indian reality—that the majority of women-loving-women in India are already married, a fact noted by almost all grassroots organizations.

Significant scholarship on the masculinization of Hinduism in contemporary India shows that antecedents traced as far back as Swami Vivekananda, who called for virile young men to come forward and work hard to lift India out of the morass of crippling traditionalisms. The antidote to the masculinity in *A Married Woman* is the queer female subject, whom Astha embodies at several levels—that of the female artist, the woman troubled by (heterosexual) monogamy and conjugality, and finally, the woman who desires woman. This female subject, however, grows out of precisely the realm of the familiar—the strong Hindu family replete with 'family values'—to challenge it not by her obvious departure from this space, but by her re-spatialization of this apparatus. Astha as resisting subject grows out of a very passive femininity, forced to account for every rupee or minute of the day it spends, a category of existence that heterosexual patriarchy finds useful to keep at home, ostensibly so the children are reared better to make good national subjects. Astha makes excuses to go away on a three-week trip with Pipeelika, with the two of them as part of a group of observers following a major national leader's Rath Yatra, the Ekta Yatra, from Kanyakumari back to Delhi part of the way. At Kanyakumari, the Vivekananda Rock, where Swami Vivekananda is supposed to have pledged to uplift the Indian masses only awakens Astha's guilt at being away from her family, away from the work she had been doing all these years, the labour that she seems to have been ordained for: the 'home work' of child-rearing. This national journey, however, conducted as it is in the teeth of resistance from everyone including Astha's widowed mother who herself spends months in the company of her guru at his ashram in the hills, represents Astha's equivalent of the celibacy that Vivekananda exhorts, though Astha's celibacy has to be defined as her resistance to functioning any longer within the patriarchal panopticon of her husband's home. Where Astha's mother's widowhood gives her the sanction to renounce sexuality, Astha realizes that as a 'married woman,' or a woman in the peak of her sexual and emotional career, religion does not offer her avenues other than blissful devotion to conjugal duties for the realization of autonomy. Astha's personal circumscription within the family as wife, mother and daughter are thus challenged by Astha's assumption of the role of unencumbered traveller—at least in theory—on this trip. Travel emerges as an alternative to the life of the family that Astha wants to partake of, but finds inadequate because it de-recognises her selfhood. At the same time, in such a Rath Yatra, Astha's and Pipeelika's lesbian relationship is itself a challenge to the heteropatriarchal nature of most religious fundamentalisms, many of whom have characterized lesbian love as an inducement to race suicide. Astha does not get to spend as much of her time on this journey loving Pipeelika as she would have wanted, for the latter is now beginning to think of life ahead, of research and higher education, both of which she can plan for rather than dream of, being unencumbered. Despite the distance, for Astha, the Rath Yatra, though a fundamentalist initiative to foment communal violence through religious mobilizations, becomes her only vacation from family and home ever: freed of everyday duties, Astha is able to think.

The virile heterosexual masculinity demanded of the *kar sevaks* who would build a Ram temple at Ayodhya finds its radical other in the almost ineffable homosexual desire Astha feels for Peepeelika. The (un)familiar homoerotic desire that catalyzes the crystallization of Astha's now quiescent subjectivity haunts her home, the marital home, in various ways. There is a spectrality to both this desire and to the resistance to it: her husband, children and in-laws all disapprove of her increasing autonomy. But what are they to disapprove of? That their daughter-in-law/wife/mother was doing very well at both motherhood and attaining social regard for her non-maternal labour as an artist? These dual responsibilities have an effect on Astha of course: her headaches function throughout as an externalized register of Astha's unconscious perception of her 'sick' role. The sick person has to be validated by society in many ways; medical practitioners must first certify the sick person is indeed sick, and this diagnosis must be confirmed at periodic intervals so that a non-sick person does not get away with deceiving society with non-performance of his/her social responsibilities. However, headaches function in a peculiar way in the sickness firmament: headaches do not have physiologically indubitable symptoms like say, a fever would have; thus, headaches in a sense function as sicknesses that leave room for performances that cannot necessarily be corroborated by physical evidence. Headaches, in that sense, are spectral diseases almost—non-sufferers think the sick person is slumming, while the sick person feels victimized that others around her do not find her disease important enough to care for her.

Astha's headaches, which first apear somewhere after her successful production of a male son and heir, mark her repressed rebellion and her unacknowledged pain at being 're-cast' to fit the moulds that patriarchy and heteronormativity demand of her. It is important to note that during the course of her affair with Peepeelika, Astha is 'cured' of her headaches altogether, a feat that surgery and other medical interventions had not been able to accomplish. The headaches reappear when Peepeelika leaves India for the US and a PhD. The medicine for Astha's sickness then, was homosexual desire and its fulfilment; Astha's emergence from 'sickness' into health is mediated by her lesbian relationship with Peepeelika, who takes Astha's freedom from sickness as her due. But upon her return home, the law of the Father takes over. Astha is racked by jaundice, and the nation too falls 'ill,' descending into the relative anarchy of the early 1990s marked by communal violence and political assassinations accompanied by economic turmoil. The paterfamilias literally personified in figures like leaders of the Rath Yatras and leaders who spearheaded the destruction of the Babri Masjid will have their due, it seems. The nation and Astha both find their mirror images immediately after they descent into sickness repulsive; their convalescence is troubled. The nation has to let go of its old socialist principles in asking for World Bank assistance, provided upon condition of economic transformation. The woman has to accompany her husband—pushed to the brink by factory troubles—on a family holiday to the USA so he has time away from the multiple factors that threaten him with heart disease. In the end, when Astha returns from the family holiday abroad, Pipeelika is ready to leave and Astha is abandoned, it would seem, to the strained fabric of heteronormative conjugality just as the nation is to the hyperbolic masculinity of a Hindutva that attains its culmination at the end of the novel with the tearing down of the Babri Masjid. Does fundamentalist patriarchal reinscription of religion, defined into homogeneity that denies difference, win at the end of the day?

> Astha feels 'like a woman of straw, her inner life dead, with a man who noticed nothing, with whom for that very reason it was soothing to be with. Her body was his, when they made love, it was Pipee's face Astha saw, her hands she felt. She accepted the misery of this disloca-tion as her due for being a faithless wife. (Kapur 2002: 287)

Astha's spiritual death is akin to the decomposition of the body politic. But Astha is still able to hold a parting art exhibition in Pipeelika's honour. Among other canvases of Pipeelika and herself masked as Every woman, is 'Women Travelling'. The plot comes full cycle here—Astha no longer travels in auto-rickshaws; she has just returned from two major journeys—one spanning the length of India, and another to and from the USA; she is also a seasoned traveller between 'flimsy possibilities' and their 'mangled and inert' comfortless real life manifestations (Kapur 2002: 287). Realizing that 'life was made up of these things' (Kapur 2002: 285), namely disaffection, emptiness, and perpetual seeking, but unlike her mother, Astha is unable to see the virtue of detachment, wanting instead to be able to fight like Pipeelika or Aijaz. Instead, all she, Astha, whose name means Faith, has is 'Faith in herself' (Kapur 2002: 299). Hitherto, Astha's lack of self-confidence, the corollary of her almost total orphanhood within her married existence, is also reminiscent of the morbid self-negation of colonized India, but that Astha's self-confidence should spring from homosexual fulfilment is the important departure Kapur's imagining of the nation makes. The tenuousness of this relation to the self, however, is evident when, in the last pages of the novel, Astha is not allowed to say a dignified goodbye to Pipeelika; the narrative's refusal to provide a stately closure need not be interpreted as a disempower-ing dis-articulation. On the other hand, in leaving Astha 'stretched thin, thin across the globe' (Kapur 2002: 307), *A Married Woman* suggests a homosexual subject that cannot be pinned down, and thus disciplined. Astha, like faith, is a free floating subjectivity whose needs cannot be met by the home that she nominally inhabits as familiar—a willing pair of hands for difficult and easy tasks, sexual gratifications and care-giving—and who may, thus, by virtue of her seeming omnipresence, also travel without anyone's noticing.

***

(Un)familiar forms of nation, family, diaspora and home are key themes in the texts in this chapter. Leilani in *Bodies in Motion* finds her vocation as poet only after she discovers she loves women, not men. But while Mohanraj is able to produce spaces of individual autonomy albeit different in nuance both for young Leilani and the very aged Mangai, Manju Kapur's novel ends as Kamala Das's short story does, with a woman returning from the airport after having seen her lesbian lover off to a country she cannot follow. While Das's Sheela could have run away with Kalyani to Australia, her self-conditioning and years of habituation have made a living 'corpse' of her, such that she cannot move or act to satisfy herself any longer. Similarly, Manju Kapur's *A Married Woman* is quite pessimistic about the possibilities for the inclusion of queer challenges to normative scripts for family, tradition and nation and femininity in the new, possibly Hindu nationalist future that awaits India. Kapur's novel when it ends, anticipates the arrival of free India's first Right-leaning national government with a dismay that is clearly informed by its understanding of how Hindu fundamentalism has marshalled the chaste body of the Hindu woman as both territory to defend against the Muslim (rapacious male) Other, as well as territory to police against miscegenation (volitional or otherwise). This corruptible body of the female Hindu is symbolized by Astha, whose life story again covers very important political events, from the destruction of the Babri Masjid to political unrest and violences unleashed by the event, to the Rath Yatra of the BJP through India for mass mobilization to the cause of Hindu nationalism. Why place the history of a relationship between two women in parallel to the trajectory of the entry into mass-politics of the ideology of Hindu fundamentalism? Making the public intrude into the private in more than one way, feminist and queer, once again, we could read Manju Kapur's *A Married Woman* as a narrative that writes homosexual love between women into the causes of producing an Indian nation that is secular, feminist, and queer. The themes of self-fashioning that are implicit in the previous texts are explicitly focalised here too, as Kapur's protagonist's coming of age as an artist also coincides with her theorization of her own oppression as a woman by structures of family, marriage, child-rearing, and domesticity. Alongside of her lesbianism, Kapur's protagonist achieves a measure of self-worth through her discovery of the artist in herself but this process is mediated by a journey in search of community and belonging, missing within prescribed, normative heterosexual structures. Placing the (un)familiar geometry of a female–female–male triangle within the terrain of modern India under attack from Hindu fundamentalism makes clear that Kapur sees religious nationalism as heteropatriarchal, even as the prior, apparently secular modern Indian nation's failure to address gendered oppressions even for the relatively empowered middle-class woman is signalled by her protagonist's lack of a sense of self-worth, or indeed self. The ideologies of Hindu nationalism and secular nationalism are not very different then, in their gender-negligent quotidian-ness, but Hindu nationalism on the other hand, is further threatening in its explicit containment of female desire within the exclusive space of traditionally sanctioned wifely and/or filial domestic duty. Thus, special roles for men and women within traditional 'Hindu' prescriptions (the quote marks signal that Hinduism in this case is the reading fixed on it by rightist religious fundamentalism, not necessarily reflective of larger Hindu practice) are a new entrant to the civil society dialogue. While Hindu fundamentalism did not necessarily take birth in the 1980s, its political avatar was certainly consolidating at a pace completely new. The voices that refract through the protagonist's search for ways to deal with her erotic and thanatic impulses then are that of secular feminism and Hindutva ideals of womanhood; what the two spaces have in common though is that they negate the homoerotic or the homosexual possibilities of desire thoroughly, at least in terms of what might be revealed anywhere in public. Astha gets around this proscription by using art as a piece of unconscious that reveals the repressed and thus forces private reflection if not open dialogue at the level of plot. Texts like Kapur's *A Married Woman* offers a counterplot of female homosexual desire that strategically harnesses the very dis-articulations imposed upon the incipient and tentative female subject by heteronormativity and patriarchy to make possible a selving. The sheer (un)familiarity of the queer female subject does place her beyond the scope of life-giving affirmations within patriarchy, but at the same time, its (un)familiarity also allows it to appropriate the disarticulation of invisibility to subvert it into becoming a means of articulating a desire that is not normative.

References

Das, Kamala. 1995 (trans. V. C. Harris and C. K. Mohamed Ummer). 'The Sandal Trees', *The Sandal Trees and Other Stories*. Hyderabad: Navya Printers.

Divakaruni, Chitra Banerjee. 1999. *Sister of My Heart*. London: Doubleday.

———. 2002. *The Vine of Desire*. London: Abacus.

De Certeau, Michel. *The Practice of Everyday Life*. Berkeley: California: California UP, 1984.

Faderman, Lillian. 1981. *Surpassing the Love of Man: Romantic Friendship and Love between Women from the Renaissance to the Present*. London: Junction Books.

———. 1991. *Odd Girls and Twilight Lovers: A History of Lesbian Life in Twentieth-Century America*. New York: Columbia University Press.

Fanon, Franz. 1967. *Black Skin, White Masks*. New York: Grove Press.

Fernandez, Bina and N. B. Gomathy. 2003. *The Nature of Violence Faced by Lesbian Women in India*. TISS, Mumbai: Research Centre on Violence against Women.

Fernandez, Bina. 2002. In Humjinsi (ed.) *A Resource Book on Lesbian, Gay and Bisexual Rights In India*. Mumbai: Combat Law Publications.

Fletcher, John. 1989. 'Freud and His Uses: Psychoanalysis and Gay Theory', in Simon Shepherd and Mick Wallis (eds) *Coming On Strong: Gay Politics and Culture*. pp. 90–118. London: Unwin Hyman.

Irigaray, Luce. 1985/1977. *This Sex Which is Not One*. Cornell University Press: Ithaca [(translation) original from 1977].

Joseph S. 2005. *Social Work Practice and Men Who Have Sex with Men*. Thousand Oaks, CA: Sage Publications.

Kale, Madhavi. 1994. 'Projecting Identities: Empire and Indentured Labor Migration From India to Trinidad and British Guiana, 1836–1885', in Peter Van Der Veer (ed.) *Nation and Migration: The Politics of Space in the South Asian Diaspora*. Philadelphia: Pennsylvania University Press.

———. 1998. *Fragments of Empire: Capital, Slavery and Indian Indentured Labor Migration in the British Carribean*. Philadelphia: University of Pennsylvania.

Kapur, Manju. 2002. *A Married Woman*. New Delhi: IndiaInk.

'Lesbians Forced to Live in Anonymity', 10 April, 2009. http://www.ndtv.com/convergence/ndtv/story.aspx?id=newen20080048221

Mohanraj, Mary Anne. 2006. *Bodies in Motion*. Harper Perennial.

Mootoo, Shani. 1993. *Out on Main Street.* Vancouver: Press Gang Publishers.

———.1996. *Cereus Blooms at Night.* London: Granta.

———. 2008. *Valmiki's Daughter.* Toronto: Anansi.

Parameswaran, Uma. 1999. *What Was Always Hers.* Canada: Broken Jaw.

———. 2001. 'Contextualizing Diasporic Locations in Deepa Mehta's Fire and Srinivas Krishna's Masala', in M. Paranjape (ed.) *Diaspora: Theories, Histories, Texts.* pp. 290–300. New Delhi: Indialog Publications.

PUCL-Karnataka. 2001. 'Human Rights Violations against Sexuality Minorities in India'. A Report.

Rao, R. Raj. 2000. 'Because Most People Marry their Own Kind. A Reading of Shyam Selvadurai's Funny Boy', in Ralph J. Crane and Radhika Mohanram (eds) *Cross Continents / Colliding Cultures: Diaspora Writing of the Indian Subcontinent.* Amsterdam: Rodopi.

Reddock, Rhoda. 1985. 'Freedom Denied: Indian Women and Indentureship in Trinidad and Tobago, 1845–1917', *Economic and Political Weekly,* 20.43: 79–87.

Rubin, Gayle. 1975. 'The Traffic in Women: Notes on the "Political Economy" of Sex', in *Toward an Anthropology of Women,* ed. Rayna Reiter. New York and London: Monthly Review Press, pp. 157–210.

———. 1993. 'Thinking Sex: Notes for a Radical Theory of the Politics of Sexuality' in Henry Abelove *et al* (eds) *The Lesbian and Gay Studies Reader.* New York and London: Routledge.

Sukhthankar, Ashwini (ed.). 1999. *Facing the Mirror: Lesbian Writing from India.* New Delhi: Penguin.

Vanita, Ruth. 2005. 'I am an Excellent Animal: Cows at Play in the Works of Bahinabai, Suniti Namjoshi, Rukun Advani and Others', *Gandhi's Tiger, Sita's Smile.* New Delhi: Yoda.

Vicinus, Martha. 1993. '"They Wonder to Which Sex I Belong?" The Historical Roots of the Modern Lesbian Identity', in *The Lesbian and Gay Studies Reader,* eds. Henry Abelove, Michèle Barale, and David M. Halperin. New York: Routledge. pp. 432–452.

4

Unbecoming Women
Shaping (Un)Familiar Lives

'But what's the big deal? I too was crazy about Najma once, but Apa bi told me we should be crazy about boys, not girls.'
'What? How awful!' Shaman jumped.
'Yes, because we can marry them and live with them forever, isn't that right?'
'But ... this is ... Allah, don't talk such rubbish, Bilquis.'

(Chughtai 2003: 78)

Is growing up the same for all genders? The Bildungsroman or novel of growth is a genre of writing debuted as a universal narrative of growing up. In the early modern period, particularly within the Romantic tradition, the Bildungsroman was a genre that persuasively modelled for readers the ideal virtues of a good citizen. The good citizen of course was always male; the theory that there are two separate spheres, one for women, one for men is almost completely hegemonic in the territory scholarship earmarked as canonical for the genre. It is instructive that for a genre that showed young people outgrowing inappropriate dreams in order to take up acceptable positions in society had no place for women; one can read this as an externalization of the political exclusion of women from the public sphere. There is after all no space for the young woman to grow into and occupy in the public sphere, unlike her male peer. Thus, inflections of the genre that centres on women have often dealt with the 'growing down' rather than the growing up of the protagonist when they were written at all. The death of the female protagonist is one particularly significant kind of growing down: Maggie in *The Mill on the Floss* (1860) finds that there is no space for her in small-town England once she has successfully asserted moral and economic autonomy. Marriages to male 'mentors' who break the spirit of the female protagonist are another trope for containment. Caroline in Charlotte Bronte's *Shirley* (1849) marries the cold and hard Robert whom she has always been in love with, but the successful culmination of this marriage only occurs after she has almost been chilled to death by his ability to coldly disdain her passion. Another of Bronte's novels, *Jane Eyre* (1864), uses the conventions of the fairy-tale to clinch the romantic narrative without alienating and breaking the spirit of the female protagonist. In *Jane Eyre*, it is Rochester who will be broken, and it is other women, such as Bertha who will be alienated and annihilated to accomplish the protagonist's wholeness at the end of the narrative. In contrast, the male version of the bildungsroman will often use a woman, or the image of a woman, as markers of the successful attainment of adulthood by the male protagonist, the most famous example being Stephen Dedalus's epiphanic sighting of a girl in the sea in *A Portrait of the Artist as a Young Man*. Dedalus will leave Ireland for the European Continent to further his dreams of becoming an artist, to forge in the 'smithy of my soul the uncreated conscience of my race' (Joyce 1968: 252–53). Here the artist as representative of humanity's conscience, as well as the artist as keeper of Ireland are both that a young man on the threshold of adulthood can expect to occupy without the slightest hint of presumption; instead, his confidence is reflective of his heroism, of his strength as an individual and last, but not least, of his social acceptability as a symbol for this undertaking. This canonical Bildungsroman tradition 'embodies the Goethean model of organic growth—cumulative, gradual, and total. Originating in the Idealist tradition of the Enlightenment, with its belief in human perfectibility and historical progress, this understanding of human growth assumes the possibility of individual achievement and social integration' (Abel 1983: 5). If as Franco Moretti proposes, the bildungsroman is the 'symbolic' form of modernity' (Moretti 2000: 5), then the male protagonist, symbolically is also the rightful heir as well as parent of this modern culture. Moretti argues that the Bildungsroman as a form conveys 'youthful attributes of mobility and inner restlessness' (Moretti 2000: 5), but by extension, mobility, and dynamism become identified as male, and by a seamless and invisible manoeuvre, stasis becomes the characteristic attribute of the binary other, the female/feminine.

Further, in its traditional development, it 'reinscribes the myth of the evolution of a coherent self, giving mankind precisely the illusion of a distinct, self-present subjectivity. The dissonances and conflicts of life appear as the necessary growth points through which the individual must pass on his way to progressively higher stages of maturity and harmony' (Abel 1983: 42–3). This maturity and harmony, Abel identifies correctly as patriarchal ideals set for women to aspire to and never be able to fully attain; Rita Felski reads women's failure to attain these ideals itself as an act of successful 'self-discovery' (Felski 1989: 133) instead, an awakening of the female protagonist to the constrictions and impediments in her way in a patriarchal universe. Felski recognizes 'the historical process of women coming to consciousness of female identity as a potentially oppositional force to existing social and cultural values' as being at a tangent to the integrative ambitions of the patriarchal 'novel of awakening' (Fraiman 1993: 131). Thus, the bildungsroman for the female protagonist cannot be an act of accepting one's place if women's place in the world is so circumscribed already; the process of self-discovery may be painfully atomizing rather than therapeutically affirmative. Susan Fraiman describes the female protagonist's process of growing up and attaining selfhood as 'not ... a single path to a clear destination, but as the endless negotiation of crossroads' (Fraiman 1993: x). Hinting at the complex processes of socialization into patriarchy that women must undergo in order to become appropriately adult, she says 'the myth of bourgeois opportunity has little place for the female protagonist, and to reinvent the genre around her is to recognise a set of stories in which compromise and even coercion are more strongly thermalized than choice' (Fraiman 1993: 6). If we follow Fraiman's suggestion that we see the Bildungsroman 'less [as] the progress of an alienated individual than ... her or his constitution by manifold social relations' (Fraiman 1993: 123), the genre becomes inseparable from the agendas underlying these social relations, including agendas of sexual normativity and racialization. The bildungsroman seen as part of the project of producing a normative kind of interiority then also produces subjects who are sited within normative sexuality; so what is the space available to subjectivities that are (un)familiars? Heteropatriarchal constructs of what is ideal and harmoniously adult may have much in common with patriarchal ones, but also be substantively different. How far apart are the queer and feminist projects of rewriting the bildungsroman? The Goethean ideals of organic national and community membership will be untenable for subjectivities struggling with the heteronormativity of these nationalist ideals, for one. Postcolonial nationalisms for their part may have many arguments with how hegemonic Anglo-American visions of citizenship have both depended on and peripheralized the racialized non-Western/Southern Other. Thus, Maria Helena Lima, in her analysis of the novel *Lucy* by Jamaica Kincaid, asks:

> I cannot help but continue to wonder what dangers lie in the form itself, given its central historical role in determining our notions of human identity. Since humanism's unstated goal ... was to constitute a 'center of humanity' ..., what is the Bildungsroman genre, recognizably one of the main carriers of humanist ideology, indeed helping to reproduce? (Lima 2002: 859)

Yet, this sort of inquiry helps broaden the definition of the term rather than abandon it altogether; rather than concede the term 'Bildungsroman' to Western modernity alone, critics today have been able to theorize how different life-stories of coming to selfhood are available in other places. Mark Stein, for example, proposes that the Black British Bildungsroman has the dual function of 'the formation of its protagonist as well as the transformation of British society and cultural institutions' (Stein 2004: 22). This formulation helps us move beyond the idea of society as an eternally stable matrix for the individual's development in allowing for the 'transformation' of the world around them. Claudine Raynaud theorizes on the divergence in the kind of 'epiphanies' or catalysts for transformation available to the racialized protagonist: 'in African American narratives ... the discovery of American society's racism is the major event in the protagonist's development and in his "education"' (Raynaud 2004:106). This chapter examines two novels that fit in this broadened definition of the genre to examine how the post-colony's narrativization of the (un)familiar protagonist's growth becomes a meditation on the growth of the nation. Frederic Jameson's theoretical premise that 'all' Third World literature is 'necessarily' allegorical, 'a form long discredited in the west' (Raynaud 2004: 324), and must be read as national allegories is a useful thesis here, despite Jameson's totalizing and homogenizing of the 'Third World' into another unitary category. If this 'Third World' literature is 'situational and materialist despite itself' (Raynaud 2004: 336) and is directly linked to the political unlike First World texts, which valorize the private and the libidinal, then 'the story of the private individual destiny [that] is always an allegory of the embattled situation of the public third-world culture and society' (Raynaud 2004: 320) offers us a useful point of entry into the often insistent heteronormativity and heteropatriarchality of nationalist ideologies that the queerness of the female protagonist allows us to reflect on.

The figure of the woman was a key focal point for both religious reform movements in the nineteenth century as well as for the formal political decolonization movement from the late nineteenth century. Education and the amelioration of social restrictions were key concerns for most campaigners, but the figure of Bharat Mata—Mother India is a figure that points not to the mainstreaming of gender-liberation work, but to the appropriation of the figure of woman for a variety of political ends to which feminism was not primary. The figure of Indian womanhood thus was paradoxical—temporally modified in that she was now better educated and therefore more efficient, hygienic and a better companion to her modern, Westernizing Indian spouse, but at the same time, temporally static in that she was still fundamentally and essentially Indian, the repository of eternal authentic Indian values. The figure of the woman thus is an arena wherein meanings of nationhood, decolonization and sovereignty were being contested right through the twentieth century. The women's movement (beginning with the All India Women's Conference from the 1920s), of course redeployed the struggles differently, participating in a number of important political campaigns against the colonial government alongside of raising awareness for women's liberation from gendered oppressions. Feminist scholarship on South Asia has shown, for example, that the production of the idealised feminine in nationalist discourse as domestic, virtuous and asexual was made possible by separating this typically upper- or middle-class feminine from her working-class counterparts, that is, from those with access to the public sphere, including those who had access by virtue of their work as courtesans and prostitutes, for example, (Sangari, Kumkum and Vaid 1990; Chatterjee 1993; Sinha 1995; 2006) This privatized feminine has counterparts also in modern national legal premises like 'personal law', which as Amrita Chachchi has shown, is underwritten by the inviolate, chaste female body always in need of protection. As the Shah Bano case in India has amply shown, personal law can also today be harnessed by religious fundamentalists on either side of the Hindu/Muslim divide for purposes of community consolidation as much as for producing sectarian strife. In both possibilities, it is the body of the woman that is deployed as the site of struggle through which ethnocentric and partisan 'meaning' can be produced. As many scholars have shown, anti-colonial and religious nationalisms have had this methodology in common. However, it awaited the work of queer scholars to show that colonial and anti-colonial/religious nationalisms also shared another narrative of continuity—their common employment of sexual deviance as a trope through which to produce governable bodies. The script of sexual normativity thus shapes the governable subjects that colonialism and its resistances sought to produce, subjects and citizens both having in common heteropatriarchality, not merely patriarchy as defining rubric.

This scholarship is useful in trying to understand a text like Ismat Chughtai's *Terhi Lakeer* (1942), where Shamman, an uncomfortable 'daughter of reform' to use Gail Minault's phrase for young Muslim women who benefited from reform within the community, has to find a place for herself as a young and independent (Muslim) woman in the new Indian nation that seems about to take birth. The narrative of *The Crooked Line* makes visible the various loci of this contest via Shamman's articulations of resistance or outright rebellion to the hallmark of the normative idealised secular nationalist/religious nationalist modernity as the virtuous, domestic, asexual woman. However, the place then to look for alternative formulations of community and nation is not only, as Gayatri Gopinath (2005) suggests, the space of what is deemed 'primitive, irrational and perverse' (Chughtai 2003: 139), but within the very terrain of a civil society taking birth, the exploding space that is not the colonial state and not quite the private sphere when focalised through a female protagonist.

Ismat Chughtai's *Terhi Lakeer*

As stated in the previous paragraph, Shamman, the protagonist of *Terhi Lakeer* (trans. *The Crooked Line*), is so appalled by what she hears about marriage that she is struck speechless. Ismat Chughtai's bildungsroman is a monument to the difficult road to adult female heterosexuality, a journey of 'learning' how to like heterosexuality—learning to firstly give up the almost parthenogenetic delights Shamman has been accustomed to until early girlhood, and secondly, of learning how to become 'straight' to use retrospectively upon this 1940s novel a term that became current much later. Shamman, or Shamshad Fatima, is herself the crooked line, an ungendered substance who from the unwelcome moment of her birth, resists being straightened into an uncomplicated psycho-sexual subjectivity. One of the meanings the Oxford English–Urdu Dictionary provides for 'Shamshad' is 'tall, and upright:' Shamman, then, paradoxically, is someone whose 'straightness' is remarkable, forcing a reassessment of what it means to fashion oneself along non-normative designs. Chughtai's own resistance to being exclusively identified as the author of a 'lesbian' text like 'Lihaaf' alerts us to what might be the restrictive impact of the term 'lesbian' in understanding the life of so polymorphously perverse a heroine as Shamman of *The Crooked Line* is. Though lesbian eroticism is certainly a part of *Terhi Lakeer*, our reading must also acknowledge that the use of 'polymorphous perversity'—desire as unrestrained by a particular form, and perverse in refusing to thus fit into more monotonous social categories—may help comprehend Shamman's desires better than the homogeneity of desire implied by 'lesbian'. Reading desire in *The Crooked Line* as (un) familiar allows the forging of a heterogeneous politics of challenge to normative orders of desiring, allows interrogation of the dominant if straitlaced homonormative politics of seeing homosexuality as a process of 'coming out' and remaining visible, intelligible within the public realm of international political work. Judith Butler argues that the term 'queer' must never claim to fully describe those it claims to represent if it is to retain any of its radical valences at all (Butler 1998: 230). That is, a successfully queer description would always have room for more than one trajectory of representation without ever claiming to be 'the' representation. Emphasizing that the politics of visibility might make subalterns of those who cannot claim visibility, Butler asks that we explore the politics inherent in the demand for 'universal 'outness' that today marks much of LGBT organizing (Butler 1998: 227).

The Crooked Line requires such a queer approach literally because it provides more than one script for desire. The analytical value of the term (un)familiar is evident in the consideration of texts like this one, where the homosexual is part of a spectrum of sexualities, and therefore is in dialogue with heterosexuality and heteronormativity rather than in an oppositional, closed dichotomous relationship. Further, the sheer everyday familiarity, even normativeness of homosexuality in some contexts like the girls' school can be conveyed very easily by the term (un)familiar as we have defined it thus far. Shamman's career defies easy acceptance of gendered, and more importantly, sexual norms that structure social beings; Shamman's efforts at self-fashioning resist easy identities of her subjectivity with either heterosexuality, or homosexuality. Shamman in many ways defines what, again retrospectively, may be called a normative homosexuality in refusing staunchly to be confined by any homogeneity. *The Crooked Line* cannot be made sense of within accounts of lesbian feminism that see the development of 'lesbian' identities as necessarily a progression from previous, more regressive forms of selfhood. In fact, it often refuses any alignment of sexual identity with selfhood insofar as selfhood might be understood to be unitary: Shamman forgets more parts of her self than the concept of unified identity would suggest. If anything, the author uses difference of various kinds, sexual difference being one, to fracture notions of unified consciousness and personality. Its location in the period of the Second World War and the Great Depression previous to it also encourages a reading of this novel as an account of modernity in the face of crumbling meta-narratives, but also, as a post/colonial text, an account of the pain of narratives being created. Chughtai's account of the development of female subjectivity is impressive along many planes in its splendid whimsy, intuitive grasp of female worlds, and its tender and at the same time blistering irony, hard as it may be to compass the two in the same utterance. Using the realistic convention to burn holes in the veil that hung between lived female experience and its conventional, normative depictions by most Urdu authors till her time, irrespective of gender, she routinizes what Geeta Patel calls the 'uncivil woman,' a reference that holds for both Chughtai's own propensity to upset the proprieties of the day, refuse decorum in her unerring instinct for depicting the everyday realities of often humble female lives, and for Chughtai's thinly-veiled autobiographical protagonist, Shamman (Patel 2004: 133).

Eve Kosofsky Sedgwick defines two 'tendencies' in Western streams of thought about sexuality: the 'minoritizing' and the 'universalizing' (Sedgwick 1985: 1). The first she defines as the endeavour to treat of homo/hetero categories as confined solely to the self, to the person, to the interiority of the subject. The second sees the homo/hetero binary as providing an epistemology for existence itself, as not only the sexual facets of our existence, but virtually every aspect of life, from which queue to stand in to be frisked at an aeroplane queue, or which toilet to choose, is governed by the how the subject has been gendered. Extending her views to gay and lesbian studies, we might ask, is the polymorphous perversity of literature only relevant to a small minority or to the world at large? Of *Terhi Lakeer* it is safe to say that it refuses to be pushed into the minoritizing imperative; instead, in locating concerns about gender and sexuality within the modern Indian nation as it attains Independence and tries to make a way for itself, like Shamman our protagonist, Chughtai queers the fledgling Indian nation through Shamman's unbecoming childhood, a useful reminder that:

> If adolescence for boys represents a rite of passage (much celebrated in the Western literature in the form of the bildungsroman), and an ascension to some version (however attenuated) of social power, for girls, adolescence is a lesson in restraint, punishment and repression (Halberstam 1993: 938).

Shamman as a girl-child is an important trope for how femininity in India is infantilized or otherwise made an adjunct of masculinity, but Shamman's many acts of independence from male masculinity also locate her as a critique of this very infantilization and secondariness. Contesting the implicit masculine bias within notions of self and nation through its privileging of autonomous female creativity sometimes metaphorically, such as when Shamman imagines she has had a child by means of parthenogenetic or immaculate conception like Mother Mary, or later, literally, when Shamman finds out she is actually pregnant, but after her white husband has disappeared from the story, *Terhi Lakeer* delinks motherhood from heteronormative coupling, marriage and cohabitation. In making her heroine behave this way, Chughtai ensures that Shamman's perversities do not remain the substance of private pathology, but instead become questions that queer the public realm wherein sexualities are boxed away for public identification or disavowal. Writing a novel that is as much female bildungsroman as much as female protagonist's personal narrative of modernity come newly to a post-colonial country, Chughtai's challenge to entrenched normative notions of woman's place within this post-colony do not place her writing under the rubric 'lesbian novel.' Yet, in presenting a protagonist who refuses to do many of the things conventional heroines in plots with heterosexual resolutions do, *Terhi Lakeer* leaves open the door for a clearly queer reading, one that must take into account both Shamman's idiosyncrasies and their functions within a national allegory told from a female standpoint.

Further *Terhi Lakeer* challenges many normative paradigms, homosexual and heterosexual, in refusing any easy equation of a unified sexuality with identity. This novel, then, must be read in the light of its own internal logic, not filtered through paradigmatic notions of what a lesbian text should be, because in its placement of queer desires in a web of other life-defining or mundane experiences, the explication of Chughtai's text requires a paradigm other than the now normative Euro-American one of 'coming out.' Again, to go back to Eve Sedgwick, she said, some coming-out[s] have more discretion than others: coming out as a Jew, she reasons, is different from coming out as 'Black' or 'female' (Sedgwick 1985: 75). Sedgwick's latter premise—the difficulty of coming out as something that you are already recognized as being, is in some sense evident in Shamman's predicaments: how to become a woman? Especially if you are already defined as one though you do not quite understand what it means. Monique Wittig in *The Straight Mind* says that to be lesbian is to be not-woman: Wittig's radical argument is that femininity or woman-hood is itself a function of heterosexuality, and that to be lesbian would thus involve a stepping out of the female gender instead of just an exit from heterosexuality (Wittig 1992: 13). Wittig's radical position, of course, does not leave room for expressions of lesbian identity that do not challenge gendered norms: most notably, as Cheshire Calhoun has argued, gendered and sexualized oppressions are not the same, and all lesbians do not have to be at cross-purposes with patriarchy all the time, or at least not to the extent to which lesbianism becomes inevitably oppositional vis-a-vis heterosexuality (Calhoun 1996: 9). Yet, in contesting normatively gendered visions of femininity, unharnessing femininity, as it were, from exclusive reciprocal libidinal linkage with the male gender, lesbianism is performing a useful service to womanhood, positing alternative models of existence, which may or may not partake of erotic same-sex genital contact. Chughtai's text may be seen in the light of these debates as one that examines the place of the desiring woman: does she belong to heterosexuality or homosexuality if she has feelings for women sometimes, and is not entirely unfeeling towards men sometimes? Does her asexuality—or sex negativeness to use a phrase from late nineteenth-century sexology—place her necessarily within a sexual economy or outside it? What is her relationship with her gender given these queernesses? And above all, what potential does this queerness have for the rest of us?

Vanita (1996) traces a history of homoerotic love and affectional kinship between women from the medieval to the modern period within the Western Tradition offers an extremely valuable paradigm for the construction and cognition of female homosexuality. Vanita argues that love between women can be considered along two planes: the Sapphic model of intense lyrical emotional, erotic and/or sexual connection between women, and the Marian model of eroticized mother–daughter relationships that form the basis for all-women triangles later on. Both models, Vanita shows, involve community, affectional ties, love of learning and the search for creativity, and faith in friendships that do not have to be congealed into blood-ties later. The Sapphic model however differs from the Marian one in that it might lead towards death while the Marian model is life-sustaining, but here Vanita's reference is towards the literal mythical histories of Sappho and the Virgin Mary. Vanita's book is a remarkable trove of research on the plenitude of expressions of same-sex love in the Western tradition, an achievement similar to what Terry Castle achieves in her monumental and extremely valuable anthology of lesbian writing, *The Literature of Lesbianism*. Vanita's argument that we replace the phallic model of desire with one that looks for plenitude instead of looking for phallic lack is also persuasive and to my mind is a major strand of resistance within queer scholarship to the fetishization of Freudian and Lacanian theory (Vanita 1996: 2). *The Crooked Line*'s construction of relationships between women does not arise from a vacuum. As can be seen from Ruth Vanita's and Saleem Kidwai's anthology *Same-Sex Love in India*, there are traditions and tropes of female–female bonding and love within Indian literature and art that the novel subliminally uses and responds to. Some of these more traditional tropes are revised in order to incorporate Shamman's location as a modern young woman rather than a woman still within the zenana. As such, any analysis of Shamman's emergence from the inner space of childhood into the public realms of her girlhood and youth necessitates that both be taken into account. In what follows, I shall examine the implications for *The Crooked Line* when read broadly within the terms of reference provided by the Marian and Sapphic models as Shamman's movement into the mainstream is also a movement towards engaging with other faiths than Islam. The viability of such a reading is evident from the emphasis the novel places on relationships between women: with the exception of two or three male characters who impose themselves in between women, *The Crooked Line*'s primary traffic is indeed between women in a fashion very different from the male–male–female triangle of homosociality posited by Eve Sedgwick as the foundational erotic geometry of western literature.

The crooked line of Shamman's search for love, companionship and emotional anchorage starts, predictably for a novel of growth, with her mis-timed birth into a household of many children, in the middle of an elder-sister's trousseau-sewing. Shamman's arrival in this world is 'ill-timed' in many ways: she the unwanted last of about a dozen children, born into a world transitioning between the precolonial and the modern. Their mother's one desire with regard to this child had been to call in an English midwife—that shadowy representative of the slowly modernizing world outside most likely to make her way into the women's area of the home; but this is thwarted by the unborn Shamman's eagerness to take birth. Her arrival is greeted with a curse, rather than with the customary blessings: 'May God curse this baby sister! Why won't Amma's womb close up now?' (Chughtai 2003: 1). This excessive fecundity on the part of her mother is put down by Chughtai as all the father's fault—he never did let his wife nurse her own babies, and in the absence of any more sophisticated means of contraception, Amma has too many opportunities for conception. Shamman emerges into a turbulent childhood in a household that is more bestiary than human habitation, and whose fecundity parallels if not rivals that of the Buendia household in *One Hundred Years of Solitude* (1985). Born into a relatively well-off middle-class family, her arrival nevertheless marks an excess:

This was the limit! A sister, a brother, then another sister and brother— it seemed that beggars had found a way to their house and now there was no keeping them out. Were there not enough mouths already? Why all these newcomers? Coming in like cats and dogs, every hungry, they had depleted the grain reserves, milk had become scarce even though there were two cows in the house, and still the bellies of these newcomers remained empty. (Chughtai 2003: 1)

That Chughtai should begin her novel with such excoriating remarks points her out to be the spiritual heir of her idol and mentor Rasheed Jahan, the doctor-turned-writer and member of the Progressive Writers' Association. Jahan drew flak—and a ban that was not to be withdrawn for many decades for *Angaarey*—for her forthright presentation of Muslim women in the throes of a colonial encounter that they are forced into and often forced to watch, rather than enabled to enter, unlike Chughtai's Shamman (Gopal 2005).

There is a great deal of historical scholarship on the social and sexual controls set in place by the British in India, and the consequences these had for both nationalism, and indigenous patriarchy, with the latter updating itself in accordance with and in parallel to state-endorsed changes (Oldenberg *et al.* 1994). Control over the lives and bodies of women was often central to a number of these changes, social, educational, economic and political. It is interesting to note how the domestic space of the home was always the locus of contest between the gendered discourses that sought to create the 'good' housewife, mother and well-brought-up girl, and the forces of subversion, resistance and autonomous self-realization that the targets of such en-gendering brought to the contest (Liddle and Joshi 1986; Sangari and Vaid 1989; Mazumdar 1999; Everett 1981; Sarkar and Butalia 1995). The narrative of *The Crooked Line* makes visible the various loci of this contest via Shamman's articulations of resistance or outright rebellion. Shamman is a meeting place not only for indigenous womanhood and modernity, but also of disciplinary restraints placed on the creative (female) spirit. Shamman's resistance makes unfamiliar a number of otherwise naturalized tropes, such as idyllic childhoods spent in the bosom of nature; the child's transcendence of fleshly desire; the emotional camaraderie of the joint family; the force of female desire, and so on. The Indian child, in most narratives, is stoically de-eroticized. Further, this child is almost universally male, and if female, is more likely to be a decorous, overachieving dear rather than the 'witch' that Shamman is perpetually accused of being in her childhood. The pulls and tugs of the flesh feature pre-eminently in Shamman's life-story, a departure from the decorum most authors even today seem to maintain with regard to childhood at least. She is also one of the few serious delineations of the girl child in Indian fiction; it is hard to think of any other, besides perhaps Durga of *Pather Panchali* whom the reader gets to know so well by the end of the novel. But Bibhutibhusan Bandhopadhyay still works within the conventions of romanticization—though Durga is impoverished, steals and lies, she (and for that matter, that other famous Indian child of the time, Swami of *Swami and Friends*), resides in the realm of the spirit, while Shamman's narrative, with its refusal to excise the impurities and the joys of the flesh, forces us to open up a new category of cognition for childhood that is neither sentimentalized, nor romanticized, nor idealized.

Chughtai's Urdu is such a rich *begumati zubaan* that one cannot but notice how this supple vocabulary makes the home a rich and important resource for its very sociable female inhabitants. Shamman herself is, however, an uneasy inhabitant of this home. Here, Shamman, after the usual pattern of the Indian joint family, is brought up by a community of elders, siblings and servants, but Chughtai's mimetic characterization of this household does not yield the expected picture of one happy joint family of rosy-cheeked indulged children. Instead, the emotional deprivation of such a terrain, with children and adults jostling for resources and emotional succour marks Shamman indelibly; this emotional deprivation Shamman is constantly in rebellion against, the bestial images of family living in the first phase of *Terhi Lakeer* are at the very least, a feminist critique of the norms of the time. Growing up in a house that the narrator describes, on behalf of Shamman's primary caregiver, her elder sister or Bari Apa, as 'more like an animal shed than a house' (Chughtai 2003: 2), Shamman's crooked line of growth into normative femininity and heterosexuality may best be read as the female subject's challenge to the familiar world of 'civil women'. Shamman herself is the familiar, the uncivil sprite who, from the very moment of her arrival in this world with 'a thunderous howl' has been showing up the world itself as a sham. Shamman's unruliness places her in a queer location—she is neither absorbed into the kinship of familial bonds, nor able to establish bonds with more convention-governed children outside. The familiar places of babyhood and childhood are all complicated, for instance, by Shamman's eroticized desire for both her (female) caregivers as by her desire to ingest the earth. She is likened to 'a mad bitch who had just finished tossing about in an earthern platter filled with sludge' (Chughtai 2003: 5), and eating dirt thus, ends up having a 'son', the slimy roundworm. This nightmarish adventure, with its disturbing resonances with actual conception, finds its formal counterpoint in Shamman's actual pregnancy, the last event reported in the novel, creates a phantasmagoric vision of herself as a repository, an oyster in which grew thousands and thousands of snake-like worms, a vision terrifying enough for the life ahead. Her erotic desires are unlinked however to her reproductive urge: Shamman's own infant corporeal response to caregivers' bodies is taken account of by the omniscient narrator and made available quietly as generalizable for other mother–child relationships shattering the de-eroticization of relationships that feature children, moving us away from the pieties of an uncritical Madonna-and-Child representation to a ruggedly Freudian one. Manjhu's marriage sunders her from Shamman; bereaved, Shamman finds herself cut off from all civilizing influences, becoming like a 'fetid gutter' with people avoiding her as 'the stench emitting from her became unbearable.' Shamman's punishment is by grime and itchiness, she would wake up crying at night' after having spent the day skulking about the house loveless (Chughtai 2003: 17). This is the first of Shamman's many traumatic separations from an object of desire. Shamman's later career may be summarized just as well by this one episode—tearing apart the artifices and cloaks of conventional marriage, Shamman finds herself punished by her solitude; till she becomes pregnant. Chughtai's selection of episodes from the young child's life permits us to reflect upon the constructedness of gendering, just as the earlier episodes from her infancy suggested that desire itself ranges free till restricted to prescribed objects. In an overturning of the law of the father, the maternal is singularly the most powerful civilizing—which here is care and love, not only brute discipline—force in Chughtai's depiction of the female subject's difficult road to normative heterosexual development. If the first several chapters of the novel can be read as a display of the 'Id' that provides the material upon which society will fashion an 'ego,' then this 'id' is untrammelled refusal of the self's incorporation into heteronormativity.

Shamman's actual pregnancy at the end of the novel, on the other hand, is her first opportunity to nourish something—a constructive conception unlike this parasitic visitation in childhood. Chughtai's narratives often appear to ramble along with no sense of time; but despite what seems to be a careless episodic structure, a closer look reveals a structure that does not explicitly mark temporal change, but at the same time, functions metaphorically to show the passage of time. The earth-eating Shamman is representative of the Freudian oral-anal stages of childhood, where the child's pre-social persona has not as yet internalized the art and science of performance; the masquerades of socialization are yet to take root. All of Shamman's childhood, following that artless, parthenogenetic 'conception' of worm-children, is an endless rehearsal for the performances of mother and less significantly, wife, that Shamman will also, if she lives long enough, be expected to undertake when she is deemed old enough. Shamman's refusal to be docile and her insistence on producing a child that never does seem to have anything to do with a man refuses the dominant Freudian narrative of femininity as a lack that seeks to be plugged by a child—given to her by the man (or his substitute) she wants to become. Instead, childbirth throughout this novel is a parthenogenetic act untied from heterosexual sex or marriage.

After this first failed attempt at Immaculate Conception, the earth-eating, 'free' Shamman, haunted by the worms that emerge from her body, is replaced by the Shamman who of late 'had been experiencing a desire to hit people' (Chughtai 2003: 9), which again, however, has maternal connotations, as Shamman is seized by a great urge to hit Manjhu in particular. Manjhu's daily tactics for sobering Shamman include as many beatings as she thought fit. Shamman's parodic internalization of this aspect of her caregiving results in this reciprocal desire to hit Manjhu into a shape that she, Shamman, finds more suitable. Where more conventional girls 'generally nurse a desire to get married' (Chughtai 2003: 9), Shamman will make do with motherhood. These ultimately parthenogenetic aspirations lead to Shamman's adoption of a doll who is then suitably feminized, for the project of motherhood also involves the project of creating a suitable femininity. This femininity in turn seems to be intimately connected to motherhood—the *cholis* that grown women wear are tied, in the child's associations, with giving suck to babies; perpetual motherhood in the zenana must of course have accustomed Shamman to this sight. Nevertheless, these signs of successful femininity are hidden away as if they 'were a foul word to be uttered only in secret' (Chughtai 2003: 14). Shamman, wearing nothing but a towel—and thus aggressively naked in the eyes of all concerned when she is cornered later—sets off to explore the *cholis* in Manjhu's trousseau. She wears as much as she can, and immediately 'assumed the bearing of a housewife,' (Chughtai 2003: 15). Her stream of thoughts takes her from satisfying thus imaginatively, the child's desire for as many sweets as she can eat, to the ultimate desire—for a child:

'Arree, Rasulan, O Rasulan, where have you gone off to, wretch! Go and quickly tell Ali Bukhsh not to get any provisions ... yes, instead tell him he should get mung daal, and yes, roasted peanuts, and for Shamanbi some sugar candy.' She scolded the imaginary ayah. While she was talking, she thought, 'Oh, the baby is asleep in my lap!' Why, he was awake. She shook her knees pretending to rock the baby.

'No, no, my precious, my dearest ... are you hungry? Do you want milk? Mmmmm...' She lifted her shirt front, but in that instant her attention was drawn to a mosquito bite and forgetting the baby and everything else… (Chughtai 2003: 15)

Where amma must hide herself in her bathroom to put her choli on, little Shamman's half-naked participation in thus playing 'mother' to her imaginary children signifies her resistance to both the de-eroticization of female bodies and their appurtenances, and of the normative rendering of these as 'foul' meant to be confined to the proximity of other impure commodities like the hamper of unwashed clothes in the bathroom. Reflecting how games socialize girls into becoming women, the 'wedding game', where 'Noori's girl doll and Shaman's boy doll were married every day' (Chughtai 2003: 42), with the children learning 'many new wedding rituals' at a wedding they are permitted to attend, soon becomes an urgent need. Finding themselves in the 'grip of a strange longing' to have 'to go to the storage room and play the wedding game right away,' they fabricate femininity out of as-yet un-gendered bodies such as Shamman's:

And then one day, summoning up great courage, they secretly stuffed two balls of cotton in the doll's *koti*. They felt such shame, they couldn't even look at her. Draped in a filmy crepe dupatta, the doll with the cloth nose and the string fingers now looked like a woman alive and real. God forgive them! They were not interested in anything else and all day long they played wedding games with her. But one day, while searching for some swatches in the rag basket, Bari Apa stumbled upon the doll and their secret was exposed. Such a beating they received that soon they were praying for death. Bari Apa tore off the koti and stitched up the shirt. From that day on they lost all interest in the doll. What was she except a bundle of rags with a piece of cloth for a nose and strings hanging from palms instead of fingers? (Chughtai 2003: 43)

The games end soon, and Shamman must go to school, itself a luxury for young (Muslim) girls at the time. *The Crooked Line* is also the story of those whom Gail Minault calls 'the daughters of reform'. Where in earlier times, girls had to procure an education through stratagems like learning to write with blacking from the fire when the elders were not looking, or by bribing the boys of the house to teach them unbeknownst to those who would disapprove, Shamman shows no awareness of the gift of an education, unbecomingly going to school wondering where the 'enemy' of civilization would strike her from.

The school offers a different regimen from the sociable and chaotic home spaces Shamman has both inhabited and ruptured all this while with her Kali-like resistance to stasis. In the home, female labour and female homosociality dominated, but at the same time the women in question are all seen primarily as caregivers or as adjuncts to men, with no independent role-models for a young girl like Shamman to emulate, excepting for a profile for motherhood. School for the first time brings to her purview women with any economic independence—earlier, such a role had been the monopoly of the lower castes: the 'sweepress' the midwives, and the like were the only women who weren't being reared for a life in purdah. In school, on the other hand, Shamman sees women like Miss Mumtaz and Miss Charan, and new designs for living soon begin to occur to her. At the same time, the environment of the school and the home share continuities—both seek to discipline her via regulations on clothing, studies and behaviour; further, both offer pleasures that are rarely replicated in the life outside: at home these pleasures included pretend-play at various games; at school, these included real games with real people. Thus, both the home Shamman comes from and the school she goes to may be seen as 'home' spaces because Shamman is most at home here. The world she goes to thereafter, once she leaves the school—college, employment, marriage—may be productively read as *unheimlich, unhomely*, destabilizing spaces where Shamman's Kali-like exuberance shrinks, finally, into pitiable little, with comely Durga-like normative femininity coming through. Shamman's house and the space of the girls' boarding school constitute the space of the familiar, whereas the space of the world beyond them marks the unfamiliar. Shamman's familiarity with the homosocial labours, pains and pleasures of the first gives her at least the strength for critical rebellion in the first; her ignorance of the unfamiliar transactions of heterosexual labours, on the contrary, force her into deeper and deeper self-erasure.

At the same time, Chughtai's representation of the home as bestiary, and this home as symbolic of the nation, as evident from the later, grown-up Shamman's meditations on life give us pause:

Chughtai was accused along with some of her other Progressive companions of revelling in filth for its own perverse pleasures (Bhalla 1997; Chugtai 1998). *The Crooked Line's* fierce characterization of this home and its habitations not as nostalgically imagined pure space, but as being unloved by the women who inhabit it is a vital component of its author's desire to refashion home. Shamman's self-fashioning is characterised not simply as her coming of age in terms of experience, but also in terms of her coming to terms with space—both spaces she inherits, like the spaces of the home, and spaces she makes, such as her own many homes in various educational institutions both as student and as teacher. Priyamvada Gopal examines the engagement of Muslim women writers like Chughtai as self-reflexive participants in the imperatives of modernity, gendering and thus transforming notions of modernity in the Urdu-speaking literary universe of pre-Independence India. However, while Gopal's points about the 'gendered and classed subject of the transition to national modernity' (Gopal 2005: 67) hold, it must be noted that not only does Chughtai *gender* the narratives of modernity, but she also *queers* them in remarkable ways. Homoerotic and homosexual desire in Chughtai's novel provides us with a complex understanding of newly emergent modernities that an analysis focussing solely on gender cannot uncover. Among the many interpretative possibilities the novel affords is one that queers patriarchal and feminist approaches to desire with its frankly homoerotic concerns. Shamman moves, as it were, in a crooked line between both the traditional space of the home, under pressure from the world outside, and the spaces opened up for her as a young middle-class woman by modernity. *The Crooked Line* does not polarize the inside from the outside; instead, Shamman herself is what one can designate a Moebius Strip, arching, flexing and twisting between both, and in the course of the journey, redefining both. Rather than break the modern from the traditional, Shamman's trajectory illustrates, as Gail Minault points out, that the 'processes of interaction between colonial and indigenous ... created change' (Minault 1998: 3).

While the modernizing imperative secures for Shamman an education, it also provides access to institutional female homosociality—that is, access to the company of women with the public sphere rather than within the domestic sphere. Shamman finds a mentor in Miss Charan, a teacher who treats her civilly; Shamman does not understand what to do with this because 'no one had ever talked to her like this'. Though she has only just met Miss Charan, Shamman finds herself 'laughing and chatting like old friends' (Chughtai 2003: 48), sharing stories of home and before long, housework, becoming familiars in other words. For Shamman, Miss Charan offers an opportunity for the only kind of life she craves—a life where she is valued as an individual, where ceremonial attention is given to her instead of the bestial community existence that home prescribes. Miss Charan's mentorship sees Shamman gain a double promotion as well as civility; female homosociality is the sobering force for the wild girl. The all-girls school is a space of female community and sharing is very similar to other all-female spaces like the convent, which is central to the Marian scheme that Ruth Vanita outlines. Unlike the zenana, where the men are on the fringes but still central in spirit to the zenana, demanding sexual and other labours of the women within it, the all-girls' school is a far freer space as it literally frees the girls within it to work on and for *themselves and for one another* willingly rather than be compelled to render services of various kinds within the various mechanisms of heterosexual privilege that the zenana underwrites.

Miss Charan's mentorship of Shamman establishes a paradigm wherein the intellectual and spiritual broadening for young women or girls is achieved when they are in contact with one another, a fact rendered starkly noticeable by its absence in most of Shamman's relationships with men, with the salient exception of the male Rai-Saheb, with whom, again, she can be said to have a tutelary relationship similar to the one she has with various women, rather than often predatory interactions she has with men. The Marian and the Sapphic models both present the intellectually curious female subject as central, but the Marian model also permits eroticism across a cohort of ages and generations: the teacher–student relationship in Shamman's case is eroticized as an analogue of the lost mother–daughter relationship. Here the teacher is an attractive, sophisticated model upon whom all young girls wish to form ourselves. The young girls's homoerotic desire for the teacher thus has not merely sexual, but very important aesthetic satisfactions: 'She was the first person after Manjhu to create a place in Shamman's heart, to have the power to influence her' (Chughtai 2003: 49). The teacher's role is to provide to the student a design for living. Often, this design for living, within the space of the school itself, loses its valences with regard to the world outside. This mentorship of the student by the teacher does not directly feed into the discourses of marriage and the active sexualities it brings; instead, this mentorship provides the young girl certain autonomous concepts for living, where a career, a postive self-image, self-esteem and the like are ratified as worthy aims in themselves rather than as unnecessary adjuncts to conjugality. Shamman's desire for Miss Charan is thus all-pervasive in her adolescent being: 'At Miss Charan's behest, she accomplished the most difficult of tasks; she would not hesitate even to kill for her' (Chughtai 2003: 49), words which could well have been lavished upon a young boy trying to woo his first girlfriend.

Shamman's 'pash' for her teacher is evident to all the other students; that it has sexual and erotic components is also evident: 'Miss Charan's name was on her lips all the time. The girls tried to tease her, but her fixation intensified, gradually becoming tinged with a romantic feeling that overwhelmed her thoughts' (Chughtai 2003: 49). Chughtai's description of Shamman's emotions at the time, with their language of heightened emotion clearly indicate that homoerotic desire to be similar to the vicissitudes and follies of heterosexual love: Shamman makes a fool of herself by constantly thinking of and watching for Miss Charan to pass; she is speechless when she finally appears before her; she is all atremble at the sound of her laughter, and while 'everyone was of the opinion that Miss Charan was extremely dark and ill-looking,' Shamman 'couldn't imagine anyone more beautiful' than Miss Charan. Miss Charan means more to her than family or God do; Shamman literally worships Miss Charan, 'passionately and with great devotion.' Miss Charan helps Shamman finally become a 'civil woman' albeit briefly; Shamman for the first time begins to engage with her books: 'her humming softly [was] a sound that seemed to help Shamman when she was stuck at a difficult question in her book; the tiny waves of Miss Charan's humming stabbed at the knot in her question, unravelling it for her' (Chughtai 2003: 53). Under Miss Charan's tutelage, Shamman acquires a love for the finer things in life: that in her earlier, Kali-like avatar, she had rejected; an able female mentor is able to do for Shamman what legions of surrogate mothers had not been able to. Soon Shamman's love for Miss Charan becomes literally a haunting:

> She began to feel her teacher's physical presence even when she was not there. She's standing and Miss Charan's image rushes by her side; she is sleeping and Miss Charan is petting her; she's thirsty, her throat is parched and Miss Charan is dripping cool, fragrant juices into her mouth. (Chughtai 2003: 49)

The wants of the body—thirst must be slaked, sleep must be had—join with the needs of the spirit. Shamman needs not only 'cool, fragrant juices' to slake her bodily thirst, but also her desire for love. Erotic affirmation in the shape of Miss Charan's acceptance and support of her, their easy sharing and love for one another give Shamman confidence, but her idolatry also shapes fears—she is afraid the spell will break, the ball will drop, the 'dream will be shattered.' Even the adolescent Shamman is aware, unconsciously, that this will not last long, for with visions of a satiated Paradise come anxious ones:

> Sometimes she sees herself rambling in the night, crying, then finds herself on the frosty grass, shivering with a chill, and suddenly Miss Charan picks her up and puts her on the bed, her head resting on her down-filled pillow, and there Shamman pretends to be unconscious because she's afraid if she opens her eyes the dream will be shattered. (Chughtai 2003: 49)

The tropes of desire are all there—the bed, the pillow, the sleeping girl and the waking care-giver. Yet, Shamman's anxious repressions of desire are in keeping with her subliminal awareness of the dangerous desires she was feeling. Shamman knows the dream will shatter if she awakes; at nights, she finds herself walking all over the school. Miss Charan's separation was prefigured in the many nightly rambles that found Shamman in front of Miss Charan's room, 'sobbing hysterically' (Chughtai 2003: 50). Shamman does not know what is happening to her: 'Was it she or her spirit that dragged her about at night?' One night, finding herself crying in front of Miss Charan's room, she thinks she has seen a ghost, that familiar apparition of desire that may not be acknowledged. Shamman is also terrified, though 'she wasn't a coward and she wasn't afraid of cats, but she ran as if pursued by supernatural creatures' (Chughtai 2003: 50); she runs into the matron, shouting 'Ghost, Ghost!' only to hear the latter tell her 'Where? You stupid girl, this is your own shadow' (Chughtai 2003: 50). Why should Shamman see ghosts? Why should her own shadow seem ghostly to her? This is Shamman's moment of encounter with the fantastic in literal terms: she cannot tell if there is indeed a ghost till Matron resolves the conundrum. The uncanny answer is that there's no ghost, only her shadow; homosexual desire then, is part of the real world, not of the fantastic, however unfamiliar its incursions may seem. Shamman is unprepared for this encounter; yet, her spirit desires it, and drags her toward the encounter.

Shamman's somnabulistic entry into the realm of (un)familiar desire suggests her unconscious knowledge that this desire was to be repressed because it contravenes permitted consensus reality for her times. Her desire becomes literally a phantasy in the Freudian sense; the girl is unable to express these desires in waking existence. Thus, they take on an uncanny existence separate from her consciousness, through her unconscious, taking her literally to Miss Charan's bed. However, the culmination is not in the form of consummation, but that of eviction. One night, Shamman wakes up sobbing in Miss Charan's bed, 'A real bed! Not the bed of her dreams, no, there was the pillowcase with the embroidered green flowers, the brown coverlet with the reddish-gold edging' (Chughtai 2003: 51). This descent from dream to reality brings Shamman and Miss Charan both within the reach of the law that decrees this is unacceptable: The principal, who comes to Miss Charan's room where Shamman starts screaming in her sleep, tells Miss Charan that 'her influence on the girls' morals was questionable.' (Un)Familiar desire thus ruptures the everyday realm of femininity that the school seeks to educate its pupils into, the principal's censure revealing societal valuation of homoerotic feelings as dangerous and destabilizing to conventional morality, for the morals the girls are being educated in are the morals of heteronormativity, as the opening epigraph shows. Miss Charan is dismissed after the principal interrogates Shamman, who 'kept her mouth shut. How was it possible that she tell her all the things she thought, felt and saw?' (Chughtai 2003: 52).

After Miss Charan's departure, Shamman 'walked about guiltily without a word' thinking 'the fault lay somewhere with her, and she was ready to accept that fact now' (Chughtai 2003: 51). What the fault is Shamman does not know; the slur of lesbianism is disarticulated as it is never spoken. Shamman too is unable to verbalize the loss of this mother figure, as with the loss earlier of earlier mother figures like Manjhu, Unna her wet-nurse, etc. Memories of Miss Charan leave her in 'spiritual agony,' so she actively forgets, wiping out memory though 'the wound associated with Miss Charan's memory seared her mind' (Chughtai 2003: 53). Shamman, now moved to a different school, turns to religion to look for a mentor, and finds the Virgin Mary. Unnerved by the changes in her body due to the onset of menstruation, the pubescent protagonist undergoes her second encounter with what she thinks mistakenly is motherhood—influenced heavily by the Bible's narratives of Immaculate Conception. Soon, however, to her dismay she finds out that she certainly does not have a child. These episodes follow in a phantasmagoric and often incomprehensibly interiorized set of passages immediately after Shamman's removal from the earlier school, still pursued by memories of Miss Charan. The placement begs the question: is Chughtai locating Shamman's desire for a child within the homoerotic/homosexual imaginary rather than within the heterosexual? Shamman feels pregnant with child even as she is isolated and segregated from other children by the inhibitions induced by menarche; however, her childish identification of pregnancy as the cause of her isolation takes us back to her parthenogenetic early childhood diagnoses of her ills. Shamman is constantly prepared for motherhood, it would seem; Miss Charan's mentorship of Shamman deprives Shamman of a mother-figure, the lack of which Shamman immediately seeks to fulfil by herself becoming a mother. Rather than lead lesbian desire as a lack that must be immediately filled, Chughtai's text encourages us to see the child's desire for a familiar as *creative*. Shamman is possessed with the thought of motherhood almost in the same way as she was earlier possessed by the thought of Miss Charan. Motherhood aided by a female partner like Miss Charan might be the dream of every lesbian who finds her dream of motherhood impeded by the lack of the male seed. Chughtai's location of the Miss Charan episode just before Shamman's newest imaginings of motherhood encourage us to consider once again a parthenogenetic conception where Miss Charan serves as a spiritual parent along with Shamman the physical parent in the production of a long-desired child.

After disease, in the form of a confinement that mimics the confinement of pregnancy has 'cured' her, permitting the trauma of the loss of Miss Charan to be dealt with, Shamman is able to enter once again the world of the living, having made 'compromises' with those absent who haunt her unconscious. At Mission School, Shamman for the first time discovers partners among and desire for her peers. The pleasures, joys and sexual jealousies of a girls' school are descried with such verisimilitude and truth by Chughtai that it is hard to believe more than sixty years have passed since the writing of this novel. That girls fall in love with one another is taken for granted; even ridicule does not deter those who fall in love because these devotees 'become unusually thick-skinned and shameless and some of them were so persistent that even their families were fed up with the obsession' (Chughtai 2003: 75). Reprimanding them would only produce hysterical grief, so 'everyone was compelled to be lenient with them' (Chughtai 2003: 75). Every successive romance allows Shamman some training in the primary emotions of life: among others the emotions of loving unrequited or of being unable to possess the object of one's desire; Shamman also learns what it is to refuse love: her room-mate Rasul Fatima's slavish passion for her only earns phantasmagoric and corporeal disgust:

> In her dream she saw the mouse again, crawling, and before she could push it away it vanquished her completely. All the veins in her body became taut, stretching like a wire, all her strength seemed to ebb from her, and she was sure she would never be able to move again. Rasul Fatima's bony fingers dug into her like nails, but she couldn't stop her. Just as a lion wrestles with its prey before swallowing it, just like that ... Terrified into silence, she remained still and unmoving and the mice kept scurrying. (Chughtai 2003: 59)

Rasul Fatima is unlike Miss Charan, and with her clingy physicality is repulsive to Shamman who can see in her nothing of aesthetic value though Rasul spends her days doing menial tasks for Shamman without being asked, and her nights groping Shamman and uses besides the language of love, calling Shamman 'tyrant,' and 'Goddess of my heart's temple' much to Shamman's indignation. Chughtai's representation of these homoerotic expressions as unwelcome to Shamman complicate the homo-eros *The Crooked Line* brings to life by revealing that homoerotic feelings are neither an accident of cohabitation, nor a pathology generated by living with the 'sick.' At the same time, despite her anger towards Rasul 'for no reason at all' (Chughtai 2003: 58), Shamman lacks both a language of desire, and a language for rejecting desire, but Rasul's presence permits Chughtai to present a spiritual side for (un)familiar loving even amongst adolescents, to establish that desires for an eros that does not go via the body alone are felt by the young too.

Shamman's new room-mate Saadat is her new object of adoration, but soon she has also fallen in love with Saadat's own 'pash' Najma. The homosocial spaces of the girls' hostel is eroticized by the frank, routinized descriptions of how young girls' adorations both take place and are polyamorous. As with Miss Charan, Shamman cannot control herself when Najma is in the room: 'Seeing Najma disturbed Shamman in some strange way; as long as Najma was in their room chatting with Saadat, her heart beat uncontrollably and she would try and distract herself by taking up some useless bit of work. But when Najma was gone Shamman felt sorry she hadn't looked at her properly' (Chughtai 2003: 66). The pleasure Shamman has in gazing at Najma is a shared pleasure that many women feel in gazing at other women; often, this pleasure may be sought by women who aren't themselves aware of lesbian or bisexual feelings for the objects of their gaze. Shamman's pleasure in Najma belongs to the realm of the erotic, yet de-sexualized joy that women get in gazing at one another, a queer pleasure that functions within a feminine realm in ways that give female desire the agency of not only looking, but also taking pleasure in looking and being looked at. However, Shamman's feelings for Najma are also definitely sexual: the touch of Najma's clothing is enough to make her 'benumbed' as if 'a snake had dropped from the ceiling.' The touch of Najma's hand is veritably orgasmic—'a convulsion spurted in her palm and it began to devour Najma's finger's' (Chughtai 2003: 73), and the potency of the touch is evident to Saadat, who fears displacement. Her intent observation of Najma would provoke Najma into angry refusals of her gaze, whereupon Shamman would be forced to occupy herself with meaningless tasks though she would 'become flustered and a chilly perspiration began crawling down her spine, her stomach convulsed and she would feel thirsty' (Chughtai 2003: 67). Her physical responses to Najma's presence are clearly also sexual; she is shy and bashful in Najma's presence just as she once was with Miss Charan, and later will be with a series of men. The culminating moment of this sexually aroused phase happens during the fancy dress party—that staple of all lesbian novels—where all the girls compete to dress as boys. Shamman in a black suit, looking 'just like a boy' is not meant to be paired with Najma who is dressed as a washerwoman, but appears to Shamman to be a veritable Padmini instead; Saadat however, understands from Najma's and Shamman's blushing display of shyness around one another that she is no longer the focus of Najma's attention. Shamman has her moment of joy with Najma, laughing and flirting with her even as Saadat grows more and more silent with jealousy. Shamman's own jealousy of Saadat which now Saadat reciprocates indicates that the relationship is no longer asexual or merely one of friendship. Najma's repulsion of Shamman puts her in mind of her own cruelty to Rasul: 'All night she heard the rustle of snakes hissing around her bed, the sounds leaving her spent and lifeless' (Chughtai 2003: 72). However, no wounds are will remain unhealed just yet: Najma will be replaced with Bilquis—with whom Shamman takes a photo with the pair in costume as Orlando and Rosalind—and so on, till finally, Shamman leaves school for college.

Here begins 'the second phase' of Shamman's life. Shamman will gain an education, learn that the objects of one's affection are not girls, but dark black snakes—*koriyale*, the slang word Chughtai uses doing duty for both snake and man. From this point on, as Shamman advances in age, there is a diminishment in the novel's own energy: Shamman's own sobering down by life and social mores finds an objective correlative in Chughtai's use of language. Verbs that convey movement and change soon give way to verbs that reflect and consider, and Shamman's increasing frustration trapped in the mind-games between the sexes is reflected by many gaps in the narrative that are never bridged: in a sense, the novel is written in the tradition of the Urdu and Persian *afsaanaah*, not the realist novel, as scene after scene is strung on, but with little comment as to how they relate. Shamman's sense of fragmentation, which earlier betrayed itself in her watchfulness when she leaves home for school, wondering where the next blow is to come from, is replaced by Shamman's progressive loss of her alertness: despite her constant vigil, Shamman finds herself befuddled. The lacunae in the chronology and development of the plot are, to my mind, to be taken as the growing girl's increasing sense of confusion and lack of sure knowledge. These narratival lacunae are a contrast to the increasing sureness of knowledge that permits characters in a conventional bildungsroman to grow (Moretti 2000; Abel 1983; Fraiman 1993; Felski 1989): the reader knows, because the author devotes time to the explication of things the protagonist cannot comprehend wholly as yet, that there is a teleology and a rationale. With *The Crooked Line*, however, Shamman loses sight of her earlier selves after the fashion of life itself, where we are unable to recollect wholly what moved us awhile ago, or what exactly it was that we had learned in an epiphanic moment of wisdom dawning upon us at just the previous bend. This technique, I argue, is a central technical tool for Chughtai: it is through *The Crooked Line*'s refusal to collect Shamman's life as entirely visible and cognizable to either the reader or the protagonist at any given point of time that Chughtai is able to reconcile the normative homoeroticism of the first phase with the female homosociality of the second phase of Shamman's life. In the third phase, even this feminine continuum is disrupted by the arrival of long-term male partners, till pregnancy with an absent husband brings Shamman back to the beginning of the book. *The Crooked Line*'s refusal to make Shamman's life entirely recuperable within the logic of memory and rational reflection enables it to provide within the frame of the realist novel a very serious consideration of why it is that love of the un/familiar is so easily forgotten: the powerful nature of social conditioning, the interpellation of the subject, if you will, tears apart any sense of wholeness of experience across vast stretches of time. *The Crooked Line* treats of Shamman as a piecemeal protagonist, actuated not by a vast historical memory of herself in toto but by immediate responses to immediate crises. When homoeroticism recedes from its position of normativity, heterosexuality takes over: this movement need not necessarily mean the 'ultimate' of cross-sex love is the only valid emotion. Rather, the 'penultimate' nature of homoeroticism, of un/familiar love is made available as a delightful oasis of life that is almost forgotten as an idle dream of paradise in the wake of the nightmarish thirsts one is subject to through life.

In the second phase of the novel, Shamman's search for love takes her from the girl-crushes of her Muslim school to the less overt though still homoerotic relationships she has later in life with other women, especially Alma. Even if intra-female desire does not become the central visible locus of Shamman's life, it is still the organizing principle. Shamman's journeys are shaped by the presence or absence of various women—her father for instance, is a conspicuous absence in a world teeming over with women of all ages and kinds. Shamman falls in 'love' first with Rashid, then with Rai Saheb, still later with Satil and Iftikhar, and finally with Taylor, but each of these romances stands on an ever-declining arc with respect to the previous one's levels of passion, energy, and excitement generated in Shamman, though her attractions are real: Shamman is in this sense polymorphously perverse, as argued earlier. However, each of these affairs reveals Shamman at her emotionally most clueless, unable to fathom what is required of her and what she might reasonably expect. Male–female relationships, unlike female–female relationships, seem to Shamman to be conducted in a code she does not understand. Shamman's various infatuations and accidents with men signal her need for a male presence or principle in her life, but paradoxically, it is these relationships that are constructed as laboured and difficult to carry through. The narrator's tone also changes subtly at first, from the sympathetic description of Shamman's relationship with the Najma–Saadat duo, to the heterosexual courtships she now depicts. Heterosexuality is dangerous and men are snakes—*koriyale*, which when Shamman looks up the word in the dictionary she learns they are 'spotted, black and white snakes, very poisonous' (Chughtai 2003: 79). Fortunately, as 'Shaman wasn't allowed to step outside the hostel, so the question of falling in love did not arise' (Chughtai 2003: 83) remarks the narrator wryly, but at the first chance, she loses her heart to the mercenary wooer, Rashid. Interludes between romantic afflictions allow Shamman an opportunity to get to know her family better. Once home, she finds her niece Noori has also 'learned about being in love from a distant cousin' (Chughtai 2003: 102) and could also pretend to have lovers just like Shamman's school-mates would. Marriage plots are hatched, in particular one with a cousin

Ajju who constantly gropes Shamman under cover of darkness, much like Rasul Fatima in school. The similiarity between male and female abusiveness highlights the similiarity, rather than the dissimilarity between the desires they seek to carry out through Shamman. Here she dreads the family's communal sleeping arrangements which literally truss her up as easy prey for the likes of Ajju every night; wishing him dead just as she had once wished Rasul Fatima, Shamman finds her wishes come true when Ajju contracts typhoid. Male desire however in this phase comes into its own as predatory—when they were children, Shamman and her niece would watch the Mullahji in the neighbouring mosque masturbating: to the children, it seemed like 'he stood for hours engaged in behaviour that seemed strange and frightening' (Chughtai 2003: 41), and for hours afterwards, they would be paralysed, like 'injured birds' (Chughtai 2003: 40), or like those retching from contact with an exposed corpse. The same nausea greets Shamman when she realises what Ajju is up to at night, and similar queasiness accompanies her distressed reaction to another cousin who comes looking for one wife, besieged all the girls with 'his intimate playfulness' (Chughtai 2003: 114) which seems demeaning to Shamman, but is looked at as the 'playful antics of the children' (Chughtai 2003: 112) by the family elders who hope he will marry one of the household's many marriageable girls.

Shamman resists these casual expectations placed on young girls to sexually service growing boys; she is happy to be punished with a college stint. At American Mission college, Shamman is for the first time is exposed to the society of young men (and also young women) seeking to enter the world. College in some ways is an extension of her nightmares about Ajju, but also a place where Shamman learns she can also find a place in the public sphere. Other students are part of the national movement, but as the narrator satirically observes, only because it helps preserve their family monopoly on indigenous industry; yet others like Iftikhar posture as radical Communists and anarchists but their positions on gender and marriage are reactionary, to say the least; still others like Satil appear 'liberal and progressive' but are chauvinistic and hide-bound. College is also where Shamman engages with other faiths. Her adult queer subjectivity shaped by encounters with all of India's three major religions: Islam, her own, does not offer a position that can enable women to come into their own; her break with Islam is her break from home. Her life alone is less religious, more secular, starting with college, when her first crush is on the Rai Saheb, a Hindu, and then Alma, a Christian, whose beauty and defiance are magnetic. The first is a teacher she mistakes for a lover; the second is a lover (spiritually) who is first a teacher, then a patient in need of Shamman's ministering and finally a lost woman who appears to prefer enslavement to a husband's love to her own liberty and self-respect. But at first, Shamman is friends with Prema, contact with whom brings her closer to the Hindu religion, which Shamman thinks to be a very exalted one. Part of her quest of belonging in this framework manifests itself in the form of her falling in love with Prema's father, the Rai Saheb.

Love at first sight plays out at different levels in the book: Shamman is taken with all the men she meets in late adolescence. After Rashid, her peers Iftikhar and Satil respectively offer her mental and physical fulfilment, presumably; while Shamman's innate virginity preserves her from an attachment to Satil, her very deep quest for love and kinship make her a veritable slave to Iftikhar. The Rai Saheb is the only one whose powerful masculinity is itself not corrosive. Symbolizing the best of Hinduism for a young Muslim girl, the Rai Saheb's beautiful dancing and the cultured family life he and his children lead draw Shamman equally. Rai Saheb's attractions are on par with if not better than what drew Shamman to Miss Charan—aesthetic refinement and sophistication. Rai Saheb is an accomplished dancer and painter, and Shamman's craving for the finer things in life lead to her proclaiming her love for him. Prema is, predictably offended, and the friendship comes to an end. Hinduism, in this period, offers for Shamman an alternative to the restraints of Islam. Music and dancing are staples in the Rai Saheb's household, a far cry from the domestic noises of Shamman's own house. The Rai-Saheb is a Hindu alternative which links the female and male together in a dynamic relationship as between the Ardhanarishwara conception of Shiva and Parvati literally united, a conception lacking in Shamman's Islamic world perhaps. The Rai Saheb's own Shiva-like dancing, further, calamitously ignite in the young girl a desire to be part of this beauty. However, Shamman's ecstatic enjoyment of the immense degree of pleasure she experiences in the artistic is again something she cannot identify immediately as erotic and aesthetic appreciation that need not necessarily be converted into a physical claim upon the performer. Just as she is susceptible to Miss Charan for the civilizing influence she had upon her, now Shamman finds herself enthralled by a sudden vision of the sublime in Rai Saheb's dancing. The character of Rai Saheb can also be seen as advancing the possibility of an enriching teacher–student relationship, which, however, must remain a celibate one, unconsummated if its powers are not to be withdrawn. Of course, making the cardinal mistake of identifying the dancer with the father of her friend—proscribed for sexual access by the rules of propriety and loyalty to her friend—Shamman excludes herself from this circle of joy in art. Shamman's cultural deprivation in her quotidian life produces a near-religious experience, akin to her earlier belief that she had given birth; seeing in Rai Saheb a beauty and grace she can appreciate with an almost mystic surrender, Shamman is willing to convert from Islam to Hinduism in order to supply herself what she has been wanting. Her adolescent misdemeanour is almost immediately paid for when Rai Saheb dies suddenly of a heart attack. Shamman's guilt produces a nervous breakdown, and one of the images that lead up to it is that of her hallucinating that she is in the graveyard where a Shiva-figure like the Rai Saheb is doing a Tandav. However, it is safe to say that the ideal in love for Shamman remains this Shiva–Parvati figure of male and female united to form a harmonious and powerful dancing whole. Rai Saheb also unfortunately dies a few days later, visions of death haunt her, till reprieve comes when 'for three months, typhoid brutally pounded her body' (Chughtai 2003: 144). This period of quarantine where Shamman is perforce confined to the home is again disorienting, cementing Shamman's fears about the lives that she will be allowed to lead. Soon enough, return to the world of the healthy, is a return to the world of claustrophobic, untenable roles for women. Shamman sees she neither belongs in the household's interiors as a monogamously chaste woman like Noori—a wife who 'demanded payment for [her] bod[y] … from only one man'—nor in the world of the Ladies' Club where she runs into her old school-friend Bilquis who collects admirers. Rather than remain a pus-ridden sore within the zenana, Shamman refuses vehemently to join it, 'slipping from every hold' (Chughtai 2003: 156), going back to college.

This time, she finds a mentor in a woman. Alma, who embodies in the largest way the travails and joys of an autonomous femininity, oversees Shamman's re-entry into the parthenogenetic after her familiar heterosexual pitfalls. Shamman's peer group of young men is much taken with Alma, who with her brown complexion, her eyebrows that arch arrogantly like those of a temple statute, and her 'poisonous teeth' is a new kind of feminine for Shamman, who heretofore has not come upon women with intellectual desires after those implied in Miss Charan. Literally fascinated by Alma, who becomes Shamman's mentor, tutoring her implicitly into the world, away from the shackles of traditional Islamic femininity, Alma appears initially to be a pastiche of the 'reformist' imperative that draws women away from the home. Alma's volatile independence, her impetuousness and her fierce curiosity about the limits of her own self's powers are reminiscent of Shamman herself though the latter does not initially see this. Retrospectively, we find she had earlier become fast friends with Alma, though Chughtai clearly does not develop this figure before now: we find out that Shamman 'could pass through the fires of hell with a smile on her face if she had her hand on Alma's shoulder' (Chughtai 2003: 156). And so it is: Alma, a popular student leader and the darling of innumerable admirers remains in various ways Shamman's companion till the very end. Shamman and Alma nurse one another through many calamities, including an unwanted marriage and an unwanted child. Alma is also the first person for whom Shamman makes such a positive affirmation—Shamman's personality has been as resistant to displays of love as to receiving demonstrations of it. Alma is also a mentor: she is an old rebel who will lead a young rebel, Shamman, once Shamman has decided to free herself of home. Where contexts that set up heterosexual tensions produce a constant urge to throw up, as if 'someone had filled her throat with the filth of a putrid gutter' (Chughtai 2003: 127), homosociality comes naturally. Satil's lecherous gaze makes Shamman feel 'as if she had been taking a bath and someone had opened wide the doors of her bathroom' (Chughtai 2003: 167), but there is no pleasure, only nausea in this forced baring of her body. Satil's extravagant physical presence, gorgeous and handsome though that he is to look at, is undercut by the withered connotations conveyed by the meaning of his name. Satil, whose name in Urdu means a shrivelled-up growth like a mushroom that springs up in decay, is an embodiment of physicality, and it awakens alike in Shamman and Alma a sense that they have been corrupted by his presence in their vicinity. Fresh-faced and well-muscled like 'the statue of Adonis,' Satil is to Alma and Shamman a 'ghoul' who is bound to corrupt them. Iftikhar, on the other hand, presents himself as transcendental romance, but is finally unmasked as diseased, lecherous of mind if not of body, deceitful and unreliable, besides being a secret philanderer. Iftikhar and Satil thus prove the impossibility of 'normal' heterosexual love relationships: masculinity is impaired, and this makes heterosexuality like 'eating canned fish. You needed to train yourself to eat this particular fish and that training had to be undertaken in the bathroom and could be successfully completed only after having vomited several times' (Chughtai 2003: 127).

Dispute still rages around the meaning of the word 'Alma'. The Hebrew root of the word 'Alma' means young woman according to many translators, but has been normatively translated into the word 'virgin,' leading also to the controversy that the Virgin birth of Jesus in the Bible is itself a mistranslation that gained extraordinary currency (Metzer and Coogan 1993). *Terhi Lakeer* gives Alma's character both meanings; she is both a young woman who bears a child and an eternal virgin through her initial refusal to accept motherhood and her later bereavement from the child she has just learned to love. Shamman's virgin-companion becomes an unmarried mother after her encounter with Satil, whom she claims to hate, but nevertheless has an affair with. Alma who till then had been a spirited and fiery anti-establishment figure, suddenly collapses: childbirth seems to be too much for one who should have remained a virgin given the nature of her personality, which refuses to be dominated or subject to patriarchal command. Shamman and Alma as educated women refuse Satil's misogyny, preferring Iftikhar's more subtle domination, but Alma's secret relationship with Satil is a meditation on the high price women have to pay for society's enjoining of perpetual chastity and monogamy on the body of woman. Alma's entry into motherhood thus follows Shamman's return from Noori's wedding knowing that she cannot be the woman that the world expects her to be. The word 'wife' makes Shamman shudder, and the sight of Noori, sleeping content the night before her wedding, makes Shamman feel that 'there were dozens of babies and thousands of worries sucking on Noori's young body like leeches,' ratifying Satil's earlier taunt, that 'A woman has only one function...' (Chughtai 2003: 171). Ashamed at the thought of becoming a sexual commodity, Shamman begins to be able to think about her plight in relation to humanity in general, to theorize her quiescent feminism, which, however, is complicated by her empathetic identification with the plight of men, an empathy required in Shamman's mind to permit room to Iftikhar's own presumably radical 'sufferings' within a conservative society. In her reverie, she remembers her exchange of blood with Iftikhar at their conversation at the union camp at night-time, a rite that mimics the shedding of blood when the hymen is broken. Located within the chapter where Noori prepares for her own defloration, but within the ceremonial of marriage, Chughtai calls attention to Shamman's own metaphorically lost virginity even as Shamman can afford to be angry at Noori's mulish acquiescence to traditional precedent. Noori is content to be 'adorned like a slice of halva and presented to a new guest ... bathed and doused with fragrance so that if there was any odour at all it would not be detected' (Chughtai 2003: 171), thinks Shamman contemptuously, forgetting all the while that she had signed her own name in blood to be true to Iftikhar without demanding emotional responsibility in return. Lying next to Noori, Shamman feels 'pride and satisfaction' that she will not become like Noori who 'will diminish and exist only as a man's woman' (Chughtai 2003: 178); in the distance she finally 'saw a long road emerging' but we know this is not the road to utopic heterosexual love.

In the third phase, Shamman's presence in a homosocial continuum of affection and deep emotional interaction with women will be severely interrupted by a variety of personal and professional demands. Returning to college, she enters a phase of emotional exploration where Satil's present attentions, and Iftikhar's absent memories seem adequate till suddenly she finds out that Alma is pregnant. Alma as Shamman's unfamiliar double bears the child that Shamman (and Alma) wants from Iftikhar; we find however that Satil instead is the biological father. Now finally sympathetic to Alma's predicament, aware that 'society demands a tax' only of women who break the rules, not men, Shamman finally theorizes the absolute frailty of womankind within the patriarchal economy, a

frailty she had dismissed earlier as the unique, private manipulative-
ness of individual women like Noori. With Alma pregnant, however,
Shamman sees that the 'open-mindedness [she] was proud of' was of
no practical use to either of them (Chughtai 2003: 191). Alma aban-
dons her education to go home to Bangalore to secure an abortion,
but failing to, becomes an aggressively resentful mother. Shamman
as Alma's familiar double goes on to do the other task assigned to the
normative feminine—the maternality that brings up the nation.

Shamman's life soon becomes oppressive. Her job as principal of
a girl's school brings on a psychic collapse after years of hammering
at obtuse social precedents and loneliness: Shamman as the principal
has become that unfeminine exponent of strictness that all female
school principals are supposed to become in order to be thought
successful. Because of her education, Shamman is above the lowly
teachers who must either like Razia Begum, have affairs with already
married men, or become beggars and petty thieves. Shamman finds
in the course of her work that though women have begun to enter
the workforce, their entry has often not been self-chosen: Chughtai's
novel at this point provides a space within which to consider the
consequences of modernity might be considered for women outside
the middle class that Shamman belongs to. Not wanting to inhabit
this space outside feudal and traditional roles and spaces, Shamman's
peers, lacking her education and the confidence her class gives her,
are abject creatures whose performance on the whole hampers the
cause of independence for women. Shamman tries to serve the nation
without becoming either a communist or an anarchist or a soldier,
but a series of Dickensonian chapters, pours forth beautiful vitriol
on the condition of the Indian nation: schools are built where earlier
feudal lords had housed courtesans; municipal pits for rubbish disposal not being available, trashy books are donated to school librar-
ies, schools are places where nothing is taught except the ceremonies
of prevarication, dissembling and laziness. In trying to 'reform' her
school, Shamman even becomes a pseudo-creator: blackboards and
benches blossom in the wilderness of the old courtesan's lodging, girls
are enrolled and teachers hired. Chaos, however sets in soon: the
school is due for an inspection it cannot ever pass because nothing
is ever learnt there except new tricks to unsettle Shamman, with all
her subordinates unwittingly or willingly undoing her every effort

at 'reform' 'operating with a western-style patience and seriousness, Shamman tried to pick up the rapidly dispersing pieces, but it seemed as if some unknown force was at work' (Chughtai 2003: 200). This unknown force is the force of old traditions that refuse to be moved by the modern unfamiliar professional woman. The manager like Madame Beck in Charlotte Bronte's *Villette* (1853), makes it his business to know everything about Shamman, and any independence on her part is immediately assailed by insinuations about her character, which make Shamman feel guilty though no one other than Iftikhar visits her occasionally. But finally, Shamman gives up, deciding in the vein of Alma and Iftikhar earlier, that the school inspectoress' statement that 'we are forced to be lenient with an underdeveloped nation' was the last straw, considering that everything she had done to provide decent education for girls at her school had only served to push 'baseness towards even greater baseness' (Chughtai 2003: 224).

Shamman decides to go on a journey, but with destination unknown, having given up her job as principal because the many unsustainable absurdities of her position have been compounded by the Second World War's increasingly larger menace. At the railway station, having decided to get into the first train she sees, all she finds are 'sick, broken, ungainly human beings, dressed in dirty, foul-smelling, shabby rags, headed for God knows where. Perhaps they too didn't know what their destination was' (Chughtai 2003: 231) any more than she did. Completely distraught, Shamman contemplates suicide among other things when, while waiting to change trains her attention is riveted by a small child with an *ayah*. Shamman, sitting on her bundle of things clearly finds herself to be an anomaly: neither in purdah nor male, she is the object of lascivious enquiry and looks, all of which make her public position on the station as distasteful to her as her professional position in the school had become. Young and able, she is an anomaly because she is neither dependent, nor a victim: as an active agent albeit in spiritual crisis, Shamman's sense of self is schizophrenically fragmenting in the weltering angsts produced by a world where:

> Every vendor seemed intent on selling his wares to her. She was tired of saying no to them. In addition to the beggars, she was attacked by orphanage workers, people toiling for shelters for widows and those

engaged in the sacred work of caring for the cow. She was extremely irritated by what she saw. If you go to an orphanage you are hard pressed to find a single orphan there, and a shelter for widows has no reason to exist when there are so many men around. And why do you need these shelters when there are streets available for orphans and for the women there are the kothas? Anyway, these are matters that are best left alone. (Chughtai 2003: 232)

The extreme cynicism of this position is both a comment on a colonial nation, where Shamman cannot rest in the railway station's waiting room because there's a white man in the first-class waiting room and the others are locked up, and a comment on the impecuniosity of a people who are both unable and unwilling to help themselves. Unable to belong either to self or to nation, it takes Alma's sudden metamorphosis on the scene for Shamman to come back to life. Five years after she sees the pregnant Alma off at the railway station, Shamman by chance runs into her again at another railway platform on a journey she has taken on a whim to escape the terrible psychic battering her role as unacknowledged nation-builder, mother to the nation, has made her take. From a point where she wanted to 'lie down on the tracks so that this tiring journey could end once and for all' (Chughtai 2003: 231), Shamman revives to the extent that she is able to repair the 'stifling atmosphere' of Alma's house and bring Alma herself to life. The chapters of this journey intercut two episodes of furtive meetings between Shamman and him, in both of which Iftikhar foregrounds the contagion of tuberculosis that he is carrying around. In comparison to what goes before and comes after, Shamman's visit with Alma is an oasis of self-renewal that is in contrast to her cross-sex relationships: after Rai Saheb's death Shamman is battered by typhoid; Iftikhar's tuberculosis has to be staved off by gifts of money, knitted sweaters and sweet dreams about how her blood, which she intends to have transfused to his body, will achieve that corporeal mingling with his body that she is denied because of his disease. Of course Shamman's dreams are never achieved, but with Alma, the theme of disease and moral corruption that accompanies Iftikhar, is often reversed in a life-giving way. In the meanwhile, Alma has been bringing up her child secretly; her refusal to give Satil any role in his upbringing makes it literally her son, and this pattern attains completion in Shamman's own pregnancy, where her husband

Ronnie is unaware that he is to have child, having opted to go to the warfront rather than to stay with Shamman. Shamman and she set up what appears to be an un/familiar parental unit when they jointly bring up this child, with Shamman staying well beyond her allocated holiday time to be with Alma and Rolf. Shamman, Alma and Rolf make a triangle that is akin to that of St. Anne, Mother Mary and Jesus in structure, with the absence of the father not being noticed by any one Rolf and his mother are re-united. Where Alma hated her son Rolf because he is also Satil's son, Shamman however is able to counsel Alma into imagining maternity as creative, not oppressive. Asking, 'why should the mother quake' if a child is though born out of wedlock: a child is still 'a benefaction' offered to the mother, Shamman argues, reinstating motherly love as a natural response, in comparison to the unnatural social condemnation of autonomous female reproduction. In the chapters with Alma, the reader is able once again to glimpse the free-spirited adolescent Shamman who in her innocence could ask the washerman's daughter, who long after being widowed had also become the unwed mother of a baby, 'So what if you are a widow? Who can interfere with the Heavenly Father's will? He can do what he wants' (Chughtai 2003: 53). Unable then to understand why the girl kept saying she had sinned, what the sin was, and why the girl had then committed it, Shamman's ardently Catholic worldview then had believed also in the Immaculate Conception. Now again she tells Alma, 'I never think that Satil has a part in his creation. He just seems like my dear Alma's pretty little toy' (Chughtai 2003: 242). Where Iftikhar affects broad-mindedness and feels superior, it is Shamman who is constantly made to feel inferior who has grown into a genuinely compassionate but still clear-sighted being. Shamman, earlier Alma's fascinated admirer, is now able to see Alma fully: as someone afraid of society but never able to admit it. However, Shamman does not make of Alma a fallen idol, unlike the men all of who would see her as a soiled creature rather than merely a changed one. Counterpointing the metaphors of aridity and fertile wetness, Chughtai describes Alma's earlier rejection of maternity as barren and her acceptance of it later as nourishing, both for herself and her child. Shamman's sympathy for Alma, whose self-censure had weakened her all these years, isolating her from the world, also helps Shamman herself recuperate from the soul-damaging effects of other kinds of isolation, censure and self-abnegation, together with undue exposure to corrosive public forces as a result of her 'modern' job-role. Shamman's visit to Alma thus advances views on maternity that are far ahead of social mores for the times the novel depicts. Chughtai's interrogation of this modernity as it is being shaped shows these women as not only spectators in the games of a changing world, but also as shaping spheres of resistance to male notions of purity and profanity.

The inner sphere for the period when nationalism comes to be is, following Partha Chatterjee's very widely-cited argument, that place where the Indian nation preserved its cultural and traditional values intact, via its women, while the outer, public sphere was the one that was buffeted by the changes that account for 'modernisation'. Chughtai's novel, however, shows a different perspective: the inner sphere is as much shaped by male, masculine views of living as the outer one was, as evident from Alma's crisis about the facts of her motherhood. That outer and inner worlds impinge on one another can be seen from Shamman's parallel nervous breakdown: even as Alma is trying to raise a child she hates and who for her is the focus of her erased social presence, Shamman is trying to raise a country—or at least its schools—out of the mire of colonial and self-legislated negations. Both Shamman and Alma find that their 'private' worlds are the subject of the outer world's invasive attention. Shamman's work robs her of a private existence as much as Alma's status as an unwed mother places her within a private realm so distant from the rest of the world that the austerities of imprisonment are beginning to rob her of her sanity. Alma and Shamman are both in negotiation with male modernity in late-colonial India, as well as with new prescriptions for a suitably 'pure' femininity. Cut off from the sustenance of traditional ties, it is significant that their parallel lives should meet at a railway station like 'shunted rail carriages coming together' (Chughtai 2003: 243). While the metaphor looks mechanistic, the modern space of the railway station is that un/familiar place where two women unhoused from traditional spaces can meet and restore themselves back to being able to cope with a censorious world.

Shamman and Alma thus offer one another a sustenance that helps them build new rituals that will once again make them functional in a world that threatens constantly to shiver them to pieces. The advancing war and the Great Depression have already set atremble much of the world Shamman knows, and new forces of 'reform' have already arrived in the wake of this expected destruction. The progressive movement arrives, stuffed with *khadar*-wearing zamindars and poets whose favourite material is the filth of the *kotha* but never the less glamorous filth of the 'pure' home, ripe and ready for reform. While Shamman is able to minister Alma back to health, she can only watch the world go awry, even as her family follows all its old ways producing innumerable children, who can perhaps, Shamman thinks, at a later date serve as cannon fodder. Shamman is perforce a spectator now, denied action: as the only 'modern' young woman in her family, Shamman's is already a queer presence; neither producing endless children nor staying at home as a dependent, Shamman's role within the traditional framework has been all but removed. No one seems to care about either her presence or its lack even when she visits home after a whole year away. Chughtai questions here the unearned claims of the family to love, but also asks, through Shamman's despair to have something to hold her fast, for she feels she 'was being pulled along by the cord of a kite, and tossing about on destiny's hands, she was getting closer to the wheel' (Chughtai 2003: 247). Shamman's own removal from all vital human relationships signals the un/familiar woman's loneliness—not having anyone else to fall back upon is the condition of those resistant to the normative order. Further, her own forgetting of different women—indicative of deep conditioning into the norms of heterosexuality—exonerate the others from having to remember or be remembered by her. The next several chapters are consumed in a fury of anxiety, in a world where the Second World War had sown the seeds of rampaging inflation and the British repression of the Independence movement in India had produced complex social upheavals. Only Iftikhar's presence restores her, but this consolation is thoroughly marred when Shamman has a visit from his wife that disabuses her of what she had all along felt was their sacred love. The platonic high-minded love that she feels for him, and which he had always given her to understand was his emotion for her too, is revealed to be completely rotten, but not before another call comes from Alma.

Repeating the pattern of one Iftikhar chapter followed by an Alma chapter, the call from Alma comes when she returns from Iftikhar's tuberculosis sanatorium in the hills. This time, Iftikhar's disease seems to take over and Shamman's vitality, at a low ebb already because of the War in addition to her prevailing emotional lowness, cannot restore order to a world where 'Germany has incinerated France,' and the 'liberated fantasies of all the nations which were buried under Nazi pressure came together in England' (Chughtai 2003: 244). She goes to Alma's to find that Rolf has died; Alma herself, in deep grief at the bereavement, is ill. Shamman does the best to pick up the pieces for her friend, and after effecting a consolation of some sort, goes home. This visit home, following soon upon the previous one, furthers the theme of Shamman's isolation from her biological family and her desperation to find her way back to life. 'Germany began showering fire over London' (Chughtai 2003: 259), and the Indian political scene is all aflame, with demands for Independence and Partition being voiced. Shamman is a participant and detached spectator in the 'non-revolutionary activities of revolutionary parties,' but tires soon enough of progressive meetings where the very rich speak of communism, women are made office-bearers for offices that have nothing to do with reform or social service and where Shamman herself becomes a mere figurehead revolutionary simply because she is female. The meltdown of her being continues to the extent that after Hussain Bibi's revelations about her husband Iftikhar, Shamman cannot think of anything but calling for her mother:

> 'Mother! Mother!' she called in silence. She wanted to scream for her mother, not the mother who was in her father's house, who used to satisfy her needs, who gave life to her and then forgot all about her. No, she wanted the mother in whose warm, loving lap she could curl up like a tiny bundle and forget this chill in her soul, whose soft delicate hands would rub her tired back and, pressing her eyelids, squeeze out the tears that were trapped inside her temples. (Chughtai 2003: 275)

Shattered by Husain Bibi's revelations, Shamman finds 'her maternal instincts commingling with the child in her' (Chughtai 2003: 276); breaking her earlier blood pact with Iftikhar literally, Shamman smashes a set of drinking glasses, and walks on the pieces, in a scene reminiscent of a scene from *Pakeezah* that was probably yet to be written when Chughtai wrote this novel. Bloodied once again, Shamman is separated from Iftikhar, but this time the blood is her separation from ideals of romance altogether: now Shamman takes up with many male admirers, even feminizing her appearance all the more by paying uncharacteristically careful attention to her clothes and makeup. As Nazi Germany extended its sway, 'Shamman meanwhile embarked on romantic relationships' (Chughtai 2003: 279). The war is clearly equated in this last set of chapters with Shamman's own personal war on heterosexuality where she tries to get the upper hand in a misguided struggle to worst men at their own game. Shamman goes down fighting: after Iftikhar's love has failed so miserably, her trust in other men is also deeply impaired. She coquets and pirouettes, but is unsatisfied within, as none of this comes naturally to her and further, irritates her whenever she has to keep it up for a while. The men leave one by one, and Shamman's disillusionment is confirmed when the ones who remain—a Professor and a poet—take her to task for behaving capriciously when she in turn is berating them for romanticizing the plight of prostitutes when their own wives are in captivity. Shamman's critique of them as dissemblers and poets manqué is not well-received: the Professor finally descends to the level of telling Shamman that she would not be behaving so frigidly with them if only she would condescend to 'love' someone. The futility of prescribing such a combative 'love' however, Shamman is aware of, and instead, she decides that her next project is the adoption of a baby: one of the several daughters that her sister Manjhu has borne, but this baby dies, a testimonial to Shamman's inability to cope with her family's wanting to monitor her motherhood. But the theme of motherhood as a restorative, so long dormant in Shamman's 'celibate' phase as a national reformer out to educate women into stepping into the public realm like herself, returns Shamman closer to the girl she used to be before the interruptions of heterosexuality arrived.

When this adopted baby dies, the War is at its height and Shamman is once again near a breakdown whereupon she decides to take a journey. By way of Agra and Delhi, which, far from being repositories of Indian civilizational glories, she finds to be 'magnificent corpses[s]' (Chughtai 2003: 300) which depress her even more, she finds her way again to Alma whose name appears as the natural answer to Shamman's question to herself about whom to ask for help. At Alma's she finds great change; Alma is finally recovering from the shock of Rolf's death in the company of Professor Nathan, whose helpmeet she has become. Here she meets Ronnie Taylor, a white Irishman serving in the British Army. Set against the backdrop of the last phases of India's movement towards political independence and Partition, Shamman's and Ronnie's relationship is a curious combination of mutual hatred, antagonism, and attraction. However, it is important to remember that where Shamman is unable to have a frank relationship with an Indian man, she is able to attain a degree of forthrightness with Ronnie, though he later holds this against her; at the same time, Taylor's white skin ensures that the last heterosexual relationship in the book before Shamman reverts to her parthenogenetic self-sustaining world functions across an overpowering racial barrier compounded by the state of the world around them. The Indian colony's demands for political decolonization had only been met with India's being entered into the British War effort without dialogue; Shamman's anger towards Ronnie, and Ronnie's less acknowledged anger towards Shamman thus find an international canvas: cross-sexual antagonism is connected to questions of colonialism, decolonization and recolonization. A further shock to Shamman is that 'the impassioned Alma of the college days was dead, it seemed, and this vanquished Alma was lowering her head in deference to every restriction' (Chughtai 2003: 304). Now that Shamman knows the one companion she had unconsciously fallen back on all along has also crossed over, Shamman unwittingly blunders into a heterosexual campaign herself. Taylor reveals himself to be as insidiously chauvinistic and reactionary as any of the other men before, but Shamman's resources are at an all-time low, and despite doubts about marrying him, she does so. Taylor's reason for wanting to do so are 'together we can do a great deal for humanity' but the poor logic of this is evident even then to Shamman when she says 'why get married for that?' (Chughtai 2003: 321).

Externalizing through racialization the impossibility of cross-gendered loving companionship, the novel finds 'night and day can't ever coexist with each other' (Chughtai 2003: 323), given further the location of this Othello–Desdemona relationship analogue within the mounting demand for political decolonization in India. Taylor and Shamman are cut off from the world but this does not enhance their treasonous romance, only curdles it, in mockery of the notion of honeymooning after one's wedding: 'An unknown fear and dread floated in the air' in a 'silence quiet as death' when the two of them go to Shimla after their hasty wedding, more to avoid people who think their marriage preposterous than to be with one another (Chughtai 2003: 327). Their pride in not wanting to admit they have made a mistake in cohabiting with one another tears them apart shortly; Taylor's 'frenzied lovemaking left Shamman feeling uneasy' once again with the artifice that seems to be necessary for heterosexuality to function (Chughtai 2003: 331). Their marriage is soon likened to a 'ripened sore' whose growth depleted both of them (Chughtai 2003: 335) and against the backdrop of the final months of the Second World War, when Japan over-ran Asia and Russia joined the War, the marriage disintegrates. After Ronnie has made an angry and acrimonious final exit, Shamman finds out she is pregnant; another 'baby' conceived at roughly the same time was 'Pakistan' slowly taking shape under the troubled final watch of the colonial administration. Shamman does some famine relief work and tries once again to help the world, but now, her resources are completely exhausted, much like India's own till she reads the letter Ronnie's mother had written him, welcoming Shamman into their lives: finally, 'the defeated mind, wrapped in slumber, saw dreams filled with fresh green rice shoots' (Chughtai 2003: 361), an image that attains its poignancy in contrast with the earlier ones of barrenness that Shamman had used, and in conjunction with the famine abounding. With the arrival of Ronnie's mother on Shamman's emotional landscape, Shamman feels she has once again gained an anchor. Of course Ronnie does not return, but nevertheless, Shamman feels that life is not so empty again though she does think herself free in a negative sense: 'Free like the spirit when it leaves the body, alone and lost!' (Chughtai 2003: 367). Her newfound freedom does make her pregnancy appear a parthenogenetic one again, born of the earth almost, as she 'remembered the glass marbles she and Kaddan had planted in the flower patch when they were children' (Chughtai 2003: 361). The implications of this pregnancy for Shamman are unmistakeable: she is literally brought back to life in being able to give birth.

> But at this moment, she felt as though the whole world had shrunk into her own being. Her loneliness was inhabited by such a hustle

and bustle today, how well-lit was the isolation of her quarters, how incredulous she was today, but so happy! She had never felt so weak and so courageous, so anxious and so content. And how beautiful the world appeared, how precious life was!

And Ronnie!

Her heart sank. Poor Ronnie, alone and empty-handed! She felt sorry for his impoverishment, just as she would feel sorry for a wretched beggar shivering in the cold outside her palace window!

(Chughtai 2003: 369–370)

This pregnancy restores and reduces—both—Shamman to her own world, a home that she will build for this child all by herself in Ronnie's or her family's absence. She will become a mother, it is true, but in the absence of a mother for herself—except in Ronnie's distant, though loving, as yet unmet mother—Shamman is truly an orphan, free of ties of blood to all but her child, who having come after so many efforts need not necessarily be seen as a child of Ronnie's but instead as Shamman's exclusive child. Shamman's life-story is one that seeks to make a home both in the house where she is born and the nation this house is part of. Shamman is a familiar in the home—a 'witch' who listens to none, who rips her Urdu-primer apart and wallows in the mud all day and then comes home to swear at everyone else; later in life, she is the bearer of both civilization and modernity—hers is the only room in the house where there is any peace and quiet, but she is now only an occasional visitor, a guest in a 'house that seemed like an inn' (Chughtai 2003: 197). That Shamman should be able to remake these familiar spaces better when she is a young child is perhaps indicative of the tragic burden of gendering that catches up with her upon adolescence. Once she has relinquished her hold upon this familiar space by moving, albeit initially unwillingly to non-domestic spaces, Shamman slowly loses both her childhood's resilience and her resourcefulness—the world becomes too much for her—till she herself is able to have a child who will provide her with a sense of order in chaos. The protagonist's womb becomes the space of home, literally a home for the new being growing within it, and figuratively home for the mother too, who has found, in the opportunity to mother, an opportunity also to administer a corrective for what has been visited upon her. Yet, in a literal sense again, there is indeed a spatial shrinkage even as she finds new spaces literally develop within herself. Shamman finally comes to find a home not within the *zenana* where she grew up, nor within the 'modern' nuclear family with her spouse, but as a veritable single parent in a world as yet unused to single parenting. Here, her story mirrors that of Alma who has borne and raised Satil's child single-handedly. However, Alma was a resistant mother, Shamman welcomes maternity, in fact, has yearned for nothing else all her life. Shamman and Alma serve as doubles of one another. Where one for all her feminist and progressive logic is torn apart by her imagining of motherhood as a gendered liability, the other is able to revel in the parthenogenetic possibilities mothering offers. In having Shamman discover her pregnancy only well after Ronnie has left for the War, Chughtai's text suggests that we read this as a delinking of mother-hood from the purview of masculinity, for Chughtai's disposal of Ronnie Taylor by sending him off (to be killed, Shamman fears) to the Second World War permits Shamman to break the Oedipal logic of lineal descent from father to child. The father is 'beggared' by his escapism, while she is enriched by motherhood to the extent that her strength and willingness to live return.

Crookedness of course has many connotations, many winking at 'alternate' or non-normative sexualities; colloquially, the Hindi word 'terhi' can often serve to identify a woman as non-heterosexual much more efficiently than most others. Whether Chughtai intended this identification or no is disputable, given her many statements disavow-ing any 'lesbian' or 'feminist' intentions. However, Chughtai's fash-ioning of largely autobiographical material can be productively seen as an instance of 'queering' de-familiarizing the heterosexual in ways that an entirely 'lesbian' text—if such exists—may not be able to do. A queer project, centering upon a female subjectivity, is precisely what Chughtai undertakes in *The Crooked Line*. Written within the tradi-tion of what might be called 'social realism' *The Crooked Line* neverthe-less cannot be fully described by this technique alone. Shamman's life offers us a bildungsroman like *Jane Eyre*, the novel that 'affected her the most' (Chughtai 2003: 134), but at the same time, unlike Jane's return 'to her blind master,' Shamman finds she has no one to return to but herself. Where *Jane Eyre*, as also many other deservedly great books, are located within the diegetic conventions of the romance, even the fairy tale—Jane's return to a diminished Rochester when she herself has been enriched and ennobled is nothing less—*The Crooked Line* stands staunchly outside this convention in leaving its heroine significantly alone at the end of the text, like Lucy in Bronte's *Villette*. Shamman's solitary closing note draws attention to many aspects of her persona that can be read as virginal: Shamman's desire for learning, her own work in the field of education, her celibate interactions with various 'progressive' facets of the 'reform' traditions being created in India between the Wars. This novel is shaped by Shamman's desire to be mothered as well as to mother, albeit this desire may be read as parthenogenetic. As a child, Shamman's desire for a child as a child herself was innocent of any knowledge of the male's necessity to such an endeavour, and the later Shamman is flummoxed by her inability to understand the conventions of heterosexual courtship. As an adult, the *deus ex machina* of making Shamman's child's father a racial 'other'—arguably one of the least autobiographical sections in this novel—makes sure that the overpowering sexual antagonism the sexes are educated into through normative upbringings destroy any hopes of 'brotherhood' of the sort E. M. Forster for one can contemplate in novels like *A Passage to India*. As Neela Bhattacharya Saxena (2004) notes in one of the few studies of this novel, Shamman is really looking for a connection to her self, her *wujud*, through her many loves, but in the end, finds this self within her own self, in her womb in fact, when she realizes she too can mother a child. Chughtai routinizes the idea of the 'lesbian'/the homoerotic/the non-heterosexual/the celibate by describing homoerotic and homosocial events in Shamman's life with the same blistering nonchalance as she employs in describing familiar, more normative activities like flirtations with men, thus making all sexuality 'queer' a departure from the self at rest.

Shamman with her fervid refusal to become a 'civil woman' like her elder sisters or their daughters, reduces bystanders to hysteria. But as her various dreams and nervous breakdowns through the text suggest, *The Crooked Line* is also a reflection of how society figuratively and literally castrates the woman by conditioning her in manifold ways. Well into the novel, in her twenties, Shamman thinks of herself as a crooked line, but her very 'deformity' makes her head throb—the pain that crookedness produces is palpable. That Shamman is not merely one intransigent woman is obvious when Chughtai says on the blurb of the Urdu version of this novel that Shamman's story is the life-story of all women in a world that forces them to abdicate their own desires in favour of others. Shamman's disruptions provide a new template for the experience of (gendered) modernity in India that queers notions of self, community and nation alike. Chughtai draws Shamman unbecoming the normative feminine through her possession of motherhood as parthenogenetically, autonomously creative.

Bare Lives: Notes from the Underground

All the texts dealt with so far have been located in what can be safely called the privileged classes: middle- or upper-class representations of (un)familiar love do depict relative lack of autonomy their women members face in economic and physical terms, but at the same time, these texts also work to normalize, at least to some extent, the privileges that accrue from belonging to relatively affluent classes in society. While directly not having access to resources themselves, their membership in classes that sometimes have a monopoly on resources of various kinds means that the women inhabiting these texts may still be beneficiaries of their social group's relatively high class standing. In this section, I locate (un)familiar desire within humble places, writing lesbian desire upon humble bodies. One narrative out of six in Anita Nair's *Ladies Coupe* and constitutes the slender archive upon which we must depend for representations of (un)familiar loves located in socially and economically less-privileged classes.

Using the metaphor of a train journey in the 'ladies coupe' to anchor narratives of feminist emancipation through small acts and big, Anita Nair's *Ladies Coupe* presents a version of (un)familiar desire that locates female same-sex love within the heart of not only the family, but also within what appear to be rigidly heteronormative feudal structures. The larger narrative of this novel focuses on the life of Akhila whose youth, energy, and money have been invested in the nurture of her family after her father's death. Having taken up his place as the 'head' of the household, Akhila finds that her sexual autonomy and selfhood are completely disregarded due to puritanical and pecuniary vested interests within her family, which plainly, in Nair's scheme of things, stands for the patriarchal family anywhere in India. Nair explicitly shows patriarchy as functioning with the active cooperation and cooptation of women into the policing of other women: thus, some of the women in the story are undercut by other women, as Akhila is by her mother and her younger sister at many points in the narrative, and disciplined into remaining 'chaste' and inviolate; further, Akhila's earning power results in her masculinization and consequent othering from any agential feminine identity. Expressions of will on Akhila's part are unacceptable interruptions within the functioning of the family she supports, so small things like eating an egg—Akhila belongs to a very strict Brahmin family—become acts of rebellion and subversiveness. Akhila decides all of a sudden to take a train journey for the sheer pleasure of it, to go to Kanyakumari, a symbolic journey all the more because she is herself a virgin though in her forties already; unlike the deity at Kanyakumari, though, Akhila's virginity is disempowering. Never treated as an adult because she is single, even though she is the sole breadwinner, Akhila's selfhood finds expression in this pilgrimage of the self she goes on where her interlocutors are the women passengers in the ladies' compartment of the long distance train she has booked her seat on. Akhila's co-passengers are all middle-class or affluent, English-speaking women with a place in the world except for one woman who:

> [W]asn't one of them. She didn't look like one of them. It wasn't that she was dressed poorly or that there was about her the stink of poverty. It was simply the expression on her face. As if she had seen it all, human fickleness and fallibility, and there was very little that could happen that would take her by surprise. In contrast, their faces, though much older than hers, were unmarked by experience or suffering.
>
> Besides, they were sure she didn't speak English as they all did. That was enough to put a distance between them and her. (Nair 2001: 18)

All night they talk in turns to Akhila, sometimes sharing their stories in groups, sometimes singly, but not till the next day, when the others have already got off the train and Akhila and this last women are alone is an inclusive conversation possible. This woman who 'wasn't one of them' tells Akhila the story of her life, the violence and the pain of which puts the others' privileged lives in relief, setting

their victories up as the victories of those who are already successful. This woman, Marikolanthu, 'Sister to the Real Thing' tells of
her life spent in Kancheepuram, where she was born and raised to
work in the *kottai* or fortress-like bungalow of the local Chettair,
successful businessmen engaged in the booming silken fabric trade,
making the world-famous zari-laden sarees of Kancheepuram.
Marikolanthu's father, a devoted but very poor subsistence farmer
is extremely connected to all the earth's creatures, transferring to
his daughter his insight that the silk-industry a brutal one because
it strips 'the poor, naked worms' of even their natural covering of
silk. Calling the Chettiar a 'slave king,' Shanmugham tells his wife
that he does not want to become the Chettiar's minion, but after his
death, Shanmugham's children grow up on the fringes of this household, taking employment either in the household itself, or in the
silk-factories the family owns. In this economy, the labour of people
like Marikolanthu's parents did not have any avenues other than the
monopoly industry of the Chettiars; Anita Nair connects economic
bondage and servitude with sexual bondage through Marikolanthu's
fascination with, and later relationship with the woman caring for
whose child becomes Marikolanthu's first job when she finishes
primary school, and cannot be sent to high school. School is far
away, and sending the girl alone would mean putting her chastity,
as valuable a possession in the rural Tamil country as it is in Akhila's
urban Brahmin community, at 'too much risk' (Nair 2001: 214).
So Marikolanthu's education is truncated while her two brothers,
unburdened by 'chastity' get educated at this distant school even
as Marikolanthu becomes a domestic care-worker at the Chettiar
household. As Prabhu-pappa's (Baby Prabhu) nanny, Marikolanthu,
herself only about ten at the time, is in constant contact with his
mother, Sujatha-akka, the newest daughter-in-law and wife of one of
the Chettiar's sons. She is also attracted to Sujatha, who to her naive
village-girl's eyes, is a veritable film-star, like Savitri, B. Saroja Devi,
Vijayakumari or Jayalalitha, the reigning goddesses of the Tamil
screen till the 1970s:

> The first time I saw Sujata Akka, I lost my heart to her. Sujata Akka
> was fairer than anyone I had ever seen. She had long black hair and
> she wore an orange and green sari. Her blouse had sleeves that ended

halfway down her upper arms. A diamond nose-stud sparkled and on her wrists were gold and green glass bangles. There were flowers in her hair and talcum powder on her face. And she wore spectacles. She looked like a film star and all I wanted to do was worship her. (Nair 2001: 219–20)

The hyperbolic femininity of these stars will, retrospectively, once Marikolanthu's (un)familiar road to self-acceptance is traced, reveal possibilities for fetishization for queer readers/viewers; the femininity of these screen-icons, for viewers like Marikolanthu, enables a repertoire of identifications that, at second remove, suggest psychological explanations for why Marikolanthu is drawn to Sujata in the first place. Marikolanthu's (un)familiar role in the 'ladies coupe' that Akhila is travelling in is to reveal to Akhila a world where learning to swim, wear western clothes or say goodbye to one's virginity or to a dead grandparent are not the most important crises: hunger, rape and abuse are part of the troubles Marikolanthu must surmount in order to produce a subjectivity that goes beyond the masochism suggested by these long-suffering film-heroines' movie characters. While Sujata's spectacle-wearing might not immediately identify her with a cine-star, the rest of her appearance, bejewelled and powdered till it is fit for a life of constant leisure as a prized trophy wife in a huge household, is very similar to the majority of the female parts available to Tamil movie heroines for a long time, perhaps even today. Sujata is, in the terms of this book, the beloved whose femininity is itself a magnet for the (un)familiar lover, though Marikolanthu is as yet unaware of the portents. It is only a matter of time before 'Sujata Akka made me her slave with her cast-off glass bangles' (Nair 2001: 217), just as the Chettiar, according to Marikolanthu's father made slaves of his workers; the star-struck Marikolanthu has, in her way, fallen in love not only with the grace that accompanies the trappings of great living, but also with Sujata Akka's femininity which is different from the spare, dark visages of her own people. Living in the Chettiar-kottai, Marikolanthu is constantly in contact with the ways of Sujata's world, with its largesse to its members and scant regard for her class; Sujata is kind to her, and indeed performs the role of interested elder sister or fairy godmother, preparing clothes for Marikolanthu after she comes of age, teaching her to sew and the like. But the things she gives Marikolanthu are intimate cast-offs—

used but clean undergarments, jewellery that has lost its fineness, old clothes—all portents, perhaps, of how Marikolanthu's emotions will, in the time to come, be treated as 'sister to the real thing' and never the thing itself.

For poor Marikolanthu, the Chettiar-kottai is a cornucopia of wonders as much as the femininity of these film-stars is; full of things like refrigerators and televisions that she in her own world has no access to, the Chettiar-kottai suggests innumerable possibilities that Marikolanthu must train herself to never desire. Once she attains puberty, Marikolanthu becomes one of these consumables; her own body becomes a commodity that she cannot control. Where Sujata had earlier been a comfort to Marikolanthu in the tough days following puberty when she is chafed by restrictions and proscriptions, when the men of the Chettiar household stop to look at the blooming Marikolanthu, Sujata, in a 'voice thick with tears' decides to deal with the 'difficult situation' that Marikolanthu's womanhood has made of her, by sending her to the household of two white women doctors, Missy K and Missy V. Marikolanthu there becomes Mari, here for the first time acquires plans for the future, deciding with the doctors' help to finish her school education and to train as a nurse, exchanging one kind of care-work for another, somewhat more socially acceptable kind. Mari also becomes wiser about the ways of the world, seeing among other things that the women secretly sleep together at night. Where 'the sensible thing to do would be for them to share a bed,' Missy K visits Missy V secretly at night and 'in the early hours, she crept back to her bed' (Nair 2001: 323). Mari wonders 'why this secrecy,' understanding only years later what Missy K's 'caressing Missy V's face with her eyes' means (Nair 2001: 233). But Mari is soon taken back to the Chettiar-kottai from this all-female world when her mother breaks a leg and wants Marikolanthu replace her at the Chettiar household. Mari however is no longer enthusiastic about Sujata's presents: dreaming now of 'independence and dignity' she sees the Chettiars' household as rapacious and alienating in comparison to the sparse but free home in Vellore where Mari is not a feudal semi-slave, but a person whose individuality is acknowledged.

But in Vellore, Mari is seen as not feminine enough, told that she looks like a 'widow even before you are married.' The correct gender presentation in rural Tamil Nadu demands more: 'Girls of your age should be seen with flowers in their hair, collyrium rimming their eyes, bangles on their wrists, and the tinkle of anklets should echo every step that they take' (Nair 2001: 236), but this femininity shortly reveals itself to be a terrible liability when Mari is raped by Sujata's brother-in-law, Murugesan. Thinking himself entitled to the 'pickings' of the Chettiars as a relative, even though a poor one, Murugesan finds it behoves him to 'remind' Marikolanthu of her proper place in the scheme of things, as a slave, not an individual with any rights, independence or dignity (Nair 2001: 240). Murugesan finds it abominable that a Chettiar servant girl should wear a watch, or 'drawers and a bra' like a 'town girl' when his own sister had been sent back by the Chettiar as too ignorant to be married to his son (Nair 2001: 240). In the scheme of things that Murugesan sees himself as part of, the Chettiar and Murugesan both are possessed of power to make the lives of individual women miserable; Murugesan claims his power in the form of rape while the Chettiar is supposed to have maddened his wife by having taken a mistress. Reminding Marikolanthu of her menial position through this molestation, Murugesan laughs away her threats that of exposure. After the act, Marikolanthu goes home and scrubs herself clean just as she had done at the end of the day's work all these weeks when she had been cooking for the Chettiars. But this of course is the wrong move in a society where victimologies are the only narratives that women can undertake:

> What should I have done? What would you have done? Now I know
> ... I should have rushed to the Chettiar's courtyard the way I was,
> with torn clothes, mussed up hair, his fluids and mine trickling down
> my legs, and terror in my eyes. I should have threatened suicide and
> demanded justice. I should have wept and stormed and let the world
> and the Chettiar see me as a victim. (Nair 2001: 241)

A combination of naivety and wounded dignity makes Mari think, in common with most rape victims who cannot bring themselves to recollect the trauma yet again, that wiping the terrible event out of memory was the best approach but this also leads to her inevitable suspicion within the evidentiary paradigm of 'justice.' When the truth comes out in the form of a pregnancy, Mari's mother is still disbelieving that it was rape and not a consensual encounter that was responsible. Mari herself now understands that 'not even the village elders would dare point a finger at Murugesan and that was the truth Amma was reluctant to accept' (Nair 2001: 244). When Sujata suggests to Mari that had she told her on the night of the rape, she would have 'brought it up with the Chettiar and insisted that Murugesan marry' Mari, Marikolanthu rejects the idea as preposterous and insulting, to the surprise of Sujata and to the outrage of her mother (Nair 2001: 244). Repeating the dialogues of film-heroines in similar spots, Marikolanthu enjoys a moment or two of attention when her intention of killing herself to avert the disgrace that so troubles her mother is voiced. While Murugesan's guilt is self-evident to Sujata, the combination of patriarchal and socio-economic power in the Chettiar household ensures that the only 'solution' to the problem is a secret abortion paid for by Sujata; Marikolanthu is sent to a distant aunt to convalesce and get rid of the baby.

The Chettiar-kottai is also home to the Chettiar's mad wife, maddened by childbirth: after the birth of her last child, whom she had refused to feed and had on occasion even tried to kill, the Chettiar's wife had been kept in solitary confinement with a nurse in a part of the house set aside for her. Marikolanthu's response to the trauma of rape is to descend into herself just as the Chettiar-wife's resistance to childbirth and childrearing is manifested in madness; Marikolanthu leaves the child to her mother's care and goes back once again to Vellore. Here, Violet is no longer happy with either Kate or with India, and wishes to leave both; Mari's trauma is manifested in nightmares of such violence that Violet gives her strong narcotic sedatives despite Kate's objections to artificial means for dealing with suffering. Mari does not pay much attention to the disintegration of Kate's and Violet's relationship, but in the end, the Vellore household is disbanded, and she goes back once again to the Chettiar-kottai where she is now entrusted the task of being Sujata's 'eye,' as also the old Chettiar-amma's caretaker. Like Grace Poole in *Jane Eyre*, Marikolanthu looks quietly after the Chettiar-amma who 'in her madness ... escaped from the long iron chain that manacled her to this world' of reproduction and wifehood (Nair 2001: 256). Marikolanthu, similarly, escapes, through sedated sleep, 'from the child that grew in my mother's house' (Nair 2001: 256); not wishing to go near the offspring of her rape, Marikolanthu stays always in the

Chettiar-kottai, patrols the house, helping Sujata retain control over it through her loyal and trustworthy espionage as her 'proxy.'

But soon came 'the day when she let me read her eyes and I was reminded of the Missies in Vellore' (Nair 2001: 258): Marikolanthu's drugged stupors slowly recede to show a Sujata who is reluctant to perform her conjugal duties, and eager to constantly talk about 'the Missies again,' wanting to be told all the time about life in that Vellore house. 'Tell me what you saw' she asks Marikolanthu every afternoon as they retire for rest (Nair 2001: 259). Soon, Marikolanthu realises Sujata is, like Missy K repulsed by men and desirous of being only with women. Mari finds that she 'loved her with my heart for so long, it seemed natural that I love her now with my body' (Nair 2001: 261). This (un)familiar love however is marked by lack of reciprocity right from the beginning; while Mari is able to love and wishes to receive love, like the cautious servant she has been trained to be, she must understand that Sujata would never make love to her body: 'Her fingers slid through my palm. That was all she would do for me. It was I who had sought to give her pleasure and in her pleasure lay my reward' (Nair 2001: 261). Her own loving of Sujata is far more generous and giving, transforming Sujata into a happy creature through their union every afternoon, described with heart-breaking beauty by Nair. Things fall apart with great speed hereafter; happy finally with being 'sister to the real thing' now, Mari does Sujata the ultimate favour in performing sexual favours for Sridhar so that he leaves his wife alone. Having done this to secure her beloved's happiness, Mari is completely surprised when she comes back after a short visit home to bury her dead mother to find that Sujata wants her to leave the Chettiar-kottai forever. Having found out about Sridhar and Marikolanthu, Sujata exercises her class and heterosexual privilege in accusing Mari of infidelity and disloyalty. Mari is shattered at the thought of leaving the only person she is able to leave but she does leave, proceeding to sell the son born of the rape to Murugesan himself by a gruesome stroke of utilitarian calculation, for two years of bond-labour in Murugesan's own looms. The poor boy, Muthu, is loving and trusting, but knows he has been betrayed by his mother when he realizes the promised 'school' is actually a place of back-breaking labour but nothing will deter Mari just yet from her path of vengeance.

Wandering, serving as a maid in one household after another, Mari's life after this point is devoted to never staying long enough for any household to take over her affections. But the gravity of her own brutality to Muthu, her son, comes home to her when she sees him dancing at his own father's funeral pyre; following it to the burial ground, she sees the poor boy has also been made a 'chandala' when he is asked to stay back to feed the fires so that the dead body, stubbornly resistant to fire, is properly burnt.

> Hidden by the night, I stood there and watched the boy gather wood to light the pyre again. I saw him walking through the grounds foraging for leftover kindling from other pyres, twigs, branches, dried grass … anything that would break into flame. The boy's face was clenched in sorrow; or was it pity? (Nair 2001: 267)

Moved finally by the injustice of a ten-year-old having to assist a 'half-charred, half-intact corpse' that adults could not bear to look at, Mari reflects on her behaviour, wondering how she was any different from all the others who had used her so ill. 'There was so much work to be done before I could claim him for my own' (Nair 2001: 268), Mari tells Akhila; in order to literally buy back the son she had sold to the mills, she goes back to Missy K who helps. The bond between mother and child, denied so long, is finally ratified by the 'quickening in my phantom womb' (Nair 2001: 268); ten years after he was born, Mari is finally able to accept her son as hers, becoming the 'real thing,' a real mother to her child after all these years of being a surrogate, a 'sister to the real thing' (Nair 2001: 268).

Mari's narrative places within a dense background a number of very interesting observations about (un)familiar love. In Mari's world as in Shamman's relationships between parents and children seem unclouded by the rancour and remorse that heterosexual relationships produce only when motherhood is a self-chosen and lovingly-cherished role in the event of the opposite, when motherhood is thrust upon women, as in the case of the Chettiar-amma and Mari herself, after their 'rapes' literal or metaphoric, at the hands of the world, these women are incapacitated in their performance of everyday normative roles as 'good' women, wives or children. Where the Chettiar-amma's madness seems to stem from maternity itself, catalyzed, as Sujata's personal anxieties suggest, perhaps from her dislike of sexual contact with her husband, Mari's unloving and cruel motherhood stems directly from explicit physical and psychic abuse and molestation. Mari seeks to avenge her violent rape by Murugesan by paying him back in the same coin, but the sight of her defenceless child doing the work of a 'chandala' in the crematory awakens her compassion finally, after about a decade of its masochistic suppression in the interests of serving her masters, the various Chettiars. Acknowledging the brutality of her desecration of her child, and seeing it finally as similar to the depredations and brutality occasioned by her 'kind' Chettiar employers, Mari's desire to be different from these masters enables her to make a place for herself within a different economy. Once again to be part of a woman-centric household along with Missy K and Muthu, Mari will have opportunity to realize herself as she did the last time she was in Missy K's home in Vellore. Nair's novel seems to suggest that within the space of the feudal Chettiar home, women like Mari and children like Muthu will never be given a space of their own because class-privilege will make objects of them. At the same time, within these households, it is women like Sujata who are active vehicles for the exercise of heterosexual privilege as evident in her disbelief at Mari's explanation for sleeping with Sridhar: Mari's desire to protect Sujata had led her to do this, but for Sujata, Mari is a menial woman who is 'unnatural' because she turns away from her own child and prefers a 'mad woman's company' to that of her mother (Nair 2001: 263). Mari's departure from normative feminine performances of duty, whether towards children or parents, is in Sujata's eyes an expression of sexual abnormality consisting in her making love to Sujata, which the latter puts down to 'black magic to make me your slave ... make me do things no woman would' (Nair 2001: 263–64). Mari's (un)familiar love for Sujata is ascribed to wickedness and control over the powers of evil, making of Mari a familiar in the literal sense of the term. Mari's position as a lowly subject of the Chettiars' will, however, makes her also less than human in another more corporeal sense: Mari's love for Sujata is not regarded as an emotion worth any recompense at all; Mari's emotional labour towards making Sujata happy is completely disregarded and unrequited. For the time Mari's attitude to Muthu mirrors that of her masters, Mari was willing to be 'sister to the real thing,' but when Mari decides to claim her son's individuality as equal to Murugesan's at least, Mari looks to the representative of another paradigm. Missy K, as lover of women and good counsellor, is the opposite of Sujata or any of the 'benevolent' Chettiars; willing to make slaves of none, Missy K's power to love is similar to Mari's. At the close of the novel, one wonders more about Mari's life rather than about the central protagonist, Akhila's.

A superficial critique of the novel might see Nair's location of a viable alternative upon the white body of Missy K as disempowering. Through a queer lens, however, it is possible to read this location as enabling: Missy K's confirmed lesbianism places her in a position of 'family outlaw' similar to Mari's. But free of many of heteronormativity's constrictions, Missy K is able to function with less violence to those around her just as Mari's father Shanmugham long ago had been able to. In their minimization of violence, Missy K and Shanmugham, at the end and beginning of Mari's narrative respectively, suggest ways forward for the production of critical subjectivities. While Missy K suggests a critique of both patriarchal and feminist characterisations of the independent woman and the lesbian, Shanmugham presents the narrative's strongest and most memorable critique of indigenous capitalist violence towards creatures big and small, animal and human. Missy K as family outlaw is able to help Mari realize the family that more entrenched participants in the life of the same family, but uncritical of its normalized assumptions—such as her mother, brothers or Sujata Akka—had been unable to do. At the same time, Mari's father Shanmugham's characterisation of the silk-trade as the needless traumatization and murder of silk-worms must be read in conjunction with Mari's own sale and later repurchase of her son Muthu. Shanmugham's treatment of the little worms as also entitled to dignity, love and freedom from needless pain stands in contrast to the mechanized, reifying worldviews that the various Chettiars have and which come to colour Mari when she has worked too long with them. Mari's freedom from her alienation then comes in the form of her recognition that the (un)familiar love she gives Sujata is also tainted by the same ugliness as the Chettiar-scion's attitude to her as a mere toy for sex-education. Once Mari makes the connection between her (un)familiar love for Sujata and what this love might mean for a more worthy object, Mari can free herself, which she does by reclaiming her son. The same-sex narratives within *Ladies Coupe* need not be seen as extraneous to the narrative: coming as Mari's story does just before the train finally reaches its destination, Mari's account of her existence's lovelessness contributes to Akhila's own decision to find bodily and spiritual love. Mari's (un)familiar narrative makes Akhila's own struggle less difficult in comparison; Mari's otherness, her (un)familiarity also makes it possible for the reader to place female same-sex love within a less privileged economic class.

***

(Un)familiar narratives of nation are produced by both Chughtai and Nair in their coming-of-age stories where women learn about un/becoming women. Where the Congress-led Independence movement wanted feminist liberation to come after political liberation, alienating many in the women's movement, the latter movement was also marked by the fissures of religion that ran in the first, with Muslim women feeling alienated in what was largely a movement dominated by elite, urban Hindu women. Chughtai's protagonist relays these conflicts through her own biography but with one complicating factor—where national and feminist movements all presumed absolute female heterosexuality, Chughtai's protagonist is at best sceptic about her membership within reproductive heteronormativity. Her career is most strongly marked by attachments to other women, some tenderly homoerotic, others 'only' homosocial but nevertheless life-defining. The challenges to heteronormative life scripts that Chughtai's novel poses articulate a queer challenge to the difficult dialogue between gender and the public sphere. Can (un)familiarity—here I use (un) familiarity to signal disturbances to the heteronormative—belong in the dialogue of the new nation with itself? Anita Nair's narrativisation of lower-class or lower-caste subjectivities allows *Ladies Coupe* to take issue with the commonly advanced (feminist) claim that feminism cannot take up the cause of lesbianism or sexual autonomy as long as the problems of caste and class have not been resolved. In plaiting all these three kinds of 'problems' together, this book enables a complex critique of how structures of heterosexual and class privilege often function in tandem to eliminate or occlude more marginal or subaltern subjectivities that undercut these assumptions.

The precarious quality of life as subjects in a colonized nation or as lower-caste/class subaltern subjects within a free nation produces bare life-scripts that reveal different kinds of difficulty entering the 'national' imaginary. The (un)familiar personal resistance of Shamman and Mari is supplemented by instances of what we could term 'reflective solidarity' with other women of their class and/or time—like Shamman's beloved friend Alma and for Mari, Miss K. and the strangers on the train. This reflective solidarity helps Alma and Shamman, and Akhila and Mari reach out to one another or other women in times of intense crisis or when in need of sharing joys, marking out female homosociality as an important mode of interpersonal association, one that sometimes contravenes the imperatives of female heteronormativity. However, this space of female homosociality is privatized or rendered secondary in the 'public' economy of their lives, despite the omnipresence of female-only institutions, like schools, colleges, train coupes, and of traditional gender-segregated living arrangements such as those necessitated by purdah. Is the public sphere then, is not only one that is gendered male, but also sexualized as heterosexual? Alma's own struggle with getting an abortion for a pre-marital pregnancy, her subsequent reluctant acceptance of single motherhood, her terrible bereavement at the tragic loss of her young child, and her final craven return to normative matrimony suggest that the space of non-domesticity is only open to the latter female, just as Shamman's own trajectory strongly sets out the obstacles in the way of a young unattached woman's making her own way in the world, be it a colony or a young nation. Mari is so violently scarred by different kinds of subalternization that she is not an identifiable self at her entry into the novel—practically unseen by others in the coupe, and ignored when seen, Mari is the cipher that is the lower-caste woman within narratives of privilege. Who will show solidarity with Mari once she is off the train? Both novels end not with a return to tradition, or a lament for the death of tradition, or the death of the protagonist, but with a hallucinatory passage to what appears to be an almost parthenogenetic maternity for Shamman, suggesting the creation of a new home for the next infant, the new nation and with the reclamation of a child born of rape for Mari, a reclamation thus of her own self as author of her experience rather than as a receptacle for others narrativizations of her. *Terhi Lakeer* and Mari's piece in *Ladies Coupe* are almost apocalyptic in terms of the tropes employed at the close of the narrative—the earth is indeed melting under the Blitzkrieg in Northern Europe and perhaps it will perish altogether, but Shamman as a newly conscious mother suddenly has the strength to will her way to survival, because of the hope she has now for doing things differently; Mari likewise sees her son's infinite sufferings and realizes how malformed her life and thus his have been and that the power to at least end his exploitation is within her. The (un)familiar as resistance to heteronormativity, thus, does not come upon a bad end in either novel. Shamman's disruptions provide a new template for the experience of (gendered) modernity in India that queers notions of self, community and nation alike. Mari's story punctures the homogeneity of the (un)familiar narrative showing queering as undertaken by all manner of subjects.

References

Abel, Elizabeth. 1983. *Voyage In: Female Fictions of Development*. Dartmouth Publishing Group.

Bhalla, Alok. 1997. *Life and Works of Saadat Hasan Manto*. Indian Institute of Advanced Study, Shimla.

Butler, Judith. 1998. 'Critically Queer', *GLQ A Journal of Lesbian and Gay Studies*.

Calhoun, Cheshire. 1996. 'The Gender Closet: Lesbian Disappearance under the Sign "Women"', *Feminist Studies*, 2(1): 7–34.

Chatterjee, Partha. 1989. 'The Nationalist Resolution to the Woman's Question', in Kumkum Sangari and Sudesh Vaid (eds), *Recasting Women: Essays in Colonial History*. New Delhi: Kali for Women.

———. 1993. *The Nation and Its Fragments: Colonial and Postcolonial Histories*. Princeton University Press.

Chopra, Radhika. 2003. 'From Violence to Supportive Practice. Family, Gender and Masculinities', *Economic and Political Weekly*.

———. 2007. 'Invisible Men: Masculinity, Sexuality and Male Domestic Labor', *Men and Masculinities*, 9:2.

Chughtai, Ismat. 1992. *The Quilt and Other Stories* (trans. Tahira Naqvi and Syeda Hameed). New Delhi: Kali for Women.

———. 1998. 'On Lihaf'. Kaghazi hai Pairahan. Trans. M. Asaduddin. Manushi 109 (Nov-Dec 1998). 28 April 2006. Retrieved from <http://www.free.freespeech.org/manushi>.

———. 2001. *Lifting the Veil: Selected Writings of Ismat Chugtai* (trans. M. Asaduddin. New Delhi: Penguin Books.

———. 2003. *The Crooked Line*. Translated by Tahira Naqvi. Heinemann Educational Books.

Chugtai, Ismat. 1993. *The Heart Breaks Free* (trans. Tahira Naqvi). New Delhi: Kali for Women.

Dalmiya, Vrinda. 2000. 'Loving Paradoxes: A Feminist Reclamation of the Goddess Kali', *Hypatia* 15.1: 125–150.

Everett, J.M. 1981. *Women and Social Change in India*. London: St. Martin's Press.

Felski, Rita. 1989. *Beyond Feminist Aesthetics: Feminist Literature and Social Change*. Harvard University Press.

Fraiman, Susan. 1993. *Unbecoming Women: British Women Writers and the Novel of Development*. Harvard University Press.

Gilbert, Sandra M. and S. Gubar. 1984. *The Madwoman in the Attic: the Woman Writer and the 19 Century Literary Imagination*. Yale: Yale University Press.

Gopal, Priyamvada. 2005. *Literary Radicalism in India: Gender, Nation and the Transition to Independence*. London and New York: Routledge.

Gopinath, Gayatri. 2005. *Impossible Desires: Queer Diaspora and South Asian Public Cultures*. New Delhi: Seagull.

Gupta, Alok and Arvind Narrain. 2010. 'Introduction'. *Law Like Love*. Delhi: Yoda Press.

Halberstam, Judith. 1998. *Female Maculinity*. p. 6. Duke University Press.

Halder, Baby. 2006. *A Life Less Ordinary*. New Delhi: Zubaan Books.

Jameson, Frederic. 1986. 'Third World Literature in the Era of Multi-national Capitalism', *Social Text*, 15: 65–88.

Liddle, J. and Joshi, R. (1986). *Daughters of Independence: Gender, Caste, and Class in India*. London: Zed Books.

Lima, Maria Helena. 2002. 'Imaginary Homelands in Jamaica Kincaid's Narratives of Development', *Callaloo*, 25(3): 857-867.

Mazumdar, V. and Agnihotri, I. 1999. 'The Women's Movement in India', in B. Ray & A. Basu (Eds.), *From Independence towards Freedom: Indian Women since 1947.* New York: Oxford University Press.

Minault, Gail. 1998. *Secluded Scholars: Women's Education and Muslim Social Reform in Colonial India*. Oxford University Press.

Moretti, Franco. 2000. *The Way of the World*. Verso.

Nair, Anita. 2001. *Ladies Coupe*. New Delhi: Penguin.

Parasher, Archana. 1992. *Women and Family Law Reform in India*. Delhi: Sage Publications.

Patel, Geeta. 2002. 'On Fire. Sexuality and Its Incitements', in Ruth Vanita (ed.) *Queering India*. London and New York: Routledge.

———. 2004. 'Homely Housewives Run Amok: Lesbians in Marital Fixes', *Public Culture* 16.1: 131–57.

Ray, Raka and Qayum, Seemin. 2009. *Cultures of Servitude: Modernity, Domesticity and Class in India*. Palo Alto: Stanford University Press.

Raynaud, C. 2004. 'Coming of Age in the African American Novel', in Maryemma Graham (ed.) *The Cambridge Companion to the African American Novel*. pp. 106–21. Cambridge: Cambridge University Press.

Rege, Sharmila. 2006. *Writing Caste, Writing Gender*. Delhi: Zubaan.

Ruether, Rosemary Radford. 1994. 'Ecofeminism: Symbolic and Social Connections of the Opression of Women and the Domination of Nature', in Christopher Key Chapple (ed.) *Ecological Prospects: Scientific, Religious and Aesthetic Perspectives*. Albany: SUNY.

Sangari, Kumkum and Vaid, Sudesh. 1989. *Recasting Women: Essays in Indian Colonial History*. New Delhi: Kali for Women.

Sarkar, T. and Butalia, U. 1995. *Women and Right-wing Movements: Indian Experiences*. London: Zed Books.

Saxena, Neela Bhattacharya. 2004. 'In the Beginning IS Desire'. *Tracing Kali's Footprints in Indian Literature*. New Delhi: Indialog.

Sedgwick, Eve K. 1985. *Between Men: English Literature and Male Homosocial Desire*. New York: Columbia University Press.

———. 1990. *Epistemology of the Closet*. Berkeley: California University Press.

Sinha, Mrinalini. 2006. *Gender and Nation*. Washington, D.C.: American Historical Association.

———. 1995. *Colonial Masculinity: The 'Manly Englishman' and the 'Effeminate Bengali' in the Late Nineteenth Century*. Manchester: Manchester University Press.

Sinha, Chitra. 2007. 'Images of Motherhood: The Hindu Code Bill Discourse', *Economic and Political Weekly*.

Stein, M. 2004. *Black British Literature: Novels of Transformation*. p. 22. Columbus: The Ohio State University Press.

Vanita, Ruth. 1996. 'Sappho and the Virgin Mary', *Same-Sex Love and the English Literary Imagination*. New York.: Columbia University Press.

Wittig, Monique. 1992. 'One Is Not Born a Woman', *Feminist Issues I: The Straight Mind and Other Essays*. Boston: Beacon.

Conclusions

Mainstreaming (Un)Familiarities

The workers at 'Sappho for Equality', a Kolkata-based organization that works with women-oriented women, have an interesting anecdote to relate about how the representation of visible 'lesbian' identities enters public cultures.[1] In Bengal's street culture, it is quite common for young, self-appointed male observers to catcall and heckle heterosexual couples over their performance of gestures of affection in public; however, after the release of *Fire*, this street-side surveillance now incorporates female homosociality too. The street's gatekeepers of affectional propriety are now liable shout 'fire, fire' whenever women holding hands walked by. *Fire* has indeed entered the cultural lexicon available to Indians, however much one may quarrel with the film's disputable and self-promotional congratulation of itself as having 'invented' lesbian sexuality in India. What can popular cultural production tell us about discourses of sexuality in modern-day subcontinental India? By way of conclusion, I examine how (un)familiar femininities have been mainstreamed in public cultures in India today.

In stark contrast to texts diegetically located in the diaspora, texts like *Fire*, located diegetically in India cannot routinize coming out as entirely within interiority; some engagement with ambient homophobia is part of the plot. Depicting the act of coming out for the non-western woman as an act of outing that she pluckily subverts to attain psychic and/or physical independence, *Sancharam* as we have seen above represents the lesbian (un)familiar as noble warrior against heterosexuality. Narratives centering around female protagonists and set in India (*Fire* and *Dedh Ishqiya*) further consolidate this (un)familiar as feminine, femme, and as almost invariably either upper- or middle-class (and/or -caste too) and unencumbered by children. While these normalizations, homogenize the image of the 'Indian lesbian', producing her as exclusively feminine-looking and relatively free to 'exit from patriarchy', they also disengage the gender display of femininity by women as exclusively oriented towards heterosexuality. I argue here that while the 'lesbian' figure might be important for a certain politics of visibility, conceptualizations of the (un)familiar as queer person prove more useful for challenging heteronormativity, as can be seen from the mainstream Hindi film *Dostana*, a film about male homosociality and male homosexuality which twists the male-brotherhood trope to make erotic meanings and in the process mainstreams the word 'gay' in Indian public cultures. Rather than see the coming-out story only in terms of coming out of the closet and finding one 'true self-expression' to borrow a phrase from Saxey (2008: 89), the terms of the coming-out story can be broadened to include films that perform the vital functions of providing people a vocabulary with which to participate in their conversation with non-heterosexual selving and of providing people with models for self-fashioning that are not heterosexual. This functionalist view of the coming-out narrative becomes all the more important when posed in terms of movies that, whether mainstream or multiplex, seem to have larger fields of circulation within public cultures than many other kinds of texts as the opening anecdote illustrates.

Fire's translation of feminine home-making labours as inadequately rewarded within patriarchy is a masterful critique of the normalization of heteronormativity in mainstream Indian cinemas, which, even as they give space to memorable female protagonists, will often represent them, as the previous section has shown, as compliant in their own oppression. Many classic mainstream texts inscribe normative femininity, defined thus far as a femininity that validates reproduction, both through motherhood and through passing forward the values of the nation, whether defined as welfare state/modern neo-liberal state etc. Earlier decades within the history of Hindi cinema, for example, yield at least one 'canonical' cinematic text where the diegetic focus was the woman: *Bandini* (dir. Bimal Roy, 1963), *Mother India* (dir. Mehboob Khan, 1957), *Pakeezah* (dir. Kamal Amrohi, 1972), *Umrao Jaan* (dir. Muzaffar Ali, 1981), or *Rudaali* (dir. Kalpana Lajmi, 1993) and within the contemporary era, a case may be made for films like *Page 3*, *Chandni Bar* (dir. Madhur Bhandarkar, 2001), *Astitva* (dir. Mahesh Manjrekar, 2001), *Fashion*, though it is too early to tell if they might be treated as exemplars of their times. However, the focus in most of these films is the heterosexualization of the heroine: educating the young woman on her place in the normative order, these films most often privilege heterosexual marriage, companionship, motherhood and related family roles. Where the first crop of films is firmly located within normative heterosexualities for both genders, films like *Page 3* and *Fashion* displace the burden of being homosexual onto male characters who are also members of the fashion fraternity, and thus presumably always-already predisposed to the effeminacy which is Bollywood's most visible trope for male homosexuality. In many of these imaginings, the woman protagonist is alone, unique, in her resistance, if she resists, to patriarchal conditioning. The isolation of women from one another can be read as an externalization of the desire to uphold patriarchal dominance as norm, and resistance to this norm as anomalous rather than systemic. Thus, a film like *Fire* (and in turn later films like *Sancharam*, etc.) are attacking one paramount convention in mainstream cinematic representation when they allow socialities between women to take centrestage and their contribution is the sensitivity and seriousness with which they approach *sakhya* between women. In presenting explicitly the continuum between female homosociality and female homoeroticism, these films function as a 'cinema of attractions' (Gunning 1984: 56) for the spectator who can have the pleasure of watching a certified spectacle. Films like *Dedh Ishqiya* however, ask the spectator to become a 'perverse spectator,' in Janet Staiger's phrase, to mine its depictions of female friendship and homosociality for queer valences (Staiger 2000: 2), in a fashion how written texts like 'Lihaaf' function when they use a child narrator whose understanding is so literal that we must read between the lines to read at all.

The Old Boys Network and Heterodominance

The conventions of the (male) buddy film largely anchor the plot around male bonding, 'celebrating the seemingly asexual, homosocial companionship among men as the pivotal concern of a narrative logic that defines 'masculinity' as norm and power' (Muraleedharan, 2010: 153). Male homosociality routinises patriarchality, particularly hetero-patriarchality in this kind of narrative by producing positions from where the audience is empathetic to/can identify with the male leads and desire similar friends/friendships for themselves. Hindi cinema, located as many mainstream cinema industries are within a largely patriarchal framework, has also expressed its ideas of normative masculinity through many kinds of 'buddy' films; in R. Raj Rao's geneology for the genre within Hindi cinema, the male 'best friend' replaces the heroine in the Amitabh Bachchan era starting the late 1970s (Rao 2000: 300). Even where the male protagonists have not been characterized as 'buddies' explicitly within the plot, the cinematic focus on male biographies within the plot have kept the action 'between men', to borrow Eve Sedgwick Kosofsky's phrase for how male homosociality tends to keep agency and subject-status 'between men' even when women are involved in transactions between these men (Sedgwick 1985: 25). Thus, many times the romantic plot between hero and heroine might be non-dominant in cinematic time and/or intensity in relation to the action depicted as happening between male contenders for the same woman's hand. Where romantic competition does not occupy the screen, the hero's friendships with other men serve to underline his organic role within society, to underwrite his integral, cohesive functioning within the prevailing social system. Buddy films of this genre can take the high serious road in characterizing this friendship as the purest, noblest human tie, such as in *Dosti,* or explore ironically how male friendships are a component of masculine self-fashionings, as *Main Khiladi tu Anari* (1994) does; still others like *Kal ho na ho* (2003) are self-conscious and ambivalent about male homosociality's intersection with male homoeroticism even as heterosexual arrangements are being negotiated. Almost all of these films at least suggest that these powerful homosocial relationships with their undertow of homoeroticism are in a fierce, anxious struggle with the normative heterosexual relationships whose establishment these narratives are ostensibly centered around; in other words, the buddy film is an interesting site of tension where earlier heteropatriarchal forms of male bonding are being challenged by and sometimes replaced by bourgeois, 'modern' formulations of ideal romantic (heterosexual) love and coupledom, followed by the production of ideal nuclear families. This segment studies two films, *Dostana* (2008) and *Dedh Ishqiya* (2014), to examine what these tensions might have in store for a feminist politics—where do female subjects after all stand between men? Then, where earlier 'bromance'/buddy films needed to be first made 'perfectly queer', to use Alexander Doty's suggestion for how to find queerness in a world that looks perfectly straight, the latter films are far less circumspect and instead often explicitly reference 'modern' 'gay' (male; much less often 'lesbian'/bisexual identities) identities. Both films are mainstream comedies located within the buddy film convention; the plots of both centre around the marriage of one female protagonist; both express and explode (hetero-) normativities about what it means to be globalized, 'modern', sexual and Indian at the same time. This chapter will examine the interplay between representations of queerness—including desires that are not heterosexual—and more normative notions of homosexual identity—gayness, lesbian-ness, etc—as they play out in the terrain of recent Hindi cinema through the two films chosen to examine if and how popular forms in Hindi cinema today produce and subvert normativities of both homosexuality and heterosexuality.

Dostana features young, mobile carriers of India's new globalized modernity, though it locates them in the never-never of the beaches of Miami. The plot revolves around its two male characters faking gayness in order to secure accommodation. The comedy of the plot is based upon its acceptance of the dictum that 'the sexes must never mix', normalizing at the same time the idea that heterosexual men are bound to feel immediate sexual attraction towards (sexy) young women. One of the male protagonists, Sam (short for Sameer) is a nurse and the other, Kunal, is a model-photographer; the woman they desire is Neha, who has a top job at a fashion magazine. The film shows them inveigling Neha's aunt into accepting them as tenants by persuading her that if the niece has two gay and male roommates, there is no question of 'baby'—the aunt's term for her niece—herself engaging in sexual action with any male visitors might be the normative guests of any female room-mates the prescriptive aunt wants Neha to have. Then they see the niece and have second thoughts, but somehow their ploy holds up and all three become best buddies: their friendship is the 'dostana' of the title.

Soon, their desire for US citizenship next prevents them from disclosing their straightness, especially once they apply as a gay couple at Neha's suggestion. Neha's attraction to her boss however upsets the applecart and the men reveal their 'real' straight selves; however, they have an opportunity for restitution and their 'dostana' resumes. While some reviewers have said that this film is valuable in that it brings gay issues into the 'mainstream', it is also important to examine the implications this 'mainstreaming' of gayness—Dostana is a big-budget film with major stars—has for nascent discourse on non-heterosexuality in the Indian public sphere; films in this sense are an important tool in civil society in terms of how the representations they create and disseminate in many ways become both actualizations of what society thinks as well as prolegomena for the future. At the same time, it is important to examine how a mainstreamed gay discourse might perhaps split from a feminist discourse: in other words, can a queer politics end up being not a feminist politics?

The buddy-film plot can contain anti-feminist positions even when women are one of the buddies. Dostana's opening conceit is that two male gay room-mates are better than any number of female room-mates for a female resident because the two gay men, being male, will also provide security in addition to keeping the woman chaste by virtue of themselves never bringing in any unattached males as they're a (presumably) monogamous couple. In one stroke thus, the film is able to normalize not only female sexual purity, but also monogamy. The film's opening sequence however, is an 'item' song titled 'Shut up and bounce', where the 'item', in an important departure from mainstream conventions, is one of the male leads. The body of 'actor John Abraham is the body that the female actor in the song is shown to be attracted to and appreciative of; the exhortation to 'shut up and bounce' is suggestive of sexual intercourse in the song within the larger metaphor of energetic dancing. The women in the song are shown to be desiring, acting on their desires; the two male leads are gazed at by women both individually and collectively in a kind of carnival of desire for the male body. Yet, in the film itself, this roving female desire is conspicuously absented; at the same time, in presenting the male protagonists as gay, the narrative perforce interrupts the Hindi cinema screen's default assumption that all gaze is directed towards heterosexual pleasure. Even though ones desires may be gay/non-heterosexual, it is still rather difficult to imagine the desiring subject as female because ultimately, the camera still keeps a strongly scopophilic eye on the female body's heterosexual desirability and sex appeal. The song sequence 'Shut up and Bounce' opens with the female actor (Shilpa Shetty) actively desiring one of the male leads; a few frames later, the object of desire is the other male lead. While it is tempting to see this as an instance of a woman desiring multiple men, it is also important to notice that this is also an instance where two men seem to unproblematically sharing one woman, as suggested by the choreography of the song and sometimes even costume changes. The rest of the film however obscures any sexual desire of the kind so frankly enjoined by 'shut up and bounce' despite replicating a similar trio of two men and a woman; in keeping with Hindi cinematic convention then, the item song is indeed still very much a place to displace sexual desire from the film's heroine onto the 'item girl' despite both entities now being similarly costumed in identifiably 'sexy' garments. One of the film's posters features an image of Neha wearing a short nightdress sitting between two apparently undressed men lying in bed: the playful suggestion, echoed by a remark her boss makes, is that she is in bed with both of them even as they are in bed with one another. However, the film normalizes emphatically the impossibility of such a non-monogamous sexual relationship by placing Neha in the pure space of the 'desi girl', untainted by sexual desire. Only one man can have her, and he will marry her first. For the men, however, sexual desire can be expressed within the frame of the narrative: immediately at the end of the 'Shut up and bounce' sequence, the film opens with shots of Sam and Kunal waking up after a night of sex; their sexual partners do not have any further role in the film—they are there only to attest to the sexual potency and irresistibility of the two men. This verification is especially necessary for the plot to counter another popular normativity—if straight men are sexual (or hyper-sexual), then gay men are effeminate. In beginning the film the morning after successful coitus, *Dostana*'s biography for the two men establishes that 'playing' gay at the very least does not make a man impotent or un-manly. At the same time, the two young men play gayness as itself by definition un-manly, but their definition of manliness/masculinity is exclusively in terms of heterosexuality. In other words, to be gay would be to be emasculated—gayness here is inability to be normatively sexual, that is heterosexual. Gayness for this film is male homosociality minus heterosexuality; 'normalcy' is then male homosociality plus heterosexuality.

Dostana's invocation of the buddy convention is many-layered and quite queer. Sam and Kunal meet for the first time in the kitchen, post-breakfast when they both awake in the morning post-coitus, in the apartment where Kunal has been a squatter with benefits apparently, the last three years. Kunal emerges onto the frame yet again in 'item boy' avatar, clad in nothing but his briefs (in the preceding song sequence, he is in tiny yellow swimming trunks). The spectacle of the desirable male body is once again presented for audience delectation as in the song sequence, but now, Sameer is also shown looking at the body, especially its only clad portion, even assessing and acknowledging its superiority with some resignation. Sameer's gesture of acknowledgement of Kunal's undressed body is a gaze that I think upsets the normative scopophilic relay from male audience/camera eye gazing on female body. The film's fetishization of the male body itself as object, as consumable even, makes the gaze queer; writing about the changing Hindi film hero, Ashok Row Kavi says that the increasing narcissistic focus on the male body, accompanied by the minimization of the role of the heroine, is an invitation to the audience's homoerotic desire for the hero's body (Kavi 2000: 312). Where in 'Shut up and bounce' we are fed a male body in swimming trunks adored by female onlookers also mostly similarly clad, here the male body is placed in the quotidian environment of the breakfast table, with cereal and orange juice on the table, an eye-mask added for personality. Sameer's shrug in the direction of Kunal's bulging trunks and his otherwise bulked-up physique produce the rare occasion of a male gaze contemplating, at least within the narrative, another male body. Visual pleasure in this case is not heterosexual; rather than assume that the gazing, desiring eye is only looking at a body it wants to be like, it is also possible, in light of the action that follows both immediately and in the rest of the film, to speculate that the gazing eye might also desire this body it comes to rest on. Sameer is presented as the more mischievous one with more derring-do and Kunal as the 'straight' one of the pair when they embark on their gay-charade; it is Sameer who is shown to be more malleable in body language and style, smoothly playing the camp, girly gay man alongside of being quite the normative masculine manly-man. Thus, having Sam look at Kunal thus, the film registers that men look at one another, model their styles of themselves based on what they see in other men and what they see of other men; at the same time, in having Sameer look at Kunal thus, the film also suggests that it is the men who look who are more likely to be self-consciously capable of moulding their masculinities in different ways. Masculinity is thus not a static script, but protean, infinitely changeable to meet different needs.

Dostana decouples gayness from its earlier Hindi cinema associations with overt effeminacy and/or *goondagardi*: its pretend-gay male leads are glamorously styled by the film so that they are part of the consumables the film can sell even as they conspicuously consume in and from a house in which rooms rent for two thousand USD each; at the same time this lifestyle does not seem to need any labour at all to sustain. *Dostana* is underwritten by a number of patriarchal codes. Much labour goes into keeping Neha, pure for marriage. While Sam and Kunal are both shown at the outset in bed with their respective female lovers, Neha is carefully produced as sexually inactive though twenty-seven years old. Later, when she has feelings for her boss, the plot provides this character with a child from a previous wife, such that a maternal Neha can be called up immediately as the prospect of a potentially sexually active Neha materializes. The chemistry Neha shares with her housemates is palpable to the viewer—this is a heterosexual Dostana at the very least—but Neha's desire according to the plot is to have *one* man of her own in preference to these two. A patriarchal heteronormative logic is preserved in spite of friendship—*dostana*—Neha must marry a third person, ensuring thus not only the separation of love and friendship, but also the de-recognition of any path other than that of 'pure' heterosexual monogamy for Neha.

Neha's international mobility and her costuming in the most cutting-edge fashions of the day do not seem to translate into any dynamism as far as personal relationships are concerned: Neha remains devoted to maintaining patriarchal heteronormative appearances as the 'desi girl' in the diaspora. Neha's character is carefully preserved in an intense sexual stasis to retain the chastity that makes her such a desirable 'desi' girl in the patriarchal heteronormative political economy of homeward looking diaspora. *Dostana* wants us to feel that Neha is, at the heart it all, still the same authentic person she would have been if she had been in her '*des:*' morally and sexually *a tabula rasa* to which platonic 'friendship' with men is touted as a new, radical attraction but sanitized of the truly radical potentialities it would have had if the representation did not have to quickly convert Neha into a wife and mother—the 'third man', Neha's beau, also has a child from a previous marriage. At the same time, in showing the quick normalization of Neha's singleness to monogamous self-chosen companionate marriage, the film is able to produce a vignette of the 'modern girl', whose heteronomativity is a necessary condition of her modernity. Thus, within *Dostana*'s apparent mainstreaming of male gayness, the logic of patriarchal heteronormativity is not simply apparent, but central: despite a central male pair with an interesting, increasingly better and independent chemistry of its own, the film must diegetically reify all this, along with Neha's incipient autonomy, into excesses within a patriarchal logic of conjugality, monogamy and 'family' defined as consisting of an ideal heterosexual pair. The installation of the single NRI girl within this idealized heterosexual couple as the 'desi girl' completes a manoeuvre that the director has had to stage abroad: once Neha inhabits this couple, she is again the symbol of an unchanging tradition that is nevertheless spunky enough to be Roman in Rome, choosing her own spouse, living more or less on her own terms, choosing her own friends and her own entertainments, being career-oriented and professionally competent all the while. Thus, even if *Dostana* does permit the male homosexual and male homosexuality—though continuously disavowed and rendered comedic through the film—to take centrestage, this is made possible only by investing simultaneously in an alternormativity that valorizes mono-gamy and mono-sexuality (the film is also in a perpetual bisexual panic): producing thus a sexually static representation of the female protagonist through leaving the patriarchality of male homosociality unchallenged.

Thus, within *Dostana*'s apparent mainstreaming of male gayness, the logic of patriarchal heteronormativity is not simply apparent, but central: despite a central male pair with an interesting, increasingly better and independent chemistry of its own, the film must diegetically reify all this, along with Neha's incipient autonomy, into excesses within a patriarchal logic of conjugality, monogamy and 'family' defined as consisting of an ideal heterosexual pair. In other words, *Dostana* is instructive as an instance where the 'gender' system is stacked against the 'woman', even as the 'sex' system is stacked against the homosexual. At the same time, this logic is not adequate, slippages are evident, and these moments can be fetishized to mean something that runs parallel with the film's recuperations of heterosexuality and male privilege: in fact, the film ends with a song sequence that retrieves all the slippery moments from earlier in case you missed them, all set to a sound track with a voiceover that screams 'gay gay gay'. In this series of moments — played after Sam and Kunal think, though reluctantly, of their penance to get back into Neha's good books: they have to kiss one another—are the false stories of love in Venice they have to tell to keep the fiction of togetherness up, the blessings Sam's mother must modify to suit a gay and thus unproductive couple—the traditional blessing is *phoolo phalo*, and then she recollects herself, shrugging, *Khair chodo*—when she finally 'accepts' Kunal as a *bahu*, complete with *shagun* bangles. In other words, the film's employment of the comedic genre can correct many of the anomalies of heterosexual privilege that the latter produces, at least for the duration of the film. But in ending with the phrase 'they lived happily ever after' forming over Kunal's and Sam's 'framed' moments, the film is cheekily telling us here's a new way of living. Thus, *Dostana* does permit the male homosexual—though continuously disavowed and rendered comedic through the film—to take centrestage, even as it produces a sexually static representation of the female protagonist. Male homosociality in fact becomes the tool that enforces Neha's sexual purity. In the film, Sam and Kunal are already in love with Neha, but when the third man arrives, they strategize and form a team to sour Neha's budding romance so that she remains exclusively available to them. Their stratagems are built on their knowledge of Neha's desires and tastes; friendship has given them special access to the woman, but their sense of heterosexual privilege manifests in their attempt to control this woman's erotic field. *Dostana's* romantic plot thus suggests male homosociality to be an additional tool in the patriarchal arsenal of mechanisms for the regulation of women. *Dostana's* achievement in addition to the positive space it provides for Indian male homosexuality is its willingness to be diegetically critical of the patriarchal implications of male homosocial bonding. As a mainstream film however, all this only happens in good fun—once Neha finds her way to true love, all is forgiven. At the same time, patriarchal sexual regulation is given its comeuppance when card carrying heterosexuals are forced to kiss one another in order to get back into their straight female friend's good books—the policemen for heteropatriarchality find themselves crossing the line from normative to non-normative, bridging the gap between the homosocial and homoerotic.

Women with Friends

While the (male) buddy movie is a space for the expression of male homoeroticism, the buddy movie is also a space wherein sexist ideologies, along with the 'rejection of effeminacy and any other version of non-heteronormative masculinity' can be extremely pronounced (Gopinath 2000: 291). *Dedh Ishqiya* explores two kinds of homosociality—male and female; explorations of the latter are extremely rare in Hindi cinema, and this makes the film thus doubly exciting in that it not only produces female characters with friendships with other female characters in the narrative, but also explores how female homosociality can be a space from where female empowerment can be nourished. In contrast to *Dostana* where gayness was only a game and one sweetly ratified by familial and social acceptance, in *Dedh Ishqiya*, female homosexual desire is literally impossible—its existence is not suspected by any, and once it is revealed to be, it makes the women vulnerable to extreme violence including threat of death. Begum Para is bound by her husband's dying wish that she make another marriage to give Mahmudpur its Nawab; like Penelope from the Greek myth, Begum Para has held off her suitors for a few years, but financial impecunity is making this gradually impossible. Her estates are mortgaged to her most ardent suitor, the raffish local MLA, Jaan Mohammed, who will not take no for an answer; so this year she must indeed make a choice. The delightful film shows her choice to be non-heteronormativity; Begum Para names Jaan Mohammed her husband, but has already arranged for her own kidnapping so as to be free of male suzerainty altogether, for Begum Para's heart is no longer for a male lover—she wants to be with Muniya, her handmaid and devoted companion instead.

Begum Para's backstory bears tremendous similarity to Begum Jaan's in Ismat Chughtai's 'Lihaaf' (1941; 'The Quilt')—both characters have neglectful husbands who are also themselves homosexual; both characters are veritably brought back to life by their female personal attendants. Ismat Chughtai's 'Lihaaf' offers an ante-text to *Fire*, as Gayatri Gopinath (2000) notes in her sensitive and nuanced study of the film. 'Lihaaf' tells the story of Begum Jaan, whose husband is a closet homosexual, finding vitality and life through her affair with a maidservant after a moribund interment as a grass widow of sorts to his flamboyant pursuit of boys. Begum Jaan is visited by the narrator of the story, a pre-adolescent child then, who learns from observation that the Begum is rather different from other women. Slowly the story pieces together from the child's literal point of view the Begum's difference as spending impossible amounts of time getting massaged or bathed by one maidservant. In the absence of this maid, Rabbo, the Begum immediately predatorily assails the child—transforming a pleasant though strange summer visit into a fearsome one—and the end of the story follows soon with Rabbo's return and their eventual reconciliation. Rather than generating lesbianism as essential difference from Indian culture, Gopinath reads 'Lihaaf' to be part and parcel of traditional gendered homosocial segregations. 'Lihaaf's women characters struggle against patriarchal invisibilization of their selves, sexualities, labours, but are not impeded by the lack of a concomitant visible 'lesbian' identity. In fact, the lack of a visible lesbian identity keeps them safe from homophobic violence; Chughtai's use of a child-narrator allows her to both make visible the female (un)familiar as well as refuse to privilege visibility as the final legitimizing tool for subjectivity. In refusing to privilege the visible, Chughtai's text does not lend itself to assessment as a 'lesbian' one, but at the same time, as Gopinath shows, the various subversions of heteronormativity we see in the story do make it a very queer work. Lihaaf is thus no coming-out story; if anything, its characters refuse to come out into visibility, even as interlocutors refuse to see them as anything other than fantastic, as (un)familiars. The total monsterization of the queer subject is circumvented by the projection of fears of this subject onto a child-narrator: while children might well be fearful of a great deal, adults have no such excuses. Since Chughtai's grown-up narrator also ends the story stating not even a fortune will persuade her to disclose what she saw under the quilt, the 'Lihaaf' that covered the two women protagonists, Rabbo and Begum Jaan, the secret is still safe even though the overall valences the "quilt" releases are faintly or overtly negative. However, an element missing in Gopinath's consideration is the predatory near-assault the Begum makes on the pre-adolescent child when Rabbo goes away for a few days to visit a son. The Begum is presented here as a sensual consumer of female bodies; polyamory translates then to predatory child-abuse, as the child-narrator is distinctly uncomfortable and refuses consent to the encounter in various ways. Thus 'Lihaaf' despite its brilliant, intuitive translation of female homosociality into female homoeroticism is still a text that creates a monster out of the female homosexual. Begum Jaan is not very far from the culture's representation of the homosexual or the lesbian as hypersexual, monstrous through her inability to control her fleshly desires. The potential of the (un)familiar thus is disturbingly negative if one weighs these implications with the rest of the picture, where the (un)familiar is indeed housed in the quotidian everyday world of everyday women. While 'Lihaaf' shows female queerness to be everywhere, especially in that space created by patriarchal dominance for the more careful surveillance of women, the *zenana*, 'Lihaaf' also shows the lesbian as inducing fear and avoidance through her sexual proclivities. If *Fire* uses 'Lihaaf' consciously as an ante-text, perhaps it is compensating for these projections onto the lesbian by presenting in its turn the woman-loving-woman as more put upon than actively harmful or negative, just as *Dedh Ishqiya* does in removing altogether the predatory sexual ardour of Begum Jaan. Next, where Begum Jaan is left locked deep within the zenana with no prospects of moving beyond her status as dependent, Muniya and Begum Para's plan willy-nilly helps bankroll their independence economically and socially. Finally, *Dedh Ishqiya* is able to give both the women access to different kinds of spaces, within and without; Begum Jaan is almost completely a dependent on the mobile Rabbo while here Begum Para, a talented dancer, is as much part of the action in her own way as Muniya is.

The world of *Dedh Ishqiya* is nonetheless a dream world, a fairy paradise whose generic convention is that of the Muslim social, itself updated rather ruthlessly here. The Muslim social's universe of Urdu poetry, mellifluous rhetoric, and courteous civility are all satirized as well as relished in this film; additionally, the marriage plot, the staple of the 'social' is turned on its head. Begum Para's quest for a husband is orchestrated through a fantastic device—the future husband must be a poet; Urdu's decline in India is both set back and registered by the flowing poetry and the need for English subtitles. However, the device itself—the husband must be a poet—is a subtle insinuation that perhaps a suitable hand might never be found; after all, only a living language will breed great poets and the competition has had to be adjourned several years already. The final victor is himself not a real poet—the victor is a poetry-stealer after all—but this lack is a comment on the death of the language, and allows us to pause to critique the circumstances that produce this death. The custodians of Urdu poetry have after all been bankrolled too by the likes of the Nawab, though this one is only interested in 'gambling, wine and the company of boys'. The world of Urdu letters was an intensely male-dominated one where women poets were rare, if they were at all, and women figured more commonly as dancers, courtesans and prostitutes. At the end of the day, where *Dedh Ishqiya* begins, it is a woman who is, ironically, custodian of this world. The film does not explain why a poet must marry Begum Para; we can safely assume that it is her way of making sure she does not have to remarry in a hurry, if at all. This plot device also allows us to see how isolating the Begum's position is: she is the only woman, absent Muniya, in a sea of men, poets all. Muniya's company, as Begum Para later tells Khalu, is what saves the Begum from the slow despair and ill-health marital neglect had brought on her. *Dedh Ishqiya* very sympathetically represents female homosociality/homoeroticism/homosexuality as a substitute for normative heterosexually organized familial relations. Begum Para is shown to have been an accomplished dancer when she is married off; her marriage is a tomb not only for herself as a sexual being, but also as a creative being. In Muniya she finds a spiritual restorative—the Begum describes Muniya as 'my friend, my sister, my life too'—and springs back to life, but the disguise the spaces of female homosociality, mandated within traditionally gender-segregated arrangements, provide for this life is absolutely vital. Shorn of the disguise, the threat of violence is absolute, and the tenability of this restored eros virtually impossible.

Dedh Ishqiya is the rare film that finds a delicate balance between representing male and female homosociality both as sympathetic without yet losing sight of many unpleasant possibilities both hold. Babban is a tool Muniya puts to work for her ends; he is outraged and immediately violent when he finds out that he was only instrumentally necessary to Muniya. Babban's heartbreak immediately transforms to violence, which, unaccompanied by the usual audio-visual cues that mark it as ironic for many other segments of the film, registers as real violence. The first time Babban is passed over is a comic one: Muniya drives in on her scooter, excited at having given Jaan the slip. A stable camera catches the woman riding in on her scooter, joyous and smiling, the brown backdrop of the plains she is riding through falling away as she comes nearer. The camera's static position in relation to the little scooter racing through the brown fields cues us to how explosively liberating the success of this kidnap plot is for Muniya; the change of music, from almost silent, suspenseful in the previous scene where she fools Jaan-bhai to chirpy and light here as she pilots her scooter to a happy place, is also expressive. The camera then cuts to a position just behind the waiting Babban; Babban is standing arms outstretched just beyond the tall bars of the gate that separates the abandoned station/warehouse near the railway line where Begum Para is hiding. She waves, Babban is shown returning the greeting; then, a long shot catches her gathering all her things and pausing to look an instant contentedly and lovingly at what initially appears to be Babban standing there with arms outstretched for a welcoming embrace. She runs towards him as we expect, but the slow motion shot shows her passing him by and ending finally in Begum Para's embrace. We do not realize at first viewing that a peripheral view of Begum Para, standing behind Babban, was to be had all along. The relief we see on Muniya's face is followed by the bathos on Babban's face; he tries to be cool, but is quite palpably disappointed. Again, at first viewing we understand little. It is only when we've seen the film once that we understand the secret was always hiding in plain sight, and that our inability to see it is precisely because of our own normative vision. But quickly Babban is angered when he realises he has been had; Muniya barely wants to talk to Babban, but he drags her aside from where she is again contentedly fanning Begum Para whilst the latter eats. Babban tells her 'I'm in love', and is once again shocked when she sharply tells him off for being unable to distinguish between sex and love; this refusal of his tender emotions is quite unpleasant for him and his response is to batter her rather violently, banging her onto the floor and pushing her around very roughly. Begum Para has to rescue Muniya from the assault by knocking Babban out on the sly. Once Babban and Khalu are both tied up and rendered mere spectators, the film shows Begum Para and Muniya enjoying their moments together, singing, dancing, joking playfully and lovingly, much like Babban and Khalu do when in a good mood. At this point in the film, the women are flickering shadows on the wall, with the men watching; the two women's shadows meld into one, but unlike in say, *Fire*, our voyeurism ends there. Babban and Khalu look at one another half in surprise, half in delight, as if themselves captivated by the sight that has taken them by surprise. Khalu says 'lihaaf maang le?' ('shall we ask for a quilt'), intertextually referencing for the viewer the Chughtai story, 'Lihaaf', but unlike in 'Lihaaf', the shadows on the wall are not a frightening (un)familiar for a terrified child-narrator. The gracefully united shadows are the final shot in this sequence, not the men watching, with the next sequence opening in a matter of fact fashion immediately thereafter. *Dedh Ishqiya* does not make scopophilic capital out of female homoseuxality, choosing instead to foreground masculine/heteropatriarchal blindness to its existence.

This does not of course mean that female homoeroticism/homosexuality are condoned: when Jaan finally catches up with his antagonists, Begum Para asks for Khalu and Babban to be released. Jaan and his hoodlums order Khalu and Begum Para to perform an 'item number'—a la *Sholay* (1975)—but the police and the source of Jaan's poetry catch up for the quick righting of wrongs. The interim, however, once again sees the two women vulnerable to all manner of humiliations synoptically encoded in Jaan's ordering of the performance: making his spouse dance in front of his assembled retinue of goons will render her no longer a woman worthy of respect. Jaan will thus avenge his order by commoditizing his spouse to be much as Babban handles rejection by being violent towards the woman who rejects him. Both responses fit within the economy of heteropatriarchal management of female sexual desire and autonomy. Begum Para was unable to divorce her dissolute and neglectful husband when he was alive; societal pressure kept the marriage intact. It is important to note that the Nawab's role as neglectful husband is not a careless negative stereotypification of gay men, but rather an attempt by the film to locate the husband's privilege as husband within the same patriarchal economy. Chughtai's 'Lihaaf' is also similar in its presentation of the homosexual husband of Begum Jaan—the character's unkindness to the woman is not primarily a function of his homosexuality, but rather, a function of his patriarchality. Both texts are aware of how masculine subjects might still benefit from membership within patriarchy despite identifiying with non-normative sexual subject positions. Locating its 'discovery' of female homosociality's slide into homosexuality in the life of a male pair of buddies, the film allows for reflection on how male homosociality often discourages and indeed prevents female homosocialities from developing.

However, in terms of cinematic representation, *Dedh Ishqiya*'s casting drives home a message just like *Dostana*'s does. Begum Para is played by A-list actress Madhuri Dixit. Part of Dixit's renown as a popular actress centres around the iconic dance numbers she starred in; in most if not all of them, the economy of desire is always taken to be the normative one of heterosexual eros: male spectator looking at female performer. *Dedh Ishqiya* subtly plays on this economy even as it performs it, with Khalu being drawn to Begum Para's dancing from a long time ago, but when the Begum reveals her heart has been elsewhere for a very long time, the economy of looks directed at the dancer at the centre of the screen is significantly supplemented. The performer's spectators might include female beloveds, women looking at a woman dance, thus interrupting the normative heterosexuality of a key spectacle in Hindi cinema—its song and dance sequences. *Dedh Ishqiya* like *Dostana*, because both films feature A-list actors, is able to suggest that this homospectatorial exchange is key, not peripheral, to the set of pleasures available to the viewer. In allowing a *Thelma and Louise* like film to end on a positive note for the female protagonists, *Dedh Ishqiya* like *Dostana* produces a radical rehabilitation for the non-heterosexual subject within the popular circulation of representations, placing the non-straight person within the cultural conversation, the *locus communis*. In allowing a *Thelma and Louise* like film to end on a positive note for the female protagonists, *Dedh Ishqiya* however, unlike *Fire*, produces a radical rehabilitation for the non-heterosexual subject within the popular circulation of representations, placing the non-straight person within the cultural conversation, the locus communis as not dead, not exiled, and instead as free, spunky and complex, perhaps like the rest of us. When Muniya and Begum Para drive away in their getaway car and live to tell the tale, they break the mould of possibilities available to the transgressive, desiring woman. *Dedh Ishqiya* explores how female homosociality can be a source of strength for women isolated within heteropatriarchal structures within which male homosociality can be a prominent tool of violence and oppression. While *Fire*'s understanding of traditional female homosociality allows it make the 'hindu home' a queerscape, *Dedh Ishqiya* revises the conventions of the buddy film in various ways to articulate the (un)familiar as woman-loving-woman into all manner of public spaces—the dance hall, the *swayamvar*, the *mushaira*, the road, the railway station, everywhere in India is the (un)familiar feminine's haunt. When Sam's mother accepts Kunal as a spouse though she is not sure whether to call him her son-in-law or daughter-in-law, the male homosexual no more stays beyond the threshold of the family. However, *Dostana*'s rearticulation of the male homosocial/homoerotic/homosexual bond into the space of the family comes, as shown above, at the expense of the female protagonist who is carefully positioned within a discourse of monogamous, chaste heterosexuality. Both films revise the conventions of the buddy film in various ways to articulate critiques of heteronormativity. In recuperating these critiques into mainstream popular culture, these films are trying to engage anew with sexual normativities as well as imagine subjectivities that stand at an angle to such normativities.

In conclusion then, these films centre around the person of the femme heroine, whose need to 'come out' as homosexual is necessitated by the otherwise seamless annexation of her body, unmarked by explicit markers of homosexuality, into a heterosexual economy. Thus, unyoking femininity from heterosexuality through their use of 'femme' heroines, these films make possible an imagination of (un)familiar love that goes beyond the elisions of anxious ridicule or misogyny or inevitable heterosexuality. This section has shown that 'the status of women and the whole question of arrangements is deeply and inescapably inscribed even in the structure of even relationships that seem to exclude women – even in male homosocial/homosexual relationships' (Sedgwick 1985: 25). At the same time, films like *Dedh Ishqiya* provide a new grammar for the buddy film by making it the quintessence not of an always default male friendship, but friendship itself, available in all its queer valances. In the end then, *Fire* and *Dedh Ishqiya* are critiques of normativities and also normativities unto themselves, in that they define various kinds of non-normative sexualities, queernesses, producing, in that sense, an alternormativity if you will, the other for heteronormativity. Yet, the alter-normativities thus produced are also protean, showing queerness to be lurking just under the surface straightness, known and yet unknown, lurking beneath the surface of the everyday yet quite plainly visible too. Popular culture in this sense has the effect of altering normativity thus through representations that push us think of homosexuality not as the other to straightness, but playable by straight women, and of straightness as also playable by lesbian women. In the course of the narrative, things are set 'straight', but not before we are forced to reflect on how they are indeed our sexual roles are merely roles whose success is measured not solely in terms of how well we inhabit them, but in terms of how well society sees us as habiting them—in other words, the more familiar our sexual selves look to everyone, the more normalized, routinized, normalized in fact they become.

Thus far, I have examined a variety of cinematic and literary texts that document different representations of the (un)familiar feminine, studying the eruption of the (un)familiar feminine in various textual sites as events that allow the discussion of homosexuality in society in general. *(Un)familiar Femininites* has followed the woman-oriented-woman through a variety of cultural conversations. The (un)familiar feminine as disruption of heteronormativity has, as we have seen, more often been a queer figuration than an explicitly 'lesbian' one, but her very refusal to be explicated in terms of an alternormative one, has been key to her many subversions of various gendered and sexual hegemonies.

Note

1. Personal conversation, 2007 August, Kolkata.

References

Chughtai, I. 1941/1999. 'Lihaaf' [The Quilt], M. Asaduddin (trans.) in *Manushi*, 110, 36-40.

Doty, A. 1993. *Making Things Perfectly Queer: Interpreting Mass Culture*. Minneapolis: Minnesota University Press.

Gopinath, G. 2000. 'Queering Bollywood: Alternative Sexualities in Popular Indian Cinema', in A. Grossman (ed.) *Queer Asian Cinema: Shadows in the Shade*. New York: Haworth Press, pp. 283–297.

Gunning, Tom. 1984. 'The Cinema of Attraction[s]', *Wide Angle*, 8 (3–4): 64. Also published as 'The Cinema of Attractions', *Early Cinema: Space, Frame, Narrative*. 1990. (ed.) Thomas Elsaesser. London: British Film Institute.

Kavi, A. R. 2000. 'The Changing Image of the Hero in Hindi Films', in A. Grossman (ed.) *Queer Asian Cinema: Shadows in the Shade*. New York: Haworth Press, pp. 307–312.

Muraleedharan, T. 2010. 'Women's Friendship in Malayalam Cinema', in M. Pillai (ed.) *Women in Malayalam Cinema: Naturalising Gender Hierarchies*. Hyderabad: Orient Blackswan, pp. 154–177.

Rao, R. R. 2000. 'Memories Pierce the Heart: Homoeroticism, Bollywood-Style', in A. Grossman (ed.) *Queer Asian Cinema: Shadows in the Shade*. New York: Haworth Press, pp. 299–307.

Saxey, Esther. 2008. *Homoplot: The Coming-Out Story and Gay, Lesbian and Bisexual Identity*. Peter Lang.

Sedgwick, Eve Kosofsky. 1985. *Between Men: English Literature and Male Homosocial Desire*. New York: Columbia University Press.

Staiger, Janet. 2000. *Perverse Spectators: The Practices of Film Reception*. New York: New York University Press.

Index

About the Author

Aneeta Rajendran is Assistant Professor in the Department of English, Gargi College, University of Delhi. This is Aneeta's first book, anchored in her doctoral work from Jawaharlal Nehru University, New Delhi, and post-doctoral work as Erasmus Mundus Fellow at Lund University, Sweden. Her academic interests lie in all kinds of cultural texts, especially popular ones including comics and cinema.